# PEARSON myeducationlab™

W9-BYU-545

## Videos and Practical Tools for Your Classroom and Career!

*MyEducationLab* helps bring the classroom to life with a wealth of resources to help you prepare for practice teaching and the job of teaching itself.

## Managing to Teach

An interactive, virtual learning environment, Managing to Teach has been designed to help teachers-in-training develop effective classroom management skills. Users will watch videos of classroom scenarios, complete interactive assignments, assume the role of decision maker in simulated teaching experiences, and receive valuable feedback from the Program Guide on their classroom decisions. Based on the three corner-stones of effective classroom management—prior planning, establishing constructive behaviours, and exhibiting desired modes of behaviour—**Managing to Teach** is the *MyEducationLab* resource that soon-to-be teachers have been waiting for!

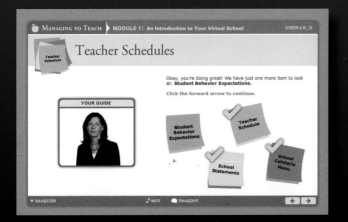

## Web Resources for Education in Canada

A comprehensive aggregation of provincial- and board-level links, a robust suite of weblinks will provide you and other students across the country with valuable information about programs and standards that will start you on the right path to becoming a teacher!

## Career Resources

Access the Careers section of *MyEducationLab* to prepare your portfolio, sample a rich array of lesson plans, and learn more about getting a job in teaching.

# INCLUSIVE CLASSROOMS
# IN ONTARIO SCHOOLS

NANCY L. HUTCHINSON
QUEEN'S UNIVERSITY

ANDREA K. MARTIN
QUEEN'S UNIVERSITY

*Steve —*
*Thanks for*
*your*
*support,*
*Nancy.*

**Pearson Canada**
Toronto

Library and Archives Canada Cataloguing in Publication

Hutchinson, Nancy Lynn, 1949-
Inclusive classrooms in Ontario schools / Nancy L. Hutchinson,
Andrea K. Martin.

Includes bibliographical references and index.
ISBN 978-0-13-814640-5

1. Inclusive education—Ontario.  I. Martin, Andrea K. (Andrea Kirman), 1946–  II. Title.

LC1203.C3H86 2011          371.9'04609713          C2010-906306-6

ISBN 978-0-13-814640-5

**Vice-President, Editorial Director:** Gary Bennett
**Editor-in-Chief:** Ky Pruesse
**Acquisitions Editor:** David Le Gallais
**Marketing Manager:** Loula March
**Developmental Editor:** Rema Celio
**Project Managers:** Marissa Lok and Renata Butera (Central Publishing)
**Production Editor:** Mohinder Singh
**Copy Editor:** Dina Theleritis and Sanchita Massey
**Proofreader:** Kapil Arambam
**Compositor:** Aptara®, Inc.
**Art Director:** Julia Hall
**Cover and Interior Designer:** Anthony Leung
**Cover Image:** Masterfile

Statistics Canada information is used with the permission of Statistics Canada. Users are forbidden to copy the data and redisseminate them, in an original or modified form, for commercial purposes, without permission from Statistics Canada. Information on the availability of the wide range of data from Statistics Canada can be obtained from Statistics Canada's Regional Offices, its World Wide Web site at www.statcan.gc.ca, and its toll-free access number 1-800-263-1136.

1 2 3 4 5    15 14 13 12 11

Printed and bound in the United States of America.

To our mothers, Ailene Holts and Sylvia Lea Palmer, who believed in us, encouraged us, and continue to inspire us.

# Brief Contents

# Contents

# Preface

We hope this book helps you to challenge your assumptions about including exceptional students while it helps you to find ways to teach and include all the students in your classes. Canadians have embraced inclusion, but writing this book has reminded us of the incredible challenges facing parents, educators, employers, and exceptional individuals in making inclusion a reality. Our hope in writing this book is that it may serve as a research-based, practically-focused resource on inclusive education for teachers and teacher educators in Ontario additional qualification courses. Whenever possible, we have used Ontario and Canadian examples and, at times, may be guilty of citing Canadian research without including references to major research programs in other countries. We hope that the extensive listings of Canadian books, websites, and programs will help teacher educators, teachers, and parents to locate our resources and our experts, of which there are many.

## Perspective

All the years we have taught at Queen's University, we have organized our courses about exceptional learners around topics such as planning, classroom organization and climate, collaborating with parents, and differentiating teaching and assessment—a *non-categorical* approach. We are constantly reminded, as we work in the university and in our community, of how much is expected of classroom teachers. And we believe that, to meet these expectations, teachers must think about the range of individuals in the class from their first thoughts about planning to their final reflections about the lesson, the unit, and the term or school year. The question to ask is not, "How do I individualize for each student?" but rather, "How do I differentiate to include all my students?" That is the perspective we have taken in this book. We have focused on the information, skills, and strategies that we have seen effective teachers using in inclusive classrooms, and have tried to present these ideas in a way that is thought-provoking as well as practical. It has been important to us to acknowledge that the challenges and dilemmas of practice are different in elementary and secondary panels and to provide examples from both panels in diverse contexts, including urban environments, suburban schools, small rural schools, and Aboriginal communities.

## Organization

This textbook is informally divided into two sections. The first four chapters provide fundamental background knowledge in the field of exceptional education in Ontario and beyond. Chapter 1 describes the current situation in Ontario and sets our experience in the context of the other provinces. As well as a brief history of how we came to be where we are, the opening chapter includes a step-by-step strategy for differentiating or adapting teaching and assessment called ADAPT, that will help you to meet the needs of exceptional learners. Chapter 2 describes the role of the classroom teacher in the education of exceptional students and the kinds of collaborations that teachers forge with parents, educational assistants, and other professionals. Chapter 3 focuses on teaching students with six high-incidence exceptionalities (from giftedness to learning disabilities). Teaching students with low-incidence exceptionalities and a range of health conditions is the focus of Chapter 4.

The second section of the book presents the focus of any course on inclusive practices: instructional approaches that emphasize teaching all students effectively regardless of their exceptionality or special education needs. Chapter 5 provides strategies for differentiating teaching and Chapter 6 describes approaches to adapting assessment. We have included many examples representing a range of grades, exceptionalities, and teaching subjects. Chapter 7 focuses on the climate, organization, and management of inclusive classrooms, while in Chapter 8 you will find information on enhancing social relations of exceptional students. The Conclusion turns the focus from exceptional learners to you, the teacher, and to how you can survive and thrive on the challenges of including exceptional learners.

## Features

This book offers the following features designed to help readers learn effectively:

- Current information specific to teaching exceptional learners and learners with special education needs in elementary and secondary schools in Ontario.
- Chapter opening vignettes and vignettes throughout the chapters to help readers relate the chapter content to the challenges of teaching in Ontario schools.
- Learner objectives at the beginning of each chapter point to key content.
- Key terms throughout the chapters appear in boldface type.
- Chapter summaries highlight important information.
- Margin notations are designed to extend readers' thinking by introducing weblinks, resources, challenges, and applications to practice.
- *Focus* boxes introduce readers to inspiring Canadian families, schools, programs, and educators.
- *Theory and Research Highlights in Educational Psychology* boxes provide theoretical grounding in the psychology that informs the teaching and inclusion of exceptional learners in Ontario schools.
- *Challenge* boxes at the end of each chapter offer review questions to help students consolidate and apply what has been learned.

Ontario and Canadian references throughout help students locate practical supports, resources, Ontario Ministry of Education documents, research, teaching materials, people, and websites within the exceptional education community.

## Student Supplements

MyEducationLab is a completely interactive, research-based learning website that brings teaching to life. Through authentic in-class video footage, interactive simulations, rich case studies, examples of authentic teacher and student work, and lesson-building tools, MyEducationLab prepares you for your teaching career by showing what quality instruction looks like.

### COURSESMART FOR STUDENTS

CourseSmart goes beyond traditional expectations by providing instant, online access to the textbooks and course materials you need at an average savings of 50 percent. With instant access from any computer and the ability to search your text, you'll find the content you need quickly, no matter where you are. And with online tools like highlighting and note-taking, you can save time and study efficiently. See all the benefits at www.coursesmart.com/students.

# Instructor Supplements

## INSTRUCTOR'S MANUAL

Instructors can log onto Pearson Education Canada's password-protected online catalogue (http://vig.pearsoned.ca) to access the **Instructor's Manual** for this book. Each chapter of the Instructor's Manual includes an overview outline, teaching ideas, activities, and discussion questions.

## COURSESMART FOR INSTRUCTORS

CourseSmart goes beyond traditional expectations by providing instant, online access to the textbooks and course materials you need at a lower cost for students. And even as students save money, you can save time and hassle with a digital eTextbook that allows you to search for the most relevant content at the very moment you need it. Whether it's evaluating textbooks or creating lecture notes to help students with difficult concepts, CourseSmart can make life a little easier. See how when you visit www.coursesmart.com/instructors.

# Acknowledgments

Many people have contributed to the completion of this project, making it possible for us to name only a few of them. We wish to thank our supportive families and friends. Nancy is especially grateful to all the gang—Hugh, Jenny, Deb, Jim, and Sandy—no one could ask for a more supportive and fun-loving family. And to her friends, especially Linda Greenwood, who has always been there. Andrea thanks her children, Jocelyn and Nicholas, for their ongoing encouragement and her stalwart circle of friends, particularly Margaret Harrison, Judy Durocher, and Cheryl McKercher, for their constant support. Outstanding graduate students have worked on many projects that have contributed to this book, most recently Connie Taylor, Jenn Dods, CJ Dalton, Jenn deLugt, and Michelle Villeneuve. Many thanks to the professionals at Pearson Education Canada who have seen us through the challenges and the exhilarations—to Cliff Newman who first set Nancy on this road, and to David LeGallais, Brian Simons, Dina Theleritis and Sanchita Massey our copy editors and Mohinder Singh, our project manager at Aptara, for their outstanding service.

We especially want to thank Rema Celio and Deanne Walle at Pearson for their timely assistance. Finally, thank you to all the pre-service and in-service teachers who have inspired us and to all the exceptional students and their families for whom this book is really written. May we continue to work together to reach our high ideals for including exceptional children in Canadian society by making them valued and full members of our classrooms.

Nancy L. Hutchinson
Andrea K. Martin
Queen's University
Kingston, Ontario, Canada
June 2010

# Introduction

## Life as a Teacher

> One teacher's perspective: "I wish I had been made more knowledgeable about and sensitive to the realities of teaching real kids in a real school."
>
> Seymour B. Sarason (*You are Thinking of Teaching? Opportunities, Problems, Realities,* 1993, p. xii)

In Canada in the early twenty-first century, being a classroom teacher means that you are certain to have exceptional children or adolescents in your classes. This is because, as a country, we have made a commitment to the inclusion and participation of persons with disability in Canadian society. This commitment is expressed in federal and provincial legislation and supported by many court decisions in the past few years. Canadians, including educators and employers, repeatedly express that, while they support inclusion and want to treat everyone fairly, they simply don't know enough about disabilities and about the changes that must be made in schools, workplaces, and the rest of society.

Our intent in writing this book has been to help you and your fellow educators to access the information you need to be confident and competent when you teach in inclusive classrooms. And to remind you that a number of recent studies point to the same conclusion: many of the teaching approaches used to increase the learning of students with disabilities also increase the learning of students who are low achievers, average achievers, or gifted (e.g., Baker et al., 2002; Montague & Applegate, 2000; King-Sears, 2008). These teaching approaches represent a paradigm shift from educators' earlier beliefs that "one size fits all" to ensuring that variety and flexibility for diverse learners, including exceptional learners, are built into instructional design, delivery, and assessment. We would never say that such approaches are without dilemmas or that we have all the research we need to inform our teaching decisions. However, a host of researchers from Ontario and throughout Canada are members of the international research community that has focused intently on advancing our understanding of the issues associated with these approaches to teaching. You will meet these researchers and their work in the pages of this book. You are a member of the teaching profession at an exciting time for advances in practice and research in the field of inclusion.

## The Role of Classroom Teachers

Schools and classroom teachers have a pivotal role in the creation of an inclusive society. First, unlike other institutions, schools are legally responsible for preparing children and adolescents with disabilities to participate meaningfully as educated adults in a democratic society. This means that as teachers we are expected to teach exceptional children and adolescents the same kinds of knowledge and skills that we teach all other students, but in ways that are meaningful to them. Second, schools have a legislated responsibility to prepare all children and adolescents to participate in an inclusive society and to accept individuals with disabilities as peers, co-workers, employees, employers, etc. This responsibility follows from one of the primary purposes of public education: preparing citizens to live in the democratic society that we have shaped, with its values, laws, and high expectations for participation.

It is important for you as an individual teacher to remember that you are neither the cause nor the solution to all the problems that arise in your classroom. Crucial to your surviving and thriving as an educator is judicious and frequent use of the resources available to support classroom teachers and their exceptional students, the focus of much of this book. We encourage you to think of your advancement as inseparable from the advancement of the collective of educators in your school, your board, and the province. Seeing yourself as part of a collective and learning to collaborate are essential to your effectiveness and to your well-being as an inclusive educator.

# The Place of Inclusion in Canadian Society

In Canada inclusive education is an issue within the context of Canadian society, not just within the context of Canadian schools. The *Charter of Rights and Freedoms* guarantees rights for minorities and specifically names persons with disabilities. It also specifies responsibilities of the Canadian government, of provincial governments like Ontario's, and of institutions to ensure that these rights are attained and maintained. On June 13, 2005, the government passed the Accessibility for Ontarians with Disabilities Act (ODA, 2005) which has recently come into force with provisions to ensure a barrier-free Ontario—including physical barriers, attitudinal barriers, and barriers to accessing information. Thus in Ontario and throughout Canada, inclusion is closely related to equity, and inclusion of exceptional learners follows from our commitment to equitable treatment guaranteed in the *Charter* and in subsequent legislation like ODA. Inclusive schools are a natural part of inclusive society, and equitable treatment of students regardless of (dis)ability is closely related to equitable treatment of students regardless of gender, race, and so on. In Ontario, and elsewhere in Canada, if we choose to teach, we are choosing to teach in inclusive settings.

## Dilemmas in Inclusive Schools

Dilemmas are a constant and pressing feature of teachers' lives (Berlak & Berlak, 1989; Norwich, 2008). Rarely do we get through a day of inclusive teaching without confronting some kind of dilemma. Many of these may look, at first analysis, like they are only decisions about teaching methods. However, upon critical examination, they frequently turn out to have ethical implications. Do I allow a student's insensitive comment to an exceptional classmate to go unanswered? How much time do I spend differentiating teaching for two students, one with a physical disability and another who is gifted, when I know I have not spent enough time thinking about the learning outcomes of the core activity? How far can I push my commitment to every student participating in hands-on learning when some can only complete the activities with so much assistance that, by the time they have finished, they feel more helpless than empowered? How much adaptation of assessment is fair, and why is it easier for us and our students to accept these changes for blind students than for students with learning disabilities? The reality is that we live on the horns of complex ethical dilemmas every day of our teaching lives (Brookfield, 1995) and that these dilemmas are only intensified by our commitment in Canada to an inclusive society and inclusive classrooms.

## Voices

Throughout this book, you will hear the voices of exceptional learners, their parents, and teachers who are working together to enhance the learning experiences of exceptional students in regular classrooms. We hope that their words will strengthen your resolve and inspire you to use all the resources available to you to meet the challenges of inclusive teaching.

# Chapter 1
## Special Education in Ontario: Where We Are Now

Gurjit is a bright and articulate girl in grade 3 who was identified as gifted in grade 1. On the first day of the social studies unit about Canada, Gurjit answered all of Ms. Wang's questions about the provinces. She asked questions the teacher had not thought of, especially about Nunavut, which joined Canada as a separate territory on April 1, 1999. In a bored voice, Gurjit asked how long they would have to "do Canada." Gurjit read reference books independently, surfed the internet on her family's computer, and wrote pages while most of her classmates penned a few sentences. Gurjit had already met the unit's outcomes and needed a challenge. The next day, Ms. Wang assigned a province or territory to each group of students. She placed Gurjit in the group working on the Northwest Territories and challenged her to research the human and physical geography of Nunavut. Gurjit found information about Nunavut on the internet and also contributed many ideas to her group about life in the Northwest Territories. While the rest of the class prepared booklets about their provinces, Gurjit developed activities for her classmates to complete at a centre on Nunavut, which remained available to the grade 3 class for the next two months.

Ben has a learning disability that was identified in grade 9. His grade 9 teachers said he rarely handed in assignments or contributed to class discussions, but when he did speak he had good ideas. Ben was often late for classes and forgot his books. His report card comments included, "Could work harder" and "Ben is disorganized." An assessment showed that Ben's reading comprehension was below grade level. He skipped over words he didn't understand and could not answer interpretive questions. At Ben's request and with the approval of his teachers, Ben transferred from the academic to the applied stream at the beginning of grade 10. The resource teacher, who then began to work with Ben and his teachers, focused on organizational strategies. She showed him how to use an agenda book to keep track of activities, classes, and assignments, and how to break an assignment into parts and set a date for the completion of each part. The resource teacher also taught Ben to use the RAP strategy—Read, Ask yourself questions, Paraphrase—for comprehending one paragraph at a time. She encouraged Ben's teachers to make adaptations, that is, to differentiate their teaching. One teacher used a paired reading strategy, another taught RAP to the entire class, and the chemistry teacher adopted occasional open-book tests. Ben passed all his applied courses in grade 10 but says that the courses were too easy. Now he wants to return to the academic stream.

## Learner Objectives

After you have read this chapter, you will be able to do the following:

1. Describe the current state of social inclusion in Ontario.

2. Describe the categories and definitions of exceptionalities in Ontario.

3. Trace highlights in the development of inclusive education in Ontario and in Canada.

4. Analyze the controversy over inclusive education for exceptional students.

5. Discuss recent developments in responsive pedagogy related to universal design for learning (UDL), differentiated instruction (DI), and progress monitoring including response to intervention (RTI).

6. Discuss what it means to differentiate or adapt teaching and classrooms to meet the needs of exceptional learners, and describe the steps of a strategy for adapting teaching to include a wide range of exceptional learners.

1. Why are both Gurjit and Ben considered exceptional students?

2. How common do you think it is to teach an exceptional student like Gurjit or Ben in your classroom?

3. What should teachers be expected to do to meet the learning needs of students like Gurjit and Ben?

4. What expectations might Gurjit have after engaging in the enriched experience about Nunavut while her classmates completed more traditional projects?

5. How do you think Ben's teachers and parents should respond to his request to return to the academic stream?

# Introduction

Gurjit and Ben are two of the approximately 200 000 exceptional learners in Ontario schools. You will probably find students like Gurjit and Ben in every class you teach because learning disabilities and giftedness are common exceptionalities. On occasion, you will teach students with less common exceptionalities, including students who are deaf or blind. You will find that kids like Gurjit and Ben are similar to other students in most ways. They are children or adolescents, like all others, who happen to have exceptionalities.

This chapter introduces you to the Ontario context in which we educate exceptional students. The discussion focuses on the current state of inclusion of persons with disabilities and of inclusive education, and introduces an overview of policies across the country, historical and legal roots, and controversies. Throughout, we are concerned with how you can help exceptional students reach their potential by responsive teaching and differentiated instruction. The chapter includes Ontario categories and definitions of exceptionalities, and introduces the ADAPT strategy for differentiating or adapting teaching to include a wide range of exceptional learners.

# Exceptional Education in Ontario

Ontario defines an **exceptional student** as a "pupil whose behavioural, communication, intellectual, physical or multiple exceptionalities are such that he or she is considered to need placement in a special education program" (*Ontario Education Act*, subsection 1(1)). Students are identified according to the categories and definitions of exceptionalities (which include giftedness) that are provided by the Ontario Ministry of Education (see Figure 1.1). A **special education program**, in turn, means, "in respect of an exceptional pupil, an educational program that is based on and modified by the results of continuous assessment and evaluation and that includes a plan containing specific objectives and an outline of educational services that meets the needs of the exceptional pupil" (subsection 1(1)). This Individual Educational Plan (IEP) and the **special education services** that it includes refer to the "facilities and resources, including support personnel and equipment, necessary for developing and implementing a special education program" (subsection 1(1)).

Once a student has been identified as exceptional (Ontario Ministry of Education, 2000a), he or she is then entitled to an adapted or differentiated education program. According to Ontario guidelines (2000a, 2000b, 2004), these adaptations are divided into three types: accommodations, modifications, and alternative learning expectations. **Accommodations** refer to changes to how a student is taught, which may involve instructional accommodations, environmental accommodations, and assessment accommodations. In each case, the student is still learning from the grade-level curriculum. *Instructional accommodations* refer to changes in teaching strategies that allow the student access to the curriculum (e.g., visual cues, cognitive strategy instruction, use of interpreters, or different formats like Braille or books on tape). *Environmental accommodations* involve changes to the classroom or school environment (e.g., using sound field systems to improve the listening and learning environment, using wall coverings to baffle sound, or preferential seating for a visually impaired student). *Assessment accommodations* involve changes needed for a student to demonstrate learning (e.g., highlighting the important words in a question on a test).

@

Weblinks

SPECIAL NEEDS OPPORTUNITY WINDOWS (SNOW)
http://snow.utoronto.ca

COUNCIL FOR EXCEPTIONAL CHILDREN
www.cec.sped.org

PUBLIC HEALTH AGENCY OF CANADA
www.publichealth.gc.ca

## FIGURE 1.1 ONTARIO CATEGORIES AND DEFINITIONS OF EXCEPTIONALITIES (EDUCATION ACT, APPENDIX D)

**The five broad categories include the following definition, as clarified in the memo to school boards of January 15, 1998:**

**Behaviour**
A learning disorder characterized by specific behaviour problems over such a period of time, and to such a marked degree, and of such a nature, as to adversely affect educational performance, and that may be accompanied by one or more of the following:
   a) an inability to build or to maintain interpersonal relationships
   b) excessive fears or anxieties
   c) a tendency to compulsive reaction
   d) an inability to learn that cannot be traced to intellectual, sensory, or other health factors, or to any combination thereof

**Communication**
Autism
A severe learning disorder that is characterized by the following:
   a) disturbances in
      – rate of educational development
      – ability to relate to the environment
      – mobility
      – perception, speech, and language
   b) a lack of the representational symbolic behaviour that precedes language

**Deaf and Hard-of-Hearing**
An impairment characterized by deficits in language and speech development because of a diminished or non-existent auditory response to sound.

**Language Impairment**
A learning disorder characterized by an impairment in comprehension, and/or the use of verbal communication, or the written or other symbol system of communication, which may be associated with neurological, psychological, physical, or sensory factors, and which may
   a) involve one or more of the form, content, and function of language in communication
   b) include one or more of the following:
      – language delay
      – dysfluency
      – voice and articulation development, which may or may not be organically or functionally based

**Speech Impairment**
A disorder in language formulation that may be associated with neurological, psychological, physical, or sensory factors; that involves perceptual motor aspects of transmitting oral messages; and that may be characterized by impairment in articulation, rhythm, and stress.

**Learning Disability**
A learning disorder evident in both academic and social situations that involves one or more of the processes necessary for the proper use of spoken language or the symbols of communication, and that is characterized by a condition that
   a) is not primarily the result of any of the following:
      – impairment of vision
      – impairment of hearing
      – physical disability
      – developmental disability
      – primary emotional disturbance
      – cultural difference
   b) results in a significant discrepancy between academic achievement and assessed intellectual ability, with deficits in one or more of the following areas:
      – receptive language (listening, reading)
      – language processing (thinking, conceptualizing, integrating)

## FIGURE 1.1 (*Continued*)

    – expressive language (talking, spelling, writing)
    – mathematical computations
  c) may be associated with one or more conditions diagnosed as
    – a perceptual handicap
    – a brain injury
    – minimal brain dysfunction
    – dyslexia
    – developmental aphasia

### Intellectual

Giftedness
An unusually advanced degree of general intellectual ability that requires differentiated learning experiences of a depth and breadth beyond those normally provided in the regular school program to satisfy the level of educational potential indicated.

### Mild Intellectual Disability

A learning disorder characterized by
  a) an ability to profit educationally within a regular class with the aid of considerable curriculum modification and supportive services
  b) an inability to profit educationally within a regular class because of slow intellectual development
  c) a potential for academic learning, independent social adjustment, and economic self-support

### Developmental Disability

A severe learning disorder characterized by
  a) an inability to profit from a special education program for students with mild intellectual disabilities because of slow intellectual development
  b) an ability to profit from a special education program that is designed to accommodate slow intellectual development
  c) a limited potential for academic learning, independent social adjustment, and economic self-support

### Physical

Physical Disability
A condition of such severe physical limitation or deficiency as to require special assistance in learning situations to provide the opportunity for educational achievement equivalent to that of pupils without exceptionalities who are of the same age or development level.

### Blind and Low Vision

A condition of partial or total impairment of sight or vision that even with correction affects educational performance adversely.

### Multiple

Multiple Exceptionalities
A combination of learning or other disorders, impairments, or physical disabilities that is of such a nature as to require, for educational achievement, the services of one or more teachers holding qualifications in special education and the provision of support services appropriate for such disorders, impairments, or disabilities.

**Modifications** are changes made to the grade-level expectations for a subject or course that meet a student's learning needs. These include changes to outcomes, or what an individual is expected to learn, that draw on outcomes from a different grade level in the curriculum or that increase or decrease the number and complexity of the regular grade-level curriculum expectations. A group of gifted grade 3 students may have modifications that include outcomes from the grade 5 math curriculum; a 10-year old student with developmental disabilities may have reading outcomes from the grade 1 curriculum. **Alternative learning expectations** are related to the development of skills deemed essential to learning in areas not represented in the curriculum policy documents. Alternative expectations include alternative programs such as orientation/mobility training for blind students, social skills development, anger management for students with behaviour exceptionalities, and personal care instruction. These programs are provided at both elementary and secondary panels. In addition, there are alternative, non-credit courses at the secondary level that are individualized for the student. These courses have a "K" course code; for example, Culinary Skills (KHI) or Money Management and Personal Banking (KBB). The next section provides the context for inclusion and highlights the significance of rights guaranteed in the *Charter of Rights and Freedoms*.

## Canada: Inclusive Society, Inclusive Schools

Since Confederation, each province has had the authority to pass laws about education. However, all laws in Canada must be consistent with the *Constitution Act*, which contains the **Charter of Rights and Freedoms** (Government of Canada, 1982, http://laws.justice.gc.ca/en/charter/index.html). The **equality rights** that apply to education are contained in section 15(1): "Every individual is equal before and under the law and has the right to the equal protection and equal benefit of the law without discrimination and, in particular, without discrimination based on race, national or ethnic origin, colour, religion, sex, age or mental or physical disability." When the Charter was passed, Canada became one of the first countries to guarantee rights to people with disabilities in its constitution.

Many developments worldwide contributed to Canada's adoption of the *Charter of Rights and Freedoms* in 1982. For example, all members of the United Nations adopted the *Universal Declaration of Human Rights* in 1948. Although education was one of the fundamental human rights listed in the Declaration, there was no mention of people with disabilities. In 1975 the United Nations declared that disabled persons had the same rights as other people (including community living, education, work, voting, etc.) in the *Declaration of Rights of Disabled Persons*. The *Canadian Human Rights Act* of 1977 stated that no one should be discriminated against for reasons of physical or mental ability. Subsequently, 1981 was proclaimed the International Year of Disabled Persons, heightening awareness of disabilities and enhancing the self-advocacy of people with disabilities.

### PARADIGM SHIFT

The United Nations continued to champion the rights of persons with disabilities, and in 1993 it adopted the Standard Rules on the Equalization of Opportunities for Persons with Disabilities, targeting eight areas for **equal participation**, including education (United Nations Enable, www.un.org/disabilities). On 13 December 2006, the *Convention on the Rights of Persons with Disabilities* (text is available at www.un.org/disabilities/default.asp?id=259) was adopted at the United Nations Headquarters in New York. The Convention represents a "paradigm shift" from viewing persons with disabilities as "objects" of charity, medical treatment, and social protection to seeing them as "subjects" with rights who are active members of society, and who are capable of claiming those rights and making decisions for their lives based on their free and informed consent.

**Further Reading**

For teaching about human rights:

Cassidy, W., & Yates, R. (2005). *Once upon a crime: Using stories, simulations, and mock trials to explore justice and citizenship in elementary school.* Calgary: Detselig Enterprises Ltd.

Castle, C. (2002). *For every child: The rights of the child in words and pictures.* New York: Red Fox Books in association with UNICEF.

Kiem, E. (2007). *Protecting the world's children: Impact of the Convention on the Rights of the Child in diverse legal systems.* Cambridge, UK: Cambridge University Press-UNICEF.

Darling, L.F. (2004). Teaching human rights in elementary classrooms: A literary approach. *Canadian Social Studies, 39*(1), accessed at www.quasar.ualberta.ca/css.

United Nations Human Rights, www.un.org/en/rights. Thematic issues include Children and Armed Conflict, The Holocaust and the UN Outreach Programme, and Indigenous People. Educational materials are linked, as are related resources and sites.

**Weblinks**

CANADIAN CHARTER OF RIGHTS AND FREEDOMS
http://laws.justice.gc.ca/en/charter/index.html

Canada's policy on persons with disabilities emphasizes **inclusion**. In 2006, the Government of Canada released its third comprehensive report on disability in Canada, *Advancing the Inclusion of Persons with Disabilities* (available at www.hrsdc. gc.ca/en/disability_issues/reports/fdr/2006/advancinginclusion.pdf). The 2006 Participation and Activity Limitation Survey (PALS), reported by Statistics Canada (2 December 2007, www.statcan.gc.ca/), estimated that one in seven Canadians, or 14.3 percent of the population, has a disability. Among children aged 5 to 14, learning disabilities and chronic health conditions were the most common forms of disability, and almost three-quarters of school-aged children with a disability reported having multiple disabilities. The executive summary of the *Advancing Inclusion* report found that more than 80 percent of Canadians believe there has been some progress over the last decade in including people with disabilities, but only 10 percent believe these individuals are fully included today. Overall, Canadians thought that people with disabilities should have the opportunity to participate in life to their fullest potential—that this is part of the "Canadian way" of doing things.

However, progress is not as robust as we might like. In 2002, employment rates were only 53 percent for people with disabilities, compared with 76 percent for people without. Of children with disabilities (aged 5 to 14), 95 percent attend school, most going to a regular school; about one in ten working-age adults with disabilities has a university degree, compared with one in five without disabilities; and Aboriginal people with disabilities have a lower rate of post-secondary completion than other Canadians with disabilities (*Advancing Inclusion,* 2006). In school, the supports needed by most students with disabilities are technical aids and human support. Schools play a key role as we continue moving toward inclusion of persons with disabilities in all aspects of our society.

# Where We Are Now: "Education for All" in Ontario

In 1998, a review of the policies and procedures across the country (Friend, Bursuck, & Hutchinson, 1998) showed two dominant themes in the education of exceptional learners: change and inclusion. A current review might suggest that accountability should also be included as standards for special education continue to be developed.

Many have argued that success for exceptional students depends on complex rights, particularly non-discrimination and access. Also essential are identification of their educational needs and differentiated teaching and services to meet those needs. In Ontario, this is usually accomplished through an **Identification, Placement, and Review Committee (IPRC)**, set up by district school boards. This committee makes a decision on whether or not a student should be identified and makes a decision on appropriate placement and reviews the identification and placement at least once in each school year (see Highlights of Regulation 181/98 www.edu.gov.on.ca/eng/general/elemsec/speced/hilites.html).

**What do you think?**

Read two of the following Canadian resources and contrast their perspectives on disabilities. Think about why we need a range of perspectives to fully understand the experience of life with a disability and to understand how to ensure valued recognition and social inclusion for individuals with disabilities (one aspect, but not the defining characteristic, of their lives). Talk with your peers about your differing points of view.

Bunch, G., & Valeo, A. (2004). Student attiudes toward peers with disabilities in inclusive and special education schools. *Disability & Society,* 19(1), 61–76.

Tichkosky, T. (2007). *Reading and writing disability differently: The textured life of embodiment.* Toronto: University of Toronto Press.

Bendall, L. (2007). *Raising a kid with special needs: The complete Canadian guide.* Toronto: Key Porter Books.

Rioux, M.H., Lindqvist, B., & Carbert, A. (2007). International human rights and intellectual disability. In I. Brown & M. Percy (Eds.), *A comprehensive guide to intellectual and developmental disabilities* (pp. 59–68). Baltimore, MD: Paul H. Brookes Pub.

Panitch, M. (2008). *Disability, mothers, and organization: Accidental activists.* New York: Routledge.

Usually, a range of five placement options is available. These are: (1) a regular classroom with indirect support where the teacher receives consultative support; (2) a regular classroom with resource assistance; (3) a regular classroom with withdrawal assistance; (4) a special education class with partial integration; and (5) a special education class full time. The majority of students receiving special education programs and services are placed in regular classrooms for more than half of the instructional day. Most recent figures from the Ontario Ministry of Education report that, for 2006-2007, approximately 14 percent of the total student population receives special education programs and services. Of these approximately 80 percent (82 percent of secondary) were in regular classrooms over half the school day.

After a student has been formally identified, an **Individual Education Plan (IEP)** is developed that describes the adaptations (accommodations and modifications) and services to be provided, outlines expectations and programs, indicates how progress will be reviewed. As well, for all exceptional students who are age 14 or older, except gifted students, a transition plan is developed. These processes are often more complex for Aboriginal students, whether they attend reservation schools, band-controlled schools, or urban schools (e.g., Varga-Toth, 2006).

Most students with IEPs have participated in an IPRC. In Ontario, however, it is possible to have an IEP without having been identified as having an exceptionality. Non-identified students with informal IEPs may receive a special education program and related services. In April 2010, the Ontario Ministry of Education adopted the term "**students with special education needs**" to describe these non-identified students who have IEPs. You may be wondering how many students in Ontario have been identified through the IPRC process in each category of exceptionality. In 2006-2007, 198 385 students were identified through IPRCs. The data for the various exceptionalities are shown in Figure 1.2.

**FIGURE 1.2   ONTARIO STATISTICS FOR IDENTIFIED STUDENTS**

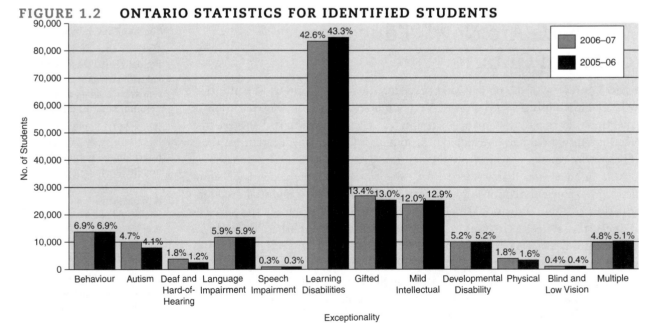

"Education for All" is the title of a report released in 2005 by the Ministry of Education: *Education for All: The Report of the Expert Panel on Literacy and Numeracy Instruction for Students with Special Education Needs, Kindergarten to Grade 6.* This report has had significant impact province-wide in operationalizing inclusive practice. Three concepts anchor the report and are key to helping you to ensure "education for all." These concepts are universal design for learning, differentiated instruction, and progress monitoring (especially one specific form called responsiveness to intervention (RTI)).

**Universal design for learning (UDL)** was inspired by a movement in architecture to design buildings that, from the outset of the design process, can be accessed by all people, including those with physical disabilities. Following the architectural model, UDL is an orientation intended to shape teaching to provide all students with access to the curriculum, right from the start of the planning process (Turnbull et al., 2002). Rather than developing a unit and making changes after the fact for exceptional students, English language learners (ELL), or students from diverse cultures, UDL encourages teachers to make a class profile and then plan from the beginning to provide means and pedagogical materials that meet the needs of all students (Ontario Ministry of Education, 2005). UDL methods fall into three clusters: (1) demonstration and presentation of new content in various ways, including instructional technology, explicit instruction, and inquiry, which are necessary for all students to learn how to acquire and use new information; (2) engagement, or practice, that takes place in numerous ways, including small groups, co-operative learning, a range of materials and activities, guided practice and independent practice as needed, and feedback and ongoing monitoring; and (3) expression, or ways for students to show what they know, including written work of various lengths, oral presentations, and real-life applications. Choice also increases meaningfulness and promotes motivation for learning (King-Sears, 2008).

**Differentiated instruction (DI)** acknowledges that students differ in interests, learning profile, and level of functioning. While UDL operates at the curriculum level, DI helps teachers to make similar student-centred decisions at the student level to address specific skills and difficulties. The principles that guide differentiation include respectful tasks, flexible grouping, and ongoing assessment and adjustment. Usually the aspects that teachers can differentiate are described as content, process, and product (Ontario Ministry of Education, 2005; Tomlinson, 1999, 2005, 2008; Tomlinson, Brimijoin, & Narvaez, 2008). You will learn throughout this book about using strategies like tiered assignments, small-group instruction, learning centres, and varied pacing (King-Sears, 2008).

The third concept is continual **progress monitoring**. Progress monitoring is important for learners of all ages. One specific form of progress monitoring, **responsiveness to intervention (RTI)**, has received considerable attention recently. It is usually focused on primary students. RTI is described as a way of thinking about how teaching can be operationalized for struggling learners. Children who are struggling after receiving excellent instruction are given a different type of instruction, which is more intense and of longer duration than regular classroom instruction. For example, if some students in a grade 1 class are not learning to read with their peers, they could be taught in a small group of two to five over ten to twenty weeks for forty-five minutes on most days. At the end of this period of special instruction, those who have learned to read return to regular classroom instruction, while those who are still struggling have individualized teaching, more intense than the previous intervention, and perhaps short-term placement in special education (Fuchs & Fuchs, 2007). RTI has emerged quite recently, though many states in the US have recognized it as an appropriate means of identifying learning disabilities.

In 2009, the Ministry of Education released a draft of *Learning for All K-12*, which builds on the guiding principles of *Education for All*. The document introduces the "breakthough system," which addresses the need to "establish classroom routines and practices that represent personalized, ongoing, data-driven, focused instruction" (p. 7). The three core components are personalization, precision, and professional learning. **Personalization** puts the learner at the centre, with assessment and instruction tailored to a student's particular learning and motivational needs. **Precision** aims to provide instruction that is precise to the level of readiness and the learning needs of the individual student, linking assessment for learning with differentiating teaching and learning activities. **Professional learning** is supported through professional learning communities of educators (PLCs) within a culture of collaboration. To aid teachers in planning focused assessment and instruction, the document has templates to assist teachers in developing a class profile and individual student profiles. The class profile would provide a snapshot of the strengths and needs, interests, and readiness of the students in the class, which could be used for planning teaching and assessment for the class. The student profile would provide a more complete and precise picture of a student's strengths and needs, as well as supports and accommodations. This information could then be used as a resource in the development of an IEP and for meeting individual needs.

## The Current State in Each Province and Territory

The figure that follows (Figure 1.3) provides a cross-Canada perspective on policies and procedures for exceptional learners in each province and territory, from west to east, and provides context for understanding Ontario initiatives.

## Cross-Country Summary

As you review the provincial and territorial documents, you will see how they reflect that our aspirations are moving toward "child-centred schools and school-centred communities" (MacKay, 2007) that embrace inclusion for all students, including exceptional students. The means to accomplish these goals include differentiated instruction and regular progress monitoring—in contexts characterized by diversity, fraught with dilemmas, and taught by regular classroom teachers—complemented by opportunities for more intense instruction in a timely fashion, as needed, in the most effective context. However, educators and researchers are experiencing tension between, on the one hand, nimble, responsive teaching and assessment with continuous progress monitoring and tiered, preventive interventions starting as soon as students begin to struggle and, on the other hand, our traditional, laborious process of in-school team meetings, IEP development, and intensive funding supports based on verified student characteristics (Philpott & Dibbon, 2007). It appears that yet again or still, "Change in exceptional education is everywhere" (Hutchinson, 2007), and yet for many exceptional students and their families, "everything remains the same." Recent reviews (MacKay, 2007; Newfoundland and Labrador's *Focusing on Students*, ISSP and Pathways Commission Report, 2007) suggest that teachers need better

**Further Reading**

Learn more about inclusive education in other parts of the world:

North America and Europe—Ferguson, D.L. (2008). International trends in inclusive education: The continuing challenge to teach one and everyone. *European Journal of Special Needs Education, 23*(2), 109–120.

India—Kalyanpur, M. (2008). Equality, quality, and quantity: Challenges in inclusive education policy and service provision in India. *International Journal of Inclusive Education, 12*(3), 243–262.

Australia—Foreman, P., & Arthur-Kelly, M. (2008). Social justice principles, the law and research, as bases for inclusion. *Australasian Journal of Special Education, 32*(1), 109–124.

Hong Kong—Chong Suk Ching, S., Forlin, C., & Lan, A.M. (2007). The influence of an inclusive education course on attitude change of pre-service secondary teachers in Hong Kong. *Asia-Pacific Journal of Teacher Education, 35*(2), 161–179.

## FIGURE 1.3 CROSS-CANADA POLICIES AND PROCEDURES FOR EXCEPTIONAL LEARNERS

**BRITISH COLUMBIA (www.bced.gov.bc.ca/specialed)**
*The Policy Document: Special Education* (2006)

- An inclusive education system where "students with special needs are fully participating members of a community of learners".

*Individual Education Planning for Students with Special Needs*

- A range of placement options are possible within a neighbourhood school, including resource rooms, self-contained classes, community-based training, or other specialized settings.
- IEPs can include: learning outcomes that may be different from, or in addition to, outcomes laid out in program guides; support services; and a list of adapted materials, instructional strategies, and assessment methods.
- Resource Guides, e.g., Teaching Students with Fetal Alcohol Syndrome, Teaching Students with Attention- Deficit/Hyperactivity Disorder, Teaching Children with Learning and Behavioural Differences; available at www.bced.gov.bc.ca/specialed/sped_res_docs.htm

**YUKON (www.education.gov.yk.ca/specialprograms)**
*Handbook for Teachers* (2007-2008): *Special Programs* (pp. 29–31)

- Students with special needs are to be educated in "the least restrictive environment," using program modifications and adaptations "to accommodate each child's unique needs" (p. 29).
- Non-categorical service delivery is practiced and no diagnosis is necessary for a student to receive "additional supports."
- IEPs are written when necessary by classroom teachers, the school-based team, and the student's parents.

**ALBERTA (www.education.alberta.ca/admin/special/programming.aspx)**
*Educational Placement of Students with Special Needs* (2003)

- The first placement option considered for special needs students should be the regular classroom in neighbourhood schools. This is based on a "philosophy of equality, sharing, participation, and the worth and dignity of individuals."
- Final placement decisions rest with school boards, but decisions should be consultative among school staff, students, and parents/guardians.
- An Individualized Program Plan (IPP) includes goals, objectives, and recommendations for services and interventions.

*Standards for Special Education* (2004)

- Programming is described as "adapted," where outcomes are achieved by adjustments to the instructional program, or "modified," where outcomes differ from the provincial curriculum.

**NORTHWEST TERRITORIES (www.ece.gov.nt.ca)**
*Ministerial Directive on Inclusive Schooling* (2006)

- Inclusive schooling means "the provision of support services as necessitated by the needs of individual students."
- Students may follow a regular program, a modified education program with outcomes from the NWT curriculum at a grade level other than that assigned to the student, or an individual education program with an IEP.
- Student support plans (SSP) document accommodations/adaptations for those in regular and modified programs.

**NUNAVUT (www.edu.gov.nu.ca/)**
*Inclusive Education in Nunavut Schools: Student Support Handbook* (2006)

- Inclusion is defined as "an attitude and a belief . . . a way of life, a way of living and working together, based on the belief that each individual is valued and does belong."
- Identification is non-categorical, by level of student need rather than by disability.
- Individual Accommodation Plans are reserved for those needing periodic support (20 percent) or more intensive supports (5–7 percent).

FIGURE 1.3 *(Continued)*

**SASKATCHEWAN (www.education.gov.sk.ca/StudentSupportServices)**
*Directions for Diversity: Final report of the Special Education Review Committee* (2000) (www.sasked.gov.sk.ca)

■ The Final Report recommended that the philosophy of inclusive schools be adopted, implemented, and supported (p. vii), while ensuring "availability of a comprehensive array of support services" (p. vi).

*Strengthening Supports* (2000), response by the Minister of Education to *Directions for Diversity Ministry of Education Intensive Needs Pupil Guidelines 2008/2009* (Saskatchewan Children's Services Branch)

■ Recommendations from a review of the "student services service delivery model: (a) focus on results, not process, (b) embrace a model of prevention and early intervention, and (c) children with intensive needs are general education children first."

**MANITOBA (www.edu.gov.mb.ca/k12/specedu/)**
*Handbook for Student Services* (2007)

■ Defines a philosophy of inclusion as "a way of thinking and acting that allows every individual to feel accepted, valued, and safe. . . . An inclusive community provides meaningful involvement and equal access to the benefits of citizen.

*Student-Specific Planning: A Handbook for Developing and Implementing Individual Education Plans (IEPs)* (2010)

■ The IEP is the basis for decision-making for exceptional students.

*Bridging to Adulthood: A Protocol for Transitioning Students with Exceptional Needs from School to Community* (2008)

■ Development and implementation of transition plans for exceptional students who require government support to enter the community, e.g., vocational rehabilitation or supported living programs.

**ONTARIO (www.edu.gov.on.ca/eng/teachers/speced.html)**
*Individual Education Plans: Standards for Development, Program Planning, and Implementation* (2000a) (www.edu.gov.on.ca/eng/general/elemsec/apeced/iepstand/iepstand.html)

■ Increased emphasis on accountability by developing standards for IEPs

*Standards for School Boards' Special Education Plans* (2000b) (www.edu.gov.on.ca/eng/general/elemsec/speced/iepstand/iepstand.pdf)

■ Every school board must submit biannually a report on the special education programs and services provided. Every board must maintain a special education plan, review it annually, amend it to meet current needs of its exceptional students, and submit any amendment(s) to the Minister.

*The Individual Education Plan (IEP): A Resource Guide* (2004) (www.edu.gov.on.ca/eng/general/elemsec/speced/guide/resource/iepresguid.pdf)

■ Provides a description of the five phases of the IEP process and IEP updates and reviews. Boards have the discretion to prepare an IEP for a student who is receiving a special education program and/or related services but who has not been formally identified as exceptional.

*Education for All* (2005) (www.edu.gov.on.ca/eng/document/reports/speced/panel/speced.pdf)

■ Focuses on differentiating instruction, using UDL and RTI to informally and quickly identify children struggling to read, putting tiered interventions in place before any labels are applied and without IEPs or IPRC meetings.

**QUEBEC (www.meq.Gouv.qc.ca/gr-pub/menu-curricu-a.htm#se)**
*Adapting Our Schools to the Needs of All Students* (2000)

■ Provision of services "in the most natural environment for the students," favouring integration into regular classrooms, and offering services in proximity to students' places of residence (p. 20).
■ The goal is to move from access to success for as many students as possible by adapting educational services and existing educational methods, and by offering program and transition plans that enable workplace participation.

FIGURE 1.3 *(Continued)*

- There is an obligation to establish an IEP that is adapted to the special needs of the student.

**NEW BRUNSWICK (www.gnb.ca/0000/publications/ss/sep.pdf)**
*Guidelines and Standards: Educational Planning for Students with Exceptionalities* (2002, Revised from *Working Guidelines on Integration*, 1998)

- Commitment to a "process of inclusive, quality education [with] every effort made to educate all students through instruction commensurate with their individual needs, in regular classes within neighbourhood schools" (p. 3).
- Special Education Plans (SEPs) provide a plan of services for exceptional students based on continuous assessment to meet students' needs.

*Inclusive Education: A Review of Programming and Services in New Brunswick* (2004)
*MacKay Report, Inclusive Education* (2007)

- Inclusive education is described as "an approach, not a place," with an emphasis on accommodating all children to maximize their potential and sense of belonging to the school community and to society.
- Recommendation is made to drop the term exceptional and use a broader term like students in need of intervention.

**NOVA SCOTIA (www.ednet.ns.ca/)**
*Special Education Policy Manual* (1997)

- An inclusive school is a "school where every child is respected as part of the school community and . . . encouraged to learn and achieve as much as possible . . . and where differences are cherished for the richness they bring" (p. 13).
- Individual Program Plans (IPPs) will contain student goals that will form the foundation for evaluating student outcomes.
- Every school must establish a program-planning team to provide and monitor programs for students with special needs.

*The Program Planning Process: A Guide for Parents* (2006)

- Describes a team approach that applies to parents and educators and the roles and responsibilities of all team members

**PRINCE EDWARD ISLAND (www.gov.pe.ca/education/index.php3)**
*Individualized Educational Planning (IEP)* (2005a) (www.gov.pe.ca/photos/original/ed_ieplanning.pdf)

- "The needs of most students will be met by classroom/subject teachers using regular provincial curriculum" (2005a, p. 1).

*Teachers and Support Staff Working Together* (2005b) (www.gov.pe.ca/photos/original/ed_tssworktog.pdf)

- Lessons that incorporate IEP goals may call for full, partial, or parallel participation.

**NEWFOUNDLAND AND LABRADOR (www.ed.gov.nl.ca/edu/k12/studentsupportservices/services.html )**
*Individual Support Services Plan (ISSP) Handbook* (1997)

- Emphasis on collaborative planning for children and youth with special needs, using a model of coordinated services among departments of Education, Heath and Community Services, Justice, and Human Resources, Labour, and Employment.

*Pathways to Programming and Graduation: A Brochure for Parents*

- Description of five pathways used in planning educational programs to meet individual student's needs.

*Focusing on Students, ISSP and Pathways Commission Report* (2007)

- Highly critical of the process for identifying and meeting the needs of exceptional students that requires interdepartmental cooperation even for classroom differentiation of teaching; "a good idea gone awry" that needs to be streamlined to focus on students, not on paperwork (p. 6).

preparation and ongoing support, and schools need more resources and flexibility. The dilemmas of legislating differentiation and inclusion alongside identification and labelling require our best problem solving and teamwork, informed by research and goodwill.

# How We Got Here: Highlights in the Development of Inclusive Education in Ontario

Over the last few decades inclusive education has evolved rapidly. Today, as we have seen, every province and territory is committed to inclusive policies and practices. However, in 1950 when the Royal Commission on Education in Ontario issued its report, the *Hope Report*, there was no obligation for schools to educate students with disabilities. The Report recommended an expansion of special education programs to serve children with learning disabilities. Although the Report was largely ignored, the recommendation was significant as an initial step. The next few sections review the history of the gradual movement toward inclusion in education in Ontario from the 1960s to the present.

## Robarts Plan and Hall-Dennis Report, 1960s

To reduce the dropout rate for secondary students, the Robarts Plan, 1962, introduced streaming, which provided three tracks to graduation: two-, four-, or five-year programs. As a result, more students remained in school, many of whom would now be considered exceptional learners. In 1968, the Hall-Dennis Report, *Living and Learning: The Report of the Provincial Committee on Aims and Objectives of Education in the Schools of Ontario*, was published. The report described special education as "a welter of complexity, divided authority, blurred responsibility, and a broad spectrum of services unevenly distributed through the province and too frequently inadequate." At that time, special education was primarily the responsibility of small township school boards whose resources were limited. The Report lent its support to those who were lobbying for the integration of all but the most severely disabled students, reinforcing "the right of every individual to have equal access to the learning experience best suited to his needs, and the responsibility of every school authority to provide a child centred learning continuum that invites learning by individual discovery and inquiry." However, throughout the 1970s, support for students with special needs was limited to self-contained and "opportunity" classes. There was no requirement for school boards to offer services or programs.

## Bill 82, 1980

In 1980, the *Ontario Education Act* was amended with the passage of Bill 82. This seminal legislation recognized the rights of exceptional students to an educational program specific to their needs in concert with the goals of education in Ontario. The five principles of Bill 82 were: (a) the right of universal access to a school program for all exceptional pupils; (b) the right of exceptional pupils to receive an appropriate education at public expense; (c) the right of parents to appeal the identification and placement of, or to request a review on behalf of, their exceptional child; (d) the right of ongoing identification and continuous assessment and review through the IPRC process; and (e) the right of exceptional pupils to a program that includes a plan with specific objectives and an outline of services to meet the needs of the exceptional pupil. Given the scope of the legislation, school boards were given five years to meet the legislative requirements.

## Comparable Legislation in the US: Public Law (PL) 94-142

Five years earlier, landmark legislation was passed in the United States that governed how students with disabilities were educated in publicly funded schools. A federal special education law, *Education of All Handicapped Children Act*, Public Law (PL) 94-142, required that free appropriate public education be made available to all students with disabilities and required procedural safeguards so that students with disabilities could challenge schools that did not live up to the provisions of the law. Where PL-94-142 was prescriptive regarding integration or segregation of pupils, mandating placement in the least restrictive environment (LRE) appropriate to the student's needs, Bill 82 left the day-to-day procedures up to individual school boards. However, subsequent regulations were developed to ensure phased-in implementation. The impact of Bill 82 was felt as programs were restructured and the regular classroom became the first choice for placement whenever possible. The legislation and policy of both Bill 82 and PL 94-142 were process driven while recent legislation has focused more on outcomes.

## Emily Eaton Case

The Charter was passed in 1982, and section 15, which named persons with disabilities as an equity group, came into force in 1985. Since then, several court cases have been heard, mainly disputing a school district's decision to place a student with a severe disability in a segregated special education classroom. In the 1995 case *Eaton v. Brant County Board of Education*, the Ontario Court of Appeal stated: "unless the parents of a child who has been identified as exceptional by reason of a physical or mental disability consent to the placement of that child in a segregated environment, the school board must provide a placement that is the least exclusionary from the mainstream and still reasonably capable of meeting the child's special needs" (*Eaton v. Brant Board of Education*, 1995, pp. 33–34). Then in 1996 the Supreme Court of Canada overturned the Ontario Court of Appeal's ruling on this case. While many saw this decision as a major setback for the equity of people with disabilities, Lepofsky (1996, p. 393) argued that the Supreme Court's approach rested on the foundation that the decision to remove a child from an integrated setting (always the preferred setting) must be governed solely by an individualized, case-specific consideration of what is in the best interests of that child. Such a decision cannot be made simply because of the existence of a disability.

### What do you think?

In June 2008, the *Globe and Mail* ran a series of articles on recent efforts to acknowledge and eliminate the stigma associated with mental illness, with considerable focus on depression. As you read this book, search for current newspaper articles on issues related to social inclusion in Canadian society. Discuss with your peers the progress we have made as a country and what we can do as educators to advance inclusion in Canada, so all people are valued participants.

## Current Accessibility Requirements

The *Accessibility for Ontarians with Disabilities Act* (AODA) (2005) aims to make Ontario a fully accessible province by 2025. Annual accessibility plans are required by every district school board under the *Ontarians with Disabilities Act* (ODA) (2001), which include initiatives for barrier-free learning environments. Barriers, under the ODA, include physical, informational, communicational, attitudinal, or technological barriers, as well as policies or practices.

## Social Inclusion

We have arrived at our commitment to inclusive education through a complex set of circumstances including United Nations proclamations, the repatriation of our constitution during the International Year of Disabled Persons, protests, innovative legislation and human rights codes, and our idealistic notions of a multicultural, diverse, and equitable society. Canadian heroes and ordinary people with disabilities alike have advocated for themselves and raised public awareness that people with disabilities are "people first." Inclusive education has been viewed as a specific example of social inclusion and is usually thought of as arising from children's rights (Hanvey, 2003). **Social inclusion** is, however, a challenging concept. In a series of working papers (www.laidlawfdn.org/cms/page1436.cfm), the Laidlaw Foundation identified five cornerstones: valued recognition, engagement, proximity, material well-being, and learning and development opportunities. Bach (2002), of the Canadian Association for Community Living, argues that emphasizing only the rights of persons with disabilities entrenches exclusion, while what is needed is for societal institutions to provide valued recognition to those who have been marginalized. Rights are necessary but not sufficient to enable the social inclusion of diverse groups and we must view social inclusion as solidarity. When we choose to teach in Canada in the early decades of the twenty-first century, we are choosing to teach in inclusive schools in a society committed to inclusion. Although our reach exceeds our grasp, we must embrace this challenge and value all our students. For a fuller historical understanding of the evolution of inclusive education within the broader Canadian social context, see Table 1.1.

# "I Don't Agree!" The Controversies over Inclusive Education

Inclusive education continues to be a controversial topic. *Inclusion* is a relatively new term. It has largely replaced **mainstreaming** and **integration**, which were used in the 1970s and 1980s and which referred to moving exceptional students from segregated settings into classrooms in the mainstream. Inclusion, however, suggests that we embrace people with exceptionalities as an integral part of society and all its institutions from birth onward. This is one of the main ways in which inclusion differs from its predecessors. Mainstreaming referred to readying students with disabilities who had been placed in segregated settings for re-entry, once they could meet traditional academic expectations with minimal support, or when traditional academic expectations were not relevant. They were often taught academic skills in a separate setting, but research suggested that exceptional students taught in segregated classes did not make more academic progress than exceptional students

### What do you think?

Many journal articles report teachers' experiences with and views on teaching a variety of subjects to a range of exceptional learners in many different contexts. Look for a source that deals with a topic that is important to you. Here are two examples to get you started. Read a paper that relates to your experience and share the findings with your peers. Listen to their reports. What similarities and differences do you see?

Scott, L.P., Jellison, J.A., Chappell, E.W., & Standridge, A.A. (2007). Talking with music teachers about inclusion: Perceptions, opinions, and experiences. *Journal of Music Therapy,* 44(1), 38–56.

Lohrmann, S., & Boggs, E.M. (2006). Elementary education teachers' beliefs about essential supports needed to successfully include students with intellectual disabilities who engage in challenging behaviors. *Research & Practice for Persons with Severe Disabilities,* 31(2), 157–173.

## Terry Fox

Terry Fox is a Canadian hero. When Canadians were asked to name their heroes in 1999, one of the most frequently chosen individuals was a young man who won Canadians' admiration and raised our awareness of people with disabilities. From Coquitlam, BC, Fox was only 19 years old when he lost his right leg to cancer in 1977. While he was recovering, he dreamed of inspiring others with cancer and raising money to fight the disease.

In April 1980, Fox set out from St. John's, Newfoundland, to run across Canada on a "Marathon of Hope," running 40 kilometres a day, ignoring the pain, heading for the Pacific Ocean. Newspaper reporters described his run as "lift, hop, lift, hop, lift, hop" because he rocked back and forth between his left leg and his prosthetic right leg. Then in September, after running 5300 kilometres and raising two million dollars, Terry Fox stopped running on the north shore of Lake Superior. The cancer had returned; Fox died less than a year later.

In the months following the end of his run, Canadians donated twenty-five million dollars to cancer research. Every fall, marathons are held in his name to raise funds and, annually, thousands visit the memorial marking the site where he halted his run. Since 1980, athletes with disabilities have become much more prominent in our communities and in the news, but Terry Fox was one of the first and has become a Canadian hero.

Consider how you can promote your students' understanding of the significance of Terry Fox's Marathon of Hope and continue his legacy.

## TABLE 1.1 EVOLUTION TOWARD INCLUSION

### 1800s: Establishing a Country, Establishing Institutions

| Developments in Canadian Society | Developments in Education |
|---|---|
| 1815–50 The Great Migration brings thousands of new settlers to Upper and Lower Canada | 1830–60 Orphanages open in Halifax, Montreal, Kingston, and Toronto |
| 1850s Railway building joins the colonies together | 1831–86 Schools for blind and deaf children open in Quebec, Ontario, Nova Scotia, and Manitoba |
| 1867 Confederation—education becomes a provincial responsibility | 1893 Children's Aid Societies start in Ontario |

### 1900–50: Change and Growth

| Developments in Canadian Society | Developments in Education |
|---|---|
| 1914–18 First World War, followed by the economic boom of the 1920s and the Great Depression of the 1930s | By the 1920s special education classes are offered in urban elementary schools |
| 1939–45 Second World War increases Canada's international reputation | By 1923 summer courses for teachers of special classes are available |
| 1945 Fifty-one nations first meet to establish the United Nations, with one of its goals the promotion of equality among peoples | 1940s Residential institutions are "home" to many people with disabilities (e.g., Smiths Falls, ON); local associations are formed by parents of children with mental retardation |

### 1950–70: The Impact of the Baby Boom Generation

| Developments in Canadian Society | Developments in Education |
|---|---|
| 1950s Baby boomers and immigrant families cause population increases, cultural diversity, and the construction of suburbs | Formation of the Canadian Association for Retarded Children (1958) and the Canadian Association for Children with Learning Disabilities (1963) |
| Cold War and Sputnik lead to huge developments in science and technology | Parent associations establish schools and developmental centres for the education of retarded children |

*(continued)*

TABLE 1.1 **EVOLUTION TOWARD INCLUSION (Continued)**

| | |
|---|---|
| Television brings global events into Canadian homes; youth movement for civil rights and social justice worldwide | Growth of segregated programs for gifted students and students with disabilities |
| 1964 Pearson government funds the Company of Young Canadians to give young activists the opportunity to work toward social change through local programs | Growth of post-secondary education: universities and community colleges |

### 1970s and 1980s: Advocacy and Rights

| **Developments in Canadian Society** | **Developments in Education** |
|---|---|
| 1975 United Nations Declaration of the Rights of Disabled Persons | In 1970 *One Million Children,* the CELDIC Report (Roberts & Lazure), advocates the integration of exceptional children and instruction based on individual learning needs; in 1971 Standards for Education of Exceptional Children in Canada (Hardy, Minto, Perkins, & Quance) sparks teacher education on exceptional children at Canadian universities |
| 1977 Canadian Human Rights Act | 1977 deinstitutionalization became the priority of the Canadian Association for the Mentally Retarded |
| 12 April 1980 Terry Fox begins his Marathon of Hope to promote public awareness of the abilities of persons with disabilities and to raise funds for cancer research | In 1979 Bill 188, the Handicapped Persons Rights [Protection] Act was advanced and then withdrawn in Ontario due to pressure from a coalition of disability groups, who described it as "separate and unequal" |
| 1981 United Nations Year of the Disabled | 1980 Bill 82 in Ontario guarantees the right of all exceptional students to an appropriate education with a new funding model |
| 1981 Demonstrations by Canadians with disabilities on Parliament Hill to demand they have Charter rights | Early 1980s provinces develop IEPs; Ontario phases in the IPRC |
| 21 March 1985, Rick Hansen sets out on his "Man in Motion" tour of thirty-four countries to raise money for spinal cord research | Mid-1980s Integration is adopted as the prevailing approach to educating exceptional students |
| 1988 People with mental disabilities receive the right to vote | Late 1980s Educational reviews begin across Canada, including reviews of special education |

### 1990s: Inclusion, Reform, and Challenges

| **Developments in Canadian Society** | **Developments in Education** |
|---|---|
| Cutbacks in government funding to schools, social services, and universities | Parents demand inclusion of children with disabilities in regular classroom settings |
| August 1994 First inclusive Commonwealth Games, hosted by Victoria, British Columbia | 10 October 1996 Supreme Court of Canada rules that Emily Eaton receive appropriate education to meet her individual needs in a segregated setting, reversing an earlier decision of a lower court |
| 1997 Release of the Report of the Royal Commission on Aboriginal Peoples | Reviews and changes in exceptional education policies across Canada make inclusion the dominant policy |

### 2000–2010: Social Inclusion and Differentiated Classrooms

| **Developments in Canadian Society** | **Developments in Education** |
|---|---|
| 2002 Release of the Laidlaw Foundation's *Working Papers Series on Social Inclusion* | 2005 Ontario Ministry of Education releases *Education for All,* promoting differentiated instruction |
| 2006 Convention on the Rights of Persons with Disabilities is adopted by the United Nations | 2006 SET-BC, which focuses on technology in classrooms, begins initiative to advance practice in BC based on UDL |
| 2008 Exhibit at the Royal Ontario Museum titled "Out from Under: Disability, History, and Things to Remember" | Increases in every province in numbers of students identified with autism and Asperger syndrome |
| 2008 Canadian government formally apologizes to Aboriginal peoples for treatment during era of residential schools | Greater emphasis on curriculum development and on policy frameworks for Aboriginal education, e.g., *Ontario First Nation, Métis, and Inuit Education Policy Framework,* 2007 |

taught in mainstream settings (e.g., Dunn, 1968). With few exceptions, parents wanted their exceptional children to participate in society, and segregated classes did not provide good models of social participation. If segregated classes did not produce better academic learning, then how could they be justified?

There have always been differing views on inclusion. Angela Valeo and Gary Bunch (1998) of York University interviewed six experienced elementary school teachers. Modifying curriculum was not a role these teachers saw themselves taking on. One teacher said, "It would be easier if he had someone [other than the classroom teacher] working with him" (p. 13).

In contrast, Paula Stanovich (1999) of the University of Toronto reported on a focus group composed of four classroom teachers, one special education teacher, and one resource teacher from a grade 7–8 school, who spoke of the benefits of inclusion and of "realities" rather than costs. Benefits included opportunities for students with disabilities to learn appropriate social behaviour and for students without disabilities to develop respect for their exceptional classmates. "There's a mutual respect now, and they're talking to each other outside of class" (p. 56). The success of inclusion was also contingent on curriculum adaptations that included using materials of various reading levels; changing the length, time, or complexity of assignments; breaking assignments into smaller parts; and using cooperative groups. To foster inclusion, the teachers identified supports including more time, appropriate teaching materials, assistants in the classroom, and administrative support.

Stanovich and Jordan (1998, 2004) found that teachers who are effective in inclusive classrooms tend to have principals who believe that all children can and should learn in regular classrooms and that teachers should differentiate their modes of instruction rather than expect exceptional children to adapt. The second important predictor of effective teaching behaviour was teachers' responses to the same questionnaire about beliefs completed by principals; inclusive teachers held beliefs that exceptional children should learn in regular classrooms. Exemplary inclusion teachers focused on helping exceptional learners become independent members of the classroom community and made many adaptations, which applied in varying degrees to all students (Jordan & Stanovich; 1998, 2004; McGhie, Underwood, & Jordan, 2007). Our beliefs about exceptional learners are closely related to our teaching actions.

Recent studies suggest that effective regular classroom teachers in inclusive classrooms have an important characteristic in common with excellent special education teachers. Stough and Palmer (2003) found that expert special education teachers consistently referred to the needs and strengths of individual students rather than speaking in generalities about the class as a whole. Paterson (2007), who studied junior high school teachers teaching in inclusive classrooms in Australia and Canada, found that they demonstrated a similar knowledge of individual students as well as awareness of categorical notions of exceptional learners. This research demonstrates the close links among teacher beliefs, knowledge, and inclusive teaching.

## Community and Inclusive Education

There are a number of ways in which community is important to inclusive education. A **community** is a group of people who have shared interests, who mutually

**Put into Practice** 🖱

Community Inclusion Initiative (www.communityinclusion.ca) aims to strengthen community capacities to secure inclusion and citizenship for people with intellectual disabilities and their families. Are there ways that you can develop ties between your students and community organizations like Community Living that support people with intellectual disabilitiies?

pursue the common good, and who usually share an acceptance of group standards and a sense of identification with the group (Dewey, 1916; McCaleb, 1995). A community ensures that students are well-known and that they are encouraged by adults who care about them (Strike, 2008). As discussed earlier, inclusion involves the acceptance and participation of all, and inclusive classrooms ought to be communities. We can act on our belief that community is important by conducting classroom meetings, using a sharing chair, teaching active listening, providing students with choices, and building mentoring relationships (Obenchain & Abernathy, 2003). High school practices that facilitate community, inclusion, and authentic learning include high expectations, teacher commitment to inclusion, intellectually demanding tasks, and making accommodations for assessment (Phelps, 2003).

## Using the ADAPT Strategy for Adapting Teaching to Include Exceptional Learners

This chapter introduces you to a systematic strategy called **ADAPT**, for adapting or differentiating teaching to include exceptional learners. This strategy is similar to others that serve the same purpose, but it also considers the perspectives of those influenced by the decision to ADAPT and the consequences for them of the adaptation. This approach is elaborated throughout the text with many examples, especially in Chapters 3, 4, 5, and 6. This strategy recognizes that both the characteristics of the student (**strengths *and* needs**) and the demands of the classroom environment have to be considered when devising adaptations.

The **ADAPT** strategy for adapting teaching to include exceptional learners has the following five steps:

- Step 1: **A**ccounts of students' strengths and needs
- Step 2: **D**emands of the classroom
- Step 3: **A**daptations
- Step 4: **P**erspectives and consequences
- Step 5: **T**each and assess the match

These five steps constitute a procedure that you can use in both elementary and secondary classrooms with learners who have a variety of exceptionalities.

## Step 1: Accounts of Students' Strengths and Needs

This first step requires that you know each exceptional student well. Start with the student's Ontario Student Record (OSR), which usually contains the IEP, psychoeducational assessment reports, teachers' anecdotal comments, and relevant medical information. It is your responsibility to be familiar with this file from the first day the student is a member of your class. The IEP includes specific statements of strengths and needs in three general areas: (1) social, emotional, and behavioural; (2) physical; and (3) academic.

**Put into Practice** 🖱

*An Act to Protect Anaphylactic Pupils: Sabrina's Law* came into effect on 1 January 2006. The law ensures that all Ontario school boards have polices and procedures in place to deal with anaphylaxis in schools. This was groundbreaking legislation and the first of its kind anywhere in the world. www.edu.gov.on.ca/eng/healthyschools/anaphylaxis.html

What is your board's policy? How can you help your students to understand anaphylactic reactions and recognize the need to seek immediate assistance? See www.eworkshop.on.ca/edu/anaphylaxis/ for the Ministry of Education online anaphylaxis training for teachers, administrators, staff, and board personnel.

Social, emotional, and behavioural strengths may include carrying on a conversation with peers, turn taking in a group activity, controlling anger, or being highly motivated to improve. You can use a strength, such as high motivation, to help a student focus on meeting personal goals. Conversely, social, emotional, and behavioural needs could mean that a student requires significant instruction and support because she cries when frustrated by academic tasks or taunts from peers.

Physical strengths and weaknesses include motor skills, neurological functioning, and vision. A student may have strong mobility skills in spite of low vision and may be able to move around the school independently; however, her low vision may mean she needs significant instruction or adaptations to read using a communication aid such as Braille or large print.

Academic strengths and weaknesses include the basic skills of reading, mathematics, etc. They also include strategies for studying and problem solving. Students can demonstrate strengths in completing calculations (with or without a calculator), organizing, and answering questions orally. Student needs can include requiring significant instruction and support to develop beginning reading skills, comprehend a textbook, or solve word problems in mathematics.

## Step 2: Demands of the Classroom

Next, consider the social, emotional, and behavioural demands of your classroom. Do students learn individually or are they working with peers most of the time? A student with attention difficulties may find it hard to focus on and remember the steps in complex assignments without peer support, but may also be distracted by learning groups that are never really quiet. How long is the lecture or information-sharing section at the beginning of the class, and is it reasonable to expect a student with behavioural challenges to listen for that amount of time? Do you model positive interactions and respect for all students?

When you consider physical demands, think about the frequency with which you move the furniture in the classroom. Could changes be dangerous to anyone—especially to a student who is blind or in a wheelchair? Do you rely on an overhead projector or an ELMO projector, and might some students have difficulty seeing the projected images from where they sit? What are the demands of your physical education classes, and could they endanger a student with asthma?

The academic demands of the classroom are manifested in the instructional materials you use, including textbooks, audiovisual aids, and manipulative devices. Do all of the children in grade 1 have the same basal readers, or do some have readers, others chapter books, and others instruction to learn the sounds in words, followed by the reading of highly predictable rhyming books?

The academic demands of the classroom are also shown in your assessment and evaluation methods. Look for means of assessment that enable exceptional learners to show what they know rather than to show their disabilities: for example, written reports, oral reports, drawings, three-dimensional models, and PowerPoint reports.

## Step 3: Adaptations

In this step you compare a student's learning needs to the demands of the classroom and identify potential mismatches and adaptations or ways to differentiate teaching and assessment that will eliminate these mismatches. Think about adaptations that take advantage of the student's strengths, as the above examples demonstrate.

You can ADAPT the fundamental organization and instruction of the classroom. For example, in a secondary history class one group may read speeches made by Canadian politicians during the Second World War and articles that appeared

**Cross-Reference**
In Chapter 2 you will find strengths and needs as described in a student's IEP. The IEP will supplement your own observations of a student.

**Cross-Reference**
Chapters 3 and 4 contain detailed information about all of the exceptionalities introduced in this chapter, focusing on educational implications for you as a classroom teacher.

in Canadian newspapers of the same era to study divergent views on conscription. Less competent readers may study political cartoons and view videos of historians discussing the issue of conscription. Both groups could use combinations of visual, oral, and written means to communicate their findings (with the emphasis on written communication varying between 20 and 80 percent).

Bypassing a student's learning need minimizes the impact of a disability. Chung has not mastered the multiplication tables. In grade 5, his teacher shows the class how to use a calculator efficiently and reminds Chung to use his and to request a "booster session" if he forgets any steps. Bypassing his weakness in calculations enables Chung to work on the same authentic problems as his peers. A peer editor or spell checker bypasses poor spelling, and Braille bypasses lack of vision.

Teaching students basic learning skills is also a way to ADAPT. Chung was taught two basic skills to use a calculator well: how to identify the series of operations required to solve a math problem, and how to estimate the answer. Secondary teachers teach basic skills about note taking and test taking. While study skills may be an urgent need for students with LD, others in the class are likely to benefit too.

## Step 4: Perspectives and Consequences

Reflect critically on adaptations and consider them from many perspectives. To get the most return for your effort, choose adaptations whenever you can that are beneficial for many (if not all) students in your class and choose adaptations that have demonstrated effectiveness. Validated practices are described in textbooks, in professional journals, and on websites. For information on pertinent journals, see Table 1.2; for guidelines on evaluating websites, see Figure 1.5.

TABLE 1.2 **READING THE JOURNALS**

| Journals about exceptional learners | General education journals |
| --- | --- |
| Exceptional Children | Adolescence |
| Exceptionality Education International | Alberta Journal of Educational Research |
| Focus on Autism and Other Developmental Disabilities | Canadian Journal of Education |
| Gifted Child Quarterly | Canadian Journal of Native Education |
| Gifted Child Today | Education Canada |
| Intellectual and Developmental Disabilities | Educational Assessment |
| Intervention in School and Clinic | Educational Leadership |
| Journal of Emotional and Behavioral Disorders | Elementary School Journal |
| Journal of Learning Disabilities | High School Journal |
| Journal of Special Education | McGill Journal of Education |
| Learning Disabilities Research and Practice | Middle School Journal |
| Learning Disability Quarterly | Phi Delta Kappan |
| Remedial and Special Education | Psychology in the Schools |
| Roeper Review | Reading Research Quarterly |
| Teaching Exceptional Children | Reading Teacher |
| Topics in Early Childhood Special Education | Review of Educational Research |
| | Theory into Practice |

Next, take the perspective of the exceptional student. Is the adaptation age appropriate? Can it be conducted without drawing undue attention to the student? Is the return for effort worthwhile for the student? If you don't consider the student's perspective, you may find yourself putting in great effort while the student is investing little. Observe and listen to the student to understand his or her point of view, and ADAPT in a way that is respectful of the student.

There are other perspectives to consider as well. How does the rest of the class view the adaptation? Do they notice? Are they concerned, involved, and respectful or do they feel ignored or bored while you speak slowly to accommodate another student? How do the parents of the exceptional student view your adaptations? What are other parents' views? More widely, what is the community view of adapting teaching?

Consider consequences, intended and unintended. What are the consequences for the exceptional student—are participation and learning evident? Are there drawbacks? What are the consequences of the adaptation for others in the class? Do any dilemmas arise? If you provide an open-ended assessment, you may be disappointed when students capable of writing an essay choose to develop a graphic representation of what they learned.

## Step 5: Teach and Assess the Match

Ask how well the adaptation has matched student strengths and needs to classroom demands. Remember that "things take time"; it is important to persevere and give an adaptation time to be effective. If you have tried everything, you may not have stayed with anything long enough. You can assess the match by observing how engaged the student is, asking how he or she finds the changes, charting the student's marks, analyzing any errors, and talking with the pupil's parents. You will think of many other sources of information to help you decide whether to continue or to rethink an adaptation.

## Using the ADAPT Strategy for a Wide Range of Exceptional Learners

In Figure 1.4 you will find brief descriptions of a wide range of exceptionalities, all students for whom you may find the ADAPT strategy helpful. These generic descriptions will not apply to all students with these exceptionalities, and you will refine them as you gain experience with these learners. In Chapters 3 and 4 you will see more detailed research-based descriptions.

> **Cross-Reference**
>
> Chapter 5 focuses on differentiating teaching, and Chapter 6 focuses on adapting assessment.

## Evaluating Internet Resources

Internet sites are identified throughout this book. Each site address was verified shortly before this book went to press. Before beginning to use any new information resource—print, online, or Web-based—take a few minutes to examine and evaluate the resource. Figure 1.5 contains a brief set of criteria to help you evaluate Web-based resources.

## Reading the Journals to Remain Current

Until internet resources undergo rigorous peer review, they will not take the place of journals. Most peer-reviewed journals publish roughly 25 percent of the papers submitted. Table 1.2 contains a list of peer-reviewed journals about exceptional learners that will help you stay current as a professional educator.

FIGURE 1.4 BRIEF DESCRIPTIONS OF EXCEPTIONAL LEARNERS

**Students who are Gifted or Developmentally Advanced**

- Have exceptionally high abilities in one or several areas including specific academic subjects, overall intellect, creativity; may show depth of interest, task commitment, maturity of thinking

**Students with Learning Disabilities (LD)**

- Have dysfunctions in processing information (e.g., dyslexia [reading], dysgraphia [writing] or, dyscalculia [arithmetic calculations]); discrepancy between ability and achievement despite average or better ability

**Students with Attention Deficit Hyperactivity Disorder (ADHD)**

- Show a persistent pattern of inattention or hyperactivity, or both inattention and hyperactivity that hinders academic and social success; usually diagnosed by physicians; students may be prescribed medications to help them focus

**Students with Speech and Language Exceptionalities**

- Have a speech impairment (e.g., lisp or stutter) or impairment in expressive language or receptive language or both; often these occur when students have autism or other exceptionalities

**Students with Behaviour and Emotional Exceptionalities**

- Have dysfunctional interactions with the environment (e.g., classroom, home, community); these behaviours are persistent and interfere with educational performance

**Students with Intellectual Disabilities (ID)**

- Have slower rate of development of cognitive abilities and adaptive behaviours than their peers; can often participate and lead productive lives; IDs range from mild to severe

**Students with Autism Spectrum Disorder (ASD) (Autism or Asperger Syndrome)**

- Have limited development of communication and social interaction with severe delay in intellectual development (Autism) or severe and sustained impairment in social interaction, restricted patterns of behaviour but no cognitive or language delay (Asperger Syndrome)

**Students who are Deaf or Hard-of-Hearing**

- Have complete or partial hearing loss that interferes with acquisition of speech and oral language; often rely on visual sources of information to learn

**Students with Visual Impairments and Students who are Blind**

- Have partial or complete loss of sight; depend on auditory and tactile sources of information

**Students with Physical Disabilities**

- Have a range of conditions restricting physical movement or motor abilities due to nervous system impairment, musculoskeletal conditions or chronic medical conditions; each is slightly different in cause, characteristics, and classroom implications
- **Nervous System Impairment**
  - **Cerebral Palsy** is a group of disorders impairing body movement and muscle coordination
  - **Spina Bifida** is developed prenatally and disturbs development of the spinal cord
  - **Epilepsy** produces disturbances in electrical functions in the brain and seizures
  - **Tourette Syndrome** involves motor tics and uncontrollable vocal sounds, and obsessions
  - **Traumatic Brain Injury (TBI)** involves sustained damage to brain tissue as a result of an accident or head injury; causes physical problems and cognitive problems including memory loss
  - **Fetal Alcohol Syndrome Disorder (FASD)** results from prenatal exposure to alcohol and manifests in physical and cognitive delays; often a characteristic pattern of facial features

# FIGURE 1.4 (Continued)

- **Musculoskeletal Conditions**
  - **Muscular Dystrophy** is a group of muscle disorders characterized by progressive weakness and muscle wasting
  - **Juvenile Arthritis** involves chronic inflammation of one or more joints with stiffness and pain; eyes can become involved
- **Chronic Medical Disorders**
  - **Life-Threatening Allergies (Anaphylaxis)** involve an abnormal reaction to a normal substance (e.g., peanuts); require an immediate injection (epinephrine); may require that a student be rushed to hospital
  - **Asthma** involves obstructed airways that hinder breathing and cause wheezing; can be life-threatening and an attack may require that a student be rushed to hospital
  - **Cystic Fibrosis** causes severe respiratory problems and digestive difficulties due to excessive mucus; students may need to do breathing exercises at school; frequent hospitalization
  - **Cancer** involves uncontrolled division of cells which spread; leukemia is a form of cancer in the bone marrow; students may return to school during treatment because school may play a normalizing role

# FIGURE 1.5 QUESTIONS TO ASK WHEN EVALUATING INFORMATION FOUND ON THE INTERNET

### Who is the author?

- What are the author's credentials on this subject and the institutional affiliation and address?

### Who is the publishing body?

- Does this entity make sense as the publisher of this information? (Look in the first portion of the URL between http:// and the first slash [/] after that.)
- If there is a sponsoring organization, is it straightforward about its nature and function? Are there links such as "About us" or "Background" or "Philosophy"?
- Is there a way of verifying the legitimacy of this organization by an address or phone number?
- Has the information undergone peer review or an equivalent process?
- What kind of domain does the page come from? What does the URL tell you? Does it show the website is (a) educational (it names a university or ends in .edu in the United States); (b) the product of a government (the URL may include .gov); (c) personal (the URL usually includes a name following "~" or may cite users, members, or other people); (d) commercial (the URL ends in .com); or (e) posted by an organization, likely nonprofit (the URL ends in .org)? Or does the URL end in a country code like .ca?

### What is the point of view or bias?

- Information is rarely neutral. What is the purpose of this internet information?
- Is the intent to sell you something or convince you of something, perhaps an extremist view?
- What political or religious views might underlie the information provided?
- Are there links to other resources on the topic? Do the links work and are they current?

### Are there references to and evidence of knowledge of the discipline?

- Does the document include a bibliography? What kinds of publications or sites are cited?
- Does the author display knowledge of theories, schools of thought, or techniques usually considered appropriate in this discipline? Is there documentation to support claims made?
- If the author's treatment of the subject is controversial, does the author acknowledge this?
- Are there indicators that the information is timely, contains a copyright date, and was updated?

**Further Reading**

For more information on evaluating websites, consult:

Sauers, M.P. (2008). *Reference librarian's guide to mastering internet searching*. London, UK: Facet Publishing.

Adams, T., & Scollard, S. (2005). *Internet effectively: A beginner's guide to the World Wide Web*. Toronto: Pearson Canada.

Barker, J. (2005). *Evaluating Web pages: Techniques to apply and questions to ask*. www.lib.berkeley.edu/TeachingLib/Guides/Internet/Evaluate.html

Tillman, H.N. (2003). *Evaluating quality on the net*. www.hopetillman.com/findqual.html

Kirk, E.E. (1996). *Evaluating information found on the internet*. www.library.jhu.edu/researchhelp/general/evaluating

UC Berkeley. (2010). *Teaching library internet workshops: Finding information on the internet: A tutorial*.

www.lib.berkeley.edu/TeachingLib/Guides/Internet/Evaluate.html

**Weblinks**

MEDIA-AWARENESS NETWORK
www.media-awareness.ca

KATHY SCHROCK'S GUIDE FOR EDUCATORS—CRITICAL EVALUATION INFORMATION
http://school.discoveryeducation.com/schrockguide/eval.html

QUEEN'S UNIVERSITY STAUFFER LIBRARY PAGE FOR EVALUATING WORLD WIDE WEB INFORMATION
http://library.queensu.ca/inforef/tutorials/qcat/evalint.htm

## FIGURE 1.5 (Continued)

**Do I trust this source?**

- Is it as credible and useful as the print and online sources available through my library?
- Could I be the victim of irony, fraud, or falsehood?
- Are my expectations fair; too lenient or too harsh; objective or biased?
- Am I accepting a lower standard than I would in a print source?
- Have I asked hard questions and remained skeptical?

———

Adapted from sources available on the internet:

Barker, J. (2005). Evaluating Web pages: Techniques to apply and questions to ask.
www.lib.berkeley.edu/TeachingLib/Guides/Internet/Evaluate.html

Tillman, H.N. (2003). Evaluating quality on the net. www.hopetillman.com/findqual.html

Kirk, E.E. (1996). Evaluating information found on the internet.
www.library.jhu.edu/researchhelp/general/ evaluating

# Summary

Exceptional education refers to the differentiated teaching and specialized services that thousands of exceptional students in Ontario and in Canada receive every day. Current practices have developed out of our history, legislation, research, and commitment to an equitable society. The dominant approach currently is inclusive education—with educators experiencing expectations that are a hybrid of our focus for the past twenty-five years on the identification of exceptionalities according to provincial categories and definitions and subsequent development of IEPs, and recent demands for responsive teaching and assessment. In Ontario, current initiatives embrace universal design for learning (UDL), differentiated instruction (DI), and progress monitoring. With these expectations come dilemmas of practice for classroom teachers. As a teacher, you will be expected to differentiate your teaching and adapt your assessment for exceptional learners. The ADAPT strategy will help you meet the needs of exceptional students as you teach, and it will guide you as you learn strategies for the inclusive classroom in the upcoming chapters.

# Key Terms

exceptional student (p. 3)
special education program (p. 3)
special education services (p. 3)
accommodations (p. 3)
modifications (p. 5)
alternative learning expectations (p. 6)
Charter of Rights and Freedoms (p. 6)

equality rights (p. 6)
equal participation (p. 6)
inclusion (p. 7)
Identification, Placement, and Review Committee (IPRC) (p. 7)
Individual Education Plan (IEP) (p. 8)

students with special education needs (p. 8)
universal design for learning (UDL) (p. 9)
differentiated instruction (DI) (p. 9)
progress monitoring (p. 9)
responsiveness to intervention (RTI) (p. 9)

personalization (p. 10)    mainstreaming (p. 16)    strengths and
precision (p. 10)    integration (p. 16)    needs (p. 20)
professional learning (p. 10)    community (p. 19)
social inclusion (p. 16)    ADAPT (p. 20)

# Challenges for Reviewing Chapter 1

1. Prepare a brochure for the various communities associated with a school with which you are familiar (including families and educators). Your topic is the highlights—as you see them—of the path to inclusive education in Ontario.

2. Make a list of the various exceptionalities identified in Ontario. Then make a personal list of these exceptionalities from the most challenging for you to include to the least challenging. Identify the three that are most challenging for you. Research these three and develop an approach to teaching that makes you feel more confident about teaching students with these exceptionalities. Compare your list and your strategies with your peers'. Make a plan for implementing this approach.

3. Develop an example of using UDL and DI to plan teaching for a class that includes an exceptional learner. Use the ADAPT strategy implicitly or explicitly, and justify the actions it led you to. Translate your example into a series of classes that enable this student to succeed. Add more complexity to the classroom by describing groups of students in the class as well as individuals who need differentiated instruction. Then develop a plan for including all these students using UDL and DI. Discuss with your peers how to implement your plan.

4. Describe to an acquaintance what social inclusion means in the context of Canadian society and why educators have such an important role to play in inclusion.

# Chapter 2
## The Educator's Role as Teacher and Collaborator

### Learner Objectives

After you have read this chapter, you will be able to do the following:

1. Describe the role of the classroom teacher in identifying the needs of exceptional learners.

2. Discuss the role of the classroom teacher in carrying out the pre-referral process.

3. Describe collaboration and outline how a school-based team collaborates to meet the needs of exceptional students.

4. Describe the IPRC and the IEP and the teacher's role in both.

5. Describe your responsibilities in collaborating with educational assistants to enhance the learning of exceptional students.

6. Discuss how you can collaborate with parents in the education of exceptional students.

**Joan Hughes telephoned Silver Birch School to make an appointment with her son Andy's grade 2 teacher, Ms. Sauvé.** Joan told Ms. Sauvé that Andy's report card—with many comments of "Needs improvement" and "Is progressing with close supervision"—seemed poor for a bright young boy who likes to read, gets his friends to take part in plays, and is intensely curious. One comment sounded familiar: "Cannot follow instructions and complete his work independently. Is easily distracted and has a difficult time organizing his work and his belongings." Joan's older son, who is now in grade 7, had brought home similar report cards and was subsequently identified as having attention deficit disorder. Joan suggested to Ms. Sauvé that Andy be referred to the in-school team. Having an IPRC and an IEP had helped her older son—classroom teachers had adapted teaching and a resource teacher had taught him strategies to focus his attention and complete tasks. Ms. Sauvé was reluctant to make a referral based on a parent's request. As a new teacher, she was not certain if parents could make such referrals, or if teachers had to act on them. Ms. Sauvé kept thinking about the three students who seemed to have more difficulty learning than Andy did. She wondered, "How can I take Andy's case to the in-school team if I don't take their cases, too?" Ms. Sauvé does not want the principal to think she cannot resolve her own challenges. She is not sure how she would feel about sharing her students with a resource teacher. Ms. Sauvé doesn't know what to do.

**Brenda Piet has a learning disability and an IEP.** It is September and she is hoping to complete grade 11 this year. Brenda has asked her home room teacher, Frank Bogg, to help her to refine and act on the brief transition plan in her IEP. She is worried about what she should do after secondary school. She has always wanted to be an architect, but she has heard recently that the local community college offers a program in architectural technology. She is wondering whether that might be a better option for her. It is not clear to Mr. Bogg how much he needs to know about all of these career options. He understands that exceptional students have a transition plan, but he does not yet know the extent of his responsibility for helping Brenda to implement hers. There are so many changes taking place in schools, and teachers are expected to take on so many new roles. Mr. Bogg used to feel that he knew what was expected of him. Now he's not so sure.

1. What is a teacher's responsibility when a parent or student asks for a referral to an in-school team, an assessment, or help in developing a transition plan?

2. What steps should Ms. Sauvé and Mr. Bogg take to respond to the requests made of them?

3. Whom should each of these teachers consult to help them decide what to do?

4. As the classroom teacher, what role might Ms. Sauvé expect to play if the in-school team decided to hold an IPRC meeting and develop an IEP for Andy?

5. What can classroom teachers like Mr. Bogg do to advise students effectively about academic and career planning?

# Introduction

As a classroom teacher, you know your students. In an elementary classroom, you may be with them all day. In a middle or secondary school, you may meet more than a hundred students each day, but you will come to know these students—their interests, friends, and strengths as learners. When you encounter students in difficulty, you may wonder if they should be identified as exceptional students by an Identification, Placement, and Review Committee (IPRC) and have Individual Education Plans (IEPs). What is your role in this process? How do teachers, parents, and educational assistants work together for students? You are introduced here to the many roles of classroom teachers in inclusive education. Following a teacher through the steps, this chapter describes the process after a teacher recognizes that a student may have special education needs. The teacher's roles on the in-school special education team and in assessment of the student are emphasized. Depending on the assessment findings and on how successfully the student's needs are met, an IPRC could be held and an IEP could be developed for the student. The teacher has key responsibilities to inform and support parents as well as to direct the duties of educational assistants.

**@**

**Weblinks**

SPECIAL NEEDS ONTARIO WINDOW (SNOW)
http://snow.utoronto.ca/index.php

**Cross-Reference**

Chapter 4 contains descriptions of low-incidence exceptionalities and strategies for teaching students who have the various exceptionalities.

# The Role of the Classroom Teacher in Identifying Needs of Exceptional Learners

Classroom teachers and parents usually have the most detailed knowledge about the strengths and needs of students with documented or suspected exceptionalities. Many exceptionalities, especially low-incidence exceptionalities, are identified early in a child's life. These include developmental disabilities, blindness, deafness, and physical disabilities like cerebral palsy. Teachers are usually informed about these exceptionalities before students enrol in their classrooms, can read the relevant student files and the IEP, and are responsible for carrying out the recommended accommodations and modifications. Observing these students, talking to previous teachers and to parents, and learning relevant teaching strategies will help. You will also be involved in reviews of the IPRCs of these students.

High-incidence exceptionalities such as learning disabilities, attention deficit disorder, and giftedness are most often identified after students enrol in school. All teachers need to be aware of the characteristics associated with these exceptionalities and of key teaching strategies. However, secondary teachers often find that these students have been identified and have IPRCs and IEPs before they reach grade 9. Usually, the challenge for secondary teachers is adapting complex curricula and teaching approaches to provide accommodations or modifications. Thus, while any teacher may be involved in recognizing students' special education needs, elementary teachers, especially those in the primary grades, have a key role in the initial identification of exceptional students. Teachers and parents bring individual students to the attention of the principal and other professionals when they suspect that a student needs intervention beyond the regular program.

In the case at the beginning of this chapter, Ms. Sauvé recognized that Andy was not thriving in the classroom, but she was not sure that Andy was experiencing

## FIGURE 2.1 FIRST STEPS

1. Document the student's characteristics, behaviours, and needs that led to your concern (or to the parent's concern). Also document the student's strengths. Analyze the demands of your classroom. Observe the student in your classroom.

2. Reread the student's file, test results, psychological reports, attendance records, and comments by previous teachers. Consult the protocol for identifying exceptional students.

3. Talk with the resource teacher. Share your observational notes, documentation, and ideas about how to address the student's needs.

4. Ask the resource teacher for suggestions and resources, including community associations. Plan pre-referral interventions. Inform the principal or the student's counsellor. The resource teacher may observe the student in your classroom.

5. Contact the parents to share your concerns and ideas for pre-referral interventions. Listen to the parents. The resource teacher may take part in this meeting. The protocol may recommend that you contact the parents before meeting with the resource teacher.

6. Make pre-referral adaptations or differentiations, keeping brief records of these and the student's responses. Use ADAPT and stay with any adaptation long enough for it to be effective. Reflect on your teaching. Could you be contributing to the student's learning needs? (This step may take from three weeks to three months.)

7. Analyze your records and make recommendations. Focus on the clearest examples of needs and strengths and the most effective adaptations. Look for patterns. Is there a need for further assessment or additional services?

enough difficulty to warrant a referral. With experience, she will learn that the first steps she can take focus on collecting relevant information to help in decision making. These steps are described in Figure 2.1. A recently developed tool that may help primary teachers collect relevant information is a web based teaching tool.

# Using a Web Based Tool to Identify Needs

Recently the Ontario Ministry of Education developed a web based teaching tool (WBTT) in partnership with the Learning Disabilities Association of Ontario, which may have been helpful for Ms. Sauvé. WBTT consists of several quick, predictive screening measures in beginning math, early literacy (phonological awareness), and school readiness. The intent is for primary teachers to screen the whole class at the beginning of the year, followed by intervention and continual monitoring. Research has shown that using this approach during the first years of school is effective in preventing later persistent difficulties if teachers respond right away with intense interventions. WBTT provides a comprehensive and searchable database of interventions based on patterns in children's data (www.ldao.ca/WBTT/index.php). WBTT is linked to the provincial primary curriculum documents. Specific teaching strategies can be printed and added to a primary student's growth plan. Teachers can enter data for their whole class, and principals can access all the data for their school. This tool provides classroom adaptations and record keeping uniquely appropriate for primary grades. The next section describes the general process of classroom adaptation and record keeping which teachers engage in prior to referring a student, called the pre-referral process.

**What do you think?**

Discuss with your peers the benefits and the dilemmas associated with tools like WBTT that help teachers to adopt current approaches to early identification of those students at risk for learning problems. Examine the WBTT website (www.ldao.ca/WBTT/index.php), and read about the Response to Intervention (RTI) model, which involves tiered interventions of increasing intensity for students who do not respond to the preceding tier of intervention. You can begin by reading the document *Education for All* (2005) at www.edu.gov.on.ca/eng/document/reports/speced/panel/speced.pdf

# Making Classroom Adaptations and Keeping Records

Ms. Sauvé talked to the principal and the resource teacher. The resource teacher gave her a copy of the school's protocol (Figure 2.1). Ms. Sauvé began a **pre-referral process**, an informal assessment of Andy's learning strengths and needs, in collaboration with the resource teacher, prior to a formal referral. This assessment may result in adjustments to the program or learning environment and later may result in referral of the student to a formal assessment and then to an IPRC. Ms. Sauvé began recording the circumstances under which Andy did and did not follow instructions and complete assigned work. She noted when he seemed most distracted. By collecting samples of his work, she came to understand his organizational needs better. Ms. Sauvé recorded the times when Andy did not experience attention difficulties. Armed with her observations and the suggestions of the resource teacher, Ms. Sauvé telephoned Joan Hughes to report what she would be doing to differentiate the classroom for Andy. They agreed to meet in six weeks.

## Using the ADAPT Strategy

**Cross-Reference**

For characteristics, identification strategies, and teaching approaches relevant to students with high-incidence exceptionalities, see Chapter 3.

Ms. Sauvé was making **pre-referral interventions** to meet Andy's needs by following the steps of the ADAPT strategy discussed in Chapter 1. First, it suggests you develop an **A**ccount of the student's strengths and needs. Andy has many strengths, social and academic. For example, he likes to read (academic), and he has friends in the class (social). Andy also needs to learn to concentrate on his assigned work and complete it more independently (academic). He is easily distracted and needs to learn to ignore other children when they are off task (social). Developing this account of strengths and needs involves informal assessment.

Second, the ADAPT strategy suggests that you describe the **D**emands of your classroom. Ms. Sauvé observed carefully and then wrote the following list:

- Most math classes start with a fifteen-minute "lecture" that introduces a new concept or activity. Andy interrupts by talking or moving around.

- I expect students to work in groups, and sometimes the noise is distracting. I often have to ask Andy to move to the quiet table at the back of the room because he "clowns around" when in a group.

- During "catch-up time," the last half-hour of the day, I want the children to finish anything not completed and ask about anything they don't understand. Andy wanders around the classroom and talks to his friends.

The third step in ADAPT is making **A**daptations that help to eliminate the kinds of mismatches in Ms. Sauvé's list. After talking with the resource teacher, Ms. Sauvé reduced the introduction to her math lessons from fifteen minutes to ten. She told Andy to check with his friend Chen to be sure that he understood all instructions. She arranged a cue with Andy—snapping her fingers was a reminder for him to "sit up straight and listen." During group work, Andy had to "work hard" or move to the quiet table before Ms. Sauvé asked him to move. Andy was to consult with Ms. Sauvé at the beginning of catch-up time and to sit with a quiet friend.

Every day, Ms. Sauvé jotted informal observations about Andy on yellow sticky notes and later copied these onto one page. Below is her summary for one day:

- Snapped my fingers three times in ten minutes when introducing the math activity "Halloween Sets." Andy didn't understand until I explained it one-on-one.

- Andy moved to the quiet table by himself during math. He stayed quiet for about five minutes. Then he argued with the next child who came to the quiet table. Quiet table only works when Andy is there alone.

- Andy fidgeted through the Halloween story, and the only character he remembered was the witch. He had great ideas for a play after Chen told him what had happened in the story.

The fourth step in ADAPT is to consider **P**erspectives and consequences. The fifth step is to **T**each and assess the match. Ms. Sauvé felt that she had made considerable effort to change her math teaching for all students. The changes had helped, but Andy needed even more effective strategies for staying focused. Andy told her he was trying to work hard, but he didn't know how. Ms. Sauvé was concerned that the consequences of continuing to ask more of Andy would be frustration and self-criticism.

By the next parent-teacher meeting, Ms. Sauvé had recognized the need for further assessment and services. Although he had tried to follow Ms. Sauvé's cues and to monitor himself, Andy continued to be distracted and to distract others. This occurred mainly during math and following a disruption. Andy needed more consistent and intensive intervention to learn **self-monitoring** strategies than Ms. Sauvé could provide within her grade 2 classroom. Joan Hughes agreed. Ms. Sauvé informed the resource teacher and the principal about her observations, documentation, parent meeting, and recommendations. Together, they decided it was time for more collaboration—time for a meeting of the in-school team.

Self-monitoring is a specific form of **self-regulation**, a key concept in educational psychology. To learn more about **self-regulation**, see the box entitled Theory and Research Highlights from Educational Psychology.

> **Put into Practice**
>
> Interview a resource teacher from the panel in which you teach (elementary or secondary) about the pre-referral interventions that the teachers in that panel might make if they were in Ms. Sauvé's position.

> **Cross-Reference**
>
> Chapter 5 focuses on adapting or differentiating teaching, and Chapter 8 describes best practices for enhancing social relations, including collaborative learning and peer tutoring.

## THEORY AND RESEARCH HIGHLIGHTS FROM
## EDUCATIONAL PSYCHOLOGY

## Self-Regulated Learning

The overall goal of education is to help children and adolescents become self-regulated learners. Our understanding of self-regulation has been advanced by the work of many researchers, including Phil Winne of Simon Fraser University, Nancy Perry of the University of British Columbia, and Allyson Hadwin of the University of Victoria (e.g., Hadwin et al., 2007; Perry & Winne, 2006; Winne, 2005). Self-regulated learners have a combination of academic learning skills and self-control that makes learning easier. That is, they have the *skill* and the *will* to learn. Their *skill* or knowledge about learning includes knowledge about themselves, so they recognize which subjects they prefer and which tasks they do best, the strategies upon which they can rely, and the contexts in which those strategies apply. They recognize when a task requires them to rehearse in order to remember straightforward facts and

*(Box continued on next page)*

when a task requires them to make a concept map and concentrate on the relationships among complex ideas (Schunk & Zimmerman, 2007). They understand that academic learning is challenging and effortful, and over time they come to use their repertoire of strategies automatically. Their *will* to learn, or motivation, is reflected in their initiative, independence, commitment, and effort. Usually they are able to sustain learning, no matter what distractions or setbacks they encounter. When they complete tasks successfully, they recognize their accomplishments, and this increases their sense of self-efficacy for similar tasks in the future (Klassen, 2007).

Self-regulated learners "proactively direct their behavior or strategies to achieve self-set goals" (Cleary & Zimmerman, 2004, p. 538). Self-regulated learning emphasizes autonomy and control by the individual who "monitors, directs, and regulates actions toward goals of information acquisition, expanding expertise, and self-improvement." Quantitative studies have produced correlations showing a strong relationship between self-regulated learning and academic achievement, and have conceptualized self-regulated learning as an aptitude (Winne & Perry, 2000). In contrast, the measurement of self-regulated learning as an event involves recording a change in the behaviours indicative of self-regulated learning. Recently, qualitative methods have been used to expand our understanding of self-regulated learning as an event (Perry, Phillips, & Dowler, 2004). These studies have generated rich descriptive data by observing individuals as they engage in self-regulated learning.

Gifted students often demonstrate high self-regulation (Ee, Moore, & Atputhasamy, 2003), while many children and adolescents with disabilities need our help to become more self-regulated learners. For example, Robert Klassen (2007) of the University of Alberta reported that children with learning disabilities demonstrated less self-regulation than children without learning disabilities. There is also research on the self-regulation of children with language-learning disorders (Bashir & Singer, 2006), intellectual disabilities (Eisenhower et al., 2007), and ADHD (Reid, Trout, & Schartz, 2005).

Research in educational psychology and special education is beginning to demonstrate the significance of self-regulation for understanding and enhancing the learning of exceptional students.

## References

Bashir, A.S., & Singer, B.D. (2006). Assisting students in becoming self-regulated writers. In T.A. Ukrainetz (Ed.), *Contextualized language intervention* (pp. 565–598). Greenville, SC: Thinking Publications University.

Cleary, T.J., & Zimmerman, B.J. (2004). Self-regulation empowerment program: A school-based program to enhance self-regulated and self-motivated cycles of student learning. *Psychology in the Schools, 41*, 537–550.

Ee, J., Moore, P.J., & Atputhasamy, L. (2003). High-achieving students: Their motivational goals, self-regulation, and achievement and relationships to their teachers' goals and strategy-based instruction. *High Ability Studies, 14*(1), 23–39.

Eisenhower, A.S., Baker, B.L., & Blacher, J. (2007). Early student–teacher relationships of children with and without intellectual disability: Contributions of behavioral, social, and self-regulatory competence. *Journal of School Psychology, 45*, 363–383.

Hadwin, A., Nesbit, J., Jamieson-Noel, D., Code, J., & Winne, P.H. (2007). Examining trace data to explore self-regulated learning. *Metacognition and Learning, 2*, 107–124.

Klassen, R.M. (2007). Using predictions to learn about the self-efficacy of early adolescents with and without learning disabilities. *Contemporary Educational Psychology, 32*, 173–187.

Perry, N.E., Phillips, L., & Dowler, J. (2004). Examining features of tasks and their potential to promote self-regulated learning. *Teachers College Record, 106*, 1854–1878.

Perry, N.E., & Winne, P.H. (2006). Learning from learning kits: gStudy traces of students' self-regulated engagements with computerized content. *Educational Psychology Review, 18*, 211–228.

Reid, R., Trout, A.L., & Schartz, M. (2005). Self-regulation interventions for children with attention deficit/?hyperactivity disorder. *Exceptional Children, 71*, 361–377.

Schunk, D.H., & Zimmerman, B.J. (2007). Influencing children's self-efficacy and self-regulation of reading and writing through modeling. *Reading and Writing Quarterly, 23*, 7–25.

Winne, P.H. (2005). A perspective on state-of-the-art research on self-regulated learning. *Instructional Science, 33*, 559–565.

Winne, P.H., & Perry, N.E. (2000). Measuring self-regulated learning. In M. Boekaerts, P.R. Pintrich, & M. Zeidner (Eds.), *Handbook of self-regulation* (pp. 531–566). San Diego, CA: Academic Press.

# Collaboration: Working with the Resource Teacher and Other Professionals

Critical factors in a school's success in meeting the needs of students include the beliefs and actions of its teachers and administrators (Jordan & Stanovich, 2004) and their willingness to collaborate (Levine & Marcus, 2010). According to Anne

Jordan of the University of Toronto, **collaboration** entails teachers and other professionals learning from each other's experiences and working in teams where all members feel that their contributions are valued. The Ontario Ministry of Education asserts that teachers need the support of the larger community to create a learning environment that supports students with special education needs (2005, p. 4). As a classroom teacher, you are central to collaboration—you are the expert on the curriculum, organization, and management of your classroom (Stanovich & Jordan, 2004). However, you do not have to be an expert on every aspect of the exceptional student's needs. Collaboration provides you with a support network and enables you to draw on the expertise of many individuals. You will work closely with resource teachers, special educators, guidance counsellors, district consultants, and your principal. Other professionals with whom you may collaborate include speech therapists, occupational therapists, social workers, and psychologists. Educational assistants and parents also play important roles in collaboration.

Many studies conducted in Ontario demonstrate the elements that contribute to collaboration:

1. Professionals with shared goals for exceptional students and clear responsibilities to meet those goals and to communicate with families (Villeneuve, 2010)

2. Classroom teachers and resource teachers who maintain regular contact, build strong relationships, and communicate frequently (Levac, 2004)

3. Classroom teachers and educational assistants who respect each other's contributions, and who communicate daily (Ramsay, 2007)

4. Principals and resource teachers who set a positive tone for inclusion, expect collaboration to be effective, and support classroom teachers (Ramsay, 2007)

"The most important element is the quality and quantity of support for the classroom teacher [who] needs to be part of an in-school team that can provide information, strategies that work and moral support" (Duquette, 1992, p. 151).

# The Classroom Teacher and the In-School Special Education Team

To support inclusive education, school districts have developed in-school teams that share responsibility for exceptional students, usually composed of members of the school staff and parents. Sometimes professionals from the district or community may be added if they have relevant expertise not available in the school.

## Suggesting a Meeting of the In-School Team

When should you suggest that the in-school team meet to discuss a student? You and the **resource teacher** have carried out all the steps in the pre-referral stage (in Figure 2.1), and you feel that the adaptations you have tried are not sufficient to meet the student's needs. That suggests that the in-school team should consider the child's case. For example, Andy engaged in more self-regulated learning, paid more attention, and completed more assignments; however, Ms. Sauvé was sure that he would benefit from more intensive teaching and practice of these strategies. She knew she did not have time for such concentrated work with Andy.

**Put into Practice**

Read Michelle Villeneuve's recent review of research on collaboration between educators and occupational therapists. Use it to inform yourself and then interview an occupational therapist about his or her experiences collaborating with educators.

Villeneuve, M. (2009). A critical examination of school-based occupational therapy collaborative consultation. *Canadian Journal of Occupational Therapy, 76,* 206–218.

**Put into Practice**

You might be interested in taking on a personal project to improve your ability to work with others. If so, check out Sharon Cramer's unusual book, *The Special Educator's Guide to Collaboration* (published by Corwin Press of Thousand Oaks, CA, in 2006), in which she challenges readers to empower themselves and acquire the motivation, understanding, and skills to analyze and improve collaboration relationships. For a more traditional approach, read M. Friend and L. Cook (2009), *Interactions: Collaboration Skills for School Professionals* (6th ed.), Boston: Allyn & Bacon Pearson.

**What do you think?**

View the PowerPoint prepared by the Ontario Ministry of Education website at: www.ontariodirectors.ca, called Collaborating for Better IEPs, Slide Deck No. 4. Compare it to the information provided here.

## FIGURE 2.2 FORM TO BE COMPLETED PRIOR TO MAKING A REFERRAL TO THE IN-SCHOOL TEAM

**Student Name:**                                                **Student #:**

**Grade:**                                                        **Date of Birth:**

**Reason for referral:**

**Student's strengths and needs:**

**Brief listing of colleagues consulted:**

**Brief description of contact with family:**

**Relevant classroom assessment:**

**Please check off and list the interventions that have been tried in the classroom:**

| Environmental | Instructional | Assessment |
|---|---|---|
| ❏ Preferential seating | ❏ Intensive individual instruction | ❏ Oral assessment |
| ❏ Proximity to instructor | ❏ Intensive small group instruction | ❏ Alternative test/ assignment |
| ❏ Frequent breaks | ❏ Graphic organizers | ❏ Scribe |
| ❏ Alternative workspace | ❏ Calculator | ❏ Shorter assignments |
| ❏ Study partner | ❏ Taped texts | ❏ Extended time |
| | ❏ Copy of notes | |
| | ❏ Tracking sheets | |

**Additional comments:**

**Teacher's Signature:**                                          **Date**

If you and the resource teacher believe that the first level of intervention has not been effective, then you will likely approach the **in-school team**. In many jurisdictions, you may be asked to complete a form similar to Figure 2.2 prior to making a referral to the in-school team. This team is a solution-finding group whose purpose is to provide a forum for dialogue by parents, teachers, and other professionals about the needs of students. As the classroom teacher or **referring teacher**, you are a key member along with the principal and the resource teacher. Usually the parents are invited to take part, and sometimes the student is invited. Parental consent is sought for decisions that significantly alter the education of an exceptional student. Usually in-school teams work better when they are small and focused.

## The Work of the In-School Special Education Team

Usually the team appoints a case coordinator and problem solves informally. As the referring teacher, you will likely be asked to present the student data from the pre-referral interventions. The team brainstorms and suggests additional assessment strategies and additional teaching strategies, including **informal assessment** conducted by you or the resource teacher and, perhaps, **formal assessment** conducted by the resource teacher, a psychologist, or another professional.

The in-school team is the cornerstone of the process of identification, assessment, and planning. The team could recommend that other formal assessments be conducted, such as an intelligence test, behaviour observation checklists, vision, hearing, or language assessments. In some school districts there is a waiting list for assessment services, and parents may choose to pay for assessments administered privately outside the school system. When results are available, the in-school team, including the parents, meets to consider the recommendations. Ontario has a two-stage process in which an **Identification, Placement, and Review Committee (IPRC)** meets to consider whether the child is exceptional and recommends placement. This is followed by an **IEP**, usually written by the teacher and the resource teacher in elementary schools and by the resource teacher or learning support teacher with input from classroom teachers in secondary schools, along with participation by the parents or guardians. Ask about the procedures in your school, because there are slight variations even within a district.

## Clarifying Your Role on the In-School Team

Classroom teachers play a central role (Pierangelo & Giuliani, 2007). But occasionally they find in-school team meetings frustrating and threatening. What can you do to ensure that this does not happen to you? One month into her second year of teaching, Leanne was reassigned from a grade 6 class to a grade 3 class because of increases in enrolment. One of her new students, Mickey, had autism and needed many accommodations and modifications in the classroom. By the end of the first week with her new class, Leanne felt that she was beginning to make progress with Mickey. A few days later, the resource teacher told Leanne that Mickey's parents had requested a meeting to discuss his program. Leanne asked the resource teacher, "What should I do to prepare? I've never been to an in-school team meeting." The resource teacher replied that they could hardly expect Leanne to present the case when she had only taught Mickey for two weeks. On the day of the meeting, the vice-principal, who was chairing, began the meeting by asking Leanne to present Mickey's history from his arrival at the school up to the current adaptations she was making in her classroom. Leanne had read Mickey's file but had not brought her notes to the team meeting. After some initial panic she described Mickey's history from memory, feeling frustrated and defensive. The parents were pleased with the adaptations Leanne described. Everyone else judged the meeting a success, but Leanne felt that she had appeared unprepared. Leanne, Mickey, and the rest of the grade 3 class went on to have a very successful year. However, Leanne still describes this meeting as the worst experience in her professional life. What could she have done before the meeting to feel prepared? Figure 2.3 contains suggestions for preparing for and participating in an in-school team meeting.

# The Teacher and the Identification, Placement, and Review Committee (IPRC) and the Individual Education Plan (IEP)

In Ontario, a two-step process is normally used. In the first step, an IPRC identifies that a student has exceptional learning needs and recommends the placement for the student. (The categories and definitions of exceptional students are listed in

## FIGURE 2.3 PREPARING FOR AND PARTICIPATING IN AN IN-SCHOOL TEAM MEETING

**Communicate Regularly with Parents**

- Send out a monthly newsletter with space for parents' comments.
- Host a class curriculum night to communicate your curriculum and expectations.
- Make a positive contact with parents of exceptional students before you make a negative contact.
- If you have not met the parents, make telephone contact before an in-school team meeting.
- Respond to parents' notes and telephone calls promptly.

**Look at Each Student as an Individual**

- Read all of the student files before the term starts.
- Make notes on the files, reports, IEPs, and medical information of exceptional students.
- Make written observations of all exceptional students early in the term.
- Meet with the resource teacher, ask questions, secure resources, and learn strategies to adapt teaching; make written notes.
- Collect work samples that demonstrate the student's strengths and needs in your class.

**Prepare for the In-School Team Meeting**

- Read the information about responsibilities of the members at in-school team meetings.
- Ask the chair of the meeting what will be expected of you.
- Discuss the student's case thoroughly with your best source of information, probably the resource teacher; ask her opinion on what you plan to say.
- Prepare to give a brief history of the student's time in the school as well as in your classroom.
- Bring all of your written notes to the in-school team meeting.
- Bring work samples to show the student's strengths and needs in your classroom.

**During the In-School Team Meeting**

- Approach the meeting in a spirit of goodwill.
- Think about how stressful these meetings can be for parents.
- Listen actively to what others have to say; take notes; do not interrupt.
- Answer questions briefly and honestly without becoming defensive.
- Ask questions if you do not understand; do not agree to commitments you cannot keep.
- Make your presentations brief, clear, and to the point; be positive and realistic in saying what you can do to meet the student's needs.
- Ensure that the meeting is summarized and ends on a positive note; thank the parents and other team members for their participation.
- Clarify when the next meeting is likely to occur and what is expected of you.

Chapter 1.) The second step is the development of an IEP. This process is described in Focus on Ontario's Regulation 181/98, Parts I and II (on page 39 and 40). However, in Ontario, a student can receive an IEP because he or she requires accommodations, without having been identified as exceptional in an IPRC. In April 2010, the Ministry of Education in Ontario began to refer to these non-identified students with IEPs as "students with special education needs." Whenever significant changes in learning expectations, curriculum, or teaching approaches are made to a student's program over the long term, an IEP must be prepared.

## Planning to Meet Individual Needs

The IEP demands that you and your colleagues make an individual plan for an exceptional student. However, that does not mean that you must teach the student one on one. According to Gail Lennon, an Ontario teacher, "Parents and students want a program which includes the student as part of the class. The measuring stick in

## Focus on Ontario's Regulation 181/98 (Part I—Exceptional Students, the IPRC, and the IEP)

Regulation 181/98 governs the identification and placement of exceptional pupils, IPRC reviews, appeal procedures, and the role of parents (or guardians) in these processes.

The Education Act requires that school boards provide special education programs and services for exceptional pupils.

**What is an IPRC?** An Identification, Placement, and Review Committee (IPRC) must be set up by each school board, and is composed of at least three persons, one of whom must be a principal or supervisory officer of the board.

**What does the IPRC do?** The IPRC (a) decides whether a student should be identified as exceptional; (b) identifies the areas of the student's exceptionality; (c) decides an appropriate placement for the student; and (d) reviews the identification and placement at least once each school year.

**Who is an exceptional student?** An exceptional pupil, according to the Education Act, is one "whose behavioural, communicational, intellectual, physical or multiple exceptionalities are such that he or she is considered to need placement in a special education program." The Ministry of Education definitions of these five categories of identification appear in Chapter 1 (on page 4 and 5).

**What is a special education program?** The Education Act specifies that a special education program is (a) based on and modified by continuous assessment, and (b) includes an Individual Education Plan (IEP) containing objectives and an outline of special education services that meet the needs of the exceptional student.

**What are special education services?** The Education Act defines these as facilities and resources, including personnel and equipment, needed to develop and implement a special education program.

**What is an IEP?** The IEP must be developed for a student, in consultation with the parent. It must include (a) specific educational expectations, (b) an outline of the special education program and services for the pupil, and (c) an indication of how progress will be reviewed. For students 14 years and older, there must be a transition plan to appropriate postsecondary activities such as work, further education, and community living. This does not apply if the student's only identification is gifted.

**When is the IEP required?** The IEP must be completed within 30 days after the student has been placed in the program, and the principal must ensure that the parent receives a copy.

Sources:

www.e-laws.gov.on.ca/

www.edu.gov.on.ca/eng/general/elemsec/speced/issues.html

www.edu.gov.on.ca/eng/general/elemsec/speced/hilites.html

---

teacher decision making should be: To what extent can the exceptional student learn the content which is being presented to the rest of the class?" (1995, p. 24). Differentiated instruction, a term used in many of Ontario's documents (e.g., www.edu.gov.on. ca/eng/studentsuccess/lms/differentiatedInstruction.pdf), is the focus of Chapter 5.

Accommodations refer to changing the method of teaching while maintaining grade level outcomes. Modifications refer to outcomes from a different grade level of the curriculum, and alternative outcomes refer to outcomes important for the student's learning, but not in the provincial curriculum.

Tomlinson (2000) writes that "differentiation can show us how to teach the same standard to a range of learners by employing a variety of teaching and learning modes." Haager and Klingner (2005) describe differentiated instruction as ensuring that all students have optimal learning opportunities within the core academic curriculum. Assessment and grouping are key to providing differentiated instruction. Flexible grouping refers to learning groups customized to students' needs (identified through assessment) that meet the lesson objectives. The composition of such groups varies on an as-needed basis. Then intensive, focused instruction can be tailored to the needs of the group. This includes instruction different from what the rest of the class requires.

What may need to be changed is the amount of time the students take to learn the skill. As well, the content may be changed so that certain skills are selected for

**Cross-Reference**

Chapter 5 provides many examples of differentiated teaching and learning.

# Focus on Ontario's Regulation 181/98 (Part II—IPRC Meetings and Reviews)

**How is an IPRC meeting requested?** The principal requests the meeting. This must take place if the principal receives a written request from the parent. When the student's teacher or teachers believe the student may benefit from a special education program, the principal provides written notice to the parent and refers the student to an IPRC. Within fifteen days of receiving a written request or of giving the parent notice, the principal must provide a copy of the board's Parents' Guide to Special Education and a written statement of approximately when the IPRC will take place.

**What is the parent's role in the IPRC?** The parent is entitled to attend and participate in all committee discussions about the student, and to be present when the committee's identification and placement decision is made. If the student is 16 or older, the student is entitled to attend. At least ten days in advance of the meeting, the parent will receive an invitation to the meeting and will be asked to indicate whether they will attend.

**Who else may attend?** The principal, resource people (such as the student's teacher, special education staff, board support staff, the representative of an agency with relevant information), a representative of the parent or student (if the student is 16 or over) who may speak on their behalf. As well, the parent or principal may request that others attend.

**What information do parents receive prior to the meeting?** At least ten days before the meeting, the chair of the IPRC will provide written notification and invite the parent to be a partner in the meeting, giving the date, time, and place, and asking the parent to indicate if they will attend. Before the meeting, the parent will receive a written copy of the information about their child that the chair of the IPRC has received. This may include assessment results or a summary of information.

**What if parents are unable to attend?** The parent can contact the principal to arrange an alternative date and time, or the parent can indicate they will not attend. As soon as possible after the meeting, the principal forwards the IPRC's written statement of decision to the parents (concerning identification, placement, and recommendations for special education programs and services).

**What happens at an IPRC meeting?** After introductions of the people involved and the purpose of the meeting, the IPRC reviews all available information about the student—educational assessment, health or psychological assessment by a qualified practitioner if they feel it is relevant, and information the parent submits (or the student, if 16 or over), and they can interview the child (with the parent's permission) if they think it is relevant. They will discuss proposals about special education programs or services, encourage parents to participate, and then make a decision.

**What contributes to placement decision?** The IPRC first considers if the regular class with appropriate special education services will meet the student's needs and is consistent with parental preferences. If the IPRC decides on a special class placement, reasons must be provided.

**What can parents do if they do not agree with the IPRC decision?** Within 15 days of receiving the identification or placement decision, they can request a second meeting to discuss their concerns. Within 30 days of receiving the decision, they can file a notice of appeal, and can file a notice of appeal within 15 days after the second meeting.

**What happens in the appeal process?** A complex set of steps takes place in which the board establishes an appeal board, and if there is still disagreement, the decision goes to the Special Education Tribunal. Information about that process will be included with the appeal board's decision.

**What does an IPRC review decide?** Once within each academic year, the IPRC considers the same type of information it discussed originally, and reviews the student's progress, and considers whether the decisions about identification and placement should remain the same.

Sources:

www.e-laws.gov.on.ca/

www.edu.gov.on.ca/eng/general/elemsec/speced/hilites.html

www.edu.gov.on.ca/eng/general/elemsec/speced/issues.html

**Put into Practice**

Obtain a copy of the IEP form used in your school district. Compare it with the IEP shown in Figure 2.4.

the exceptional students and other skills are deleted from their program plans. In rare cases the entire content may be replaced by more appropriate learning experiences. Again, the question to be asked is, *To what extent can the exceptional student learn in the same way as the rest of the class, and how can I differentiate the way I teach, based on the student's unique learning needs?*

Exceptional students sometimes need a different way to demonstrate the learning outcomes they have accomplished. Whenever the same outcome is

# FIGURE 2.4 EXAMPLE OF AN IEP

THIS IEP CONTAINS ☑ AC ☐ MOD ☐ ALT

## REASON FOR DEVELOPING THE IEP

☑ Student identified as exceptional by IPRC

☐ Student not formally identified but requires special education program/services including modified/alternative learning expectations and/or accommodations

## STUDENT PROFILE

Student OEN: 444444

Last Name: Bylsma

First Name: Barbara

Gender: F

Date of Birth: March 1, 1994

School: Brock Secondary

School Type: Secondary

Principal: Ms. Yung

Current Grade/Special Class: Grade 11

School Year: 2010-2011

Exceptionality (identified): Learning disability

Placement: Regular class with withdrawal

Student (secondary only) is currently working toward attainment of the:

☑ Ontario Secondary School Diploma

☐ Ontario Secondary School Certificate

☐ Certificate of Accomplishment

## STUDENT'S AREAS OF STRENGTH AND AREAS OF NEED

| Areas of Strength | Areas of Need |
|---|---|
| Problem-solving skills | Expressive language skills-writing |
| Self-advocacy skills | Receptive language skills - writing |
| Expressive language skills | Organizational skills |
| Keyboarding skills | Processing speed |

## SUBJECTS, COURSE/CODES OR ALTERNATIVE SKILL AREAS TO WHICH THE IEP APPLIES

Accommodated only (AC), Modified (MOD), Alternative (ALT)

| | | |
|---|---|---|
| 1. English | ENG 3C | AC |
| 2. Math/Personal Finance | MBF 3C | AC |
| 3. Health/Physical Education | PPL 30 | AC |
| 4. History/Canadian & Politics | CHH 3C | AC |
| 5. Biology | SBI 3C | AC |
| 6. Learning Strategies/Advanced | GLE 30 | AC |
| 7. Information Technology Applications/Business | BTA 30 | AC |
| 8. Dramatic Arts | ADA 30 | AC |

## ACCOMMODATIONS FOR LEARNING, INCLUDING REQUIRED EQUIPMENT

Accommodations are assumed to be the same for all program areas unless otherwise indicated

| Instructional Accommodations | Environmental Accommodations | Assessment Accommodations |
|---|---|---|
| Assistive technology: text-to-speech | Access to outlet for assistive technology | Additional time |
| Word processing for spell check | | Computer with spell check |
| Extra time | | Speech-to-text software |
| Graphic organizers | | Verbatim scribing of responses |
| Organizational coaching | | |
| Laptop | | |

FIGURE 2.4 (Continued)

**HUMAN RESOURCES (teaching/non-teaching)**

| Type of Service | Frequency or Intensity for Staff | Location |
|---|---|---|
| Special education teacher | Daily during CLE | Resource room |
| Guidance counsellor | Monitor one time per month | Resource room |
| Support for computer programs | Minimum once per semester | Resource room |

Source: Based on sample IEPs available on the Ontario Directors of Education website,
http://www.ontariodirectors.ca/IEP-PEI/index.html

appropriate, maintain that outcome. When necessary, choose alternative formats or products that enable students to show what they have learned, not the impact of their disabilities. Widely used adaptations are more time for tests, speaking into a tape recorder, and using a scribe. Adapting assessment is the focus of Chapter 6.

## CASE STUDY WHAT SHOULD THE COUNSELOR DO TO HELP BARBARA?

Barbara Bylsma has a learning disability. It is October and she is in grade 11. She is telling the counsellor who meets with her once a month about the challenges she is facing in her classes. "Sometimes I get to class late, usually because I am mixed up about what day it is. Or which floor the room is on. And sometimes I get there with the wrong books. I really find it hard to get all my assignments done. The teachers give me extra time but there are only so many hours in the day. So I end up working late on my assignments, and having no sleep or else no time to do anything but schoolwork." When the counsellor asks Barbara about the assignments she has not submitted in her English class, Barbara explains that she didn't finish them and was embarrassed to hand in a half-completed assignment so she handed in nothing on the days the assignments were due. "I always think that I will get my English assignments done somehow, and then I get working on the next thing and I never get back to it. Not like my math homework which I love and can always get done on time. And not like having to give a speech in English or History—I love that! It's completely different than writing a paper!" When the counsellor asks Barbara how her assistive technology is working, Barbara replies, "I think I need more help using the programs efficiently. That is what I want to work on with you today. I want to figure out a strategy to get more help using my speech-to-text and text-to-speech software. When you help me prepare what I am going to say, I do a better job of convincing people of what I need to be successful. We should do this "Excerpts from Barbara's IEP appear in Figure 2.4. What should the counselor do to help Barbara?

# Changing Context of IEPs in Ontario

Recent documents prepared by the Ontario Ministry of Education suggest that the expectations for IEPs are changing and the expectations for teachers to "reach every student" are increasing. For example, the draft of *Learning for All K-12* (June 2009) focuses on the need for measurability and accountability in IEPs. At the same time, it recommends that teachers develop profiles of individual students and of the entire class to aid in planning assessment and instruction that is "good for all and necessary for some." Recommended instructional approaches include Universal

Design for Learning, differentiated instruction, and tiered approaches to prevention and intervention where the intensity and duration of intervention increase for students who have not responded to the previous intervention (e.g., responsiveness to intervention). One strategy for enhancing the measurability and accountability of IEPs is SMART IEP goals.

## SMART IEP GOALS

Writing good goals that meet the specific student's needs is critical. Many jurisdictions are starting to use **SMART goals**—**S**pecific, **M**easurable, **A**chievable, **R**elevant, and **T**ime limited. These goals describe what the student will do, how and when the student will do it, and what the time frame will be for achieving it.

When writing SMART goals, keep the following tips in mind:

1. Be very specific about the action. For example: raise his/her hand for attention; use a classroom voice; read the pre-primer Dolch Words; complete homework; point to "I want" in augmentative symbols.

2. Provide a time frame or location/context for the goal. For instance: during silent reading time; while in the gym; at recess time; by the end of second term; point to 3 picture symbols when something is wanted.

3. Decide what determines the success of the goal. For instance: how many consecutive periods will the student be on task? how fluently will the child read the words — without hesitation and prompting? what percentage accuracy? how often?

### What do you think?

What kinds of assessment practices are consistent with measurable and meaningful IEP goals?

Read the following papers and look for other resources to inform you on this topic.

Capizzi, A.M. (2008). From assessment to annual goal: Engaging a decision-making process in writing measurable IEPs. *Teaching Exceptional Children, 41*(1), 18–25.

Hessler, T., & Konrad, M. (2008). Using curriculum-based measurement to drive IEPs and instruction in written expression. *Teaching Exceptional Children, 41*(2), 28–37.

# The Teacher and the Educational Assistant

In-school teams may include **educational assistants**, also referred to as teacher assistants or paraeducators. *The Special Education Handbook* published by the Elementary Teachers' Federation of Ontario (2007, p. 8) describes this role as:

- helps the student with learning activities under the supervision of the teacher;
- assists with providing appropriate accommodations as outlined in the IEP;
- maintains ongoing communication with the student's teachers.

## The Role of the Educational Assistant

Sometimes educational assistants are assigned to work with one or more exceptional students in your classroom, while other times they are assigned to support your work with the entire class while monitoring the exceptional students and offering them assistance at key moments (Groom & Rose, 2005). Often the IEP includes information about the role of the educational assistant in the program of an exceptional student. The principal is responsible for assigning roles to educational assistants, but often the principal will consult with the classroom teacher, and usually the educational assistant works under your direction or the direction of the in-school team.

Canadian research reports that in successful inclusive schools, educational assistants and teachers work as partners (Villeneuve, 2010; Sundmark, 2003). Jennifer Ramsay (2007), a teacher in Ontario, found that in an effective working

### Further Reading

About working with educational assistants:

Carter, E., et al. (2009). Knowledge, responsibilities, and training needs of prarprofessionals in elementary and secondary schools. *Remedial and Special Education, 30*(6), 344-359.

Causton-Theoharis, J. (2009). *The paraprofessional's handbook for effective support in inclusive classrooms.* Baltimore, MD: Paul H. Brookes Pub. Co.

Giangreco, M.F. (2003). Working with paraprofessionals. *Educational Leadership, 61*(2), 50–53.

Causton-Theoharis, J. et al. (2007). Paraprofessionals: The sous-chefs of literacy instruction. *Teaching Exceptional Children, 40*(1), 56-62.

Peterborough Victoria Northumberland and Clarington Catholic District School Board. (2003). *Educational assistants: Resource guide,* www.pvnccdsb.on.ca.

## FIGURE 2.5 ROLE OF CLASSROOM TEACHERS IN WORKING WITH EDUCATIONAL ASSISTANTS

Classroom teachers who receive support from educational assistants have the following responsibilities:

- informing educational assistants of classroom procedures and rules, and methods of classroom management
- assigning appropriate responsibilities and tasks to educational assistants, taking into consideration their training, knowledge, and skills as well as student needs
- documenting identified responsibilities and tasks with educational assistants, and providing copies for principals (and special education supervisors, where appropriate)
- providing input regarding the supervision and evaluation of educational assistants
- informing principals when students whom educational assistants support are absent so that the assistants' schedules can be changed
- ensuring that time is allocated for educational assistants to meet with teachers regularly
- ensuring communication with educational assistants through communication books, logs, regular meetings for collaborative monitoring, and ongoing discussion
- recommending training and resources to support educational assistants in their roles
- modelling the confidentiality of the student–school relationship
- helping educational assistants to develop skills they need such as observation and data-collection strategies and effective behaviour management strategies
- encouraging high standards of practice
- resolving conflicts with educational assistants at the classroom level first, school level second, and regional school board level third

relationship, the EA and teacher shared beliefs about what was important for inclusive education, recognized that their roles were distinct, and received direct and indirect support from the principal and the resource teacher. An educational assistant can provide continuity for staff, parents, and exceptional learners and can contribute to the planning and delivery of services. The EA should have a work station in the classroom and the two of you need to arrive at a shared understanding of her role.

## Your Role in Working with an Educational Assistant

It is important to clarify your role before beginning a partnership with an educational assistant (see Figure 2.5). Read your district's job description for educational assistants and reread the IEPs of exceptional children in your class for information about the role of the educational assistant. Many teachers have never supervised another team member and find it difficult to assign tasks to others. Many school districts (e.g., Peterborough Victoria Northumberland and Clarington Catholic DSB; www.pvnccdsb.on.ca) have resource guides that clarify the roles of educational assistants. On successful teams, the teacher and the educational assistant meet frequently before and after school to discuss what is happening in the classroom as engaged teaching partners (Ramsay, 2007; Villeneuve, 2010).

Sometimes an educational assistant may work with the same exceptional student for many years and may know the child or adolescent better than the classroom or subject teacher. Despite that, educational assistants should always work under the supervision of a qualified teacher. It is important that they contribute to the participation of exceptional students in classrooms and not come between the students and their classmates, teachers, or learning tasks (Giangreco, Smith, & Pinckney, 2006). Consider the point of view of this member of the team. Look for his or her unique strengths and then work together for the students.

# The Teacher and the Parents

In recent years, parents have developed an increasing awareness of their own and their children's legal and social rights, and are asserting themselves more with school personnel (DiGiorgio, 2004). Being aware of these rights and making an effort to understand and support parents who exercise them may enhance your relations with parents. Families of children with disabilities spend significant amounts of time interacting with educational professionals. By becoming sensitive to parental needs, you can ensure that your meetings with families go more smoothly.

## Understanding the Parents' Perspective

A recurring theme in this book is the importance of taking others' perspectives. This section focuses on the perspectives of parents. Living with an exceptional child or adolescent can create challenges for a family, while some parents report that it is a transformative experience (e.g., Scorgie, Wilgosh, & Sobsey, 2004). See Focus on Families. Patricia Minnes and her colleagues at Queen's University report that families experience both empowerment and high levels of stress because of the responsibilities of caring for and advocating for exceptional children (Nachshen, et al., 2005; Nachshen & Minnes, 2005). Sometimes after the identification of

@

**Weblinks**

PARENTBOOKS (A BOOKSTORE)
http://parentbooks.ca

DOOR2ADULTHOOD
www.hollandbloorview.ca/door2adulthood

ONTARIO PARENT INVOLEMENT POLICY
http://www.edu.gov.on.ca/eng/general/elemsec/partnership/developing.html

## ✳ ≫ FOCUS ON FAMILIES
## Letter to Andrew

Families of exceptional children in Calgary published a book entitled *Letters to Our Children*.

Here is the letter to Andrew Ziebell, who was born three weeks prematurely with cerebral palsy that affects all four limbs. Andrew has some hearing and vision loss.

Dear Andrew,

You, my love, turned seven years old on March 3, 1993. In your short lifetime you have had a long, hard road to follow. And that road will not get any easier. Always know, Andrew, that I love you more than anything in the world and I will always be there right beside you, helping your every step, sharing in your dreams, your hopes, your tears and your fears.

You have a circle of friends who love you and love to share in your life. These friends are special in every way because they see you as Andrew, a person first and foremost, and your disability doesn't matter.

The sky was the limit when you entered preschool. Your teachers, Jill, Jo-Anne, and Val took you through two years of learning, socializing, and fun-filled experiences. Your summer program there was just as wonderful because I could see the look of excitement on your face each and every day when you came home from the Leisure Centre. You had a great year at your community school where you moved mountains and acquired lifelong friendships.

In the beginning of 1993, another chapter opened in your life. You entered the world of Scouting. In full uniform you and your brother proudly stand united with all Boy Scouts of Canada. We are all proud to feel your sense of belonging.

Your world is not always full of joy and not all people see your strength, but dwell on your disabilities. The most difficult challenge began in June 1992 when you were not allowed to continue in your community school placement. Not only did this cost you a year of education, but the emotional devastation this inflicted on your brother and sister, who could not understand why you were not allowed to go to school with them, has been very traumatic. We will continue to fight to obtain your right to a fair and equal education in your community school, no matter how long it takes.

What your future holds for you, my son, I cannot say; but what I hope it holds for you is full acceptance into society and a world that is kind and full of love; a circle of friends and independence.

Lovingly,

Your Mom, Dad, Jennifer-Lea, Christopher and last, but not least, your watchful puppy Kelsey

Source: Excerpted from D.E. Badry, J.R. McDonald, & J. LeBlond (Eds.), *Letters to Our Children*. Copyright © 1993 by University of Calgary Press. Reprinted by permission.

## What do you think?

Recently, contrasting perspectives on our work with parents have emerged. Some researchers have argued that educators must develop a new conceptualization of partnership with the community to promote community-based regeneration. For example, see Confronting failure: Towards a pedagogy of recognition in the *International Journal of Inclusive Education*, 1, 121–141 by Jon Nixon and his colleagues (1997). At the same time, educators have begun to receive advice on how to deal with aggressive parents. For example, see *The difficult parent: An educator's guide to handling aggressive behavior* by Charles Jaksec (Corwin Press, 2005) and *Working with challenging parents of students with special needs* by Jean Cheng Gorman (Corwin Press, 2004). Are these perspectives contradictory or complementary? What do you think?

**Weblinks**

BC COALITION OF PEOPLE WITH DISABILITIES
www.bccpd.bc.ca/programs/advocacy.htm

NATIONAL EDUCATIONAL ASSOCIATION OF DISABLED STUDENTS (NEADS) (ADVOCATES FOR ACCESS TO COLLEGE AND UNIVERSITY)
www.neads.ca

INTERNATIONAL LISTING OF ADVOCACY GROUPS
www.independentliving.org/links/links-advocacy.html

ADVOCACY RESOURCE CENTRE FOR THE HANDICAPPED (ARCH) (A LEGAL RESOURCE CENTRE IN ONTARIO)
www.archdisabilitylaw.ca

## FIGURE 2.6 WEBLINKS FOR YOUTH WITH DISABILITIES

**www.focusas.com/Canada.html**
Focus Adolescent Services—A free internet clearinghouse of information and resources on teen and family issues to help and support families with troubled and at-risk teens. Includes hotlines adolescents may call and provides links to many informative websites.

**www.youth.gc.ca/eng/audiences/disabled/index.shtml**
Youth with Disabilities—A government of Canada website with information about funding, accommodations, education, and employment.

**www.disabilityresources.org**
Disability Resources on the Internet—A comprehensive source including thousands of links, answers to FAQs (frequently asked questions), and publications.

**http://abilityonline.org**
AbilityOnline.org—A Canadian website with great resources and information. Worth the effort to register.

**www.focusas.com/Stress.html**
Focus Adolescent Services: Helping Teenagers with Stress—Potential sources of stress for adolescents and suggestions for how adolescents can help themselves and how adults can help.

**http://www.rcpsych.ac.uk/specialties/faculties/childandadolescent/booksforteensadults.aspx**
Royal College of Psychiatrists [in the United Kingdom]: Books for Teens and Adults—A list of books about disabilities written for individuals with disabilities.

a child's disability, parents' expectations for achievement in school are dashed (Russell, 2005). And coming to terms with this can reappear at major developmental stages (Wilgosh & Scorgie, 2006b). Figure 2.6 identifies websites that may help families and adolescents at the time of the transition to high school.

### EFFECTS ON FAMILIES

Siblings of children and adolescents with disabilities need to know about their sibling's disability because they are often expected to supply information at school and to act as a caretaker at home. Siblings may experience teasing at school. However, positive effects have also been observed. Alex Bilodeau who won a gold medal at the 2010 Olympics credited his brother Frederic, who has cerebral palsy, with inspiring him. When Michelle Pompeo (2004) of University of Western Ontario interviewed the siblings of youth with disabilities, they said that their experiences fueled their desire to become teachers and advocates for individuals with disabilities.

### PARENTS' TEACHING AND ADVOCATING FOR EXCEPTIONAL YOUTH

Parents often assume the role of teacher and advocate. They may spend long hours helping their children with disabilities complete school work. A "communication book" for children or an agenda book for adolescents, which the students carry between school and home, may remind students of assignments and enable parents to see what is expected. Sometimes parents report that their teaching role interferes with their parenting. It is more important for exceptional children and adolescents to have accepting and supportive parents than to have another academic teacher.

Teaching is, after all, your role. Many parents assume the role of **advocate**: "My child's success depends on my ability to advocate for him" (Hess et al., 2006, p. 154). Parents often express concerns about their exceptional child's prospects for the future. The case of Brenda Piet illustrates that, increasingly, IEPs contain transition plans.

## Collaborating with Parents

Many teachers recognize that the real experts on a student are usually the parents. In turn, some parents recognize the pressure that teachers are under and can be a source of support and advocacy for resources. Research suggests that the more extensive the collaboration between schools and families, the more successful children and adolescents with exceptionalities are likely to be (Carter et al., 2007). Not all parents choose to collaborate with teachers and schools, but parents are more likely to co-operate if the school, program, and teacher make them feel welcome (Rogers, 2007; Stanovich & Jordan, 2004). The qualities parents look for in teachers include patience, approachability, comfort, flexibility, a positive attitude, and adequate training (Wilgosh & Scorgie, 2006a). Parents want to feel supported (Janus et al., 2007) but, most of all, they want their children to be "fully participating, valued, and contributing members of a regular classroom of age appropriate peers . . . safe, accepted and encouraged" (Wilgosh & Chomicki, 1994, p. 30).

## Parent–Teacher Conferences

**Parent–teacher conferences** are a common means of facilitating productive partnerships. Communicate effectively with the parents of exceptional students at every opportunity. In spite of your busy schedule, you should make calls to these parents yourself, rather than asking the school secretary to call. Prepare by being informed about the student and the resources available in school and community.

### BEFORE PARENT-TEACHER CONFERENCES

If possible, contact the parents of exceptional students prior to the start of term. Introduce yourself and assure the parents that you are concerned about their child and want to develop a positive working relationship. Simmons (2002) suggests that successful alliances can be established by adhering to three basic assumptions:

1. Assume goodwill—that the parents, like you, have a deep desire to see the child do well.

2. Assume competence—that parents whose input is welcomed and valued will make constructive suggestions.

3. Assume a shared responsibility—that everyone needs to co-operate and actively participate in making and carrying out plans for a common goal.

When arranging parent–teacher conferences, be flexible about time and invite the child if that will help to reach the goals. Use child-produced invitations as well as formal announcements in newsletters, newspapers, and on the radio (in the languages of the community). Encourage parents to prepare for the conference.

### DURING PARENT-TEACHER CONFERENCES

The message you want to convey is that there is a team approach between home and school and between students and teachers. Strategies appear in Figure 2.7.

**Further Reading**

On working collaboratively with parents of exceptional students:

Simpson, R.L., & Mundschenk, N.A. (2010). *Working with parents and families of exceptional children and youth: Techniques for successful conferencing and collaboration.* Austin, TX: PRO-ED, Inc.

Turnbull, A., Zuna, N., Young Hoo, J., et al. (2010). Knowledge-to-action guides: Preparing families to be partners in making educational decisions. *Teaching Exceptional Children, 42*(3), 42–53.

## FIGURE 2.7 STRATEGIES TO USE IN PARENT-TEACHER CONFERENCES

- Create a comfortable atmosphere. Use adult chairs
- Avoid jargon and give examples to show what you mean
- Discuss frankly the goals for the next week, month, and term
- Avoid forecasting far into the future, focus on what is feasible in your classroom
- Make a plan and ensure that you have all the information and examples you need
- Invite parents to talk and remember to look at the parents and listen attentively
- After consensus has been reached, make a plan that supports the student in age-appropriate and culturally sensitive ways

**Put into Practice**

Read about the challenges of creating welcoming parent–teacher conferences in schools with diverse student populations. Then develop a plan for engaging parents who may be reluctant to attend or uncomfortable in meetings with educators. Use the strategy of putting yourself in the parents' place and thinking about what they might find helpful. Resources you could consult include:

Allen, J. (2007). *Creating welcoming schools: A practical guide to home–school partnerships with diverse families.* Newark, DE: International Reading Association.

Ontario Ministry of Education. (2007). *Shared solutions: A guide to preventing and resolving conflicts regarding programs and services for students with special education needs.* Toronto: Author. (http://www.edu.gov.on.ca/eng/general/elemsec/speced/shared.pdf)

Crozier, G., & Davies, J. (2007). Hard to reach parents or hard to reach schools? *British Educational Research Journal, 33*, 295–313.

There are many opportunities for conflict, and guides to conflict resolution remind us that conflict is natural. *Shared Solutions* (Ontario Ministry of Education, 2007) suggests there are three main reasons for conflict in special education:

1. Planning conflicts occur when parents and educators do not have the same understanding about the students' strengths and needs and the special education programs and services that are likely to be best for the student.

2. Implementation conflicts occur when parents believe that the school has not implemented the special education programs or services adequately.

3. Relationship conflicts occur as a result of differences in cultural background, ways of interacting, breakdowns in communication, or loss of trust.

We can reduce conflict by communicating effectively, treating parents respectfully, and developing a shared perspective and a positive school climate (see Chapter 8).

Exceptional adolescents can learn **self-advocacy** to negotiate with their teachers for accommodations consistent with the IEP. Participating in parent–teacher conferences may contribute to the development of autonomy. Prepare students for the conference. Student-led, teacher-supported conferences have been shown to improve student learning and communication (Goodman, 2008; Versnel, 2005).

### AFTER PARENT–TEACHER CONFERENCES

After a conference, write notes to remind yourself of the important points discussed. If any major decisions were made, write a brief note to the parents to confirm what was decided. If you agreed to take any action, carry it out as soon as possible. Inform other members of the in-school team about the outcomes.

It also can be helpful to look at the conference from the parents' perspective. While you have an important job—to teach this child—these parents also have an important job. Theirs is to love and care for this child and to be the child's advocate. This is the basis from which you can expect them to communicate with you. There may be families who do not form partnerships with you. Because of their situations—including homelessness, unemployment, discrimination, poverty, and violence—parents may not engage in collaboration. As educators, we have to respect their decisions and encourage them to attend the next conference.

# Summary

The role of the classroom teacher in the education of exceptional children is increasing. Teachers identify the needs of exceptional students, carry out pre-referral adaptations, and collaborate with in-school teams. Teachers also play a central role in IPRCs and in developing IEPs and carrying out these IEPs by ADAPTing or differentiating their teaching, assessment, and classroom organization. Strategies for meeting these challenges appear in upcoming chapters. Both parents and educational assistants are partners in the education of exceptional students and share the responsibility in these changing times.

# Key Terms

pre-referral process (p. 32)

pre-referral interventions (p. 32)

self-monitoring (p. 33)

self-regulation (p. 33)

collaboration (p. 35)

resource teacher (p. 35)

in-school team (p. 36)

referring teacher (p. 36)

informal assessment (p. 36)

formal assessment (p. 36)

Identification, Placement, and
 Review Committee (IPRC) (p. 37)

Individual Education Plan (IEP) (p. 37)

SMART goals (p. 43)

educational assistant (p. 43)

advocate (p. 47)

parent–teacher conferences (p. 47)

self-advocacy (p. 48)

# Challenges for Reviewing Chapter 2

1. Why is your role as a classroom teacher so important in identifying the needs of exceptional students?

2. Identify the steps a teacher would take before referring a child to an in-school team.

3. Using Figure 2.4 as a model, develop an IEP for Andy Hughes. Refer to sources identified in this chapter as well as the information in this chapter.

4. Identify three aspects of your role as a classroom teacher working with an educational assistant at the grade level at which you teach.

5. Describe the actions you would take at the start of the school year to ensure collaborative working relationships with parents of exceptional students.

6. Return to the opening cases of Andy and Brenda and answer the five questions that follow the cases.

# Chapter 3
## Teaching Students with High-Incidence Exceptionalities

### Learner Objectives

After you have read this chapter, you will be able to:

1. Describe the high-incidence exceptionalities discussed in this chapter.

2. Describe ways you can differentiate teaching for students who are gifted or developmentally advanced.

3. Describe differentiated teaching to meet the needs of students with learning disabilities.

4. Describe classroom differentiations for students with ADHD.

5. Describe adaptations needed by students with communication disorders.

6. For students with behaviour and emotional exceptionalities, discuss differentiated teaching.

7. Discuss classroom differentiation appropriate for students with mild intellectual disabilities.

**Urjo is 15 years old and in grade 10.** His teachers say he is non-compliant and underachieving. They describe a boy who does not complete assignments, refuses to do his homework, has difficulty following instructions, and rarely co-operates. Teachers describe him muttering under his breath, folding his arms across his chest, and shouting at peers. However, he excels in art class. While he engages in loud, verbal power struggles with most teachers, Urjo is quiet and engrossed when drawing or painting. The counsellor who interviewed him suggests that Urjo uses power struggles to avoid work he finds boring and pointless and to exert control over others. Urjo's parents report that he initiates the same battles at home and that his younger brothers are starting to engage in the same behaviours. When teachers pressure Urjo to comply, he bad-mouths them and indulges in negative self-talk. Achievement tests show that Urjo is slightly below grade level in reading, written expression, and mathematics and is easily distracted but does not have a learning disability. This is described as a behaviour exceptionality, with defiant behaviours and disruptions to the classroom.

**Scott is included in a grade 3 class and learns to read in a small group in the resource room.** Scott was born with Down syndrome. His family has always involved him in all their activities and he has always been in regular education programs. After participating in early intervention (from the age of two months to four years) and attending the neighbourhood preschool, he moved with his classmates to senior kindergarten. At his teacher's suggestion, Scott stayed in senior kindergarten for a second year. Since then he has moved to the next grade each year. Like many people with Down syndrome, Scott learns by watching. For the past two years, he has watched and asked Billy, a classmate with ADHD, whenever he didn't know what to do. Scott's parents and teachers know that the gap between his academic achievement and that of his classmates will gradually increase. However, Scott works hard, likes school, and especially likes learning to read. Scott recognizes and sounds out many words, is reading small books with predictable stories, and recognizes the names of all the students in his class. In math Scott can add and subtract numbers less than 10 and hopes to learn to use a calculator this year. He loves environmental science, discusses issues such as recycling, watches nature programs on television, and attends the "young naturalists" program in his community. Scott hopes to work in environmental protection when he grows up. His IEP lists his exceptionality as mild intellectual disabilities and refers to Scott's lower-than-average intellectual, social, and adaptive functioning.

1.  Which of the characteristics of each student are most likely to affect learning and participation in the regular classroom? What learning needs are implied by these characteristics?

2.  With such a range of characteristics and learning needs, what do exceptional students like Urjo and Scott, who are learning in inclusive classrooms, have in common?

3.  How frequently is a teacher likely to be teaching a student with each of these exceptionalities?

4.  What types of differentiation does each student need in order to be included in the social life and the group learning activities of the classroom?

5.  What community resources can a teacher draw on to supplement in-school resources when teaching each of these students?

# Introduction

This chapter focuses on the characteristics of students with **high-incidence exceptionalities** and on classroom differentiations that help them to learn. We use person-first language: exceptional students are children and adolescents *first*, and they also have *some* characteristics associated with their exceptionality. We describe the student as *having* an exceptionality. The exception is "children who *are* gifted."

Each section on an exceptionality begins with the personal story of a child or adolescent, followed by characteristics and then implications for learning and for differentiating in the classroom. There are examples of teachers differentiating in elementary and secondary classrooms, and you will find reminders that exceptional students are most successful when we set high but realistic expectations.

**Cross-Reference**

Chapter 4 focuses on descriptions of, and differentiated teaching for, students with low-incidence exceptionalities, physical disabilities, and chronic health conditions.

## THEORY AND RESEARCH HIGHLIGHTS FROM

## EDUCATIONAL PSYCHOLOGY

## The Concept of Intelligence

Definitions of a number of the high-incidence exceptionalities in this chapter include references to intelligence (e.g., gifted, learning disabilities, intellectual disabilities). However, controversy persists about what is meant by intelligence and how it should be measured. Early theories about intelligence referred to capacity to learn and knowledge already learned. In 1986, 24 psychologists attended a symposium on intelligence and provided 24 distinct views about the nature of intelligence (Sternberg & Detterman, 1986). There was little agreement about whether it was composed of a single, general ability or of many separate, domain-specific abilities. However, they agreed about the importance of higher-order thinking (e.g., abstract reasoning and problem solving), as well as metacognition—that is, thinking about thinking and knowledge of oneself.

An early theorist supporting general ability, Charles Spearman (1927) advocated *g*, or general intelligence, which he thought combined with specific abilities to enable us to perform mental tasks such as memorization. In contrast, Edward Thurstone (1938) theorized a number of distinct "primary mental abilities" for memory, numerical ability, reasoning, word fluency, etc. and no general intelligence. Howard Gardner (1993) postulated eight multiple intelligences: verbal, spatial, logico-mathematical, naturalist, musical, bodily-kinesthetic, interpersonal, and intrapersonal. He argued that intelligence is the ability to solve problems valued by one's culture.

Recent work in cognitive psychology has focused on how we gather and use information to solve problems, sometimes called cognitive processing or information processing. Robert Sternberg (1990) developed a triarchic theory of intelligence with three components: analytic or componential intelligence (abstract thinking abilities, verbal abilities, etc.); creative or experiential intelligence (emphasizing the ability to formulate new ideas and deal with novel situations); and practical or tacit intelligence (meaning the ability to adapt to changing environments).

The irony is that while these theoretical developments proceed, schools, for the most part, continue to use standardized tests to measure children and adolescents' intelligence in a completely atheoretical way. In 1904, Alfred Binet developed a test with his collaborator, Theophile Simon, intended to measure mental age. By this they meant that a child who passed the tests normally passed by an eight year old had a mental age of eight, regardless of chronological age. The Stanford-Binet Intelligence Scale has been revised many times and while the concept of mental age has been altered somewhat, no one has developed theoretical underpinnings for the test. The most-used intelligence test in Canada and the United States is the Wechsler Intelligence Test for Children developed by Jerome Sattler, which was designed to predict school achievement. It is similar to the Stanford-Binet in design and concept, and is also atheoretical. Most intelligence tests are designed so an average score is 100, and 68 percent of the population will earn scores between 85 and 115. Only about 16 percent of the population will receive scores either above 115 or below 85. However, the tests are less reliable as one gets away from the normal range, and yet they are most often used to identify those students with high scores (gifted students) or low scores (students with severe intellectual disabilities or developmental disabilities), as

*(Box continued on next page)*

well as students with learning disabilities. The tests are not likely to be valid for students from culturally diverse backgrounds for whom English is a second language or for Aboriginal students.

Controversy about IQ testing persists. Recent research suggests that working memory tests are better predictors of school achievement than IQ tests (Alloway & Alloway, 2010) and, for both clinical and non-clinical samples, attention may interact with intelligence to predict achievement (Steinmayr et al., 2010). Debates continue over whether intelligence is more a matter of nature (born with it, cannot do anything about it) or nurture (can be developed through stimulation and education). Today most psychologists believe both are important. Because we, as educators, can do little about nature, we must make every effort to influence nurture—to produce stimulating, caring classrooms in which students take risks and are willing to use and develop their intelligence.

### References

Alloway, T.P., & Alloway, R.G. (2010). Investigating the predictive roles of working memory and IQ in academic attainment. *Journal of Experimental Child Psychology, 106*, 20–29.

Gardner, H. (1993). *Multiple intelligences: The theory in practice*. New York, NY: Basic Books.

Spearman, C. (1927). *The abilities of man: Their nature and measurement*. New York, NY: Macmillan.

Syteinmayr, R., Ziegler, M., & Trauble, B. (2010). Do intelligence and sustained attention interact in predicting academic achievement? *Learning and Individual Differences, 20*, 14–18.

Sternberg, R.J. (1990). *Metaphors of mind: Conceptions of the nature of intelligence*. New York: Cambridge University Press.

Sternberg, R.J., & Detterman, D.L. (Eds.). (1986). *What is intelligence? Contemporary viewpoints on its nature and definition*. Norwood, NJ: Ablex.

Thurstone, E.L. (1938). Primary mental abilities. *Psychometric Monographs*, No. 1.

High-incidence exceptionalities include students who are gifted or have learning disabilities, attention deficit **hyperactivity** disorder, speech or language disabilities, behaviour or emotional exceptionalities, or mild intellectual disabilities. Many of these students will also have asthma, allergies, diabetes, and other chronic health conditions described in Chapter 4. The definitions for high incidence exceptionalities appear in Table 3.1. Prevalence estimates appear in Table 3.2. These students are often difficult to distinguish from peers without exceptionalities, especially outside school settings. In school, they frequently show a combination of behavioural, social, and academic needs. Gifted students usually benefit from challenges and opportunities to work with developmentally advanced peers.

@

Weblinks

COUNCIL FOR EXCEPTIONAL CHILDREN (GIFTED EDUCATION)
www.cectag.org

GIFTED CANADA
www3.telus.net/giftedcanada

UNIVERSITY OF CALGARY CENTRE FOR GIFTED EDUCATION
www.gifted.ucalgary.ca

**TABLE 3.1 STUDENTS WITH HIGH-INCIDENCE EXCEPTIONALITIES**

| Exceptionality | Description |
| --- | --- |
| Gifted or developmentally advanced | Have unusually advanced degree of general intellectual ability that requires differentiation of learning experiences; developmentally advanced in specific domains. |
| Learning disabilities | Learning disorder evident in academic and social situations that is not due primarily to (a) visual, hearing, or physical disability; (b) emotional disturbance; or (c) cultural difference. Results in discrepancy between academic achievement and intellectual ability. |
| Attention deficit hyperactivity disorder | Persistent pattern of (a) inattention, (b) hyperactivity and impulsivity, or of both (a) and (b). |
| Communication exceptionalities | Includes disorders of speech (articulation, voice, and fluency) and disorders of language (expressive and receptive). |
| Behaviour and emotional exceptionalities | Characterized by specific behaviour problems over time and to such a degree as to adversely affect academic performance; may be accompanied by inability to build or maintain relationships, excessive anxieties, a tendency to compulsive reaction. |
| Mild intellectual disabilities | Lower-than-average intellectual functioning and adaptive behaviour. Knows much about living in the community; requires instruction that can be provided in relatively non-intensive conditions. |

**TABLE 3.2 ESTIMATED PREVALENCE OF HIGH-INCIDENCE EXCEPTIONALITIES**

| Exceptionality | General Incidence in Research | % of IPRCs in ON in 2006/07* |
|---|---|---|
| Gifted | 200 to 500 per 10,000 (Belanger & Gagne, 2006; Winzer, 2007) | 13.4% |
| Learning disabilities | 400 to 700 per 10,000 (Dirks et al., 2008; LDAC, website) | 42.6% |
| ADHD | 400 to 500 per 10,000 (Alberta Education, 2006; Faraone et al., 2003) | — |
| Communication | 300 per 10,000 (Bennett et al., 2008; Duff et al., 2004) | 6.2% |
| Behaviour | 200 per 10,000 (BC Education, 2006; Lane et al., 2005) | 6.9% |
| Mild intellectual disabilities | 200 to 300 per 10,000 (BC Education, 2006; Christianson et al., 2002) | 12.0% |

\* See Figure 1.2 in Chapter 1 (Ontario Provincial Statistics for IPRCs 2006/2007)

Other students with high-incidence exceptionalities usually benefit from differentiated teaching and systematic, structured, instructional interventions such as those described in this chapter and throughout the book.

# Teaching Students Who Are Gifted or Developmentally Advanced

Teacher: How can I help you stay out of trouble?

Brian: I don't want to be bored. Challenge me. Let me work ahead on things that really interest me.

*Brian is a gifted Aboriginal boy in grade 3. This exchange took place after his teacher had intervened in a scuffle between Brian and a classmate for the third time in a week.*

Teacher: Why did you push Larry?

Brian: When I have nothing to do, he gets to me. He calls me "brainer" and tells me that I'm weird. When I'm busy, I don't notice as much. I need more stuff to do . . . please.

## Characteristics of Gifted Students

Ontario defines **gifted** students as "having an unusually advanced degree of general intellectual ability that requires differentiated learning experiences of a depth and breadth beyond those normally provided in the regular school program" (Ontario Ministry of Education, 2001, p. A20). They are usually identified by high scores on intelligence tests. Recent research conducted in Ontario schools emphasizes that gifted learners are **developmentally advanced** in specific **domains**, and reminds us to consider students' "habits of mind" and socio-emotional factors (e.g., motivation, curiosity, anxiety). Dona Matthews and her colleagues recommend that teachers differentiate curriculum to challenge students in the subjects in which they demonstrate advanced ability (Matthews & Steinhauer, 1998; Matthews et al., 2007).

Gifted students may demonstrate outstanding abilities in many areas; however, many do not excel in all curriculum areas. Some gifted students may go unrecognized, including young boys, adolescent girls, and students who are from diverse cultural groups or have disabilities (Lupart & Wilgosh, 1998; Pedersen & Kitano, 2006). Gifted students who also have disabilities, such as learning disabilities, are often called "twice exceptional" (Assouline et al., 2010; Yssel et al., 2010).

## COGNITIVE CHARACTERISTICS

In general, gifted students differ from their classmates in three key ways: the rate at which they learn, the depth of their comprehension, and the range of their interests (Maker & Nielson, 1996). Research by Bruce Shore of McGill University (e.g., Hannah & Shore, 2008; Martini & Shore, 2008) suggests they often demonstrate enhanced **metacognition**, or the ability to decide when and where to use their knowledge and skills. Characteristics to watch for include:

- a large vocabulary and high verbal fluency;
- an excellent retention of new knowledge;
- a facility for learning quickly and easily;
- a demonstrated ability to generalize information;
- a demonstrated ability to make abstractions readily;
- the capacity to identify similarities, differences, and relationships; and
- good organizational and planning skills.

Renzulli's Enrichment Triad Model (2005) describes giftedness as an interaction among three clusters of characteristics: above-average **cognitive abilities** (as described above), high levels of task commitment, and high levels of creativity. **High task commitment** refers to students' setting their own goals, embracing challenges and persevering, and can result in perfectionism. Gifted students may chastise themselves when they make a mistake, and may think they should excel at everything (Pyryt, 2007). High levels of **creativity** are demonstrated by students' contributing many ideas, transforming ideas, asking questions, and being curious.

## BEHAVIOUR CHARACTERISTICS

The behaviour of gifted students varies. Sometimes gifted students are more advanced intellectually than emotionally (Delisle & Galbraith, 2004). They may show enhanced concern for justice and awareness of complex ethical, environmental, and societal issues (Foster & Matthews, 2006). Adults can listen to children's concerns, acknowledge that there are troubles in the world, focus on how problems are being addressed, and help children to set reasonable goals for what they can do (www.sengifted.org/articles_social/).

## Differentiating Curriculum and Teaching Students Who Are Gifted

Differentiated education was first developed to meet the needs of gifted learners (Tomlinson, 1999) and then recognized as appropriate for all learners. When differentiating for gifted learners, look for curriculum areas where students are not challenged and consider how to remedy that. Assessment to inform differentiation for gifted students may include RTI (discussed in Chapter 1; e.g., Rollins et al., 2009) and embedded *assessment for learning* (discussed in Chapter 6; e.g., Miedijensky & Tal, 2009). Strategies often suggested include enabling students to

### Further Reading

On social-emotional characteristics of gifted students:

Delisle, J., & Galbraith, J. (2004). *When gifted kids don't have all the answers: How to meet their social and emotional needs.* Minneapolis, MN: Free Spirit Publishing.

Lupart, J.L., Pyryt, M.C., Watson, S.L., & Pierce K. (2005). Gifted education and counseling in Canada. *International Journal for the Advancement of Counseling, 27*(2), 173–190.

Wood, S. (2010). Best practices in counseling the gifted in schools: What's really happening. *Gifted Child Quarterly, 54*(1), 42–58.

Martin, L.T., Burns, R.M., & Schonlau, M. (2010). Mental disorders among gifted and nongifted youth: A selected review of the epidemiologic literature, *Gifted Child Quarterly, 54*(1), 31–41.

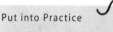

### Put into Practice

Read about students who are twice exceptional and interview the parent of one of these students. Learn about the family's experiences with identification and differentiation: Which was recognized first—being gifted or having a disability? Compare your interviews with those conducted by your peers.

Assouline, S.G., Nicpon, M.F., & Whiteman, C. (2010). Cognitive and psychosocial characteristics of gifted students with written language disability, *Gifted Child Quarterly, 54*(2), 102–115.

Yssel, N., Prater, M., & Smith, D. (2010). How can such a smart kid not get it? Finding the right fit for twice-exceptional students in our schools, *Gifted Child Today, 33*(1), 54–61.

**Further Reading**

On differentiating teaching for gifted learners:

Carver, A., & Bailey, J.M. (2010). Differentiation for 200 students: Unit pages. *Science Scope, 33*(6), 12-17.

Matthews, D.J., & Foster, J.F. (2005). *Being smart about gifted children: A guidebook for parents and educators.* Scottsdale, AZ: Great Potential Press.

Preddy, L.B. (2009). Reaching advanced readers in the middle grades. *School Library Media Activities Monthly, 25*(10), 19-21.

Reis, S.M., & Renzulli, J.S. (2002). *The Secondary Triad Model: A practical plan for implementing gifted programs at the junior and senior high school levels.* Heatherton, Australia: Hawker Brownlow Education.

Smith, C.M.M. (Ed.). (2006). *Including the gifted and talented: Making inclusion work for the gifted and able learners.* London, UK: Routledge.

pursue their interests (Gentry et al., 2007) and using tiered assignments, as discussed throughout this book (see examples for: physics in Geddes, 2010; math in Tretter, 2010, and Barger, 2009; reading in Preddy, 2009; and general examples in Rakow, 2007).

Other strategies include: introducing technologies, like spreadsheets, to increase the sophistication of student projects (Siegle, 2005); assigning self-directed projects (Hargrove, 2005); designing multicultural literature units (Pederson & Kitano, 2006); and developing accelerated programs (Renzulli, 2008). Acceleration refers to placing students based on readiness and potential to succeed rather than on chronological age (Colangelo & Assouline, 2005). Some acceleration strategies change the placement of the student, such as moving the student into the next grade for math class, having the student skip a grade and move to the next grade in all subjects, creating combined classes, giving early entrance to kindergarten or grade one, or early graduation from secondary school. Kanevsky and McGrimmond (2008) found a wide variation in the use of acceleration strategies across Canada.

Research suggests that gifted learners need to be with their intellectual peers for at least part of the school day so they are stimulated in areas in which they are advanced (Cross, 2002). They also benefit from learning with same-age peers during each school day. Teaching self-advocacy encourages gifted students to become partners in differentiation (Douglas, 2004). Strategies for differentiating the curriculum for gifted students appear in Table 3.3.

Many gifted adolescents find it difficult to focus their career aspirations, perhaps because they have so many talents and interests. Co-operative education helps them to "try out" careers (Chin et al., 2000), and gifted students value experiences that connect them with adults with similar interests (Gentry et al., 2007).

**Cross-Reference**

Chapter 5 contains practical strategies to implement phonemic awareness interventions.

Adams, M.J., Foorman, B.R., Lundberg, I., & Beeler, T. (1998). *Phonemic awareness in young children: A classroom curriculum.* Toronto: Irwin Publishers.

Cunningham, P.M., & Hall, D.P. (2008). *Making words: Second grade: 100 hands-on lessons for phonemic awareness, phonics and spelling.* Boston: Pearson/Allyn & Bacon.

Ellery, V. (2005). *Creating strategic readers: Techniques for developing competency, in phonemic awareness, phonics, fluency, vocabulary, and comprehension.* Newark, DE: International Reading Association.

# Teaching Students with Learning Disabilities

Frank watched his teacher put the afternoon schedule on the board. The list included reading. Did that mean oral reading? Frank had not practised the next story in the book. If the teacher asked him to read, he would die, the other kids would laugh, and … He tried to think of a way to get out of class before oral reading. He felt his chest tightening, his stomach flipping, and his palms growing damp. Frank hated to stutter and stumble. He slouched down in his seat and worried. He kept asking himself, "How bad can it be?" He knew the answer: "Bad!" When you can't read in grade 6, it's bad. Frank is a grade 6 student with learning disabilities in reading.

## Characteristics of Students with Learning Disabilities

In Ontario, **learning disability (LD)** refers to a learning disorder evident in academic and social situations that involves at least one of the processes necessary for using spoken language or the symbols of communication. It must not be primarily a result of any of the following:

- impairment of vision;
- impairment of hearing;

**TABLE 3.3 ENRICHMENT STRATEGIES FOR TEACHING GIFTED STUDENTS**

| Strategies | Descriptions and Examples |
|---|---|
| Sophistication | Introduce students to the theories and concepts that underlie the content being learned by the class. *Example:* When teaching about child development in a secondary course on psychology, provide gifted students with writings by Piaget and encourage them to observe in a preschool. |
| Novelty | Students explore required curricular content from different and unique perspectives. *Example:* In history, gifted students write from the perspective of the child who lived in Montreal while her father was a member of the Northwest Trading Company. |
| Authentic problem solving | Students apply their knowledge and skills to problems that are significant to their own lives. *Example:* When studying watersheds, gifted students test the water quality of a stream that collects runoff from a parking lot in their community and prepare a report for town council. |
| Independent studies | Students pursue an area of personal interest or investigate a topic from the curriculum. *Example:* Students select a character from *Hamlet* and prepare a résumé for that character. |
| Telescoping | Taking advantage of the overlap in curricula of adjacent grades, students do two curricula in a year. *Example:* Students complete grades 7 and 8 science in one year. |
| Compacting | After discerning what the student already knows, provide assignments so the student masters unfamiliar material. Then provide enrichment activities in the compacted area. *Example:* For a student who already understands much about WW II, give assignments on unfamiliar topics. Have the student choose a topic (e.g., how the war changed our society), contact the War Museum, use the Internet, conference with you, and prepare a multimedia presentation. |
| Ability grouping | Students work with their intellectual peers on a regular, part-time basis, in the classroom or outside, providing social support, emotional support, and intellectual stimulation. *Example:* An advanced reading or math work group, perhaps with peers from other classes, for enrichment. |
| Mentor programs | Students apply their knowledge and skills in a hands-on setting supervised by an adult in the community. They pursue interests and try out career paths. *Example:* A student who is a skilled artist attends the studio of a painter who invites her to help her in preparing for a show. |
| Open-ended assignments | Students are given options to complete an assignment and decide how far to take their learning. *Example:* In a kindergarten unit on whales, provide required assignments about the habitat and diet of whales; provide optional assignments that require more writing or allow children to create games for whales based on their knowledge of whales. |
| Tiered assignments | Prepare a range of distinct assignments, from simple to complex, all focusing on key learning outcomes. You may select one activity to be completed by everyone and allow students to choose another, or students may choose the level of assignments they complete. *Example:* In a secondary drama unit, the tiers include preparing a scene, an act, or a short play while employing two, three, or more actors and embodying one or more themes from a list. Each tier can be described separately so students see that they have choices about degrees of complexity. |

- physical disability;
- developmental disability;
- emotional disturbance; or
- cultural difference.

It results in a significant discrepancy between academic achievement and assessed intellectual ability in one or more of the following:

- receptive language (listening, reading);
- language processing (thinking, conceptualizing, integrating);
- expressive language (talking, spelling, writing); or
- mathematical computations. (Ontario Ministry of Education, 2001, p. A19)

The Learning Disability Association of Canada (LDAC) (2002) emphasizes 4 characteristics in its definition: neurobiological, genetic, lifelong, and felt in all areas of life. The Learning Disabilities Association of Ontario (LDAO) (2001) emphasizes impairments in psychological processes related to learning and causing difficulties in skills such as oral language, reading, written language, and mathematics.

Both these definitions, like Ontario's, include references to the discrepancy between potential and achievement. Canadian researchers (Siegel, 1999; Stanovich, 2005) have argued against using discrepancy formulas, arguing all students who show disabilities in learning should be identified as having LD. "For each LD, the primary manifestation of the disability represents specific academic skill deficits (e.g., in word recognition, reading comprehension, reading fluency, mathematics computations/problem solving, and written expression)" (Fletcher et al., 2007, p. 2). Since 2004 some US states have used RTI to identify students with learning disabilities, with a criterion that students do not respond to high-quality intervention. Teachers are the most likely people to suspect learning disabilities because the characteristics interfere with classroom learning. However, characteristics vary greatly from student to student.

### COGNITIVE CHARACTERISTICS

Students with LD demonstrate lower-than-expected achievement in one or more areas, but demonstrate academic strengths on which you can build. Often they perform poorly on tasks requiring memory, focused attention, organization, metacognition, and information processing. These characteristics are elaborated on in Table 3.4.

## TABLE 3.4 WHAT ARE CHILDREN AND ADOLESCENTS WITH LEARNING DISABILITIES LIKE?

| | |
|---|---|
| They are all different, with unique strengths and weaknesses. Often they are overwhelmed by the volume of work in the classroom and seem to be behind and frustrated. They have average or better ability, but achievement lags behind ability. | We can be attentive to their strengths and weaknesses, ensure they know that we want to help, and ask them for advice about what would help. Differentiate without drawing attention to them. Find what works. |
| **Psychological Processes** | **What We Can Do** |
| 1. PERCEPTION: Organizing, interpreting what we experience; most impact when perception is critical to learning—early years; may confuse letters more often and longer. | WE CAN: Keep pieces of information separate that are perceptually confusing until at least one is learned well; highlight important characteristics of information. |
| 2. ATTENTION: Focusing on information; coming to and maintaining attention; some identified as having ADHD; "in her/his own world"; distracted, in constant motion. | WE CAN: Break task into smaller segments; gradually build up; bring attention to key words with cues; meaning-check for instructions; help identify the important, independently. |
| 3. MEMORY: Arranging what has been perceived and attended to; many processes, e.g., problems in working memory (storing, retrieving information); too much so only take in part (e.g., note-taking in lecture); may not make connections. | WE CAN: Help develop strategies for remembering (e.g., minute hand is longer than hour hand, minute is longer word); provide more practice; remind to find relationships; make it meaningful; teach strategies. |
| 4. METACOGNITION: Monitoring and evaluating own learning; identifying most effective way to learn; key to generalizing, applying; may act impulsively or without planning. | WE CAN: Teach self-monitoring; model thinking out loud; ask the student to give reasons; give cues, give feedback, encourage, be clear, teach strategies. |
| 5. ORGANIZATION: Come without pencil; lose papers; have difficulty getting good ideas into an essay or assignment; lose track of goal, especially if it is long-term. | WE CAN: Teach routines; put checklist in notebook; break task into steps; post agenda; warn about major changes; ask questions to keep putting the onus on the student. |

Source: Adapted from Hutchinson, N.L. (2004). *Teaching exceptional children and adolescents: A Canadian casebook* (2nd ed.), p. 144. Copyright Prentice Hall. Used by permission.

Most students with LD experience difficulties when learning to read. Research supports insufficiently developed phonemic awareness as a major characteristic of primary children with reading disabilities. **Phonemic awareness** includes the awareness that words can be segmented into component sounds, identifying sounds in various positions in words, and manipulating sounds in words (Ryder et al., 2008). One Canadian study reported that phonemic processing in grade 1 was the best predictor of grade 6 reading (Cunningham & Stanovich, 1997). Explicit, systematic instruction in phonemic awareness is necessary for most children and does no harm to those for whom it is redundant (Shankweiler & Fowler, 2004), and phonemic awareness interventions are effective in helping *most* children with LD to learn to read (e.g., Ehri et al., 2001; Ryder et al., 2008). Ontario researchers Maryanne Wolf and John Kirby suggest that **rapid naming** also plays a significant role in beginning reading (Johnston & Kirby, 2006; Katzir, Wolf, et al., 2008). They study the **double-deficit hypothesis**, referring to deficits in phonemic awareness and rapid naming. Other critical reading skills include phonics, fluency, vocabulary development, and text comprehension (National Reading Panel, 2000, www.nationalreadingpanel.org). The typical characteristics of young children with learning disabilities appear in Figure 3.1 and of older students in Figure 3.2.

## CHARACTERISTICS: LEARNING MATH

**Number sense** may be the mathematical equivalent of phonemic awareness (Chard et al., 2008). Number sense refers to children's flexibility with numbers, the sense of what numbers mean, and an ability to look at the world and make mental comparisons

## FIGURE 3.1 CHARACTERISTICS OF LEARNING DISABILITIES IN YOUNG CHILDREN

**Problems in Reading**
- Often lacks awareness of sounds that make up words; does not "attack" a new word but guesses or waits for the teacher to say the word.
- Loses meaning of sentence before getting to the end; loses sequence of what has been read.
- Is painful to listen to; finds reading painful and finds creative ways to avoid reading.

**Difficulty in Copying**
- Copies better from a page beside him than from the board; appears careless.
- Loses his place frequently and ignores organizational cues.

**Difficulty with Alphabet**
- Has difficulty remembering sounds of letters and names of letters.
- Confuses letter names and sounds if learning both at once.
- Shows poor penmanship with frequent reversals or distorted shapes or sizes of letters (or numbers).

**Strengths**
- Often shows strengths in some areas and weaknesses in others, and really benefits from recognition of his strengths.
- Often expresses ideas better orally than in writing.
- Often highly motivated by small successes and willing to work very hard to succeed again.
- Often shows imagination and complex ideas when asked to draw or act out his ideas, but reverts to simpler ideas when writing to avoid errors or embarrassment.

## FIGURE 3.2 CHARACTERISTICS OF STUDENTS WITH LD IN JUNIOR GRADES AND INTERMEDIATE-SENIOR GRADES

**Characteristics in Junior Grades**

- Avoids reading aloud; reads without fluency and does not understand what has been read.
- Has difficulty understanding and representing word problems.
- Experiences difficulty expressing ideas, especially in a meaningful sequence.
- May be scape-goated by classmates because not socially aware.
- Has awkward pencil grip.
- Knows content from watching movies and television, not from classes and reading.
- May show less self-regulation than classmates.
- May be easily discouraged about lack of success.

**Characteristics in Intermediate-Senior Grades**

- Spelling difficulties persist and may now interfere with written expression.
- Reads slowly and experiences severe difficulties in comprehension, especially of textbooks.
- Difficulties persist in written expression and affect quality of written assignments.
- Difficulties with organization persist and now may affect grades (not submitting work).
- Shows weak grasp of abstract concepts; cannot read to understand nuanced meanings.
- Benefits from having models of what is expected in assignments.
- Benefits from guided practice and needs more independent practice than peers.
- Learns well in intensity of small group where teacher is responsive to lack of comprehension.
- Can be encouraged and engaged by caring, attentive teacher.
- May be much more successful in some classes than in others.
- May not have a realistic understanding of own strengths and weaknesses.

about quantities (Griffin & Case, 1997). Recent research suggests that students with learning disabilities only in mathematics have weak number sense, while those with learning disabilities in both math and reading may be characterized by weak phonological processing (Robinson et al., 2002). Challenges often arise in learning addition facts and multiplication tables, and students may ignore columns in computations and carry or borrow incorrectly, issues addressed in research by Derek Berg of Queen's University (Berg, 2006, 2008). Older students with LD often find it challenging to represent mathematical relations in word problems (Montague et al., 2000). You may see lack of understanding of the use of symbols in algebra and memorization of procedures.

### SOCIAL AND BEHAVIOURAL CHARACTERISTICS

Ontario (2001) states that LD are apparent in both academic and social situations. Research findings about social competence are inconsistent. Jess Whitley (2007) of the University of Ottawa found teachers reported that *most* students with LD experienced social skills difficulties and peers reported that *many* had low **social status**; but only a *few* children with LD report low social **self-concept** (Walker & Nabuzoka, 2007). A series of qualitative studies conducted at Queen's University reported that some students with LD showed well-developed social skills and peer relations (Lévesque, 1997), while others showed good social skills and peer relations in some contexts (Stoch, 1999) (see Hutchinson et al., 2002). Capitalizing on adolescents' interests may make social interventions more effective (Hutchinson et al., 2004).

Rob Klassen reported that adolescents with LD tend to overestimate their efficacy for spelling and writing (2007), and teachers who knew the adolescents well thought these adolescents were overconfident about their academic ability (Klassen

& Lynch, 2007). This can be challenging for teachers because we want these students to have realistic self-assessments, but we don't want to discourage them by insisting on how incompetent they are. We need to be encouraging *and* realistic.

## Implications for Learning and Classroom Differentiation: Students with LD

### ESTABLISHING AN INCLUSIVE CLASSROOM

It is important to establish a safe classroom where students with LD feel accepted. You can use interactive teaching, check that individual students understand your instructions, and eliminate bullying (Edwards, 2000). Teachers who are good at teaching students with LD are responsive to individuals (Stough & Palmer, 2003), and students see them as approachable and willing to differentiate (Long et al., 2008). These teacher characteristics enhance the confidence and engagement of students with LD.

### DIFFERENTIATING TEACHING

You can build on an inclusive learning environment by differentiating your instructional techniques to make them more accessible to students with LD by:

- providing overviews of lessons in chart form;
- varying the mode of presentation (oral, visual, activity-based);
- cueing students to listen to, or make notes about, important points;
- relating material to students' lives and using experiential teaching approaches;
- making directions short and reinforcing oral directions with visual cues;
- clarifying definitions and asking students to repeat definitions;
- breaking a large task into manageable parts with individual deadlines;
- using collaborative and co-operative learning approaches;
- offering assistance when it is needed, after students have asked their peers;
- preparing study guides of key words and concepts so students have clear notes from which to study;
- using colour-coded materials to make organization easier;
- using partially filled-in tasks to guide students;
- offering an audio recorder for taping a lecture or listening to a book on tape; and
- using cross-age tutoring of both younger students by those with LD and of those with LD by older role models.

### TEACHING STRATEGIES

It is important that you demonstrate to students how to learn and provide them with time to practise what you teach. General organizational skills, identifying main ideas, and note-taking strategies can be taught to the whole class; then provide additional practice for those who need it. Teaching organizational skills is the focus of Figure 3.3. Teach outlining by providing a partial outline of your notes for students to complete, and teach highlighting by having pairs of students decide what main ideas should be highlighted. Model on an overhead before the students begin and debrief with reasons at the end of the lesson. In a recent meta-analysis, Swanson and Deshler (2003) reported that eight instructional factors—questioning,

### Put into Practice

Read the following papers and make a plan to differentiate your teaching and ensure you are approachable for students with LD.

Faggella-Luby, M.N., & Deshler, D.D. (2008). Reading comprehension in adolescents with LD: What we know; what we need to learn. *Learning Disabilities Research & Practice, 23*(2), 70–78.

Klassen, R., & Lynch, S.L. (2007). Self-efficacy from the perspective of adolescents with LD and their specialist teachers. *Journal of Learning Disabilities, 40*(6), 494–507.

Witzel, B.S., Riccomini, P.J., & Schneider, E. (2008). Implementing CRA with secondary students with learning disabilities in mathematics. *Intervention in School and Clinic, 43*(5), 270–276.

### Further Reading

On learning disabilities:

Fletcher, J.M., Lyon, G.R., Fuchs, L.S., & Barnes, M.A. (2007). *Learning disabilities: From identification to intervention.* New York, NY: Guilford Press.

Greenbaum, J., & Markel, G. (2001). *Helping adolescents with ADHD and learning disabilities: Ready-to-use tips, techniques, and checklists for school success.* San Francisco: Jossey-Bass.

Kass, C.E. & Maddux, C.D. (2005). *A human development view of learning disabilities: From theory to practice* (2nd ed.). Springfield, IL: Charles C. Thomas Pub.

Wong, B.Y.L. & Donahue, M. (Eds.) (2002). *The social dimensions of learning disabilities: Essays in honor of Tanis Bryan.* Mahwah, NJ: Erlbaum.

Wong, B.Y.L. (Ed.) (2004). *Learning about learning disabilities* (3rd ed.). Toronto: Academic Press.

## FIGURE 3.3 HELPING STUDENTS WITH LD TO IMPROVE THEIR ORGANIZATIONAL SKILLS

**Strategies for Building Organizational Skills in Students with Learning Disabilities**

- Post an agenda at the front of class; follow it and give warning before you make changes.
- If necessary, post a personal agenda on a student's desk until the class agenda is sufficient.
- Post a calendar of deadlines on a bulletin board in the classroom.
- Encourage the student (and parents if necessary) to post a calendar of deadlines at home.
- Teach students to record homework, deadlines, etc. in an organizer/planner.
- Provide checklists so students can track their progress through activities and assignments.
- Teach students to date and title notes and assignments.
- If students move from room to room, provide a mobile schedule.
- Help students to organize their desk or locker containing books and other necessities.
- Suggest students carry books for 2 classes; they won't have to go to their lockers as often.
- Teach students to use sticky notes and highlighters as self-reminders.
- Provide time checks for the whole class at 5 or 10 minute intervals so students self-monitor.
- Provide clear, concise instructions and check that students understand what to do.
- Teach appropriate help-seeking behaviour and encourage increasing independence.
- Put organizational goals on IEPs so teachers must make accommodations; focus on improvement.
- Explicitly teach time management skills; follow up with students with LD regularly.
- Remember that students with LD require more guided and independent practice to reach mastery of any skill.
- Be clear with the students and parents about your expectations for organizational skills.
- Emphasize that organizational skills are important and everyone can learn to be organized.
- Be vigilant and persistent, especially at the beginning; the changes in behaviour are worth it.

---

### Put into Practice

Choose two of the references listed here that are relevant for your grade level and teaching assignment. Prepare reading activities you could use in your class/teaching.

Boyle, J.R. (2008). Reading strategies for students with mild disabilities. *Intervention in School and Clinic, 44*(1), 3–9.

Conderman, G., & Strobel, D. (2006). Problem solving with guided repeated oral reading instruction. *Intervention in School and Clinic, 42*(1), 34–391.

King-Sears, M., & Duke, J.M. (2010). Bring your textbook!': Using secondary texts to assess reading demands and skills required for students with high-incidence disabilities. *Intervention in School and Clinic, 45*, 284–293.

Skylar, A.A., Higgins, K., & Boone, R. (2007). Strategies for adapting webquests for students with learning disabilities. *Intervention in School and Clinic, 43*(1), 20–28.

sequencing and segmentation, skill modelling, organization and explicit practice, small-group setting, indirect teacher activities (e.g., homework), technology, and scaffolding—captured the most successful interventions for adolescents with LD. Find a way to teach more intensely—to a small group where you can be more responsive—and if that is not enough, arrange for students with LD to receive some individual teaching or practice.

**Cognitive strategies** are often used to teach reading comprehension (Boyle, 2008; Faggella et al., 2007) and math problem solving (Montague, 2008). Alan Edmunds (1999) of the University of Western Ontario suggests that teachers enter the steps of a personalized cognitive strategy into the computer, and print them on a credit card–sized space. After laminating the card and punching a hole in the corner, the student can attach the cognitive credit card (CCC) to his or her pencil case. Many adolescents with LD experience comprehension difficulties. Faggella-Luby and Deshler (2008) describe a six-tiered continuum of literacy instruction:

- Level 1: Enhance content instruction of critical content for all students.

- Level 2: Embed strategy instruction in your large-group teaching.

- Level 3: Provide more intense instruction in learning strategies and more time for practice for those who need it.

- Level 4: Develop and provide, as a team, intensive basic skill instruction for students with severe deficits.

- Level 5: Access therapeutic intervention for students with significant deficits in basic language competencies.

- Level 6: Work with your colleagues and the students' families to extend instructional time through strategic before- and after-school tutoring (p. 76).

Because there are similar challenges in teaching mathematics to adolescents with LD, Witzel and his colleagues (2008) developed a process for using their **concrete-to-representational-to-abstract (CRA)** sequence of instruction. This approach takes students through **C**oncrete hands-on instruction with manipulative objects, then through pictorial **R**epresentations of these manipulatives, to learning through **A**bstract notation including operational symbols. The seven steps in CRA are:

1. Choose the math topic to be taught.
2. Review procedures to solve the problem.
3. Adjust the steps to remove notation or calculation tricks.
4. Match the abstract steps with an appropriate concrete manipulative.
5. Arrange concrete and representational lessons.
6. Teach each concrete, representational, and abstract lesson to student mastery.
7. Help students generalize what they learn through word problems.

There is extensive research under way to develop appropriate tiered interventions that differentiate instruction for students with LD. Access journal articles online through an organization like your school district or through a subscription to journals of organizations like Council for Exceptional Children.

Many adults with LD have successful careers, while others experience underemployment (Shaywitz et al., 2008). **Career development** programs have used cognitive strategies to teach employment readiness and career awareness (e.g., *The BreakAway Company*, Campbell et al., 1994; *Pathways*, Hutchinson & Freeman, 1994). Adolescents with disabilities benefit from workplace experience and from learning to negotiate workplace accommodations (Hutchinson et al., 2008).

**Further Reading**

On teaching students with ADHD:

Greenbaum, J., & Markel G. (2000). *Helping adolescents with ADHD and learning disabilities: Ready-to-use tips, techniques, and checklists for school success.* San Francisco, CA: Jossey-Bass.

Honos-Webb, L. (2010). *ADHD workbook for teens: Activities to help you gain motivation and confidence.* Oakland, CA: New Harbinger Pub.

Lougy, R., DeRuvo, S., & Rosenthal D. (2007). *Teaching young children with ADHD: Successful strategies and practical interventions for PreK-3.* Thousand Oaks, CA: Corwin Press.

Nadeau, K.G., & Dixon., E.B. (2005). *Learning to slow down and pay attention: A book for kids about ADHD* (3rd ed.). Washington, DC: American Psychological Association.

Sleeper-Triplett, J. (2010). *Empowering youth with ADHD: A guide to coaching adolescents and young adults for coaches, parents, and professionals.* Ocean, NJ: Specialty Press Inc.

# Teaching Students with Attention Deficit Hyperactivity Disorder (ADHD)

**Put Into Practice**

Observe a teacher experienced with students with LD in an inclusive classroom. Focus on how the teacher makes everyone feel like a valued member and differentiates teaching and adapts assessment.

I have Attention Deficit Disorder, which is often called ADD for short. Dad says that I have eagle eyes; I notice everything. But eagles know when to stop looking around and zoom in on their prey. Me, I just keep noticing more things and miss my catch.

Once when Dad and Emily and I hiked at Birdsong Trail, a thunderstorm sent us rushing back toward the car. Dad tripped over a rock and twisted his knee. His face wrinkled with pain. He asked Emily to go for help, but she was not sure of the way.

"I can find it, Dad!" I interrupted. And I told him the whole route. "Ben, I knew those eagle eyes of yours would come in handy," Dad replied. "You'll find the way just fine. Emily can stay here to keep me company." As I turned to go, Dad called, "Hurry, Ben! I need you." Swift as an eagle, I zoomed off toward the ranger station and got help for Dad. I was the only one who could do it. And that's when I realized it's good to be me.

*Gehret, 1991, p. 11.*

## Characteristics of Students with ADHD

"Although ADHD is not named as a specific category of exceptionality [in Ontario], students with ADHD may present characteristics that can be identified in the various categories such as Learning Disability or Behaviour" (Tannock; *What*

**Weblinks**

TEACHING STUDENTS WITH ADHD: A RESOURCE GUIDE FOR TEACHERS (2007, BC EDUCATION)
www.bced.gov.bc.ca/specialed/adhd

FOCUSING ON SUCCESS: TEACHING STUDENTS WITH ATTENTION DEFICIT/HYPERACTIVITY DISORDER (2006, ALBERTA EDUCATION)
http://education.alberta.ca/admin/special/resources/adhd.aspx

TEACH ADHD (BY SICK KIDS HOSPITAL, TORONTO)
http://research.aboutkidshealth.ca/teachadhd

CHADD—CHILDREN AND ADULTS WITH ATTENTION DEFICIT DISORDERS (CANADIAN SITE)
www.chaddcanada.org

CENTRE FOR ADHD/ADD ADVOCACY, CANADA
www.caddac.ca

CANADIAN ADHD RESOURCE ALLIANCE
www.caddra.ca/cms4

**Put into Practice**

Develop a set of consequences for a class you have taught or could be teaching. Describe the characteristics of a student with ADHD in this class and consider how the consequences will apply in this case. Develop a plan for a lesson; describe the cognitive characteristics of a student with ADHD and how you would differentiate instruction for this student. Use resources like these:

Anderson, K.M. (2007). Differentiating instruction to include all students. *Preventing School Failure, 51*(3), 49–54.

Nowacek, E.J., & Mamlin, N. (2007). General education teachers and students with ADHD: What modifications are made? *Preventing School Failure, 51*(3), 28–35.

Rotter, K.M. (2004). Simple techniques to improve teacher-made instructional materials for use by pupils with disabilities. *Preventing School Failure, 48*(2), 38–43.

Stormont, M.A. (2008). Increase academic success for children with ADHD using sticky notes and highlighters. *Intervention in School and Clinic, 43*(5), 305–308.

*Works? Research into Practice*, Monograph #3, 2007, April). The characteristics and learning needs of students with ADHD vary. *The Diagnostic and Statistical Manual of Mental Disorders* (DSM-IV-TR) (American Psychiatric Association, 2000) defines three subtypes of this neurobehavioural condition: Predominantly **Inattentive**, Predominantly Hyperactive-Impulsive and Combined Type, and stipulates that the characteristics occur prior to the age of seven. The condition can go unrecognized in preschoolers, although it is becoming more common for them to be identified and even prescribed medication (Bakermans-Kranenberg, et al., 2010; Wolraich, 2006). Dilemmas surround ADHD for educators unsure about how to differentiate (Schlachter, 2008) and for parents who may be reluctant to inform educators, fearing bias (Kidder, 2009).

Students with **ADHD Predominantly Inattentive** display many more characteristics of inattention than of hyperactivity-impulsivity. They may ignore details, make careless errors, or have trouble staying on task while working or playing. They do not seem to listen when you speak to them directly, and often do not follow instructions or complete homework and classroom tasks. Students who are predominantly inattentive may have difficulty organizing their activities, and may lose or forget things. They dislike or try to avoid work that requires them to concentrate for long periods of time, and may be easily distracted by movement, objects, or noises in the classroom. They have a tendency to daydream and to rush through tasks.

Students with **ADHD Predominantly Hyperactive-Impulsive** display many more characteristics of hyperactivity-impulsivity than of inattention. They may fidget and squirm, leave their desks, and run and climb at inappropriate times. They usually find it challenging to play or work quietly, move constantly, and talk excessively. Characteristics include blurting out answers before you have finished asking a question, not waiting their turn or following classroom rules, and disturbing or interrupting others. This impatience can lead to acting unsafely and neglecting to consider the consequences of their actions. Transitions are often challenging.

Most students with ADHD have the **Combined Type**. They display many characteristics of both inattention and hyperactivity-impulsivity. The key behaviour patterns you may recognize are:

- not listening when you speak to them directly;
- difficulty making and keeping a schedule for assignments and activities;
- fidgeting;
- difficulty paying attention for sustained periods of time;
- answering questions before they are called on; and
- always being "on the go."

### QUESTIONING THE PREVAILING CONCEPTION OF ADHD

Prominent researchers in the field have argued, over the past 15 years, that what is important are the cognitive characteristics rather than the behavioural characteristics of ADHD. Barkley's model (1997) suggested that neurologically-based problems of response inhibition (sometimes described as impulsivity) led directly to problems in four major executive functions of cognition: working memory, internalized speech, motivational appraisal, and synthesizing past experience relevant to a current situation. Rosemary Tannock of the University of Toronto Faculty of

Education has synthesized the evidence that ADHD is associated with subtle cognitive differences in the brain and argues that ADHD be reconceptualized as a learning disorder distinct from LD (1998, 2007). Others have concentrated on weighing the evidence for genetic factors contributing to ADHD (Thapar et al., 2007), and recent studies have suggested that while children may meet the criteria for mainly hyperactive when they are young, over time many shift to the combined subtype (e.g., Lahey et al., 2005). Clearly this is a complex phenomenon about which we are still learning.

### CHARACTERISTICS OF SOCIAL INTERACTIONS

ADHD can also influence social interactions. The classroom is often a problematic environment for students with ADHD because of their impulsivity, distractibility, and overactivity (Alberta Education, 2006), as well as their cognitive characteristics (Tannock, 2007; Tannock & Martinussen, 2001). Students and teachers may react negatively when students with ADHD show limited self-confidence, are unable to contribute to a team, misinterpret social cues, have difficulty with anger management, or overreact emotionally. A recent study reported that children with ADHD were less well-liked than their peers without ADHD and had fewer reciprocal friendships (Hoza et al., 2005). It is important that you treat students with ADHD respectfully and patiently, both to enhance your relationship with them and to serve as a model for the class. Programs designed to improve the social problem solving of students with ADHD can be group facilitated (e.g., Gresham, 2002) or computer mediated (e.g., Fenstermacher et al., 2006). Chapters 7 and 8 include information about implementing such programs. Unless they learn to interact effectively, adults with ADHD can find themselves underemployed, and they often benefit from choosing careers that use their strengths (see *ADD Success Stories,* Hartmann, 1995).

## Implications for Learning and for Differentiating in the Classroom: Students with ADHD

Because students with ADHD often have difficulty getting started on assignments, help them to begin. Try scheduling frequent, but short and specific, break times (DuPaul & Stoner, 2003). **Checkpoints** for project completion and homework journals for nightly assignments can help many students. Provide students with clear numbered and written, as well as verbal, instructions to help them complete tasks. Teachers report differentiating instruction for students with ADHD by being flexible for all students, using tailored lists of spelling words, teaching strategies for reading in the content areas, allowing students to dictate to a scribe rather than write a test answer, providing copies of textbook pages so students don't have to copy math questions into their notebooks, permitting students to choose where they want to work, as well as making accommodations that allow movement in the classroom.

Teachers have reported using many approaches to promote acceptance of students with ADHD; some "hit problems head-on," while others use "subtle" means. All those interviewed said they modelled patience and acceptance, tried to "ward off" situations, and focused on accepting differences within discussions of course content (e.g., novel study) (Nowacek & Mamlin, 2007). Key elements of differentiated instruction include: flexibility, choice, and creativity in finding ways to help students develop understanding and ways to demonstrate what they have learned (Anderson, 2007). Resource teachers recommend that teachers use three strategies to make teacher-designed materials more accessible: leave more white space on the page so materials are better spaced, use large fonts on the computer instead of hand-written materials, and make the key information or directions clear to students through bolding, colour-coding, highlighting, or boxing information (Rotter, 2004). Remember that such differentiations may help many students in your class to learn.

### ADAPTING CLASSROOM ORGANIZATION

Adapting classroom organization should enhance the learning of students with ADHD and benefit other students. For example, minimize distracting factors. A **carrel** is a protected space, with wooden or cardboard walls, that blocks out distractions. Try to borrow a carrel from your school library or make one from the carton for a large appliance. If you introduce a carrel, use it yourself so it is seen as a high-status opportunity, not a punishment. Provide a predictable, structured environment so students know what you expect of them and what they can expect of you. Communicate explicitly to ensure that students with ADHD have understood prior to beginning a specific activity (DuPaul & Stoner, 2003). When you teach, ADAPT, maintain the students' interest, model by **thinking aloud**, and ensure adequate opportunities for practice. Removing recess privileges from students with ADHD when the students fail to complete their work increases levels of inappropriate behaviour, restlessness, and distractibility for the remainder of the day (Ridgway et al., 2003). Look for other ways to help all students complete their assigned work, and to enable them to exercise and socialize with their classmates during the recess breaks. Table 3.5 provides specific examples of cognitive characteristics of students with ADHD and actions you can take to meet their needs in the classroom.

### RESPONDING TO INAPPROPRIATE BEHAVIOUR

In spite of using preventive strategies, you will probably have to respond to inappropriate behaviour by students with ADHD. Try to give inappropriate behaviour as little attention as possible and instead provide positive attention for appropriate behaviour when it occurs. When a **verbal reprimand** is necessary, make it immediate, unemotional, brief, and backed up with a time out or loss of privileges. Sometimes you need to follow up with the consequences developed at the beginning of the year. For a clear description of how to use consequences effectively, read DuPaul and Weyandt (2006) *School-Based Intervention for Children with Attention Deficit Hyperactivity Disorder: Effects on Academic, Social, and Behavioural Functioning.*

A **time out** is a type of punishment which removes a student from opportunities for reward. A time out can be carried out in the classroom or in the hall, away from the immediate setting that reinforces the behaviour. Chapter 7 contains more information on time outs. A one- to five-minute time out will have the same effect as a longer one; generally assign one minute per two years of age (Roberts et al., 1997).

### STRATEGIES FOR SELF-MANAGEMENT

Self-management strategies are implemented by the student and designed to increase self-control of behaviour (DuPaul & Weyandt, 2006). **Cognitive-behaviour**

**What do you think?**

Read about both sides of the debate on medication and ADHD:

Pro:

Silver, L.B. (2003). *Attention-deficit/hyperactivity disorder: A clinical guide to diagnosis and treatment for health and mental health professionals* (2nd ed.). Arlington, VA: American Psychiatric Publishing.

Vaughn, B.S., Roberts, H.J., & Needelman, H. (2009). Current medications for the treatment of attention-deficit/hyperactivity disorder. *Psychology in the Schools,* 46(9), 846–856.

Con:

Stein, D.B. (2002). *Ritalin is not the answer action guide: An interactive companion to the bestselling drug-free ADD/ADHD parenting program.* Somerset, NJ: John Wiley & Sons.

Balanced:

American Academy of Child and Adolescent Psychiatry and American Psychiatric Association. (2010). *ADHD: Parents medication guide,* www.ParentsMedGuide.org

## TABLE 3.5 PROMOTING ACADEMIC SUCCESS FOR STUDENTS WITH ADHD

Current treatment approaches have focused on medication and behavioural interventions. However, emerging data on cognitive characteristics have implications for the classroom.

| Cognitive Characteristics | Cognitive Adaptations in the Classroom |
|---|---|
| Difficulty understanding words such as *before, after, more than*. | Make language clear at beginning of task. |
| Lack of understanding of passage of time and of temporal events. | Post a list of items to be completed. Strike through items as they are finished. |
| Mismatch of student needs to lesson content and delivery. | Model what is to be done, repeat, and explain instructions and tasks. |
| Difficulty understanding language used in teaching and materials. | Rephrase student's language when that helps others to understand student's meaning. |
| Lack of understanding about taking turns, working co-operatively. | Teach social skills (e.g., use microphone to show children whose turn it is to talk). |
| Difficulty understanding the process expected in practice activities following direct teaching. | Provide as much support—guided practice—as necessary for the student to begin the activity. Gradually reduce support and increase self-direction. |
| Difficulty focusing on the needed information to complete tasks. | Reduce demands on working memory by providing external memory aids, mnemonics, graphic reminders, lists of steps, strategies. |
| Lack of self-regulation. | Model strategies that can be used to self-regulate. Teach one strategy thoroughly and then another, helping students to discern when each is useful. Cue strategy use. |

Sources: Tannock, R., & Martinussen, R. (2001). Reconceptualizing ADHD. *Educational Leadership*, 20-25; Mariage, T.V., Englert, C.S., & Garmon, M.A. (2000). The teacher as "more knowledgeable other" in assisting literacy learning with special needs students. *Reading and Writing Quarterly, 16*(4), 299-226.

management (CBM) programs teach students to use cognition to control behaviour. Usually you and the student agree on a problem that is interfering with learning (e.g., looking around instead of completing assignments). You develop steps for the student to follow, put these on a cue card, and model their use. The student practices the steps aloud and gradually, covertly, to solve the problem. The student monitors his or her own performance of the steps. Some teachers use a signal to remind the student to begin using the CBM steps. Chapters 5, 7 and 8 contain examples of CBM programs developed for students. These take thought and time in the early stages but are worth the effort when they are effective. At first, the student can be cued, but eventually must initiate and carry out the steps independently.

### MEDICATION

Prescribing medication to children with ADHD remains controversial (*A Convenient Diagnosis*, CTV, 2007; Tannock, 2007), although data suggest that when medication is combined with behaviour therapy, low doses of medication can improve academic performance and family relationships (e.g., MTA Cooperative Group, 1999). Two classes of medication are commonly used to treat children with ADHD: **stimulant medications** (e.g., Ritalin) and non-stimulants. There has always been concern about adolescents selling stimulant medications illicitly, and the US data indicate non-medical use of Ritalin by 1.6 percent of 8th graders and 3.4 percent of 12th graders in 2008 (www.nida.nih.gov/infofacts/ADHD.html).

For 20 years, researchers have questioned whether the resultant decreases in behaviour problems and gains in attention are worth the associated risks of medication (e.g., Forness et al., 1992), and have raised concerns about medications masking opportunities for individuals to learn to cope with, or even take advantage of, characteristics of ADHD (e.g., Billiard, 2009; Graham-Day et al., 2010). The most common side effects of stimulants are insomnia, reduced appetite, weight loss, stomach pain, and irritability. Uncommon but serious side effects are heart problems, suicidal thoughts, and liver problems (www.ParentsMedGuide.org). Controlled studies show that stimulant medications, in relatively low doses and when monitored carefully, are widely regarded as effective in reducing the core symptoms of ADHD (www.nida.nih.gov/infofacts/ADHD.html). The other class of medication prescribed for ADHD, non-stimulants (i.e., **antidepressants**), can cause side effects such as cardiac complications, insomnia, and even seizures. Cantwell (1996) reported that 70 percent of children with ADHD respond to one of the stimulants on the first trial and if a number are tried, the likelihood of positive response increases to 85 to 90 percent. Current best practice is thought to combine a psychosocial approach with medication (Austin, 2003; Maté, 2000), and the recommended psychosocial approach includes cognitive-behaviour management programs for the child, family and classroom interventions, and individual psychotherapy if the child becomes depressed. While there are strongly held opinions on both sides of this issue, parents and physicians, not teachers, decide about medication. Figure 3.4 contains questions for parents and teachers to ask physicians about medication for ADHD.

## FIGURE 3.4 QUESTIONS FOR TEACHERS AND PARENTS TO ASK ABOUT MEDICATION FOR CHILDREN WITH ADHD

The most commonly prescribed medications for children and adolescents with ADHD are Ritalin (methylphenidate) and Dexedrine (dextroamphetamine). Parents and teachers should be well-informed about these medications and able to answer questions such as:

1. What is the medication? What information can I read about it?
2. Why is this medication prescribed for this adolescent? What changes should we expect to see at home? At school?
3. What behavioural program or behavioural therapy is being implemented in conjunction with this drug therapy?
4. How long will this medication be prescribed for this adolescent?
5. What are the side effects in the short term? In the long term?
6. What is the dosage? What is the schedule on which the medication will be taken?
7. How often will the adolescent be seen by the prescribing physician for re-evaluation?
8. Should the medication be stopped for a short period of time to see if it is still required? When?
9. Are there foods, beverages, or other substances that should not be consumed when one is taking this medication?
10. What kind of communication is necessary among home, school, and the adolescent to evaluate whether the medication is having the desired effect?
11. What procedures should be followed if the adolescent accidentally ingests an overdose?
12. Who explains all of this to the adolescent and what should the adolescent be told?

Source: Hutchinson, N.L. (2004). *Teaching exceptional children and adolescents: A Canadian casebook*. Toronto: Prentice Hall. Reprinted by permission.

Put into Practice

Seek resources to help you understand the level of language development of children entering grade 1. Look for books and consider videos such as *Children learning language: How adults can help* (1997). Lake Zurich, IL: Learning Seed.

Useful books include:

Beaty, J.J. (2009). *50 early childhood literacy strategies*. Upper Saddle River, NJ: Pearson Education.

Griffith, P.L., Beach, S.A., Ruan, J., & Dunn, L. (2008). *Literacy for young children: A guide for early childhood educators*. Thousand Oaks, CA: Corwin Press.

Silliman, E.R., & Wilkinson, L.C. (Eds.) (2004). *Language and literacy learning in schools*. New York, NY: Guilford Press.

# Teaching Students with Communication Exceptionalities

Writing in my journal every day helps me feel better. I used to go to speech therapy every week. Now my therapist comes to school once a month. In between, I practice my sounds with helpers. Today my speech therapist told me that I am really getting better at making my sounds. She recorded me talking and I listened to myself. I felt proud. I have to talk like that in my class. Then maybe the other kids will stop saying that I talk like a baby. I am going to ask if I can be in the next play for social studies.

*From the journal of Ruth, a grade 2 student with an articulation speech disorder.*

## Characteristics of Students with Communication Exceptionalities

Generally, communication exceptionalities include disorders of speech (**articulation**, voice, and fluency) and disorders of language (expressive or receptive). The term **speech impairment** is widely used to refer to a disorder that involves the motor aspects of transmitting oral messages. The Ontario Ministry of Education (2001) describes **language impairment** as "an impairment in comprehension and/or use of verbal communication or the written or other symbol systems of communication, which may be associated with neurological, psychological, physical, or sensory factors" (p. A19). Usually, language impairment is described as involving one or more of the form, content, and function of language in communication and is characterized by language delay—of expressive language, receptive language, or both.

Many students with communication disorders experience difficulties with both speech and language, but some students have difficulty in only one. Many students with other exceptionalities (e.g., autism, learning disabilities, cerebral palsy, intellectual disabilities) also have communication disorders. However, the designation "communication disorder" is most often used when speech or language is the primary exceptionality. Some children with severe disabilities who cannot use speech use **augmentative and alternative communication (AAC)** systems. Calculator (2009) helps teachers to integrate AAC into the daily life of the classroom. You may recognize students with communication disorders in your classroom from some of the characteristics listed in Table 3.6. Learners with communication exceptionalities often have less developed vocabularies than their classmates (Beitchman et al., 2008). If you suspect that a young child has a speech or language disorder, talk with the parents. Recommend an assessment by a speech-language pathologist who can refer the student to services in the school district and in local agencies.

## Differentiating Curriculum and Teaching Students with Communication Exceptionalities

Students can receive direct therapy or indirect therapy, alone or in a group; recent research suggests that indirect therapy with a therapist's assistant followed up by volunteers can be as effective as direct therapy from a pathologist (Boyle et al.,

**What do you think?**

It has been suggested that children adopted from abroad (especially those adopted at older ages) have a "perfect storm" of issues that increase the likelihood they will require speech and language services. This issue is addressed by Glennen in the paper cited below. After reading Glennen's paper, discuss with your peers your views of the best practices teachers can adopt to help these students.

Glennen, S. (2009). Speech and language guidelines for children adopted from abroad at older ages. *Topics in Language Disorders, 29*(10), 50–64.

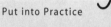

Put into Practice

Read the paper about augmentative and alternative communication (AAC) and develop a plan for differentiating instruction for a student using AAC at a grade level and in a subject that you have experience teaching. Compare your plan with those developed by your peers. Consider the kinds of support that you would need to implement your plan.

Calculator, S.N. (2009). Augmentative and alternative communication (AAC) and inclusive education for students with the most severe disabilities. *International Journal of Inclusive Education, 13*(1), 93–113.

## TABLE 3.6 SPEECH AND LANGUAGE DISORDERS AND THEIR CHARACTERISTICS

| Communication Disorder | Example of Characteristics |
| --- | --- |
| Language delay | For young students, at least six months behind in reaching language milestones; a grade 2 student uses three words rather than full sentences. |
| Receptive language | Student in grade 6 consistently fails to understand an oral instruction, even when given individually. |
| Expressive language | Student in grade 10 begins each sentence four or five times and cannot be understood by peers; refuses to speak in front of class. |
| Aphasia | Student cannot understand speech or produce meaningful sentences. |
| Apraxia | Student cannot sequence muscle movements and thus does not produce meaningful speech. |
| Articulation | Student in grade 2 cannot produce the S sound. This results in teasing by classmates. |
| Dysfluency | Student in grade 12 stutters but persists to express ideas. |
| Voice disorders | Student speaks slowly and softly in a husky voice (does not speak with normal pitch, loudness, duration, or quality); is shy about expressing ideas. |
| Orofacial defects | Student in grade 5 with cleft palate has difficulties with speech and feeding. |
| Dysarthria | Grade 9 student's speech is distorted because of paralysis of speaking muscles. |

2009). In the scenario presented at the opening of this section, Ruth practises with volunteers between visits of the speech-language pathologist. Many teachers rely on volunteers from the community for individual activities such as articulation practice. Forbes (2008) describes the knowledge that the speech-language pathologist and the teacher need in order to collaborate effectively (see also Baxter et al., 2009). You can assist students with communication disorders by:

- Creating an accepting atmosphere and never allowing classmates to mock or tease.
- Collaborating with the student, the parents, and the speech and language specialist to obtain suggestions and goals.
- Being proactive: give students opportunities to answer questions that require brief responses, and teach them to monitor their speech.

Be a good role model for other students when speaking to students with communication disorders. Speak clearly and a bit slower than normal, pause at appropriate times, and use straightforward language and simple grammatical structures. When responding to a student with a communication disorder, respond to the meaning rather than to how the student speaks. Resist the temptation to interrupt students or to finish their sentences when they stutter or pause. Make eye contact and wait for a few seconds before responding (Reed, 2005; Silliman & Wilkinson, 2004).

Many students with communication disorders experience difficulty with academics. Problems with speech sounds can result in underdeveloped phonemic awareness, which is required for reading and spelling. Receptive language delays can result in challenges producing narrative accounts and delays in the development of working memory (Dodwell & Bavin, 2008) and can contribute to difficulties in reading comprehension and in understanding specialized terms in mathematics (Stojanovik & Riddell, 2008). Language disabilities can impede content-area learning in upper grades, where lectures and independent reading

### Weblinks

TYKETALK (A PARTNERSHIP OF AGENCIES IN THAMES VALLEY, ONTARIO)
http://tyketalk.com

CANADIAN ASSOCIATION OF SPEECH-LANGUAGE PATHOLOGISTS AND AUDIOLOGISTS
www.caslpa.ca

ONTARIO ASSOCIATION OF SPEECH-LANGUAGE PATHOLOGISTS ANDAUDIOLOGISTS
www.osla.on.ca

NET CONNECTIONS FOR COMMUNICATION DISORDERS AND SCIENCES (AN INTERNET GUIDE BY JUDITH MAGINNIS KUSTER)
www.mnsu.edu/comdis/kuster2/welcome.html

INTERNATIONAL SOCIETY FOR AUGMENTATIVE AND ALTERNATIVE COMMUNICATION (ISSAC)
www.isaac-online.org/en/home.shtml

provide complex conceptual information (Miller et al., 2008). Research suggests that children with both speech and language disorders are at greater risk for reading, spelling, and language difficulties (Lewis, Freebairn, & Taylor, 2000), and an Ontario study suggests they are less ready for independence by the end of high school (Johnson et al., 2010).

Being unable to communicate effectively can contribute to social needs and cause students to feel neglected or even rejected by their peers. These pressures can be felt acutely during adolescence, when peer acceptance is so highly valued. Many adults are able to overcome speech disorders if these are their only exceptionalities. However, research suggests that employers still hold stereotypes and judge individuals with speech and language disorders, especially language disorders, as less decisive and less reliable (Allard & Williams, 2008)—a reminder of the potential ramifications of ignoring students' communication exceptionalities.

**Further Reading**

If you want to learn more about the nature of language impairments in individuals with autism and Asperger syndrome, you could read the following papers and look for other, similar sources.

Colle, L., Baron-Cohen, S., Wheelwright, S., & van der Lely, H.K.J. (2008). Narrative discourse in adults with high-functioning autism or Asperger syndrome. *Journal of Autism and Developmental Disorders, 38*(1), 28–40.

Whitehouse, A.J.O., Barry, J.G., & Bishop, D.V.M. (2008). Further defining the language impairment of autism: Is there a specific language impairment subtype? *Journal of Communication Disorders, 41*(4), 319–336.

# Teaching Students with Behaviour and Emotional Exceptionalities

I don't like the work we do here. It is boring. I can figure out the questions and after that I don't feel like doing them, so I don't. Most of the teachers back off when a student yells at them. They don't make me do it then. Other guys leave me alone when they see I can make the teacher afraid. I like to draw. I'm awesome at drawing. I should just do drawing all day so I can be an artist. I want to draw comic books and stuff like that.

*From Urjo's interview with a counsellor about his experiences at school.*

## Characteristics of Students with Behaviour Exceptionalities

Urjo was described at the opening of this chapter—refusing to do his homework, engaging in verbal disagreements with teachers—and had been identified as having a behaviour exceptionality. This term has different meanings in different provinces (Dworet & Rathgeber, 1998). In Ontario it refers to:

A learning disorder characterized by specific behaviour problems over such a period of time, and to such a marked degree, and of such a nature, as to adversely affect educational performance, and that may be accompanied by one or more of the following:

(a) an inability to build or to maintain interpersonal relationships

(b) excessive fears or anxieties

(c) a tendency to compulsive reaction

(d) an inability to learn that cannot be traced to intellectual, sensory, or other health factors, or any combination thereof.

*(Ontario Ministry of Education, 2001, p. A18)*

Students with mild behaviour exceptionalities can usually be supported in the classroom with the assistance of a resource teacher or counsellor. Students with moderate and severe behaviour disorders may require more intensive interventions.

**Cross-Reference**

Chapter 7 focuses on preventive classroom organization and classroom management, while Chapter 8 describes proactive ways of ensuring a positive milieu in which students respect and value one another.

**What do you think?**

The characteristics in this list can be seen on occasion in many students. What distinguishes those with behaviour and emotional difficulties from other students?

**Put into Practice**

Look at the following resources and develop a plan for working with a student who has experienced trauma. Compare your plan with those of your peers.

Hurlington, K. (2010). *Bolstering resilience in students: Teachers as protective factors* (What works? Research into practice.). Toronto: Ontario Ministry of Education, Literacy and Numeracy Secretariat, www.edu.gov.on.ca/eng/literacynumeracy/inspire/research/WW_bolstering_students.pdf

Hutchinson, N.L., Dods, J., & Dalton, CJ. (2009). http://partners.hpedsb.on.ca/misaeast/images/stories/files/pub_supporting_mental_health.pdf

Malchiodi, C.A. (2008). *Creative interventions with traumatized children.* New York, NY: Guilford Press.

Meichenbaum, D. (2006), www.teachsafeschools.org/Resilience.pdf

Students with moderate behaviour disorders often demonstrate one or more of the following:

- **aggression** (physical, emotional, or sexual) and/or hyperactivity;
- **negative psychological states** (such as anxiety, depression, stress-related disorders); and
- behaviours related to **social problems** (such as delinquency, substance abuse, neglect).

These students can have a disruptive effect on the classroom. They have demonstrated these behaviours over a period of time, in more than one setting, with more than one person, and have not responded to typical classroom management strategies. Students with more severe behaviour disorders are likely to require intensive intervention from community agencies as well as school personnel.

Because students with behaviour exceptionalities are a heterogeneous population, no student would exhibit all of the following characteristics. However, you are likely to see some of these characteristics even in students with mild or moderate behaviour disorders (Smith, et al., 2008):

- aggressive acting-out of behaviours, lying;
- social deficits, irresponsibility, poor peer relationships;
- hyperactivity, distractibility;
- academic difficulties; and
- depression, anxiety.

If a student has a moderate behaviour disorder, you are likely to see that the student needs some or all of the following while in the classroom (Reithaug, 1998a):

- **structure**, predictability, and consistency;
- immediate, frequent, and specific **feedback** with consequences;
- academic success;
- responsibility and independence;
- positive alternatives to current behaviours;
- enhanced self-confidence;
- positive school-to-home support systems; and
- evidence that he or she is making changes for the better.

Students with behaviour exceptionalities benefit from challenging, respectful, and cognitively engaging activities. Research shows that when students experience positive emotions in school, they demonstrate higher levels of engagement (Reschly et al., 2008). When their needs are not met, students with behaviour exceptionalities fail more courses, miss more days of class, and are more likely to drop out of school than students with other exceptionalities (Sugai & Horner, 2008).

One group of students has recently gained the attention of educators and mental health professionals: students who have experienced trauma. They could be dealing with neglect, abuse or violence, illness, injury, or death. Traumatic experiences are often accompanied by feelings of intense fear and helplessness and can cause significant psychological and physical distress. This can be exhibited in sleep disturbances, panic, aggression, hypervigilance, or exaggerated startle responses (APA, 2000). These

**Put into Practice**

Should we teach students with emotional and behavioural exceptionalities social skills for using social networking?

Cumming, T.M. (20100. Using technology to create motivating social skills lessons. *Intervention in School and Clinic, 45*(4), 242–250.

Morgan, J.J. (2010). Social networking web sites: Teaching appropriate social competence to students with emotional and behavioral disorders? *Intervention in School and Clinic, 45*(3), 147–157.

ongoing symptoms become maladaptive in the presence of any threat and may be at the root of emotional and behavioural needs in the classroom, although these students may not have been identified with behaviour exceptionalities.

## Differentiating Curriculum and Teaching Students with Behaviour Exceptionalities and Students with Mental Health Needs

Recent research suggests that a sense of **school connectedness** has a positive impact on academic and social functioning for students who have experienced trauma (Dods, Hutchinson, & Dalton, 2009). School connectedness refers to school and classroom environments that engage students through relationships and create a sense of belonging. This is dependent on teachers' holding high, manageable expectations of academic success and on students' perceiving support by teachers and experiencing a safe school environment. Students report that small teacher actions such as noticing absences, telling students they were missed, and attentive listening lead to increased engagement even in students who have appeared to resist or reject teachers' efforts (Dods, 2009). Students who feel that their teachers care about them are more resilient in the face of trauma and stress (Hurlington, 2010). Resilience refers to the capacity to return to good mental health after challenging and difficult situations; it emphasizes the importance of protective factors like caring teachers and supportive school environments. In brief, it is all about relationships. See Figure 3.5 which provides a number of strategies for supporting students with mental health needs.

### HELPING STUDENTS TO IMPROVE THEIR BEHAVIOUR

Begin by establishing caring relationships with your students, and expect that you may also need to focus on differentiating to help them improve their behaviour

> **What do you think?**
>
> There are many dilemmas associated with mental health issues and students with behaviour exceptionalities in schools. For example, are we imposing social control on students or engaging them in learning?
>
> These issues are addressed in a new book:
>
> Adelman, H.S. & Taylor, L. (2010). *Mental health in schools: Engaging learners, preventing problems, and improving schools.* Thousand Oaks, CA: Corwin.

## FIGURE 3.5 SUPPORTING MENTAL HEALTH NEEDS OF STUDENTS: IT'S ALL ABOUT RELATIONSHIPS

Your actions and words can communicate support to students who have mental health needs. It is not necessary for you to know details about a student's history to communicate that you care.

- Speak to students in a way that communicates that you are interested in them as individuals.
- Help students identify and nurture their strengths.
- Create a motivational climate that fosters "learning for learning's sake."
- Help students find social supports among their peers and in school clubs and activities.
- Provide opportunities for youth to help others.
- Convey high expectations and hope that can nurture resilience in all students.
- Provide a safe and inviting classroom and school environment for all students.
- Bolster students' connectedness to school; help them feel a part of your class.
- Encourage, and help students to engage in, help-seeking behaviour.
- No matter how many times a student rebuffs your efforts, remain supportive and communicate that you care.

Sources: Dods, J.C. (2010). *The educational experience of youth who have lived through trauma: Learning from students' stories.* Unpublished M.Ed. thesis, Queen's University. Meichenbaum, D. (2006), www.teachsafeschools.org/Resilience.pdf.

## FIGURE 3.6 PREVENTIVE MEASURES FOR STUDENTS WITH BEHAVIOUR EXCEPTIONALITIES

- Inform students of what is expected of them and of the consequences of not meeting your expectations.
- Check to ensure that the student with a behaviour exceptionality understands both expectations and consequences.

Then establish a positive climate for participating and learning:

- Model behaviour that treats everyone fairly, makes everyone feel included, and challenges but does not threaten.
- Talk with the student with a behaviour exceptionality about what each of you can do to ensure that he or she feels part of the class.
- Focus on the positive, rather than the negative, by exhibiting your self-confidence and building the self-confidence of your students.
- Encourage the student with a history of behaviour problems to believe that the two of you can work together for a positive experience.
- Recognize positive student attributes; catch students "being good."
- Focus on recognizing the positive attributes of the student with a behaviour exceptionality at optimal times; be vigilant so you don't miss the times when he or she is co-operating, etc.

and to help them learn. You can help students improve their behaviour in many ways, ranging from preventive measures to direct responses. Figure 3.6 focuses on making preventive measures effective for students with behaviour exceptionalities.

### DIFFERENTIATING THE CURRICULUM AND STRUCTURING THE CLASSROOM

Differentiate the curriculum and structure the classroom environment to take advantage of "getting off to a good start." Apply your procedures, rules, and consequences consistently and discuss any changes (reasons and implementation) with the class. Use differentiated teaching for academic instruction without waiting for students' behaviour problems to be resolved (Gable et al., 2002). For some students, academic difficulties contribute to behavioural problems (Morgan et al., in press). Positive behavioural interventions and supports (PBIS) (Horner et al., 2001) use three tiers: school-wide interventions ensure that all students understand behavioural expectations; secondary prevention, for groups of students with at-risk behaviour, follows; and finally specialized intervention for individuals with identified needs.

Recent studies show the effectiveness of first-tier or universal interventions for social and emotional learning (Conduct Problems Prevention Research Group, 2010; Kramer et al., 2010). Use the resources of the school, the school district, and the community to secure group intervention for the class, to teach **prosocial behaviours**. Consider the Values, Influences, and Peers (VIP) program, of your local police service, a joint program of the Ontario Ministry of Education and the Ministry of the Solicitor-General. Topics include peer pressure, responsible citizenship, and interpersonal skills. Persist to locate individual counselling and self-management strategies (for the students with behaviour exceptionalities) consistent with the group intervention. Differentiate your teaching; provide students with choice of activities or at least of the order of the activities, and choose high-interest activities based on your observations or informal polls of the class' preferences (Heacox, 2002; Kern et al., 2002). As Karen Hume of the Durham

### Further Reading

On teaching students with emotional and behaviour disorders:

Jensen, M.M. (2005). *Introduction to emotional and behavioral disorders: Recognizing and managing problems in the classroom.* Upper Saddle River, NJ: Pearson Merrill Prentice Hall.

Morris, R.J., & Mathers, N. (Eds). (2008). *Evidence-based interventions for students with learning and behavioral challenges.* New York, NY: Routledge.

District School Board (2008) says, "Start where they are." Cuccaro and Geitner (2007) describe a second-tier intervention consisting of direct instruction and practice in social skills that took place at lunch every day for 2 weeks, with positive results for a small group of students. This action research may inspire you to develop a systematic approach to those students who require intensive help learning appropriate behaviour.

The Manitoba Department of Education provides resources to help teachers develop behaviour intervention plans for the third step (www.edu.gov.mb.ca/k12/specedu/bip). These plans help teachers to understand:

- what a student is trying to accomplish with problem behaviours;
- what the student needs from teachers so the negative behaviour is not necessary;
- proactive interventions to prevent reoccurrences; and
- reactive interventions to end the incident and minimize disruption to learning.

You may find it helpful to develop a behaviour or learning **contract** with a student specific to his or her greatest challenge; make it realistic and immediate, and both of you sign it. Contracts are described in Chapter 7. Use the ADAPT strategy, and work with a resource teacher or educational assistant to ensure that individual tutoring reinforces your adaptations (Kamps et al., 2000). Although time-consuming and challenging, these actions can get students with behaviour exceptionalities "onside" from the first day. Programs that use literature can help students learn about themselves and about others (e.g., Circle of Courage in Regan and Page, 2008).

Students with behaviour and emotional exceptionalities lack advocates (Smith, 2004). In June 2008 the *Globe and Mail* ran an extensive series of newspaper articles, online contributions, and question-and-answer opportunities with mental health experts aimed at reducing the stigma associated with mental health conditions. They reported what the research has shown: adolescents and young adults are particularly vulnerable to depression, anxiety, and other mental illnesses, making it difficult for them to take on adult responsibilities and employment. The Canadian Mental Health Association (CMHA) (www.cmha.ca/bins/index.asp) provides employment support to individuals with emotional and mental health disorders.

## THE IMPORTANCE OF CLASSROOM PROGRAMS IN PRO-SOCIAL BEHAVIOUR

You may feel that, as a teacher, your efforts with these students are insignificant compared to the work of psychologists and psychiatrists. If so, you are underestimating your importance. A 2001 report by the National Institute for Mental Health, *Teens: The Company They Keep*, highlights the role of schools in preventing anti-social behaviour through interventions aimed at peers and other key people around the student. "The primary strategy currently employed to achieve this goal is classroom and school-based programs in social problem solving, conflict management, violence prevention, and promoting emotional and social development." In fall 2010 the CMHA implemented a mental health curriculum in Canadian high schools.

**Put into Practice**

There are many different approaches to dealing with behaviour challenges in the classroom.

Read two of these resources and develop differentiated instruction and a highly structured classroom approach to address the issues raised in the description of Urjo.

BC Special Education Branch. (2006). *Teaching students with learning and behavioural differences: A resource guide for teachers.* www.bced.gov.bc.ca/specialed/landbdif/toc.htm.

Kaiser, B. (2009). *Challenging behavior in elementary and middle school.* Upper Saddle River, NJ: Pearson.

Rockwell, S. (1995). *Back off, cool down, try again: Teaching students how to control aggressive behavior.* Reston, VA: Council for Exceptional Children.

Shindler, J. (2010). *Transformative classroom management: Positive strategies to engage all students and promote a psychology of success.* San Francisco, CA: Jossey-Bass.

**Weblinks**

CANADIAN MENTAL HEALTH ASSOCIATION: MY LIFE—"IT'S COOL TO TALK ABOUT IT!" (YOUTH MENTAL HEALTH)
www.cmha.ca/mylife

NATIONAL INSTITUTE FOR MENTAL HEALTH (CHILD AND ADOLESCENT MENTAL HEALTH)
www.nimh.nih.gov/health/topics/child-and-adolescent-mental-health/index.shtml

PRINCE EDWARD ISLAND DEPARTMENT OF EDUCATION STUDENT SERVICES, *MEETING BEHAVIOURAL CHALLENGES*
www.gov.pe.ca/photos/original/ed_mebech.pdf

# Teaching Students with Mild Intellectual Disabilities

To Ms. Starr: I want to work in recycling. Because I want to help the environment and I won't need to read too much. I'm not too good at reading or writing, but I am learning this year. I like this class. You and Mr. T. [Mr. Tymchuk, the resource teacher] make me want to learn. You let me try my way. Thank you. That's why I want to be in recycling.

*Dictated to the resource teacher by Scott who has mild intellectual disabilities (gr. 3)*

## Characteristics of Students with Mild Intellectual Disabilities

*Intellectual disabilities* (ID) is widely used in Canada to replace *mental retardation*, a term unacceptable to most people; "intellectual disability is characterized by significant limitations both in intellectual functioning and in adaptive behavior as expressed in conceptual, social, and practical **adaptive skills**. This disability originates before age 18" (Schalock et al., 2007, for American Association on Intellectual and Developmental Disabilities (AAIDD)). The AAIDD defines intellectual functioning as a general mental capability involving the ability to reason, plan, think abstractly, and learn from experience. Generally, **intelligence** is represented by intelligence quotient (IQ) scores obtained from standardized tests given by trained professionals. By adaptive behaviour, the AAIDD means the collection of conceptual, social, and practical skills that people have learned so they can function in their everyday lives.

"Persons with mild [ID] are those who know a great deal about living in the community without supervision and who require some instruction that could be provided under relatively non-intensive conditions" (Dever, 1990, p. 150). The Ontario Ministry of Education describes mild ID as characterized by the ability to profit educationally within a regular classroom with modifications, slow intellectual development, potential for academic learning, independent social adjustment, and economic self-support (2001, p. A20). Recent research has dispelled an earlier belief that individuals with **Down syndrome** necessarily function at a moderate level of developmental disability. Research shows that many individuals with Down syndrome have mild ID (Rynders & Horrobin, 1990), like Scott, whose case is highlighted at the opening of this chapter. Figure 3.7 provides information about students with Down syndrome and for teaching students with mild ID.

Usually, students with mild ID learn to meet everyday demands and develop into self-sufficient adults. However, they may have difficulty attaining the academic skills associated with their grade level, learning and passing through the developmental stages at a slower rate than their classmates. Delays can be seen in physical, cognitive, language, and social development. In physical development, fine motor coordination may be delayed, affecting skills such as cutting, colouring, printing, etc. Cognitive delays affect short-term memory, attention, and ability to generalize (Ven der Molen et al., 2008). They may be less interested in letters, words, reading, and numbers than their classmates, and are likely to find reading comprehension,

## What do you think?

Visit the websites representing the various perspectives on mild intellectual disabilities. How can teachers become effective advocates for students with intellectual disabilities?

Human Rights Perspective: Independent Living Canada www.vilrc.ca/web/guest/vilrc

Educational Perspective: J.P. Das Developmental Disabilities Centre, www.ualberta.ca/~jpdasddc/INDEX.html

Medical Perspective: Developmental Disabilities Program at the University of Western Ontario, www.ddd.uwo.ca

Weblinks

CANADIAN DOWN SYNDROME SOCIETY www.cdss.ca

SPECIAL OLYMPICS CANADA www.specialolympics.ca

BEST BUDDIES www.bestbuddies.org

## FIGURE 3.7 INFORMATION FOR TEACHING STUDENTS WITH DOWN SYNDROME

Put into Practice

Down syndrome (DS) is a chromosomal arrangement that occurs before birth and causes limitations in physical and cognitive development. All persons with Down syndrome have extra genetic material associated with the twenty-first chromosome. One in 800 live births in Canada is affected by DS. Though the likelihood of having a child with DS increases to some degree with the age of the mother, three-quarters of all children with the syndrome are born to mothers under 35.

Although all individuals with DS have some degree of intellectual disability, other factors such as environment and low expectations also affect their learning. Generally, progress is slow and some complex skills are difficult. Each individual has unique strengths and weaknesses. Learning differences, physical characteristics, and health concerns are highly variable and individualistic.

Physically, children with Down syndrome have chubby cheeks, large round eyes, a larger tongue, smaller limbs and smaller body frame, and tend to have low muscle tone and generalized looseness of the ligaments. There is also a strong susceptibility to hearing and vision difficulties and frequent upper respiratory infections. About 40 percent of the children have heart defects.

**Classroom Strategies: Social**

- Help the student to feel proud and to act independently; this will contribute to self-esteem and social relationships.
- Your behaviour and acceptance are a model for how you expect classmates to interact.
- With the co-operation of the family, help all members of the class to understand Down syndrome. Conduct discussions about individual differences, inclusion, and DS specifically.
- Encourage interaction with other students through play activities and learning activities.

**Classroom Strategies: Teaching**

- Seat the student with DS in a quiet place where he or she can see and hear what is going on.
- Discuss the schedule before the day starts; use a visual schedule and photographs to reinforce structure and sequencing. Avoid surprises.
- Break up tasks into small steps; use short blocks of time. Allow time to finish a task.
- Use concrete and visual materials, activities, and reminders, working toward the abstract.
- Help the student with DS to focus on one thing at a time; remove distractions.
- Phrase questions simply, in short sentences; give response time, allow the child to show what they mean if they cannot verbalize it.
- Encourage speech by asking the student to express wants rather than saying "yes" or "no."
- Gain attention by using simple commands and by using eye contact. Be precise.
- Expect appropriate behaviour. All students are accountable for their behaviour.
- Expect the student with DS to learn to read; be patient; do what works; read recent research.
- Co-operate with the parents in using authentic, community-based learning activities, e.g., shopping, banking, travel. Be mutually aware of what the student needs to learn.
- Use a variety of resources including peers and computer software.

---

Sources adapted from: British Columbia Ministry of Education (1996). *Awareness of Chronic Health Conditions: What the Teacher Needs to Know.* Victoria: Queen's Printer for British Columbia; Canadian Down Syndrome Society: www.cdss.ca.

Read about the cognitive characteristics of students with Down syndrome. With your peers, develop some activities at the level at which you teach that are appropriately differentiated for students with DS.

Gilmore, L., & Cuskelly, M. (2009). A longitudinal study of motivation and competence in children with Down syndrome: Early childhood to early adolescence. *Journal of Intellectual Disability Research, 53*(5), 484–492.

Lanfranchi, S. et al. (2010). Executive function in adolescents with Down syndrome. *Journal of Intellectual Disability Research, 54*(4), 308–319.

Martin, G.E., eta I. (2009). Language characteristics of individuals with Down syndrome. *Topics in Language Disorders, 29*(2), 112–132.

**Further Reading**

About collaborative and co-operative learning:

Cohen, E.G. (1994). *Designing groupwork: Strategies for the heterogeneous classroom* (2nd ed.). New York, NY: Teachers College, Columbia University.

English, R., & Dean, S. (2004). *Show me how to learn: Key strategies and powerful techniques that promote cooperative learning.* Markham, ON: Pembroke Publishers.

Gillies, R.M., Ashman, A., & Terwel, J. (Eds.). (2007). *The teacher's role in implementing cooperative learning in the classroom.* New York, NY: Springer.

*Getting results from cooperative learning* (3 video recordings and a facilitator's guide). (2005). Alexandria, VA: Association for Supervision and Curriculum Development (ASCD).

Jaques, D., & Salmon, G. (2007). *Learning in groups: A handbook for face-to-face and online environments* (4th ed.). New York, NY: Routledge.

arithmetic reasoning, and problem solving difficult (Chung & Tam, 2005). They often do best in curriculum areas where they can use experiential learning, such as Scott's expertise about recycling and nature acquired by camping and watching television.

In speech and language development, you may see delay, with expressive language less developed than receptive language. Students with mild ID may not understand long sentences or complex ideas when they are presented for the first time. Characteristics often include articulation disorders and concrete language. Challenges with social adjustment are common, including lack of initiative and **learned helplessness**. Thus they are less socially prepared to pay attention, initiate

**Put into Practice**

Read the document *Down Syndrome and You* (www.cdss.ca/images/pdf/brochures/english/down_syndrome_and_you_english.pdf), written for young people with Down syndrome. Consider how you would use it to help a young person with Down syndrome gain self-knowledge. How could you use this booklet to help other students understand a classmate with Down syndrome?

**Further Reading**

About teaching reading and math to students with Down syndrome:

Bunch, G. O. (2006). *The basics: Supporting learners with intellectual challenge in regular classrooms.* Toronto, ON: Inclusion Press.

Horstmeier, D. (2004). *Teaching math to people with Down syndrome and other hands-on learners.* Bethesda, MD: Woodbine House.

Kumin, L. (2008). *Helping children with Down syndrome communicate better: Speech and language skills for ages 6–14.* Bethesda, MD: Woodbine House.

Lemons, C.J., & Fuchs, D. (2010). Phonological awareness of children with Down syndrome: Its role in learning to read and the effectiveness of related interventions. *Research in Developmental Disabilities: A Multidisciplinary Journal, 31*(2), 316–330.

Levorato, M., C., Roch, M., & Beltrame, R. (2009). Text comprehension in Down syndrome: The role of lower and higher level abilities. *Clinical Linguistics & Phonetics, 23*(4), 285–300.

Roch, M., & Levorato, M.C. (2009). Simple view of reading in Down's syndrome: The role of listening comprehension and reading skills. *International Journal of Language and Communication Disorders, 44*(2), 206–223.

conversation, and co-operate, and they may appear immature or shy (see Canney & Byrne, 2006). During the adolescent years this can be especially difficult.

## Differentiating Curriculum and Teaching Students with Mild Intellectual Disabilities

To promote cognitive development, encourage students with mild ID to interact more. Provide sensory and intellectual stimulation, and structure and consistency. Set goals and use action-oriented activities and concrete materials (Smith et al., 2003). You can also use colour-coding, reduce choice, and highlight key text to focus students' attention on what is important (Bennett et al., 2008).

Some ways to differentiate from the BC resource *Students with Intellectual Disabilities: A Resource Guide for Teachers* (www.bced.gov.bc.ca/specialed/sid):

- preview the day plan before the day starts and materials before each lesson
- prepare a summary with blanks for the student to fill in while listening
- modify by giving more concrete assignments on a related topic

This BC resource guide reminds us "when making modifications, change only that which is necessary to meet the needs of the student, with a view to fostering inclusion." Many of these differentiations make learning easier for other students, as well.

Extend deadlines and encourage peers to create social opportunities; learn about alternative resources, such as parallel textbooks at **lower reading levels**, textbooks on tape, manipulatives that appeal to the senses, and games to practise concepts. Students with mild ID benefit from re-teaching and from practice applying skills. Using money and other authentic, manipulative materials helps in math, along with cognitive strategy instruction and worked examples (Chung & Tam, 2005).

To promote language development, simplify the language you use in instructions and relate new ideas to students' experiences. Provide opportunities for students to speak without fear of criticism. To promote social development, ensure that classmates treat the student with mild ID with respect, and create contexts in which students learn by collaborating and using strengths other than traditional academic knowledge. Canney and Byrne (2006) describe how to use circle time in primary classrooms, and the BC resource guide on ID has suggestions for working with adolescents (www.bced.gov.bc.ca/specialed/sid). To adapt assessments, simplify, shorten, and make clearer what you are looking for in an answer. Alternative assessments include oral exams, portfolios, and interviews.

What about career opportunities? During high school the focus usually shifts to functional or vocational learning, in the community and in specialized classes as well as in regular classes. Adolescents with mild ID benefit from learning through experience in programs like co-operative education (Eisenman, 2007; Lord & Hutchison, 2007). Hutchinson et al. (2008) described an adolescent with mild ID who benefited from workplace experiences with gradually increasing demands for independence. These youth may participate in programs in community colleges (Crawford, 2005) or in universities (e.g., H'Art Prep). H'Art Prep is a "ten-month program for people with intellectual disabilities, who want to learn more about goal setting while pursuing continuing education and post-secondary education experiences, and meaningful volunteer opportunities" (www.kingston.org/hartstudio/HartPrep.htm).

People with mild ID may be disadvantaged in formal school settings, but they thrive in the community, where they can use their life experience. However, fewer than half of those with ID are involved in work or training after secondary school (Yamaki & Fujiura, 2002). A recent survey in Ontario showed that most respondents believed people with ID would not negatively affect the image of workplaces and thought that lack of employment training was the major obstacle to their inclusion (Burge et al., 2007). To be successful, inclusion must prepare youth with ID for inclusion in the workplace and the community, as well as the school.

# Summary

Students with high-incidence exceptionalities include students who are gifted or who have learning disabilities, attention deficit hyperactivity disorder, communication exceptionalities, behaviour exceptionalities, or mild intellectual disabilities. You will be teaching these students frequently. They may be inefficient at making sense of what you are teaching and may require encouragement and learning strategies that help them stay on task and complete assignments.

Gifted students will thrive with assignments that offer choice, challenge them, and enable them to go beyond regular curriculum expectations. Students with speech and language exceptionalities may require opportunities to practise in the classroom what they learn with a specialist, and volunteers may assume this responsibility. Expect to seek the assistance of other team members for students who have behaviour exceptionalities; they can be challenging and often require individual counselling that you cannot provide in a classroom. Asking for help when you really need it is a sign of strength, not weakness. Students with mild intellectual disabilities will probably not keep pace with the regular curriculum, and you can expect to see the gap widen over time. However, they benefit greatly from observing their peers in a regular class, are likely to participate in regular classrooms during the elementary years, and may be enrolled in streams or programs that emphasize inclusion in the community during high school.

It is often difficult to distinguish students with high-incidence exceptionalities from their peers because their exceptionalities are not always obvious. Using the ADAPT strategy, in combination with students' IEPs, will help you differentiate elements of the classroom so that you can meet individual needs. Most of these students benefit from a structured, predictable, engaging class with a positive tone, in which everyone is treated with respect by you and taught that that is how they are expected to treat one another.

# Key Terms

high-incidence exceptionalities (p. 52)
gifted (p. 54)
developmentally advanced (p. 54)
domains (p. 54)
metacognition (p. 55)
cognitive abilities (p. 55)

high task commitment (p. 55)
creativity (p. 55)
learning disability (p. 56)
phonemic awareness (p. 59)
rapid naming (p. 59)
double-deficit hypothesis (p. 59)

number sense (p. 59)
social status (p. 60)
self-concept (p. 60)
cognitive strategies (p. 62)
concrete-to-representational-to-
   abstract (CRA) (p. 63)

# Discussion Questions

1. What high-incidence exceptionalities do you expect in your classroom? Why it is important to differentiate social aspects as well as academic instruction?

2. Read about Brian in the section on teaching students who are gifted. How could you differentiate instruction so he is engaged and less likely to be taunted?

3. Write a description of a student with LD at a grade level that you teach. Describe the challenges; consider the benefits and challenges of intensive tiered instruction.

4. You are on the in-school team for a student with ADHD, predominantly inattentive. Role-play a team meeting, focus on his strengths. How does this change the discussion?

5. Consider the learning needs of Ruth, a student with a communication disorder, described in this chapter. How do the major issues change with her age (6, 12, 18)?

6. Read the description of Urjo; he is in your class. In a chart, list his needs and strengths; use his strengths to overcome his needs. Whose support will you enlist?

7. Scott is described in the chapter. Plan to differentiate teaching and the social aspects of your class, using Scott's interest in environmental science. He is 9 or 17 years of age.

8. Return to the cases of Urjo and Scott, at the start of the chapter. Answer the questions following the cases. Identify the most surprising thing you have learned. What dilemmas stick in your mind after reading this chapter and how would you deal with them?

# Chapter 4
## Teaching Students with Low-Incidence Exceptionalities

**Pamela is in senior kindergarten at Grove Elementary School.** She likes playing with water, making towers of blocks, being near the teacher, and exploring the materials the teacher is demonstrating. The classroom is often busy and noisy. For example, today a visitor is teaching the children to drum on the tomato-juice can drums they made last week. While the others sit in a circle, Pamela is running from one side of the room to the other, waving her arms. She has a short attention span for activities with a social component and becomes agitated when the classroom is too busy or too noisy. Pamela wants to sit on the chair beside the visitor and touch his drum. When she can't have her way, she has a tantrum. She repeats, "I like the big chair, I like the big chair," and "Thump the drum, thump the drum," both lines that she has heard the visitor say to the class. Pamela communicates through echolalia (echoing what is said), gestures, and limited functional speech, including, "No," "Help me," and "Get that one." Pamela's IEP states that she has autism.

**Brittany has cystic fibrosis and coughs constantly.** Although she is in grade 7, she is as small as most girls in grade 4. She has just returned to school after being hospitalized for two months. Brittany has told teachers and students in previous classes about how her body produces abnormally thick and sticky secretions that cause problems in her respiratory and digestive systems. This mucus builds up in her lungs and also makes it difficult for her to digest her food. Brittany has always left class willingly to take her medication and receive therapy to clear her airways. Most teachers have found that Brittany needs encouragement to follow her regime of medication and treatment. This year she also needs emotional support to deal with the recent insertion of a feeding tube that will ensure that she continues to grow and has enough energy. Brittany's health condition has an impact on her school life, mainly on her social and emotional well-being.

1. Which of the characteristics of each student are most likely to affect learning? What learning needs are implied by these characteristics?

2. With such a range of learning needs, what do exceptional students like Pamela and Brittany have in common?

## Learner Objectives

After you have read this chapter, you will be able to:

1. Describe low-incidence exceptionalities and physical and health conditions.

2. Describe ways you can make modifications for students with developmental disabilities (DD).

3. For students with autism spectrum disorders (ASD), discuss differentiating teaching and helping them to participate socially.

4. Describe how you can include students who are hard of hearing or deaf.

5. Describe adaptations that would meet the needs of students with low vision or blindness.

6. Describe differentiating in the classroom for students with physical disabilities.

7. Explain how you could differentiate teaching for students with chronic medical disorders.

3. How frequently is a teacher likely to be teaching a student with each of these exceptionalities?

4. What types of differentiation does each of these students need in order to be included in the social life and the learning activities of the classroom?

5. What community resources can a teacher draw on to supplement in-school resources to teach each of these students?

# Introduction

In this chapter you will learn about the characteristics of students with **low-incidence exceptionalities**, **physical disabilities**, and **chronic health conditions**, and about how to differentiate teaching for these students and provide them with social support. They may be identified soon after birth if their conditions are severe, and they may have an IPRC before they begin school (e.g., autism) or may never have an IPRC (e.g., diabetes). Parents tend to be very involved in the lives of these children (Turnbull et al., 2010; Wysocki & Gavin, 2006). They may assume the role of **case coordinator** and may be better informed than the classroom teacher about their child's exceptionality. Remember that you are likely to teach a child with cystic fibrosis once or twice in your career, and parents teach their child with cystic fibrosis every day.

Each section begins with the words of an exceptional child or adolescent, followed by a description of characteristics and implications for differentiation. For low-incidence exceptionalities and health conditions, you can seek information on a need-to-know basis because it is almost impossible to remember all the details. We also provide information about responding to life-threatening conditions, such as allergic reactions and asthma. Table 4.1 introduces the exceptionalities and conditions in this chapter, using Ontario terminology where applicable, and Table 4.2 reports prevalence data for these low-incidence exceptionalities and health conditions.

**Cross-Reference**

For descriptions of and differentiations for students with high-incidence exceptionalities, see Chapter 3.

# Teaching Students with Developmental Disabilities

My name is Reid. I am 17 and I have developmental disabilities caused by a genetic condition called Coffin-Lowry syndrome. I am in a life-skills class at Campbell Collegiate. My favourite part is my work placement. Every morning I clean the cages and walk the animals at a pet store. I sweep the floors and do odd jobs. My goal is to live in my own place with my friend Dan. My mom says she hopes that I can do that, but she will miss me. Dan and I need people to help us. I use my wheelchair more. But I think we can do it. That is my dream.

*Generated by Reid Ford and his mother in conversation.*

## Description of Developmental Disabilities

In Ontario, **developmental disability (DD)** is defined in the *Education Act* as a severe learning disorder characterized by:

- inability to profit from a special education program for students with mild intellectual disabilities because of slow intellectual development;
- ability to profit from a special education program that is designed to accommodate slow intellectual development; and
- limited potential for academic learning, independent social adjustment, and economic self-support.

In psychological research and practice, the term **intellectual disabilities** is often used, as well as the term developmental disabilities, to refer to conditions originating before the age of 18 that result in significant limitations in intellectual functioning

**Weblinks**

ONTARIO ASSOCIATION ON DEVELOPMENTAL DISABILITIES
www.oadd.org

CANADIAN ASSOCIATION FOR COMMUNITY LIVING (NO EXCUSES CAMPAIGN FOR INCLUSION)
www.no-excuses.ca

CREATING OPPORTUNITIES FOR STUDENTS WITH INTELLECTUAL OR MULTIPLE DISABILITIES (SASKATCHEWAN EDUCATION)
www.sasked.gov.sk.ca/branches/curr/special_ed/docs/createopp/createopp.shtml

**TABLE 4.1 STUDENTS WITH LOW-INCIDENCE EXCEPTIONALITIES, PHYSICAL DISABILITIES, AND CHRONIC MEDICAL CONDITIONS**

| Exceptionality | Description |
|---|---|
| **Low-Incidence Exceptionalities** | |
| Developmental disabilities | Sometimes called severe intellectual disabilities. Severe limitation in both intellectual functioning and adaptive behaviour; focus is on the need for support to function in the community. |
| **Autism Spectrum Disorders** | |
| Autism | Impairments in verbal and nonverbal communication and reciprocal social interaction; restricted, repetitive patterns of behaviour; intellectual disability. |
| Asperger syndrome | Severe and sustained impairment in social interaction, and development of restricted, repetitive patterns of behaviour and interests. |
| **Sensory Exceptionalities** | |
| Hard of hearing and deaf | Hearing loss that has significantly affected development of speech and/or language and caused students to need adaptations to learn. |
| Visual impairments | Blind or partially sighted students who need adaptations to learn through channels other than visual. |
| **Physical Disabilities and Chronic Medical Conditions** | |
| **Nervous System Impairment** | |
| Cerebral palsy | Disorders affecting body movement and muscle coordination resulting from damage to brain during pregnancy or first three years. |
| Spina bifida | Neural tube defect that occurs during first 4 weeks of pregnancy, causing vertebrae or spinal cord to fail to develop properly. |
| Epilepsy | Neurological disorder involving sudden bursts of electrical energy in the brain. |
| Tourette syndrome | Neurological disorder characterized by tics. |
| Brain injury | Damage to brain tissue that prevents it from functioning properly. |
| Fetal alcohol spectrum disorders | Neurological disorders caused by significant prenatal exposure to alcohol. |
| **Musculoskeletal Conditions** | |
| Muscular dystrophy | Genetically based muscle disorders that result in progressive muscle weakness. |
| Juvenile arthritis | Continuous inflammation of joints in young people under 16. |
| **Chronic Health Impairments** | |
| Diabetes | Condition in which the body does not make enough insulin and has problems absorbing and storing sugars. |
| Allergies | Sensitivity or abnormal immune response to normal substance, which can cause anaphylactic shock. |
| Asthma | Chronic lung condition, characterized by difficulty breathing, in which airways are obstructed by inflammation, muscle spasms, and excess mucus. |
| Cystic fibrosis | Incurable disorder caused by inherited genetic defect affecting mainly the lungs and the digestive system. |
| Cancer and leukemia | Cancer is characterized by uncontrolled division of cells and the ability of these to spread; leukemia is a type of cancer that forms in the bone marrow, causing abnormal white blood cell development. |

and conceptual, social, and practical adaptive skills (American Psychiatric Association, 2000). Intensity of the disability can be mild, moderate, severe, or profound. These terms were used in the past to label those diagnosed with mental retardation (see the website of **American Association on Intellectual and Developmental Disabilities (AAIDD):** www.aaidd.org). Individuals with DD (or moderate, severe,

**TABLE 4.2 PREVALENCE OF LOW-INCIDENCE EXCEPTIONALITIES, PHYSICAL DISABILITIES, AND CHRONIC MEDICAL CONDITIONS**

| Exceptionality | General Incidence in Research | % of IPRCs in ON in 2006/07* |
|---|---|---|
| *Low-Incidence Exceptionalities* | | |
| Developmental disabilities | 13 per 10,000 (Arvio & Sillanpaa, 2003) | 5.2% |
| *Autism Spectrum Disorders (ASD)* | | |
| Autism | ASD: 36 per 10,000 (Fombonne et al., 2006) | ASD: 4.7% |
| Asperger syndrome | 4 per 10,000 (Fombonne et al., 2006) | |
| *Sensory Exceptionalities* | | |
| Deaf and hard of hearing | Hard of hearing: up to 1,500 per 10,000 (Niskar, 2001); deaf: 10 per 10,000 (Public Health Ontario, 2000) | 1.8% |
| Blind and low vision | Low vision: 35 per 10,000; blind: 4 per 10,000 (Maberly et al., 2006) | 0.4% |
| *Physical Disabilities and Chronic Medical Conditions* | | Physical: 1.8% |
| *Nervous System Impairment* | | |
| Cerebral palsy | 20 per 10,000 (Robertson et al., 2007) | |
| Spina bifida | 4 per 10,000 (DeWals et al., 2008) | |
| Epilepsy | 56 per 10,000 (Tellez-Zenteno et al., 2004) | |
| Tourette syndrome | 30 per 10,000 (Blumberg et al., 2007) | |
| Brain injury | Serious brain injury in children: 22 per 10,000 (Kraus, 1986) | |
| Fetal alcohol spectrum disorders | 10 to 30 per 10,000 (Barr & Streissguth, 2006) | |
| *Musculoskeletal Conditions* | | |
| Muscular dystrophy | Duchenne muscular dystrophy: 2 per 10,000 males (Dooley et al., 2010) | |
| Juvenile arthritis | 5 to 11 per 10,000 (depending on country) (Cakmak & Bolukbas, 2005) | |
| *Chronic Health Impairments* | | |
| Diabetes | Pediatric: 17 per 10,000 (www.cdc.gov/diabetes/projects/cda2.htm) | |
| Allergies | Peanut allergy: 134 per 10,000 (Kagan et al., 2003) | |
| Asthma | 910 per 10,000 (Akinbami et al., 2009) | |
| Cystic fibrosis | 3 per 10,000 (www.cysticfibrosis.ca/en/aboutCysticFibrosis) | |
| Cancer and leukemia | Pediatric cancer: 850 children in Canada annually (Ellison et al., 2009) | |

* See Figure 1.2 in Chapter 1 (Ontario Provincial Statistics for IPRCs 2006/07)

and profound intellectual disabilities) have greater limitations in intellectual and adaptive functioning than individuals with mild intellectual disabilities (described in Chapter 3). The AAIDD definition includes six dimensions: intellectual abilities; adaptive behaviour; participation, interaction, and social roles; health; environmental context; and age of onset.

The adaptive skills in which one would expect to see Reid (described above) challenged by the expectations of his environment include: communication, home living, community use, health and safety, leisure, self-care, social skills, self-direction, academics, and work. Reid has many strengths: he communicates well orally, is a hard worker, knows himself, and uses this self-knowledge to make good decisions. With excellent support at home, at school, and in the neighbourhood, he has surpassed early predictions, but he is aware that he will increasingly need his wheelchair. He wants to be independent but accepts that he needs support to participate in his environment. Reid is learning about responsibility in his work placement.

## Characteristics of Students with Developmental Disabilities

Developmental disabilities are often the result of conditions described later in this chapter, such as fetal alcohol syndrome, cerebral palsy, and spina bifida, as well as Down syndrome, Angelman syndrome, and other **chromosomal abnormalities**. Students with DD span a range of abilities, from those who acquire academic skills to those who require assistance with **self-care** throughout their lives. Usually the strengths and weaknesses of students with DD are assessed across four dimensions:

- intellectual or cognitive and adaptive behaviour skills;
- psychological, emotional, and social considerations;
- physical and health considerations; and
- environmental considerations.

Cognitive characteristics of this group include difficulties focusing attention and getting information into memory; however, long-term memory may be excellent. Language is likely to be delayed, and in the most severe cases verbal language may not develop. Adaptive behaviours refer to coping with the demands of daily living. Psychological characteristics may include frustration and impulsivity. Students with DD find social interactions challenging; often they do not know how to make friends, even though they may be loyal and caring. They may withdraw or develop repetitive behaviours that seem bizarre to their peers (Pilling et al., 2007).

Physical and health considerations depend on concomitant conditions such as cerebral palsy. Less physical dexterity and coordination than others of the same age are to be expected, and in the most severe cases there may be limited locomotion. Environmental considerations include such things as requiring a wheelchair that holds the head in a specific position or a **voice synthesizer** to produce speech.

## Differentiating Curriculum and Teaching for Students with Developmental Disabilities

Many of the ways of differentiating instruction discussed in Chapter 3 for students with high-incidence exceptionalities are suitable for some students with DD. Grade-level curriculum outcomes may be appropriate, but materials or presentation may need to be changed. For example, you can make accommodations in the environment by positioning the student where there are fewest distractions, and the desk may be adapted to suit a wheelchair. A schedule and list of assignments can be taped to the student's desk. You can highlight key points in the text and break information into steps. Use concrete examples. You could videotape a lesson so the student can review it at home. Allow extra time to complete tasks and tests. The student may draw or write individual words rather than sentences and paragraphs.

## MODIFYING CURRICULUM, DEVELOPING ALTERNATIVE EXPECTATIONS

You will need to modify learning outcomes for most students with DD. Curriculum expectations can be drawn from the curriculum for a lower grade. These students often require alternative expectations that are not found in curriculum documents; the goals section of the IEP can serve as a guide. You can consult other members of the in-school team and follow two principles to guide the development of alternative curriculum. The principle of **functional curriculum** suggests basing goals on life skills (Bouk, 2009). At his co-op placement in the pet store, Reid learned to be punctual and to speak clearly to customers. The principle of **community-based** education suggests engaging students in authentic tasks in the community (Sabbatino & Macrine, 2007). When Reid's classmates were learning about the Bank of Canada, Reid learned to cash cheques, pay bills, and withdraw cash from his bank account. Learning to use money takes much practice for youth with DD (Xin et al., 2005).

There will be great variation from one IEP to the next, but the goals of alternative programs for students with developmental disabilities usually include:

- functional academic skills;
- physical development and personal care;
- communication skills and social interaction skills;
- community living skills; and
- career development, work experience, and transition planning.

Figure 4.1 shows how to generate modified and alternative outcomes.

If students ask why Reid has different tasks, explain that fairness does not necessarily mean sameness. Use examples of different but fair treatment for exceptionalities not represented in your class. Ask whether it is fair to expect a student with no legs to climb stairs or a blind student to read a test. Students can see that not everyone needs an elevator, and that most would be disadvantaged by Braille. Make routines for exceptional students similar to the class routines. Students with DD should have challenging tasks and assignments just as their peers do.

## FIGURE 4.1 MODIFIED AND ALTERNATIVE EXPECTATIONS FOR STUDENTS WITH DEVELOPMENTAL DISABILITIES

Change only what is necessary to meet the student's needs, with a view to fostering inclusion.
- Give more concrete assignments on a topic related to that being studied by the class.
- Simplify learning tasks; provide more structure or examples for the student to use as models.
- Ask easier questions related to the same concept.
- Give the same materials to be used for a different purpose, e.g., adding instead of multiplying.
- Use high-interest/low-vocabulary resources on the same topic. For adolescents, choose age-appropriate topics; avoid texts written for primary students that may cause embarrassment.
- Provide community preparation such as:
  - trips to community locations, such as stores;
  - opportunities to apply functional skills in different settings; and
  - job-related experiences, such as running a small business.
- Individualize community tasks for each student based on need.

**@**

**Weblinks**

GENEVA CENTRE FOR AUTISM, TORONTO
www.autism.net

AUTISM ONTARIO
www.autismontario.com

ONTARIO MINISTRY OF EDUCATION, STUDENTS WITH AUTISM
www.edu.gov.on.ca/eng/general/elemsec/speced/monog4.html

SASKATCHEWAN EDUCATION, TEACHING STUDENTS WITH AUTISM: A GUIDE FOR EDUCATORS
www.sasked.gov.sk.ca/branches/curr/special_ed/docs/autism/Teaching%20Students%20with%20Autism%20Document.pdf

MANITOBA EDUCATION, CITIZENSHIP AND YOUTH, 2005, SUPPORTING INCLUSIVE SCHOOLS: A HANDBOOK FOR DEVELOPING AND IMPLEMENTING PROGRAMMING FOR STUDENTS WITH AUTISM SPECTRUM DISORDER.
www.edu.gov.mb.ca/k12/specedu/aut/pdf/ASD_Document.pdf

AUTISM SOCIETY CANADA
www.autismsocietycanada.ca

**What do you think?**

On April 12, 2010, the *Globe and Mail* reported that parents and educators were celebrating the release of the iPad because it will be a major improvement over the iPod Touch, which has helped children with autism to communicate. There are many communication applications and families can load photos that their children can point to and express their wants and needs. How do you think this kind of technology can help teachers provide accommodations for non-verbal students?

**Put into Practice**

Read about social stories in the resources listed below and develop a social story for Pamela, the kindergarten student with autism described in the case study opening this chapter. Choose a focus different from Figure 4.2 on page 91

Smith, C. (2003). *Writing and developing social stories: Practical interventions in autism.* Bicester: Speechmark.

Ali, S., & Frederickson, N. (2006). Investigating the evidence base of social stories. *Educational Psychology in Practice, 22,* 355–377.

Bernad-Ripoll, S. (2007). Using a self-as-model video combined with social stories to help a child with Asperger syndrome understand emotions. *Focus on Autism and Other Developmental Disabilities, 22,* 100–106.

Howley, M., & Arnold, E., (2005). *Revealing the hidden social code: Social stories for people with autistic spectrum disorders.* London and Philadelphia: Jessica Kingsley Publishers.

Quilty, K.M. (2007). Teaching paraprofessionals how to write and implement social stories for students with autism spectrum disorders. *Remedial and Special Education, 28,* 182–189.

Reynhout, G., & Careter, M. (2007). Social story efficacy with a child with autism spectrum disorder and moderate intellectual disability. *Focus on Autism and Other Developmental Disabilities, 22,* 173–182.

Scattone, D. (2008). Enhancing the conversation skills of a boy with Asperger's disorder through social stories and video modeling. *Journal of Autism and Developmental Disorders, 38,* 395–400.

Recent research shows that inclusive education is more likely to prepare students with DD for independent living as adults (e.g., Downing & Peckingham-Hardin, 2007). A recent survey found that a majority of adults in Ontario saw inclusive education as the best option for individuals with DD (Burge et al., 2009). Transition planning from high school to adult life must be part of the IEP, including options for employment, further education, and community participation.

# Teaching Students with Autism Spectrum Disorders

I love streetcars. I know all the routes. And I can tell you anything about streetcars in Toronto—the history, the kinds. But I wish there were no people on the streetcars. They make noise and come near me. My favourite thing is to ride the streetcar with my dad while all the people are at work. We talk to the driver. Streetcars are my hobby.

*From the free-writing book of Jason, who is 12 and has Asperger syndrome.*

This section focuses on autism and Asperger syndrome, a group of similar disorders are now collected under a broad term: **autism spectrum disorders (ASDs)**. ASDs are characterized by varying degrees of impairment in three areas: communication skills, social interactions, and repetitive and stereotyped patterns of behaviour (Volkmar, 2007; *DSM-IV*, American Psychiatric Association, 1994). The five disorders on the spectrum are autism, Asperger syndrome (AS), Rett syndrome, childhood disintegrative disorder, and pervasive developmental disorder not otherwise specified (PDD-NOS). In the following sections autism is discussed first, followed by Asperger syndrome; these are the most prevalent ASDs.

## Autism: Characteristics

The case of Pamela describes a kindergarten student with autism. Pamela communicates mainly by echoing others' words, socializes little with her peers, and runs around the room waving her arms. **Autism** affects the functioning of the brain and is believed to be genetic in origin, although diagnosis is based on a child's behaviour and must be evident before the age of three years. Autism is characterized by:

- impairments in verbal and nonverbal communication;
- impairments in reciprocal social interaction;
- impairments in imaginative creativity; and
- restricted, repetitive, and stereotypic patterns of behaviour, interests, and activities (American Psychiatric Association, 2000).

Most people with autism have intellectual disability ranging from mild to severe. Language often shows **perseveration** on one topic or echolalia. It is estimated that 50 percent of those with autism never develop functional speech. Children with autism have a high rate of tics and Tourette syndrome (Canitano & Vivanti, 2007).

It is *not* that students with autism do not want to interact reciprocally with others; rather, they are unable to understand social situations. Their lack of imaginative creativity can be seen in their inability to understand or even acknowledge the perspective of others; this has been described as lacking a **theory of mind**

(Baron-Cohen, 1995; Williams & Happe, 2010). They seem unaware that people have intentions, emotions, etc. Unusual behaviours you might observe include:

- a restricted range of interests; a preoccupation with one interest or object;
- an inflexible adherence to non-functional routine;
- stereotypic and repetitive motor mannerisms, such as hand flapping, finger licking, rocking, spinning, walking on tiptoes, spinning objects;
- a preoccupation with parts of objects;
- a fascination with movement, such as the spinning of wheels on toys;
- an insistence on sameness and resistance to change; and
- unusual responses to sensory stimuli.

## THEORY AND RESEARCH HIGHLIGHTS FROM

## EDUCATIONAL PSYCHOLOGY

## Theory of Mind

In attempting to explain the typical characteristics of children with autism spectrum disorders (impaired communication skills; impaired reciprocal social interaction; restricted, repetitive, and stereotypic patterns of behaviour; as well as impaired imaginative creativity), some researchers have developed unifying theories. The best known of these is *theory of mind* (ToM) (Baron-Cohen, 1995; Frith, 2003; Wellman et al., 2002). In locating the basis of autism, Baron-Cohen, Leslie, and Frith (1985) postulated that all people have a cognitive model of the world, or theory of mind, which is the ability to appreciate other people's mental states. However, children with autism don't see others' intentions, needs, or beliefs and, therefore, demonstrate a mind-blindness. They have a deficit in theory of mind.

Theory of mind is a cognitive capacity that represents epistemic mental states such as pretending, thinking, knowing, believing, imagining, dreaming, guessing, deceiving, etc. Theory of mind ties together mental-state concepts (the volitional, perceptual, and epistemic) into an understanding of how mental states and actions are related. Basically, this cognitive capacity is described as the ability to attribute mental states to others and to oneself, to recognize these states, to understand they may differ from one's own, and to predict future behaviour from reading these mental states (Baron-Cohen, 1995; Baron-Cohen et al., 1985).

*False belief.* The best-known test of theory of mind is called the false-belief test. It is believed that impairments in false belief lead to impairments in theory of mind, and together may be the basis for some of the impairments characteristic of autism (especially

difficulties in socialization, communication, and imagination). The best-known false belief task, the Sally-Ann task, studied by Baron-Cohen et al. (1985), involves a child representing a story of a character's false belief that an object is in one location when it is actually in another. Three groups of children were tested: four year olds with normal development, children with autism, and children with Down syndrome. The story of Sally and Ann is enacted individually to children in the three groups. Sally has a marble that she places inside a basket. Sally leaves the room and Ann takes the marble and places it in a box while Sally is away and cannot see that the marble has been moved. The child who is watching this scenario is asked three questions: a memory question, "In the beginning where did Sally put the marble?" (correct answer: basket); a reality question, "Where is the marble now?" (correct answer: box); and a prediction question, "Where will Sally look for her marble?" (correct answer: in the basket where she placed it). Only 20 percent of children with autism attributed a false belief to Sally and predicted that she would look in the basket. The other 80 percent failed to recognize that Sally's mental state had changed and that her previously correct belief that the marble was in the basket was now incorrect. Not understanding a change in mental state and not ascribing false belief implies a lack of theory of mind. In contrast, 85 percent of children with normal development and 86 percent of children with Down syndrome were able to predict correctly where Sally would look, recognizing that she falsely believed the marble was still in the basket (Baron-Cohen,

*(Box continued on next page)*

1995; Surian & Leslie, 1999). Normally developing four year olds generally answer the prediction question correctly.

*Communication deficits.* Deficits in communication are evident during the early years of an autistic child. Lord (1997) noted that all behaviours that best discriminate autistic children at the age of two involve communication of affect, i.e., greetings, seeking shared enjoyment of an event (joint attention), and responding to others' indications of pleasure (empathy) (cited in Robertson et al., 1999).

*Reservations.* There is a large issue that avoids explanation by theory of mind, and that is the characteristic of restricted, repetitive, and stereotypic patterns of behaviours, interests, and activities. This remains a huge challenge to researchers and practitioners who see theory of mind explaining the myriad characteristics that make daily life challenging for children and adolescents with autism.

## References

Baron-Cohen, S. (1995). *Mindblindness: An essay on autism and theory of mind.* Cambridge, MA: Bradford/MIT Press.

Baron-Cohen, S., Leslie, A.M., & Frith, U. (1985). Does the autistic child have a theory of mind? *Cognition, 21,* 37–46.

Frith, U. (2003). *Autism: Explaining the enigma* (2nd ed.). Malden, MA: Blackwell Pub.

Robertson, J.M., Tanguay, P.E., L'Ecuyer, S., Sims, A., & Waltrip, C. (1999). Domains of social communication handicap in autism spectrum disorder. *Journal of the American Academy of Child and Adolescent Psychiatry, 38,* 738–745.

Surian, L., & Leslie, A.M. (1999). Competence and performance in false belief understanding: A comparison of autistic and normal 3-year-old children. *British Journal of Developmental Psychology, 17,* 141–155.

Wellman, H.M., Baron-Cohen, S., Caswell, R., Gomez, J.C., Swettenham, J., Toye, E., & Lagattuta, K. (2002). Thought-bubbles help children with autism acquire an alternative to a theory of mind. *Autism, 6,* 343–363.

## Autism: Implications for Learning and Differentiation

The IEPs of students with autism usually include goals in the areas used to identify the exceptionality—communication, social interaction, stereotypic behaviours, and, sometimes, imaginative creativity—as well as in functional skills.

### ENHANCING COMMUNICATION

To enhance communication, it may be necessary to teach the student to listen by having the student face the speaker, remain still, and focus on what is being said. Speak in sentences to the student with autism; use concrete words and repeat as necessary. Visual aids are helpful; objects are the most concrete, followed by photographs, and then line drawings. A camera enables you to "catch the student doing good" and record the action. Make a schedule showing the student completing each activity of the day, or a sequence of photographs of the student in the steps of a complex activity. Encourage oral language by accepting limited verbal attempts and nonverbal behaviour as communication and using specific praise. This strategy is based on Goddard (2009) and named for **PAMELA**, as in the opening case study:

**P**uppets, games, and music can be used to increase participation.

**A**nchoring instruction in visual cues including visual schedules.

**M**aintaining joint attention through pointing and imitation.

**E**cholalia may provide clues to what the student is trying to communicate.

**L**earning through video modelling and self-as-model video.

**A**dapting teaching on the same topic being studied by the class.

### ENHANCING SOCIAL COGNITION AND BEHAVIOUR

To improve social interaction, social skills, and social cognition, students with autism require explicit teaching and practice. Carol Gray (2002) has developed first-person

## FIGURE 4.2  A SOCIAL STORY FOR PAMELA

A social story describes a social situation and includes social cues and appropriate responses. It is written for a specific situation for an individual student. The story can be used to:

- facilitate the inclusion of the student in regular classes;
- introduce changes and new routines;
- explain reasons for the behaviour of others;
- teach situation-specific social skills; and
- assist in teaching new academic skills.

Stories can be read, listened to on audio, or watched on video. The language must be understood by the child. The story should be from the child's perspective, use "I," and should direct the child to perform the appropriate behaviour. Social stories use descriptive sentences (which provide information on the setting and people), directive statements (i.e., positive statements about the desired response for a specific situation), and perspective statements (which describe the possible reactions of others).

Use two to five descriptive statements and one directive statement. Put only one or two sentences on a page. Symbols, drawings, or pictures can be included to support the meaning for the student.

Pamela tends to run and wave her arms while the other children sit on their chairs in a circle. Her teacher has made a social story for Pamela. The first page includes a photograph of the children smiling, sitting in a circle while the teacher reads a story. The second page shows Pamela smiling, sitting on her chair while the teacher holds a book. Page three shows a smiling child sitting on each side of Pamela, one speaking to her and the other offering her a toy. Each day, before the children sit in their circle, the teacher reads the story twice to Pamela and then reads each sentence and waits for Pamela to repeat it. Pamela has a videotape of the story at home that she watches with her mother.

Page 1:    Other kids like to hear the teacher.
Page 2:    I will sit on my chair when the teacher talks.
Page 3:    Everyone likes me when I sit on my chair.

———

Source: Based on Gray, C. (1993). *The Social Story Book*. Jenison, MI: Jenison Public Schools.

**Further Reading**

To learn more about teaching students with autism and Asperger syndrome, please see:

Betts, S., Betts, D., & Gerber-Eckard, L. (2007). *Asperger syndrome in the inclusive classroom: Advice and strategies for teachers.* London, UK: Jessica Kingsley Publishers.

British Columbia, Ministry of Education, Special Programs Branch. (2000). *Teaching students with autism: A resource guide for schools.* Victoria, BC: Ministry of Education, Special Programs Branch.

Griffin, H.C., Griffin, L.W. et al. (2006). Educational interventions for individuals with Asperger syndrome. *Intervention in School and Clinic, 41*(3), 150–155.

Krumins, J. (2007). *Been there, done that, finally getting it right: A guide to educational planning for a student with autism.* Peterborough, ON: Autism Aspirations.

Leach, D., & Duffy, M.L. (2009). Supporting students with autism spectrum disorders in inclusive settings. *Intervention in School and Clinic, 45*(1), 31–37.

Morrison, R.S., & Blackburn, A.M. (2008). Take the challenge: Building social competency in adolescents with Asperger's syndrome. *Teaching Exceptional Children Plus, 5*(2), Article 5. Retrieved April 21, 2010, from http://escholarship.bc.edu/education/tecplus/vol5/iss2/art5.

The entire issue of *Teaching Exceptional Children*, September/October 2009, is about instruction and autism spectrum disorders.

**social stories** that describe a situation from the perspective of the student and direct the young person to practise the appropriate behaviour. For an example of a social story, see Figure 4.2. "I will" cards use a similar strategy to help students respond to their peers (Boutot, 2009). Interventions have been developed using video to explicitly teach children with autism that others have intentions and emotions (Steiner-Bell, 1998) and, using applied behaviour analysis (ABA) principles, to teach children with autism to question peers about their "favourites" (Vieira, 2010). Remember that you are an effective model for classmates about how to interact with those with autism.

### GENERAL ADAPTATIONS AND MODIFICATIONS

When teaching, use visual approaches, **reinforcers** that you know work for this student, and task analysis to keep tasks at a level that reduces frustration. Make the theme of the learning consistent with the lesson for others in the class. When others are writing about highlights of the day in a journal, ask the child with autism to use a photograph from a magazine (and name it) to communicate "something fun" from that day. Use hands-on activities and allow as much time as the child requires.

It helps to provide a structured, predictable classroom environment. Make a customized visual schedule (Bryan & Gast, 2000) and give advance warning of any changes from the usual schedule and of transitions from activity to activity. Picture Exchange Systems are often used (Bondy & Frost, 1994). Minimize distracting auditory stimuli (e,g., fans) and distracting visual stimuli around the student's desk, and remove textures the student finds aversive for a calm learning environment.

## Asperger Syndrome: Characteristics and Differentiating

**Asperger syndrome (AS)** is a lifelong developmental condition, characterized by severe and sustained impairment in social interaction and the development of restricted, repetitive patterns of behaviour, interests, and activities (Cederlund et al., 2010). In contrast to autism, a child with AS is unlikely to experience significant delays in the acquisition of language, adaptive behaviour (other than social interaction), cognitive development, self-help skills, or curiosity about the environment.

Students with Asperger syndrome are characterized by a qualitative impairment in social interaction. They are often enthusiastic about relating to others but challenged by the complexity of the language, and approach others in unusual ways. They misinterpret social cues, lack empathy, appear socially awkward, are unaware of the rules of conversation, and need explicit instruction in social skills. With average or better intelligence, they tend to excel at learning facts but need intensive teaching in reading comprehension, problem solving, and inference making. Frequently, students with AS are **hypersensitive** to sensory stimuli. Flickering and fluorescent lights, as well as loud, unexpected noises are particular irritants, while subdued lighting may be calming. Providing earphones may help. Try reducing class noise by putting tennis balls on the feet of chairs and desks.

Students with AS may be inattentive, easily distracted, and anxious. Some strategies for teaching students with autism and students with learning disabilities will apply, but consider the student's unique learning characteristics and build on their strengths. Boutot (2009) recommends a social coach to help the student with AS daily. Develop a "safe space" in the classroom or the school (Kluth, 2004).

# Teaching Students Who Are Hard of Hearing or Deaf

Students, teachers, administrators, a lot of people in schools just don't know what hearing loss is and don't know how to treat someone with hearing loss or what they have to do so I can understand them. I have to constantly remind the teachers about what I need and I find it really tiring, and I just don't want to do it any more—I shouldn't have to!

*Valerie, 18, with moderate to severe hearing loss in both ears.*

## Characteristics of Students Who Are Hard of Hearing or Deaf

Ontario defines **deaf** and **hard of hearing** students as having an impairment characterized by deficits in language and speech development because of a diminished or non-existent auditory response to sound. There are four categories of hearing loss: mild, moderate, severe, and profound or deaf, depending on the dB (decibel) level an individual can hear. The Canadian Association of the Deaf (www.cad.ca/definition_of_deaf.php) recognizes a person to be deaf when that person has little or no functional hearing and depends upon visual rather than auditory communication. The main characteristics of students who are hard of hearing are they cannot hear well enough to use hearing as a primary channel for learning without relying on visual information and their language development is likely to be influenced. Valerie, described above, is hard of hearing.

A complex array of factors influences learning. Two students with similar hearing loss may have different experiences prior to school and may communicate in different ways. Language development and communication can be affected by:

- the age at the onset of the hearing loss, especially whether the student had already developed spoken language at that time;
- the severity of the hearing loss;
- intelligence; and
- the **hearing status** of the family (a student who is deaf tends to experience higher academic success if the parents are deaf as well).

Young children can experience hearing loss when fluid builds up in the middle ear. Primary teachers might see children failing to respond to their name, asking for directions to be repeated, turning their head to hear, speaking too loudly or too softly, or complaining of earaches. Physicians can insert tubes that drain fluid, reversing the temporary loss of hearing. Teachers who spot these characteristics play an important role in preventing hearing loss and subsequent language delays.

**Put into Practice**

The Literacy and Numeracy Secretariat in Ontario publishes brochures that focus on "Research into Practice."

Read *Using Classroom Amplification in a Universal Design Model to Enhance Hearing and Listening* (by Dr. Pamela Millett), available at: www.edu.gov.on.ca/eng/literacynumeracy/inspire/research/WW_Classroom_Amplification.pdf

Discuss with your peers how you could apply these ideas in your classroom. Consider the dilemmas that may be associated with this strategy. Most strategies work well for some and disadvantage others, or introduce troubling elements along with advantages. What do you think?

## Implications for Learning and Classroom Adaptations for Students with Hearing Loss

You are likely to teach students who are hard of hearing. At first you may experience difficulty understanding their speech, but teachers usually grow accustomed to their manner of speaking in a few days. Ask a student who is reluctant to speak in front of the class to speak with you individually so you can learn the speech patterns. Hard of hearing students may feel isolated because they miss the exchanges that go on in the classroom. Recent research suggests that hard of hearing students experience difficulties with feelings of belongingness, competence and autonomy in the classroom (Dalton, 2010). Without these basic needs being met, they may lack the motivation to put in the effort necessary for them to succeed in a hearing world. It is less likely that you will teach children who use only **American Sign Language (ASL)**, and if children who use ASL are included in your classroom, they will probably be accompanied by an interpreter (for guidance on working with an interpreter, see Atlantic Provinces Special Education Authority, 2001a). There are concerns that deaf children with interpreters may not receive all of the information teachers and peers communicate to hearing students (e.g., Langer, 2007).

### ENHANCING SPEECH-READING

There are many actions you can take to differentiate or adapt your teaching. For students who are **speech-reading**, arrange the classroom so the student can see your face at all times, and get the student's attention before speaking to him or her, but remember that preferential seating is not adequate accommodation (McCormick Richburg & Goldberg, 2005). Allow the student to move during a lesson. Ensure that you don't turn your back (use a projector instead of the board) and don't put

@

**Weblinks**

ONTARIO PROVINCIAL AND
DEMONSTRATION SCHOOLS
www.psbnet.ca/eng/index.html

SIR JAMES WHITNEY SCHOOL FOR
THE DEAF (BELLEVILLE, ONTARIO)
www.psbnet.ca/eng/schools/sjw/
index.html

SAGONASKA DEMONSTRATION SCHOOL
(LEARNING DISABILITIES) (BELLEVILLE,
ONTARIO)
www.psbnet.ca/eng/schools/
sagonaska/index.html

W. ROSS MACDONALD SCHOOL FOR
THE BLIND (BRANTFORD, ONTARIO)
www.psbnet.ca/eng/schools/
wross/index.html

THE ROBARTS SCHOOL FOR THE DEAF
(LONDON, ONTARIO)
www.psbnet.ca/eng/schools/
robarts/index.html

AMETHYST DEMONSTRATION SCHOOL
(LEARNING DISABILITIES) (LONDON,
ONTARIO)
www.psbnet.ca/eng/schools/
amethyst/index.html

ERNEST C. DRURY SCHOOL FOR THE
DEAF (MILTON, ONTARIO)
www.psbnet.ca/eng/schools/ecd/
index.html

TRILLIUM DEMONSTRATION SCHOOL
(LEARNING DISABILITIES) (MILTON,
ONTARIO)
www.psbnet.ca/eng/schools/
trillium/index.html

CENTRE JULES-LÉGER (OTTAWA, ONTARIO)
www.centrejulesleger.com/index2.
htm

HARD OF HEARING AND DEAF STUDENTS:
A RESOURCE GUIDE TO SUPPORT
CLASSROOM TEACHERS (BC MINISTRY
OF EDUCATION)
www.bced.gov.bc.ca/specialed/
hearimpair/toc.htm

CODI: CORNUCOPIA OF DISABILITY
INFORMATION—HEARING IMPAIRMENTS
http://codi.buffalo.edu/hearing.htm

**Further Reading**

Padden, C.A. & Humphries, T.L. (2005). *Inside Deaf culture*. Cambridge, MS: Harvard University Press.

Garay, S.V. (2003). Listening to the voices of deaf students: Essential transition issues. *Teaching Exceptional Children, 35*(4), 44–48.

Atlantic Provinces Special Education Authority, (2001). *Support for students who are deaf or hard of hearing in an inclusive setting.* Halifax, NS: Atlantic Provinces Special Education Authority.

your hands in front of your face. Speak normally and avoid making distracting gestures. Some words, such as *bat*, *pat*, and *mat*, sound the same when you pronounce them. Try to put words like this into context, especially during spelling dictation. If other students ask questions, repeat them so the student who is deaf or hard of hearing knows what was asked. Summaries at the end of lessons give all students a second chance to take in information. Sit the class in a circle for group discussions.

You can convey important messages visually, as well as orally; for example, many students will benefit from having an agenda and assignments listed on the board. Use visual aids, written summaries, and **manipulatives**. The student with hearing loss will benefit from your **pre-teaching** new vocabulary. Pay attention to, and try to diffuse, the student's frustration. You can plan the day's work so periods of intense concentration are interspersed with less-demanding activities. For more information about including a student who is deaf or hard of hearing, see Figure 4.3.

## SYSTEMS OF AMPLIFICATION

Classrooms often have excessive background noise and reverberation, which interfere with accurate speech perception. Degradation of the speech signal can be reduced for children who are hard of hearing by using **frequency modulation (FM)** devices in the classroom to enhance the speech-to-noise ratio (S/N) of the teacher's voice. There are three types of S/N-enhancing FM devices currently used in classrooms: FM systems linked to personal **hearing aids**, sound field system with speakers placed throughout the classroom, and personal sound field system placed on the student's desk. Carpeted classrooms are best for all these systems; alternatively, place tennis balls over the feet of the desks. **Amplification** makes speech

## FIGURE 4.3 TIPS FOR TEACHERS OF STUDENTS WHO ARE DEAF OR HARD OF HEARING

- Ensure students who are hard of hearing can see your face all the time to speech-read and to understand non-verbal communication.
- Smile to encourage, invite, and include.
- Natural lighting is important. Don't stand in front of lights or windows, as they put your face in shadow.
- Speak naturally. Talking very loudly or over-enunciating does not help; in fact, it makes it harder.
- Discuss the best seating arrangement in the room with the student. Work out the best place for receiving maximum information within the normal flow of classroom activities.
- Vocabulary lists with definitions of new terms and concepts help the student to develop a personal dictionary. Provide vocabulary before it is used.
- An outline of the class agenda—three or four points on the board—helps students get a sense of purpose, direction, and timing for short term work which fits into the long range planning.
- Course or grade outline of the topics and kind of work to be done may be useful.
- Provide an outline of a typical school day with the student's own timetable. Include room numbers and a list of people who can assist (e.g. counsellor, school secretary).
- If there is class discussion or group work, it is useful to summarize on the board or have the groups report their work on large paper that can be read as a group.
- Use of overheads, visuals, handouts, and outlines may be helpful.
- Other students in the class may be asked to volunteer as a buddy note-taker.
- Remember that fatigue sets in after hours of speech-reading and straining to understand.

Sources: Adapted from BC Ministry of Education, www.bced.gov.bc.ca/specialed/hearimpair/tip15.htm.

louder, not clearer, and also amplifies background noise (Anderson, 2003). Expect new devices based on technological advances and remember to speak clearly, stay still while talking, and allow the student to see your face.

# Teaching Children with Low Vision and Blindness

While the grade 3 students shouted goodbye, Amber painstakingly packed her books on tape, laptop, and thick pages of Braille into her backpack and then asked her teacher, "Did I get everything I need to finish my work?" Her teacher thought about how hard Amber would work at home to complete the day's lessons. "Don't work too hard tonight, Amber." Amber answered, "I'll try not to. But I still have a lot of questions in math." Her voice sounded heavy; Amber knew that when you can't see, everything takes longer.

*Adapted from Hutchinson, 2004 (2nd ed.), p. 9.*

## Characteristics of Students with Blindness and Low Vision

Ontario Ministry of Education defines **blindness** and **low vision** as a condition of partial or total impairment of sight or vision that even with correction affects educational performance adversely. These students cannot participate with ease in everyday activities and need accommodations such as **Braille**, **taped books**, and access to technology. They may also have alternative outcomes like mobility training.

Children and adolescents can experience deteriorating vision at any age, and teachers often identify students who need to be assessed. Student complaints may signal a need for correction or a condition such as a brain tumour. Pay attention to the appearance of the eyes (e.g., reddened, encrusted, frequent sties). Listen to student complaints (e.g., headaches, burning eyes, blurred print, difficulty reading the board). Also observe behavioural signs (e.g., the student squints or tilts head extremely while reading). For a complete list of characteristics, consult the *Special Education Handbook* (Elementary Teachers' Federation of Ontario, 2007). Record your observations and encourage parents to seek a vision assessment.

Students who cannot learn social skills through observation may need instruction in areas such as body language and eye contact from a **vision teacher** (Janssen et al., 2007), and educational assistants can play a role in their early literacy (Forster & Holbrook, 2005). Vision enables young children to explore their environment, so students with low vision or blindness may have had restricted exploration and movement. Without mobility and independence training in the preschool years, they may experience global delays in development (cognitive, motor, social) from lack of experience rather than from lack of ability (McAllister & Gray, 2007).

## Implications for Learning and Classroom Adaptations for Visual Impairments

Students with visual disabilities and blindness are likely to need adaptation and differentiation in four areas: presentation of information, classroom environment and organization, learning resources, and assessment.

**Further Reading**

On students who are deaf-blind:

Council for the Advancement of Communication with Deaf People. (2002). *Deafblind awareness curriculum.* London, UK: Council for the Advancement of Communication with Deaf People.

McInnes, J.M. (Ed.) (1999). *A guide to planning and support for individuals who are deafblind.* Toronto, ON: University of Toronto Press.

On students who are blind:

Hersch, M.A., Johnson, M.A., & Keating, D. (2007). *Assistive technology for the vision-impaired and blind.* New York, NY: Springer.

Landau, S., Russell, M., & Ern, J.N. (2006). Using the talking tactile tablet as a testing accommodation. *RE:view: Rehabilitation Education for Blindness and Visual Impairment, 38*(1), 7–21.

MacCuspie, P.A. (1996). *Promoting acceptance of children with disabilities: From tolerance to inclusion.* Halifax, NS: Atlantic Provinces Special Education Authority.

Schaefer, L.M. (2008). *Some kids are blind.* Mankato, MN: Capstone Press

**Weblinks**

TEACHING STUDENTS WITH VISUAL IMPAIRMENTS: A GUIDE FOR THE SUPPORT TEAM (SASKATCHEWAN LEARNING) www.sasked.gov.sk.ca/branches/curr/special_ed/docs/guides/blind/teachwithvi.pdf

SPECIAL EDUCATION TECHNOLOGY BRITISH COLUMBIA (SET-BC) www.setbc.org

SPECIAL NEEDS OPPORTUNITY WINDOWS (SNOW) ADAPTIVE TECHNOLOGY ON-LINE WORKSHOPS FOR EDUCATORS AND PARAEDUCATORS http://snow.utoronto.ca/index.php

## What do you think?

Recently, news articles have appeared stating that a decline in Braille reading among young blind people will lead to a generation of functionally illiterate blind adults. Currently, only about 10 percent of blind people read Braille, though it often is an indicator of professional success, according to the National Federation of the Blind (an American organization). More than 80 percent of blind people who are employed know Braille. What do you think is the connection between reliance on computer technology and Braille use? Research this issue in the electronic archives of major newspapers from a number of counties. How widespread is the decline in Braille use?

See The Braille Crisis by K. Engelhart in *Maclean's*, May 6, 2010, www2.macleans.ca/2010/05/06/the-braille-crisis

### Further Reading

Brown, R.T., Rickel, A.U., & Daly, B.P. (2007). *Chronic illness in children and adolescents.* Toronto, ON: Hogrefe & Huber.

Clark, C. (2003). *In sickness and in play: Coping with chronic illness.* Piscataway, NJ: Rutgers University Press.

DePaepe, P., Garrison-Kane, L., & Doelling, J. (2002). Supporting students with health needs in schools: An overview of selected health conditions. *Focus on Exceptional Children, 35*(1), 1–24.

Lightfoot, J., et al. (2001). Supporting pupils with special health needs in mainstream schools: Policy and practice. *Children and Society, 15,* 57–69.

Taras, H., & Potts-Datema, W. (2005). Chronic health conditions and student performance at school. *Journal of School Health, 75*(7), 255–266.

## ADAPTING PRESENTATION OF INFORMATION AND ORGANIZATION

In adapting the presentation of information, you may work closely with a vision teacher, educational assistant, or resource teacher. The specific adaptations depend on how the student acquires information—substituting other senses for vision (auditory and tactile), using partial vision, or both. Give directions and notes verbally, as well as visually, and provide three-dimensional models of visual concepts (for an example, see Jones et al., 2006). For students with partial vision, enlarge print (usually to 130 percent on a photocopier or 18-point font) and enhance contrast of written materials. Experiment to see whether coloured acetate (e.g., yellow or pale blue) enhances the contrast or if particular contrasts of paper and print are easiest for the student to read. A peer may serve as note taker. You can make large-print copies of chalkboard notes and overheads. You may need to order books on tape and adaptive technology from the provincial resource centre, W. Ross Macdonald School Resource Services (www.psbnet.ca/eng/schools/wross/index.html).

Organize your classroom and use a seating arrangement so that students with partial vision have the best view possible of the board and of demonstrations. Enclosed (rather than open-concept) classrooms with reduced clutter are safer for these students. Ensure that everyone keeps possessions off the floor, move the furniture as little as possible, and warn the student who cannot easily see about any changes. The organization of learning activities can foster inclusion. Form groups that enable these students to practise social and communication skills with empathic peers. Work with the vision or resource teacher, who may be instructing them in eye contact, body language, and facial expression, and helping to eliminate behaviours that stimulate the eyes, such as eye poking. For strategies, see Figure 4.4.

## ADAPTING RESOURCES AND ASSESSMENT

There are many learning resources for students with visual impairments, including large-print books and Braille books. Computer technology includes Braillers combined with word processors, programs that convert print to audio output, and

## FIGURE 4.4 TIPS FOR TEACHERS OF STUDENTS WHO ARE VISUALLY IMPAIRED

1. Point out the classroom rules to which the student must adhere.
2. Expect the same quality of work, rather than the same quantity.
3. Don't move furniture in the classroom without warning the student.
4. Reduce glare on boards, desks, etc.
5. Provide multi-sensory experiences, learning by doing, and support without dependence.
6. Stress legibility, not size, as student will tend to print or write in large size, if at all.
7. Remind individual speakers to name themselves (name the speaker if students forget).
8. Remind classmates to provide non-visual feedback (like saying "well done" instead of nodding).
9. Encourage peers to be friends, not helpers.
10. Encourage the student to talk with you so that you can understand the student's perspective and help the student feel like an integral part of the community in the classroom.

Source: Based on Hutchinson, N.L. (2004). *Teaching exceptional children and adolescents: A Canadian casebook* (2nd ed.), p. 13. Prentice Hall. Used by permission.

speech-activated word processors. An IEP usually ensures funding for technology, three-dimensional maps and tape measures, and other learning materials. You may need to plan six months ahead to ensure receipt of Braille textbooks, books on tape, and large-print or tactile learning materials before they are needed by the student.

The work and learning of students with low vision and blindness can be evaluated by extending time frames for test taking and homework assignments and by testing students orally. Braille or large-print formats may be necessary, or assessments can be completed on a computer or under supervision in a resource room.

# Teaching Students with Physical Disabilities and Chronic Medical Conditions

In Ontario, physical disability is defined in the *Education Act* as a condition of such severe physical limitation or deficiency as to require special assistance in learning situations to provide the opportunity for educational achievement equivalent to that of pupils without exceptionalities who are of the same age or developmental level.

At least 15 percent of students experience a serious illness or health condition before the age of 18 (Bethell et al., 2008). Many physical disabilities and chronic medical disorders influence the social participation and learning of children and adolescents (Wodrich & Cunningham, 2007). These conditions result from genetic, environmental, and unknown causes and may be transient, lifelong, or life threatening. Students experience unpredictable changes due to deteriorating health, recurring surgery, **remission**, and side effects of medication. Each physical condition presents differently from case to case, and how well families and individuals cope interacts with the physical condition. Read your students' files before the term starts, and familiarize yourself with characteristics, emergency responses, and teaching strategies that you will need for the students you will teach in the term ahead.

Physical and chronic health disorders are difficult to categorize depending on whether you focus on the area of dysfunction, the cause, or the impact. A student is considered to have a physical disability or chronic medical disorder, based on the need for differentiated teaching or special education services, because of one or more of the following: nervous system impairment, musculoskeletal condition, or chronic health impairment (BC Special Education Branch, 2008).

## Nervous System Impairment

**Nervous system impairment** or **neurological dysfunction** results from damage or dysfunction of the brain or spinal cord that occurred before, during, or after birth. We discuss cerebral palsy, spina bifida, epilepsy, Tourette syndrome, brain injury, and fetal alcohol spectrum disorders. Only some students have IPRCs (e.g., those with cerebral palsy), but all will need differentiated teaching and social support at some time.

### CEREBRAL PALSY

> On Wednesday, nobody understood what I wanted. Most days I can point or just wheel over. I've got lots of words inside my head, but people don't seem to hear

**Put into Practice**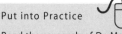

Read *On Being Sarah,* written by Elizabeth Helfman (Albert Whiman and Co., 1992). Think about how you might use a book like this to help this student feel less alone. Look for other similar books and compile a list of resources for exceptional children to read or listen to about others like themselves.

Consult:

Maples, L., & Applin, J.L. (2009). Stories that promote understanding of children with special needs. *Community and Junior College Libraries, 15*(4), 176–187.

**Put into Practice**

Read the research of Dr. Marcia Barnes of the University of Guelph on students with spina bifida and discuss with your classmates the implications for teaching. For example, Barnes (2004) reports that children with spina bifida and who have hydrocephalus have particular difficulty comprehending text even when they can decode or sound the words.

Barnes, M.A., et al. (2004). Meaning construction and integration in children with hydrocephalus. *Brain and Language, 89,* 47–56.

Barnes, M.A., et al. (2006). Arithmetic processing in children with spina bifida: Calculation accuracy, strategy use, and fact retrieval fluency. *Journal of Learning Disabilities, 39,* 174–187.

Lomax-Bream, L.E., Barnes, M.A., Fletcher, J.M., & Swank, P. (2007). Role of early parenting and motor skills on development in children with spina bifida. *Journal of Applied Developmental Psychology, 28,* 250–263.

**Further Reading**

Angell, M.E., Stoner, J.B., & Fulk, B.M. (2010). Advice from adults with physical disabilities on fostering self-determination during the school years. *Teaching Exceptional Children, 42*(3), 64–75.

Jenks, K.M. et al. (2009). Arithmetic difficulties in children with cerebral palsy are related to executive function and working memory. *Journal of Child Psychology and Psychiatry, 50*(7), 824–833.

Palisano, R.J. et al. (2009). Mobility experiences of adolescents with cerebral palsy. *Physical and Occupational Therapy in Pediatrics, 29*(2), 133–153.

*@*

**Weblinks**

SPINA BIFIDA AND HYDROCEPHALUS CANADA
http://sbhac.ca/beta

SPINA BIFIDA AND HYDROCEPHALUS ASSOCIATION OF ONTARIO
www.sbhao.on.ca

SPINA BIFIDA ASSOCIATION
www.sbaa.org

**Put into Practice**

Interview an adult with cerebral palsy. View the 11-minute video, *Never Say Never*, available from the Cerebral Palsy Association in Alberta (fax: 403-543-1168) or the 29-minute video, Kids with Courage, developed at Johns Hopkins University in Baltimore, Maryland (2004) by L. Poole et al. Consult provincial associations for cerebral palsy, such as www.cpalberta.com.

them like I do. Some days, even my mum doesn't know what I mean. Wednesday was a bad day. Nobody understood. My big yellow school bus was on my top shelf and I wanted to play with it. Dad handed me the blocks instead. Bbbusss . . . That's a hard word to say.

*Yates, 1994, pp. 3–5.*

This girl with **cerebral palsy (CP)** speaks little and cannot walk, but has thoughts to express. Cerebral palsy describes a group of disorders affecting body movement and muscle coordination resulting from brain damage during pregnancy or before age three. This damage interferes with messages between brain and body, and can lead to developmental disabilities, hearing impairment, learning disabilities, and seizures. Degree of physical disability does not indicate level of intelligence.

The effects vary widely. At its mildest, CP causes awkward movement and poor muscle control. At its most severe, CP may result in almost no muscle control, profoundly affecting movement and speech (Palisano et al., 2009). Depending on which areas of the brain are damaged, one or more of the following may occur:

- muscle tightness or spasm;
- involuntary movement;
- difficulty with gross-motor skills such as walking or running;
- difficulty with fine-motor skills such as writing and speaking; and
- abnormal perception and sensation.

Treat students with CP as normally as possible and don't underestimate their ability to learn and participate; they may need more time for everything they do, and may need to repeat themselves when misunderstood. Some use voice output communication aids, which can make it challenging for classmates to take turns in conversation with them (Clarke & Wilkinson, 2008). Learn to help to position and transfer students who use wheelchairs and to push wheelchairs by asking students, parents, physiotherapists. Felt-tipped pens and soft-lead pencils enable the student to exert less pressure when writing, and a rubber grip may help with holding a pencil. Help the student set and reach realistic goals in your classroom. For accommodations consult www.bced.gov.bc.ca/specialed/awareness/33.htm and the work of Wright and his colleagues (2004) on adapting physical activity for students with CP.

## SPINA BIFIDA

I am going to try out for the swim team this year, even though I may not be picked. I have been swimming since I was very young because my parents thought I might get hurt in rough team sports. I have always swum alone, but I really want to be on a team.

*From the diary of a 15-year-old with spina bifida who has leg braces and uses crutches.*

**Spina bifida** is a neural tube defect that occurs within the first four weeks of pregnancy. The spinal cord fails to develop properly, causing damage to the nervous system. It often results in paralysis of the lower limbs, as well as a loss of bladder control, and in 80% of cases is accompanied by **hydrocephalus**, the accumulation of fluid surrounding the brain (http://sbhac.ca/beta). This fluid can cause brain injury if not treated immediately; usually a **shunt** is installed to drain the fluid for re-absorption. Many individuals with spina bifida have developmental disabilities.

You may need to watch for signs of headaches, coordination difficulties, vomiting, and seizures—indications of shunt blockage. Lack of bladder or bowel control can be a barrier to peer acceptance. You can model acceptance and be sensitive to the student's need to leave the classroom unexpectedly. Encourage independence and ensure privacy. Often an educational assistant will help with these functions.

Sitting in a wheelchair makes one vulnerable to sores and skin breakdown. Students need to be positioned properly and moved periodically, and may be advised to use standers, braces, or crutches for part of the day. Treat changes in position as normal occurrences and assist students without drawing undue attention to them. Extended absences from school may result from medical issues. Encourage students to use aids such as computers and calculators, and give them two copies of textbooks: one for school and one for home. Counsellors and parents can help you to increase social participation and acceptance of students with spina bifida (Brislin, 2008).

## EPILEPSY

> Last week I had a seizure at school. Fortunately, my best friend was in the class and stopped some guy from sticking his pencil in my mouth so I wouldn't "swallow my tongue." She told the other kids it was no big deal and not to worry. My friend says the teacher fluttered around like she didn't know what to do. The teacher is being kind of gooey. I think my classmates would forget the whole thing if she would act normal.
>
> *Based on Kaufman, 2005, p. 99.*

**Epilepsy** is a neurological disorder characterized by sudden, brief **seizures,** bursts of electrical energy in the brain, lasting from 10 seconds to 5 minutes. If a seizure lasts longer than 10 minutes, medical attention is required (www.epilepsytoronto.org). Causes include chemical imbalance and head injury. Many children with epilepsy also have another exceptionality (Wodrich et al., 2006). The two main kinds of seizures are **partial seizures** (in one area of the brain) and **generalized seizures** (involving the whole brain). In a partial seizure there may be strange sensations and movements like plucking at clothes, smacking lips, wandering. Complete consciousness is not lost, though confusion usually follows.

Generalized seizures are of two types: simple absence and tonic-clonic. **Simple absence seizures** (formerly called **petit mal**) occur in children; they stare or daydream for up to 15 seconds. There may be small movements in the face, the eyes may roll upward, and the child may be confused about the seconds "missed." If they are not treated, serious learning problems can result. Teachers who notice these seizures should urge parents to seek neurological assessment (DePaepe et al., 2002).

The **tonic-clonic seizure** (formerly called **grand mal)** can be frightening. The student may give a sharp cry before falling to the floor; the muscles stiffen and jerk rhythmically. There may be loss of bladder control, breathing difficulty, and excess saliva. In most cases the seizure will not hurt the student; some school policies require the student be taken to hospital. Medical attention is necessary if the seizure lasts more than 10 minutes or is repeated without full recovery (Epilepsy Toronto).

A child or adolescent with seizures may experience the world as an unpredictable and scary place. Some chat in peer-to-peer networks for support from peers with epilepsy (Lorence & Chen, 2007). Adults' concerns about safety can lead to

### What do you think?

Sex and sexual activity are sensitive issues in both parenting and teaching individuals with disability. Reading on the issue may help you to understand your feelings about it and may help you to be sensitive to the needs of your students, especially adolescents. Relevant Canadian and American sources include:

Kaufman, M., Silverberg, C., & Odette, F. (2007). *The ultimate guide to sex and disability: For all of us who live with disabilities, chronic pain, and illness.* San Francisco, CA: Cleis Press.

Krishnamurthy, K.B., & Osbourne, P. (2007, September). Seizures and teens: Teens, sex, seizures and drugs, what teenage girls and their parents need to know. *Exceptional Parent, 37(9),* 80-81.

Thompson, S.A. (2005). LGBTQ (lesbian, gay, bisexual, transgendered, queer) youth with intellectual disabilities, in J. Sears (Ed.) *Encyclopedia of [Homo]Sexualities, Education and Youth* (pp. 268–272). Toronto, ON: Greenwood Publishing.

### Further Reading

Downing, J.E. (with invited contributors). (2002). *Including students with severe and multiple disabilities in typical classrooms: Practical strategies for teachers.* Baltimore, MD: Paul H. Brookes.

Haslam, R.H., & Valletutti, P.J. (2004). *Medical problems in the classroom: The teacher's role in diagnosis and management* (4th ed.). Austin, TX: PRO-ED, Inc.

Sherwood Best, J., et al. (2004). *Teaching individuals with physical or multiple disabilities.* Toronto, ON: Pearson Education Canada.

### Further Reading

Epilepsy can have an impact on the family life of any child, but especially for an adolescent. The publication *Exceptional Parent* has included a series of articles on adolescents and epilepsy. Here are a few of these articles, which will give you a much greater understanding of the lives of adolescents (and children) who live with epilepsy and seizures.

Shafer, P.O., & Israel, B. (2007, February). Seizures and teens: The practical aspects of managing seizure medications. *Exceptional Parent, 37*(2), 57–59.

Shafer, P.O., & Schachter, S.C. (2007, November). Seizures and teens: Using technology to develop seizure preparedness. *Exceptional Parent, 37*(11), 64–66.

Sundstrom, D. (2007, April). Seizures and teens: Maximizing health and safety. *Exceptional Parent, 37*(4), 77–79.

Weinstein, S.C. (2007, June). Seizures and teens: The impact of seizures and epilepsy on families. *Exceptional Parent, 37*(6), 61–62.

### Put into Practice

Watch a video on epilepsy to reduce your discomfort with intervening when a student has a seizure. Make a brief action plan and discuss it with your peers. Epilepsy Toronto has a comprehensive list of videos on its website (http://epilepsytoronto.org/resourcecentre_videolist.php). Two that are highly recommended are *Understanding Seizure Disorders*, which is eleven minutes long and includes video clips of various types of seizures; and *Seizure First Aid*, ten minutes long with demonstrations of first aid that should be provided to individuals with different types of seizures.

overprotection and contribute to feelings of helplessness; however, you may want to excuse students from activities that include climbing high ropes, operating power tools, etc. You may perceive a student with epilepsy as being unmotivated, not realizing that seizures can have a profound cognitive impact, contributing to inattentiveness and distractibility. Some students feel embarrassed and may act out, which serves to further distance them from their peers. Your support and acceptance is critical. You can consult a special educator or school psychologist to help with targeted interventions (Wodrich & Cunningham, 2007). Many children require administration of medication at school. Medications often have side effects, which range from hyperactivity to sleepiness, and include clumsiness and difficulty thinking or talking (DePaepe et al., 2002). Figure 4.5 lists the specific actions to take during a generalized seizure.

### TOURETTE SYNDROME

> Hi! My name is Russell. I am nie years old and I have TS. I have tics. They really bother me because they keep me awake at night. I get "buggie" when something is frustrating and it makes it hard to work. I don't like it when other kids ask me why I make funny noises. These are some of the tics I have: twirling my hair, arm movements, shrugging my shoulders, sticking my pinky finger in the air, and others.
>
> *Adapted from the Tourette Syndrome Foundation of Canada website (www.tourette.ca).*

### FIGURE 4.5 STRATEGIES FOR HANDLING A GENERALIZED SEIZURE IN THE CLASSROOM

**Before a Seizure**

- Meet with the parents and student at the beginning of the year. Learn the characteristics of the student's seizures.
- Familiarize yourself with the school's policies.
- Discuss with the family how to inform the class that a seizure may occur.
- Keep the area surrounding the student's desk free of objects that could cause harm to the student during a seizure.

**During a Seizure**

- Stay calm and keep the students calm. Remind them that the seizure is painless. Ask another teacher to remove excited students from the classroom.
- Ease the student to the floor and loosen clothing.
- Try to remove any hard, sharp, or hot objects that might injure the student.
- Place a blanket, coat, or cushion under the student's head to soften the impact of the seizure.
- Place the student on his or her side to allow saliva to flow from the mouth.
- Write down the time the seizure began. If a seizure lasts longer than 10 minutes, medical attention may be needed.
- Refrain from restraining the student or placing objects in the student's mouth.
- Refrain from giving the student food or drink.

**After a Seizure**

- Allow the student to rest or sleep and then offer the opportunity to resume classroom activities.
- Be attuned to the student's emotional state, as most (but not all) students can rejoin classroom activities.
- The student should not leave the school alone if weakness or convulsive behaviours persist.
- Refrain from "fussing over" the student with epilepsy. Foster an attitude of understanding and acceptance. The student with epilepsy needs support from you and peers.

**Tourette syndrome (TS)** is a complex neurological disorder modulated by psychological and social factors. It is characterized by **tics**: involuntary, rapid, sudden muscular movements; uncontrollable vocal sounds; and inappropriate words. Symptoms appear between the ages of 2 and 18 and change over time. Stress aggravates TS symptoms; thus structure and predictability at school result in fewer disruptions. Typically, tics decrease with concentration on an absorbing task, so engaging teaching helps students with TS. These children may also have learning disabilities, obsessive-compulsive behaviours, and attentional difficulties. Symptoms appear to be more severe in students with concomitant conditions like attention deficit disorder. Working closely with families can be very effective (Christner & Dieker, 2008). When teaching a student with Tourette syndrome in a classroom:

- be patient and engage all students fully;
- respond to tics with tolerance, not anger—the student cannot control them;
- encourage the student to leave the room for a short time when tics occur;
- provide a quiet place in the classroom for the student to work or take tests;
- minimize stress by differentiating, using structure, and eliminating chaos; and
- seek assistance from counsellors, psychologists, and parents.

## BRAIN INJURY

> How I hated going to school! It was almost a year after my brain injury. I was still relearning to read and write and even to remember. I felt myself getting more and more down. Most of my teachers were helpful, and I had a tutor who helped me write my assignments and read my textbooks. But it was really the counsellor who got me through.
>
> *Mark, reflecting on returning to school (based on Acorn and Offer, 1998).*

Brain injury, which happens when the brain's tissue is damaged or not able to function properly, is also called **acquired (ABI)** or **traumatic brain injury (TBI)**, or **head injury**. Many brain injuries are acquired, the result of a blow to the head from a fall, a sports injury, or a cycling or vehicle accident. Cycling and vehicle accidents are responsible for most brain injuries to youths (Bennett et al., 2003). Students with brain injury experience difficulties remembering, understanding, organizing, and planning that interfere with their ability to function in school. They often have physical effects such as paralysis and vision and hearing loss. Anti-social behaviour, impulsiveness, confusion, and inappropriate or immature language and behaviour can result (Bullock et al., 2005). For a thorough description of the learning characteristics of students with ABI, consult *Educating Educators about ABI: Resource Book* (Bennett et al., 2003). Strategies for teaching these students appear similar to those used with students who have LD. However, there are important differences between the needs of these two groups. Bennett et al. describe the strategies for students with ABI as redirecting (steering a person away from their preoccupation), restructuring (focusing on the relevant, ignoring the irrelevant), and the "back door approach" (implemented without the person being confronted). Because they know themselves as they were prior to the brain injury, students with ABI may hold onto their pre-trauma academic and career aspirations, although these have become unrealistic. Realistic goals are essential but can be discouraging (Balaban et al., 2009; Hawley, 2004). Figure 4.6 contains strategies for adaptations in the classroom.

**What do you think?**

Many people with epilepsy feel they are discriminated against. View the website of Epilepsy Toronto (www.epilepsytoronto.org) and of Epilepsy Canada (www.epilepsy.ca), and then discuss with your classmates this charge of unfair treatment.

**Cross-Reference**

Chapter 3 contains information about mild intellectual disabilities, while the current chapter contains information about developmental disabilities, which are more severe intellectual disabilities.

**Further Reading**

The Tourette Syndrome Foundation of Canada has developed a resource guide for educators called *Circle of Support* and a handbook, *Understanding Tourette Syndrome: A Handbook for Educators,* both available from the website (www.tourette.ca). *Circle of Support* includes a DVD, an interactive workbook, a facilitator's guide, symptom checklists, and a copy of *Understanding Tourette Syndrome.*

Christner, B., & Dieker, L.A. (2008). Tourette syndrome: A collaborative approach focused on empowering students, families, and teachers. *Teaching Exceptional Children, 40*(5), 44–51.

## Further Reading

Acorn, S., & Offer, P. (Eds.). (1998). *Living with brain injury: A guide for families and caregivers.* Toronto, ON: University of Toronto Press.

Bennett, S., Good, D., & Kumpf, J. (2003). *Educating educators about ABI: Resource book.* St. Catharines, ON: Ontario Brain Injury Association, www.abieducation.com.

Bullock, L.M., Gable, R.A., & Mohr, J.D. (2005). Traumatic brain injury: A challenge for educators. *Preventing School Failure, 49*(4), 6–10.

Hawley, C.A. (2004). Behaviour and school performance after brain injury. *Brain Injury, 18*(7), 645–659.

Jameson, L., & Jameson, B. (2007). *Brain injury survivor's guide: Welcome to our world.* Parker, CO: Outskirts Press, Inc.

## FIGURE 4.6 STRATEGIES FOR TEACHING STUDENTS WITH BRAIN INJURY IN A CLASSROOM SETTING

### Strategies for Physical Adaptations

- Schedule rest breaks; have a shortened day. Schedule more difficult classes early in the day.
- Provide adapted equipment or assistance, including scribes, without drawing undue attention.

### Strategies for Language Adaptations

- Use shorter, simpler sentences, with pictures and gestures to aid comprehension.
- Teach the student to ask for clarification or repetition at a slower rate.

### Strategies for Cognitive Adaptations

- Remove distractions and limit the amount of information on a page.
- Provide focusing cues and visual cues, or a set of steps to follow.
- Adjust the length of assignments to the student's attention span; limit the number of steps.
- Use rehearsal to strengthen memory; have the student practise aloud.
- Use a tape recorder or note-taker instead of having the student write notes.
- Teach the student to overcome word-finding problems by describing the item.
- Give prior warning for transitions; make transitions clear and structured.
- Role-play appropriate responses and stop inappropriate responses as soon as they begin.

### Strategies for Social Adaptations

- Make asking for assistance a student goal; remind the student to seek assistance.
- Check work after a small amount is begun to reassure the student that he can do it.
- Emphasize personal progress; discourage comparisons to classmates.
- Arrange for counselling to deal with frustration and aggression.
- Model patience and understanding to the class in your relations with the student.

## FETAL ALCOHOL SPECTRUM DISORDERS (FASD)

## Weblinks

FASLINK FETAL ALCOHOL DISORDERS SOCIETY
www.faslink.org

ALBERTA EDUCATION. (2004). TEACHING STUDENTS WITH FETAL ALCOHOL SPECTRUM DISORDER: BUILDING STRENGTHS, CREATING HOPE. (PROGRAMMING FOR STUDENTS WITH SPECIAL NEEDS, BOOK 10.)
http://education.alberta.ca/admin/special/resources/fasd.aspx

SASKATCHEWAN LEARNING. (2004). PLANNING FOR STUDENTS WITH FETAL ALCOHOL SPECTRUM DISORDER.
www.sasked.gov.sk.ca/branches/curr/special_ed/docs/misc/fasd2004.pdf

MANITOBA EDUCATION, TRAINING, AND YOUTH (2001). *TOWARDS INCLUSION: TAPPING HIDDEN STRENGTHS—PLANNING FOR STUDENTS WHO ARE ALCOHOL-AFFECTED.*
www.edu.gov.mb.ca/k12/specedu/fas/pdf/intro.pdf

CANADIAN CENTRE ON SUBSTANCE ABUSE: FASD INFORMATION SERVICE
www.ccsa.ca/eng/topics/populations/fetalalcoholspectrum/pages/default.aspx

My daughter, Faye, doesn't have an easy time in school. She doesn't have any close friends. Faye has fetal alcohol syndrome. Her birth mother's drinking during pregnancy caused Faye's mild intellectual disability, small stature, unusual facial features, and damage to her central nervous system. She needs reminders about how to behave normally around people and verbal cues for everything. Her brain just doesn't work like yours and mine.

*From a speech given by the mother of a girl with fetal alcohol syndrome.*

**Prenatal alcohol exposure** can lead to significant neurodevelopmental disabilities, now recognized as **fetal alcohol spectrum disorders (FASD)**. This includes both **fetal alcohol syndrome (FAS)**, a lifelong birth defect (with growth deficiency in height and weight, facial abnormalities including small eyes, and brain impairment), and a wider range of enduring learning and behaviour deficits often called **partial fetal alcohol syndrome (PFAS)** (with few or no facial abnormalities), and **alcohol-related neurodevelopmental disorder (ARND)** (without facial or growth abnormalities) (Olson et al., 2007). Recent research suggests that even occasional alcohol consumption during pregnancy can cause neurodevelopmental damage.

FASDs are difficult to diagnose, perhaps because the characteristics are similar to other exceptionalities and some mothers resist acknowledging responsibility for their children's disabilities. Students with FASD can be chatty and charming; however, they show impaired rates of learning, poor memory, and difficulty generalizing. They often act impulsively, exhibit short attention spans, and have difficulty recognizing patterns and predicting common sense outcomes. Parents describe a

## FIGURE 4.7 STRATEGIES FOR CLASSROOM MANAGEMENT OF STUDENTS WITH FASD

- Place the student near the front of the room to help with focus.
- Allow the student to have short breaks when necessary.
- Set limits and follow them consistently.
- Change rewards often to keep interest in rewards high.
- Have pre-established consequences for misbehaviour.
- Review and repeat consequences of behaviours. Ask the student to tell you the consequences.
- Do not debate or argue over rules already established: "Just do it."
- Notice and comment when the student is behaving appropriately.
- Avoid threats.
- Redirect behaviour.
- Monitor the student carefully.
- Intervene before behaviour escalates.
- Protect the student from being exploited. These students are naive.

lack of social judgment. Difficulty understanding cause and effect appears to be an integral part of FASD (Olson et al., 2007), and children do not "outgrow" FASD. Consistency in behaviour management across home and school usually helps. Figure 4.7 includes strategies for behaviour management for home and school. There is little research to guide effective interventions for students with FASD (Burd, 2007; Premji et al., 2006). Figure 4.8 includes strategies for teaching students with FASD.

## Musculoskeletal Conditions

Two **musculoskeletal conditions** that can affect all aspects of a student's life are muscular dystrophy and juvenile arthritis. They have different characteristics, treatments, and educational implications.

### MUSCULAR DYSTROPHY

> Having muscular dystrophy is hard. My muscles are very weak and I can't walk any more. I use a wheelchair. Some days I feel sad but mostly I am tired. I am glad I can

## FIGURE 4.8 STRATEGIES FOR TEACHING STUDENTS WITH FASD

- Use concrete, hands-on learning methods.
- Establish routines and follow them; when you vary the routine, give the student ample warning.
- Avoid surprises and loud noises.
- Post a visual schedule.
- Give short and simple directions.
- Have the student repeat back his or her understanding of directions.
- Whenever you can, use the same directions as in the past.
- Give one task at a time. Repeat tasks.
- Provide a calculator and other aids to enable the student to succeed.
- Reduce the auditory and visual distractions in the classroom.
- Put a small number of tasks on a page with white space around them.
- Notice and comment when the student is doing well.
- Work with the family to maintain consistency as much as possible.
- For younger students, use a communication book daily between school and home.
- For older students, work out a regular means of age-appropriate communication.

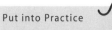

### Weblinks

ONTARIO BRAIN INJURY ASSOCIATION
www.obia.on.ca

BRAIN INJURY ASSOCIATION OF CANADA
www.biac-aclc.ca

NEUROSCIENCE FOR KIDS
http://faculty.washington.edu/chudler/neurok.html

### Put into Practice

Two recent papers report on teaching approaches that "work" for students with FASD. Read these papers and discuss the implications for regular classroom teachers with your peers.

Coles, C.D., Strickland, D.C., Padgett, L., & Bellmoff, L. (2007). Games that "work": Using computer games to teach alcohol-affected children about fire and street safety. *Research in Developmental Disabilities, 28*, 518–530.

Laugeson, E.A., Paley, B., Schonfeld, A.M., Carpenter, E.M., Frankel, F., & O'Connor, M.J. (2007). Adaptation of the children's friendship training program for children with fetal alcohol spectrum disorders. *Child and Family Behavior Therapy, 29*(3), 57–69.

### Further Reading

These sources can help you to develop an insider's perspective on arthritis:

Murphy-Melas, E., & Hartman, A. (2002). *Keeping a secret: A story about juvenile rheumatoid arthritis.* Albuquerque, NM: Health Press, NA.

Miller, D.D.L. (2002). *Taking arthritis to school.* Plainview, NY: JayJo Books.

*I am brave: Children living with arthritis*: www.arthritis.ca/local/files/pdf%20documents/TAS_I_AM_BRAVE_E.pdf [Search for "I am Brave" (Booklet written by children and adolescents with juvenile arthritis.)]

For classroom strategies see: www.arthritis.org (search for "school").

**Weblinks**

MUSCULAR DYSTROPHY CANADA
www.muscle.ca

ARTHRITIS CANADA
www.arthritiscanada.com

THE ARTHRITIS SOCIETY
www.arthritis.ca

**Put into Practice**

Obtain a copy of the IEP form used in your school district. Compare it to the IEP for Brenda Piet shown in Figure 2.4 on page 41.

**What do you think?**

Is obesity a chronic health condition?

Many think that Canada is in the midst of a childhood obesity crisis. In 2009, Health Canada reported that over the past 25 years, obesity rates in Canadian children and youth have nearly tripled. Is obesity now a chronic health condition? What role should schools and educators play in changing health habits and physical activity levels of children and youth? Glenn Young, a BC teacher, has developed a program in which "Fitkids" serve as coaches for their classmates. You can read about it in:

Young, G. (2010). Fitkids coaches: Showing classmates the way. *Physical and Health Education Journal, 75*(4), 12–14.

---

talk to my teacher. Sometimes I worry about the future and what will happen to me, but my Mom reminds me to live the best I can every day and that is what I try to do.

*Marc, 12, has muscular dystrophy.*

**Muscular dystrophy (MD)** refers to a group of genetically-based neuromuscular disorders that result in progressive muscle weakness. Muscle tissue is replaced by fatty tissue and connective tissue, which causes the muscles to weaken and eventually waste away, making it difficult to speak, breathe, or move. Each form of MD is caused by an error in a specific gene associated with muscle function; however, several individuals with the same disorder may experience the disorder and its symptoms quite differently. **Duchenne muscular dystrophy (DMD)** is the most common form, with marked physical degeneration occurring during the school years.

Symptoms of DMD are first noted between two and five years of age and include difficulty in climbing stairs. A wheelchair is usually necessary by early adolescence and breathing is increasingly affected. Behavioural issues often arise, as well as poor verbal memory, suggesting delayed language and poor social skills (Hinton et al., 2004), both of which can have wide-ranging consequences in highly social classrooms. Lifespan is shortened, with death typically occurring during the twenties.

At school, care must be taken to avoid overactivity and fatigue. Because the disease is progressive, the needs of the student are continually changing, including their needs for assistive technology (Heller et al., 2009). Because the student is coping with the prospect of a reduced lifespan, emotional support is as critical as differentiated teaching (Talbot, 2002). For information on all aspects of MD, including recent research developments, visit the website of Muscular Dystrophy Canada (www.muscle.ca).

### JUVENILE ARTHRITIS

No one knows for sure what causes juvenile arthritis. Mine was diagnosed when I was eight. I was upset because I played sports, played the piano, and was good at art. My treatment team has helped me to take charge of my life. I play the piano even though I can't practise when my hands are swollen. Now I am 18. Some days I can't get out of bed, but those days are rare. With the help of my family, friends, and teachers I do well in school and will go to university next year. You can take charge of your arthritis, too.

*From Helen's speech to children recently diagnosed with juvenile arthritis, at a conference for families.*

**Juvenile arthritis (JA),** which refers to continuous **inflammation** of one or more joints lasting at least six weeks for which no other cause can be found, is a chronic arthritic condition present before the age of 16. Juvenile arthritis can be difficult to detect. Doctors look for signs of joint swelling or loss of mobility that suggest inflamed joints. Students may complain of stiffness or pain, walk with a limp, or have difficulty using an arm or leg. The **immune system** seems to be overactive, inflaming joints as if fighting an infection when none is present. Most children have an up-and-down course for many years; treatment includes physiotherapy and occupational therapy.

Students with JA tend to feel stiffness and pain after sitting in one position and may need to stand or move around in the middle of a class. Because of low stamina, they may require a shorter day or rest breaks. Medication will probably have to be taken during the school day and usually must be taken with food to prevent adverse effects on the gastrointestinal tract. Fever is a symptom of JA and does not indicate an infectious disease. Because eyes can become involved in arthritis, you will need to be alert for any indications of a visual problem and notify the parents.

The physical education program should take into account decreased stamina and limit strenuous games that put pressure on joints or limbs (Hutzal et al., 2009). Pain can interfere with concentration, so break tasks into shorter segments. Students may have a **limited range of motion** in affected limbs and swollen fingers that prevent them from grasping pencils and pens. Timed written tests may need to be changed or extended. Because symptoms vary from day to day, you must be accepting of a wide range of variation in the student's functioning, emotional well-being, and independence (Garnefski et al., 2009). Encourage as much independence as possible while reassuring the student that support is available (Jenkinson et al., 2002). Adolescence is a particularly challenging time, and families often encourage older children to take more responsibility for managing their arthritis—that is, taking medication, monitoring side effects, and following an exercise program. This may mean that you see problems developing at school that the parents do not see, and that you need to discuss these with the adolescent and the family. Be supportive and remember that your guidance and encouragement may enable the student to adapt so arthritis has as little impact as possible on his or her life at school (Erkolahti & Ilonen, 2005).

## Chronic Health Conditions

Usually, students with **chronic health conditions,** have been assessed by a qualified medical practitioner who certifies that they require medical procedures, beyond taking medication, while at school to ensure their health and safety. Often they require ongoing monitoring and differentiated instruction because of their limited school attendance or because the condition adversely affects their educational performance (Gomes & Smith, 2007). The speed and accuracy with which teachers, office staff, and school administrators respond to a student health crisis has far-reaching implications. When you begin working in a school, ask to see the Emergency Protocols Manual, ask about an orientation session, and sign up for a CPR and first aid course. Then you will be prepared and confident to respond to school health crises.

Smooth transitions to school are critical for students with chronic illnesses who have been hospitalized (Shaw & McCabe, 2008). Children and adolescents with conditions like cancer and leukemia may spend only a day or two in hospital at a time, often on repeated occasions, to receive treatment, and then go home and return immediately to school. You may need to differentiate instruction for some time. These students often show an array of social and emotional difficulties, including increased behaviour problems, depression, anxiety, and poor peer relations. By adolescence, students with chronic illness may experience suicide ideation and engage in substance abuse (Shaw & McCabe, 2008). Discuss the student's needs with the student and the family, and include the student in all academic planning.

Conditions discussed in this section include diabetes, allergies, asthma, cystic fibrosis, and cancer and leukemia. There are many other chronic health impairments, including congenital and acquired heart disease, gastrointestinal system

**Further Reading**

Brown, P., & Kent, M. (2000). *Guidelines for the care of students with diabetes in the school setting.* Trenton, NJ: New Jersey Dept. of Education.

Maitland DeLand, M. (2010). *The great Katie Kate discusses diabetes.* Austin, TX: Greenleaf Book Group Press. (For students.)

Parker, V. (2011). *I know someone with diabetes.* Mankota, MN: Heinemann-Raintree. (For students.)

Platt, A. (2010). *100 Q and As about your child's Type 1 diabetes.* Sudbury, MA: Jones & Bartlett Pub. (For families.)

Wishnietsky, D., & Wishnietsky, D. (2004). *Helping students with diabetes management.* Bloomington, In: Phi Delta Kappa Educational Foundation.

**Put into Practice**

Talk with a student with diabetes and with the student's parent(s). Ask each of them what tips they would suggest. Also ask them what they think of these five tips. Which are most important to the student, to the parent?

1. Don't draw unnecessary attention to the child.
2. Allow unrestricted bathroom breaks.
3. Always be prepared with a snack.
4. Every child with diabetes is different.
5. Show you care with empathy, not sympathy.

## Further Reading

Chilman-Blair, K., & Taddeo, J. (2010). *What's up with David?: Medikidz explain food allergies.* New York, NY: Rosen Pub. Group. (for students)

Engel, J. (2003). *The complete allergy book.* Richmond Hill, ON: Firefly Books.

Gold, M. (Ed.) (2004). *The complete kid's allergy and asthma guide: Allergy and asthma information for children of all ages.* Richmond Hill, ON: Firefly Books.

Parker, V. (2011). *I know someone with allergies.* Mankota, MN: Heinemann-Raintree. (for students)

Thomas, P., & Harker, L. (2008). *First look at: Allergies.* London, UK: Hodder Children's Division.

diseases, such as Crohn's disease and ulcerative colitis, as well as hemophilia. In each case you can obtain relevant information from the family, community agencies, websites, and print sources, including pamphlets, resource books, and books to be read to children and by adolescents about these conditions.

## DIABETES

> I stayed after school to talk to my homeroom teacher. I told her that I have diabetes. She already knew from my file. I said I don't want the other kids to know until I get to know them better. I told her that I keep juice in my backpack and that if I ask to leave class, it will be because I need sugar or insulin and she should let me go right away. Tomorrow I have to talk with my physical education teacher because I always need to eat after exercising. Today was good—a practice run for tomorrow.
>
> *Phil, describing his first day of high school to his parents.*

With **diabetes**, the body does not make enough insulin or has problems absorbing and storing insulin. Most children with diabetes receive **insulin** daily. Adolescents also check their blood sugar regularly. Diabetes is controlled somewhat through planned eating, insulin supplementation, and regular physical activity.

There are three types of diabetic emergencies: low blood sugar, high blood sugar, and ketoacidosis. The symptoms look similar, but low blood sugar is more dangerous, so if you are unsure which is occurring, give sugar. The symptoms of **low blood sugar (hypoglycemia)** occur suddenly: cold, clammy, or sweaty skin; trembling; confusion; difficulty speaking; and eventually fainting or unconsciousness. The student may report hunger, headache, dizziness, blurry vision, and abdominal pain. If the student is conscious, give a regular soft drink or juice that contains sugar or two teaspoons of sugar. Amounts may be specified in the student's file. This should be followed by a snack that includes complex carbohydrates and protein (e.g., a nutrient bar). The student may carry a snack. Causes of hypoglycemia include too much insulin, delayed or missed meals, and more exercise than usual. Contact the parents or physician, or take the student to hospital. Follow the protocol.

**High blood sugar (hyperglycemia)** symptoms show gradually, even over days. Causes include overeating, too little insulin, and stress. The student may be thirsty, flushed with dry skin, nauseous, drowsy, and eventually unconscious. Contact the parents or physician. The student requires insulin to combat hyperglycemia. It may be necessary to take the student to hospital. The third condition you should be aware of is diabetic ketoacidosis, when blood glucose is highly elevated and the body burns fat instead of glucose for energy. This can lead to severe dehydration, loss of consciousness, coma, and even death (Touchette, 2000). Diabetes can be life threatening. Remember: you are responsible for the student (Mandall & Gordon, 2009).

Your school probably has **diabetes emergency kits** of juice, raisins, or dextrose. Know the location of these and take one with you on field trips. Most students with diabetes will carry the emergency food or juice they need in their backpack, but if they become weak and confused they may not consume what they need. Explain to younger children the importance of eating their own snacks, without focusing attention on children with diabetes. Supervise the student at all times after a reaction; inform the parents. Most students know about their condition and require only your support and information about changes in routine, especially the timing of snacks and meals.

@

## Weblinks

CANADIAN DIABETES ASSOCIATION
www.diabetes.ca/

TEN TIPS FOR TEACHERS
www.diabetes.org/assets/pdfs/schools/tentipsforteachers.pdf

HELPING THE STUDENT WITH DIABETES SUCCEED: A GUIDE FOR SCHOOL PERSONNEL (AMERICAN DIABETES ASSOCIATION)
www.ndep.nih.gov/media/Youth_NDEPSchoolGuide.pdf?redirect=true

Diabetes can affect students in the classroom. When students experience a high or a low, or the day after they have had high or low blood sugar, they may be weak, tired, irritable, and unable to concentrate. Children whose diabetes is poorly controlled experience poor cognitive functioning (perhaps as a result of seizures) (Taras & Potts-Datema, 2005). Encourage students with diabetes to signal you when they need to leave quickly (and have a buddy go with them). Talk regularly with parents of young children so they are comfortable telling you about their child's changing condition. Beware of the following misconceptions (Rosenthal-Malek & Greenspan, 1999):

- that the student will inform you of highs or lows—sometimes the student won't be aware;

- that only food affects the level of blood sugar—activity level also influences it;

- that bathroom privileges can wait—a few minutes can put a student into a coma; and

- that all the effects are physical—attention, memory, learning, and processing speed in the classroom may be affected.

In a recent study conducted by an Ontario teacher, Kate Walker (2008) interviewed four young advocates for people with diabetes. They reported that diabetes influenced every aspect of their lives, including their stamina, choice of friends and social occasions, academic accomplishments, and choice of university program and career. They believed that most of their teachers had no idea how important it is to be understanding and supportive of students with diabetes. Your understanding will make a difference to the learning and well-being of students with diabetes.

## ALLERGIES

> On September 29, 2003, Sabrina Shannon bought French fries in her school cafeteria, after checking that they were cooked in vegetable oil and not peanut oil. Sabrina's allergy triggers were peanut, dairy products, and soy, all of which put her at risk of anaphylaxis. In class after lunch, Sabrina began to wheeze; a teacher raced to Sabrina's locker to get her EpiPen® in case it was her food allergies. Sabrina went into cardiac arrest before the EpiPen® could be administered and before the ambulance arrived. She died one day later. The coroner posited that Sabrina had been exposed to cross-contamination from cheese curds because the tongs had been used to serve poutine, as well as fries. Sabrina's mother's campaign with Anaphylaxis Canada resulted in the passage of Sabrina's Law, requiring all principals in Ontario to implement anaphylaxis plans and to develop an individual plan for each student at risk of anaphylaxis.
>
> *Sabrina's Law: http://www.e-laws.gov.on.ca/html/statutes/english/elaws_statutes_05s07_e.htm*

An **allergy** is an abnormal immune response to a substance that is tolerated by non-allergic people. It results in individual symptoms that vary in range and severity and can occur up to 72 hours after exposure to the allergen. Allergies can become worse with a single exposure to an allergen. **Anaphylaxis** is a sudden, severe allergic reaction that causes breathing difficulties (Olson et al., 2009). Death can occur within minutes unless an injection is administered. As many as 40 percent of those with a diagnosed food allergy are at high risk for anaphylaxis (Sheetz et al., 2004).

**Put into Practice**

Make a contingency plan for when a student has low blood sugar and needs to be rushed to hospital. Consult:

A. Rosenthal-Malek & J. Greenspan (1999), A student with diabetes is in my class, *Teaching Exceptional Children*, 31(3), 38–43;

The Canadian Diabetes Association, www.diabetes.ca

Helping the student with diabetes succeed: A guide for school personnel (American Diabetes Association), www.ndep.nih.gov/media/Youth_NDEPSchoolGuide.pdf?redirect=true

**Weblinks**

SABRINA'S LAW (ONTARIO)
www.e-laws.gov.on.ca/html/statutes/english/elaws_statutes_05s07_e.htm

ALLERGY ASTHMA INFORMATION ASSOCIATION (OF CANADA)
www.aaia.ca

## What do you think?

Should schools be peanut free?

Read the following papers and choose one side of this issue to debate with your peers.

Grant, I. (1997). Life, liberty and peanut butter. From the *Globe and Mail*, www.calgaryallergy.ca/Articles/English/Adobe/Lifeliberty.pdf

Maldonado, N.S. (2009). Peanut butter in schools: A tough nut to crack. *Childhood Education, 86*(1), 40–44.

Olson, B.F. et al. (2009). Development of an educational packet for persons with life-threatening allergies. *Journal of Food Science Education, 8,* 73–77.

Allergens, which cause allergic reactions, can enter the body through the following means:

- breathed through the nose or mouth—including dust; pollen; moulds; odours from chemicals, markers, perfumes, etc.;
- ingested through the mouth—including foods such as peanuts, shellfish, and milk; drugs such as aspirin (ASA), penicillin, and other antibiotics;
- by contact with the skin—including powders; lotions; metals such as jean snaps; latex; peanut butter; or
- through insect stings—including the venom of bees and wasps.

For the allergic student, reactions often accompany changes in routine, and anaphylaxis is more likely to occur at school than at home. Before the start of the school year, read the school plan on anaphylaxis and the individual plan for your student, and offer to meet with the family. Because characteristics of allergic reactions vary, it is important to learn each student's signs and symptoms. The main symptoms are itchy, watery eyes and itchy, runny nose. Other signs include itching elsewhere, hives, dark circles under the eyes, headache, shortness of breath, wheezing, cough, diarrhea, and stomach cramps.

You should know the steps in the individual emergency plan that has been developed for each student with severe allergies and the location of the injector for each student (in the student's backpack, in a cupboard, etc.). The general steps in an emergency plan are as follows:

- Administer **epinephrine** immediately (**EpiPen** or **Twinject**), following directions on the injector. This can save a life, but note that it is only first aid.
- Call 911 or an ambulance. Warn them that there is anaphylaxis. More serious reactions may follow, so a hospital is essential.
- Ensure that there is additional epinephrine available. If breathing difficulties persist, it may be necessary to re-administer it every 15 minutes.
- Call the parents or next of kin, but only *after* administering the injection immediately. Don't delay by calling the parents first.

Students with severe allergies can feel anxious and isolated because they feel different. They may wear a **MedicAlert** identification bracelet and should carry an injector in a backpack or purse. Sometimes adolescents leave their injector in their lockers or engage in risky behaviours (e.g., eating cafeteria food, like Sabrina). You can help by respecting feelings and offering support. Try to include the student in all activities, even if this means providing an **allergen-free alternative**.

### ASTHMA

## Put into Practice

Learn what to do in an emergency. Consult the Anaphylaxis Reference Kit, www.ycdsb.ca/parents_students/documents/Anaphylaxis_ResourceKit.pdf

Also see Health Canada and the Canadian School Boards Association (2001), *Anaphylaxis: A Handbook for School Board*, Ottawa: Canadian School Boards Association, www.safe4kids.ca/content/schools/anaphylaxis_eng.pdf

> Ms. Aboul, I need to talk with you. Grade 9 is hard. I'm so far behind. I've missed a lot of classes this year because of my asthma and doctors' appointments. I hate carrying my puffer around at school. Most of all I'm afraid of having a really big attack and not making it to the hospital. I need to talk with you. Meghan Lowie, 9D
>
> *A note left for a guidance counsellor by a student with asthma.*

**Asthma** is a chronic lung condition that can develop at any age. The most important characteristic is difficulty breathing. The airways are obstructed by inflammation, muscle spasm, and excess mucus. The airways respond in an exaggerated way to common irritants (e.g., smoke, scents in markers), allergens (e.g., pollen, foods such as nuts and shellfish), and other triggers (e.g., viral head colds, exercise). To treat asthma effectively, the individual must know his or her triggers and avoid contact with these triggers. Two kinds of medication are used to treat asthma: **preventers** are anti-inflammatory drugs taken regularly to prevent and treat inflammation, and **relievers,** used as rescue medications to relax the muscles of the airways and give quick relief from breathing problems, are inhaled with a **puffer** or **nebulizer**.

Those with asthma are affected to varying degrees, from mild (only during vigorous exercise) to severe (with daily symptoms that cause lifestyle restrictions). Rates of asthma are higher in children who are obese and who live in poor, urban communities (Fiese et al., 2009; Nelson et al., 2009). In Canada, 20 children die annually from asthma. By identifying the warning signs, you can help prevent an episode. As breathing becomes more difficult, signs of an asthma episode become more evident (Lim et al., 2009). Such signs are:

- wheezing;
- rapid shallow breathing;
- complaints of chest tightness;
- lips and nails greyish or bluish in colour; and
- contracted and bulging neck muscles, nasal flaring, and mouth breathing.

When you see these signs, start asthma first aid treatment (see Figure 4.9). Time is critical, so you must know what to do before an episode occurs. Read the student's file and school policy on asthma, advise the principal of your upcoming meeting, then meet with the student and parents before school begins. Learn the student's triggers, warning signs and symptoms, and how the asthma medications (relievers) are administered. These are usually summarized in an asthma action plan (see Put into Practice box on this page). Have the parents detail the steps they follow in first aid treatment, and together compare these to the school policy. If the two are not the same, consult your principal. Some schools have a form that parents of students with asthma must complete to describe medications, symptoms, first aid.

Always believe students with asthma. Do not make them wait for medication; asthma can be life threatening. If a student with asthma is using symptoms to get attention, talk with the parents and encourage the student to talk with a counsellor. Social problems seem to increase with the seriousness of the condition, and

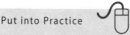

**Weblinks**

A TEACHER'S GUIDE TO ASTHMA
www.calgaryallergy.ca/Articles/English/teacherast.html

THE LUNG ASSOCIATION
www.lung.ca

THE LUNG ASSOCIATION: ASTHMA AT SCHOOL
www.lung.ca/diseases-maladies/asthma-asthme/children-enfants/school-ecole_e.php

**Put into Practice**

Conduct research on the web to learn about asthma action plans:

What an asthma action plan tells you.

What symptoms you should look for.

What the symptoms mean.

How to adjust medication according to the symptoms.

When to call a doctor or 911.

Sources to get you started:

www.asthma.ca/adults/control/pdf/AsthmaActionPlan_ENG.pdf

www.asthmanz.co.nz/files/PDF-files/childplan.pdf

www.mayoclinic.com/health/asthma/DS00021

**Further Reading**

On including children with childhood leukemia and cancer in the classroom:

Prevatt, F.F., Heffer, R.W., & Lowe, P.A. (2000). A review of school reintegration programs for children with cancer. *Journal of School Psychology, 38,* 447–467.

Sullivan, N.A. (2004). *Walking with a shadow: Surviving childhood leukemia.* Portsmouth, NH: Greenwood Publishers.

Sullivan, N.A., Fulmer, D.L., & Zigmond, N. (2001). School: The normalizing factor for children with childhood leukemia. *Preventing School Failure, 46*(1), 4–13.

## FIGURE 4.9 ASTHMA FIRST AID TREATMENT

In case of breathing difficulty:
- Have the student stop all activity.
- Help the student assume an upright position, sitting with legs crossed and elbows on knees.
- Stay with the student; talk reassuringly and calmly.
- Have the student take the appropriate medication (inhaler or nebulizer usually); it is more detrimental to withhold medication than to give the student medication when it is not needed.
- Notify the proper person, following school policy, usually a parent; if the student's condition does not improve or becomes worse 15 minutes after the medication, call an ambulance.

Source: Based on information from The Lung Association, www.lung.ca/asthma.

**Further Reading**

Fiese, B. et al. (2009). Wheezing, sleeping, and worrying: The hidden risks of asthma and obesity in school-age children. *Psychology in the Schools, 46*(8), 728-738.

Lim, J.H. et al. (2009). Understanding children with asthma: Trouble and triggers. *Childhood Education, 85*(5), 307–3111.

Nelson, B.W. et al. (2009). The continuing problem of asthma in very young children. *Journal of School Health, 79*(5), 209–215.

internalizing behaviour disorders, feelings of fatigue, worthlessness, and anxiety have also been reported, as well as difficulties with concentration, memory, and hyperactivity. Some of these effects may arise from the medications (Bray et al., 2008).

Encourage physical activities and remind students to monitor their symptoms. Inform students and parents about potential triggers likely to be introduced into the classroom. Taking medication and having asthmatic episodes at school can make students self-conscious. Arrange for the student to leave unobtrusively when necessary, provide a quiet supervised location in which the student can take medication, and ask someone to stay with your class while you monitor the student with asthma.

### CYSTIC FIBROSIS

Today my mom told me I had no choice, and here I am in the hospital with pneumonia again. I'm sorry I can't be in our class play on Friday. Mom says I probably got overtired from all the rehearsals. That might be why I am sick again. But I'm still glad I tried out for the play. I don't want CF to get in the way of having a life.

*From the diary of Brittany, a grade 7 student with CF.*

**Cystic fibrosis (CF)** is incurable, the result of an inherited genetic defect, and causes chronic lung problems and digestive disorders. The lungs become covered with sticky mucus that is difficult to remove and promotes bacterial infection. Most people with CF require frequent hospitalizations and regular use of antibiotics. (Remember Brittany, who was described in one of the cases that opened this chapter?) They take **enzyme supplements** so they can digest the nutrients in their food. Sometimes a feeding tube is necessary. Life expectancy, which was once only eight years, is now in the mid-thirties, and a lung transplant can extend that. Still, most persons with CF eventually die of lung disease (dePaepe et al., 2002).

The student with CF copes with a chronic cough and may need to have therapy during school to remove airway mucus. He or she will probably have an excessive appetite, combined with weight loss, and may need to eat during school hours. Bowel disturbances are common. Repeated bouts of pneumonia mean frequent absences, but communication with the family should ease the process of shifting learning to the hospital room. Cystic fibrosis can have a negative impact on learning, and differentiated instruction may be necessary. Cystic fibrosis has been associated with depressed mood, anxiety, memory and concentration problems, and fatigue (Koscik et al., 2004). You might find it helpful to read the Teacher's Guide to Cystic Fibrosis (www.cysticfibrosis.ca/assets/files/pdf/Teachers_Guide_to_cystic_fibrosisE.pdf). Adolescents often rebel against treatments, and need counselling to deal with delayed puberty and to accept that their life expectancy may be shortened (Chesson, Chisholm & Zaw, 2004). Recent first person accounts suggest that many young adults with CF are determined to "beat" it (e.g., Lipman, 2003).

### CANCER AND LEUKEMIA

Kristopher described returning to school after each treatment for leukemia. "I liked everything about returning to school. If you have something you like, and they take it away, and then you go back, you like it a lot." He went on to say, "I really wanted to finish my work at school. I was feeling like I wouldn't pass because I was missing so much work."

*Based on Sullivan et al., 2001.*

@

**Weblinks**

CANADIAN CYSTIC FIBROSIS FOUNDATION (CCFF)
www.cysticfibrosis.ca/en/index.php

AMERICAN CYSTIC FIBROSIS FOUNDATION
www.cff.org

BLOG OF EVA MARKVOORT DESCRIBING HER FIGHT TO THE DEATH WITH CF
http://65redroses.livejournal.com/

CYSTIC FIBROSIS WORLDWIDE
www.cfww.org

A TEACHER'S GUIDE TO CF
www.cysticfibrosis.ca/assets/files/pdf/Teachers_Guide_to_cystic_fibrosisE.pdf

Childhood **cancer**, particularly **leukemia**, is increasing. Survival rates for leukemia stand at about 80 percent (Sullivan, 2004). Cancer is relatively uncommon in children. Nevertheless, cancer is the most common disease-related cause of death in school-aged children. Although survival rates are much better than in the past, the effects of these chronic illnesses persist, and maintaining a normal lifestyle is essential to positive adaptation (Prevatt et al., 2000); this includes attending school whenever possible because school is a normalizing factor (Sullivan et al., 2001). Educators must appreciate the serious nature of the illness and be sensitive, collaborate with the hospital or home schooling teacher, provide opportunities for classmates to maintain contact during absences, and communicate frequently, proactively, and supportively with parents about the student's learning and psychosocial needs at school (Sullivan, 2004).

## MULTIPLE EXCEPTIONALITIES

In Ontario, multiple exceptionalities refers to a combination of learning or other disorders, impairments, or physical disabilities that is of such a nature as to require, for educational achievement, the services of one or more teachers holding qualifications in special education and the provision of support services appropriate for such disorders, impairments, or disabilities. This category is used to identify children with severe multiple needs.

**Put into Pracitce**

Read these books written for children and adolescents, and develop a plan for using them to inform classmates about cancer or leukemia that is being experienced by a student in your class.

Chilman-Blair, K., & Taddeo, J. (2010). *What's up with Lyndon?: Medikidz explain osteosarcoma.* Atlanta, GA: American Cancer Society, Inc.

Chilman-Blair, K., & Taddeo, J. (2010). *What's up with Richard?: Medikidz explain leukemia.* Atlanta, GA: American Cancer Society, Inc.

Hyman Fead, B. et al. (2009). *Nana, what's cancer?* Atlanta, GA: American Cancer Society, Inc.

Meyers, B., & Mays. L. (2010). *The long and the short of it: A tale about hair.* Atlanta, GA: American Cancer Society, Inc.

# Summary

There are a large number of low-incidence exceptionalities which, when taken together, affect many students in our classrooms. The number of students with chronic health conditions such as asthma and allergies is growing quickly. The students discussed in this chapter have diverse strengths, challenges, and needs. Remember that you will teach only two or three students in your career who have, for example, cystic fibrosis, and you may never be teaching more than a few students at a time who have low-incidence exceptionalities. Many of the strategies you have already learned will be effective in teaching these students, and you should draw on the experience and expertise of parents and in-school team members. While accommodations will usually be adequate, on occasion you may need to modify the curriculum or develop an alternate curriculum, especially for students with developmental disabilities and autism.

In this chapter we focused on differentiating instruction for students with a number of low-incidence exceptionalities, including developmental disabilities, autism, and Asperger syndrome. We considered adaptations for students who are deaf, hard of hearing, blind, or who have low vision. The range of needs and strengths in students with these low-incidence exceptionalities is huge. Students with physical exceptionalities also benefit from differentiation. We focused on students with nervous system impairment—cerebral palsy, spina bifida, epilepsy, Tourette syndrome, brain injury, and fetal alcohol spectrum disorders—as well as two musculoskeletal conditions (muscular dystrophy and juvenile arthritis). The final area of concentration was chronic health conditions such as diabetes, allergies, asthma, cystic fibrosis, and cancer and leukemia. It is customary to think of the physical and stamina limitations of students with physical and health conditions, as well as the possibility that they will need medication at school. However, meeting the social and emotional needs of these students is also important. Inclusion means more than the physical presence of students with low-incidence exceptionalities in regular classrooms. Inclusion means making them feel part of the social and academic life of the class and the broader community.

# Key Terms

low-incidence exceptionalities (p. 83)
physical disabilities (p. 83)
chronic health conditions (p. 83)
case coordinator (p. 83)
developmental disabilities (DD p. 83)
intellectual disability (ID) (p. 83)
American Association on Intellectual and Developmental Disabilities (AAIDD)(p. 84)
chromosomal abnormalities (p. 86)
self-care (p. 86)
voice synthesizer (p. 86)
functional curriculum (p. 87)
community-based (p. 87)
autism spectrum disorders (ASDs) (p. 88)
autism (p. 88)
perseveration (p. 88)
theory of mind (p. 88)
social stories (p. 91)
reinforcers (p. 91)
Asperger syndrome (AS) (p. 92)
hypersensitive (p. 92)
deaf (p. 92)
hard of hearing (p. 92)
hearing status (p. 93)
American Sign Language (ASL) (p. 93)
speech-reading (p. 93)
manipulatives (p. 94)
pre-teaching (p. 94)
frequency modulation (FM) systems) (p. 94)
hearing aids (p. 94)
amplification (p. 94)

Blindness (p. 95)
low vision (p. 95)
Braille (p. 95)
taped books (p. 95)
vision teacher (p. 95)
speech-activated (p. 97)
remission (p. 97)
nervous system impairment (p. 97)
neurological dysfunction (p. 97)
cerebral palsy (CP) (p. 98)
spina bifida (p. 98)
hydrocephalus (p. 98)
shunt (p. 98)
epilepsy (p. 99)
seizures (p. 99)
partial seizures (p. 99)
generalized seizures (p. 99)
simple absence seizure (petit mal) (p. 99)
tonic-clonic (grand mal) seizure (p. 99)
Tourette syndrome (TS) (p. 101)
tics (p. 101)
acquired brain injury (ABI) (p. 101)
traumatic brain injury (TBI) (p. 101)
head injury (p. 101)
prenatal alcohol exposure (p. 102)
fetal alcohol spectrum disorders (FASD) (p. 102)
fetal alcohol syndrome (FAS) (p. 102)
partial fetal alcohol syndrome (PFAS) (p. 102)
alcohol-related neurodevelopmental disorder (ARND) (p. 102)

musculoskeletal conditions (p. 103)
muscular dystrophy (MD) (p. 104)
Duchenne muscular dystrophy (DMD) (p. 104)
juvenile arthritis (JA) (p. 104)
inflammation (p. 104)
immune system (p. 104)
limited range of motion (p. 105)
chronic health condition (p. 105)
diabetes (p. 106)
insulin (p. 106)
low blood sugar (hypoglycemia) (p. 106)
high blood sugar (hyperglycemia) (p. 106)
diabetes emergency kits (p. 106)
allergy (p. 107)
anaphylaxis (p. 107)
epinephrine (p. 108)
EpiPen® (p. 108)
Twinject (p. 108)
MedicAlert® (p. 108)
allergen-free alternative (p. 108)
asthma (p. 108)
preventers (p. 109)
relievers (p. 109)
puffer (p. 109)
nebulizer (p. 109)
cystic fibrosis (CF) (p. 110)
enzyme supplements (p. 110)
cancer (p. 111)
leukemia (p. 111)

# Challenges for Reviewing Chapter 4

1. What low-incidence exceptionalities do you think you need to know about? Which physical and health conditions do you expect to encounter in your teaching? Discuss with your peers why it is important to understand the physical and psychosocial aspects of these exceptionalities and conditions?

2. Write a brief scenario that includes some of the greatest challenges to your teaching and management in a classroom with students with autism spectrum disorders—like Pamela in the opening case, who has autism, and Jason, described at the beginning of the section on ASD, who has Asperger syndrome. Describe how you could differentiate instruction to meet their needs.

3. You are currently a member of the in-school team for a student who is hard of hearing. Prepare to assume the role of one member of the team and to role play with your peers. The team includes a classroom teacher, a resource teacher, a principal, and a parent. Together develop a systematic approach to differentiating teaching and ensuring social participation of the student who is hard of hearing.

4. Develop a chart that includes the physical disabilities described in this chapter (i.e., cerebral palsy, spina bifida, epilepsy, Tourette syndrome, brain injury, fetal alcohol spectrum disorders, muscular dystrophy, juvenile arthritis). Compare these exceptionalities on four dimensions, one of which is differentiating teaching, and compare your chart with those of your peers. What dimensions are most important to teachers?

5. Consider what is meant by the term *chronic health condition*. Compare the six chronic conditions described in this chapter. Why must educators be knowledgeable about these conditions in order to meet their legal and ethical responsibilities? Provide convincing examples to support your position.

6. Re-read the case of Brittany who has cystic fibrosis. Answer the questions following the case, focusing on Brittany. With your peers, consider differences and similarities in issues raised by secondary and elementary teachers.

# Chapter 5
## Differentiating Teaching

**Ms. Ash teaches mathematics at a large inner-city secondary school.** She starts every class with an example of how the day's math can be used—perhaps by engineers to design a heating system. When she teaches new mathematical content, she teaches to the whole class, with the students seated in pairs. First she reviews, pointing out explicitly how recent lessons relate to today's class. Next she hands out a partially completed outline and places the same outline on the overhead projector. She demonstrates, questions, and fills in the overhead transparency while she explains the new content. She stops every few minutes for students to ask questions and complete their outlines. She moves to guided practice by demonstrating an example on the overhead projector while students work in pairs on the same example. Then students complete two or three examples in pairs without Ms. Ash guiding them. She takes up these examples, guides students in practising another if necessary, and then asks students to work together on two or three examples and finally to complete two or three independently. She moves to the round table and invites students who want to review the steps to join her while the rest complete a challenge task in collaborative groups. Samuel has a learning disability and has always found math difficult. This term, Ms. Ash paired Samuel with a boy who answers his questions with explanations, and Samuel is learning. He likes to go to the round table to hear Ms. Ash explain the concepts and the steps again and to have her correct his work. Ms. Ash has taught him how to use a calculator and encourages him to use it, one of the adaptations listed on his IEP. Now he feels that he is learning to solve problems rather than spending all his time trying to do calculations.

**Hema has an intellectual disability; she has a pacemaker, but it does not restrict her activities.** She is included in a grade 5 class and learns best with visual materials, hands-on activities, and pre-teaching. Hema reads common signs in the neighbourhood, recognizes the written names of family and friends, and reads calendar words. She prints her name on forms or applications, draws simple pictures, and types a couple of sentences on the computer with a model. Her annual goals (on her IEP) include sustaining a conversation; maintaining socially appropriate behaviour; using a telephone; describing events, interactions, etc.; using money; and reading to get information. For the weather unit in Hema's science class, classroom teacher Mr. Carvello, along with the resource teacher, used the ADAPT strategy. While the other students completed a full-page chart on the weather each day using the class's weather station, Hema recorded only three aspects: she recorded the temperature, drew the cloud cover, and wrote the precipitation. To meet the IEP goals of using the telephone and relaying information, the two teachers designed a learning activity: in the company of a peer, Hema would go to the school office to telephone the regional weather office daily. Eleven peers volunteered to take turns accompanying Hema. Mr. Carvello demonstrated their role to the peer volunteers twice. Hema dialed the number, listened, and repeated what the meteorologist had said. Mr. Carvello printed it neatly and prompted Hema while she practised telling the class. Hema gradually used the telephone more independently, and the peer who had accompanied Hema provided any information she missed in her summary. Hema's daily goal was to give a full account, which she was soon able to do.

1. How have these two teachers matched the strengths and needs of exceptional students—like Samuel and Hema—with classroom demands?

2. What differentiations or adaptations do these teachers make for these exceptional students? How do these adaptations relate to the students' IEPs?

3. How have these teachers considered the perspectives of and consequences for others, as well as for Hema and Samuel?

4. Consider how these differentiations are beneficial to students other than Hema and Samuel.

5. How have these teachers ADAPTed teaching without unduly increasing their own workloads?

# Introduction

In differentiated classrooms teachers begin where the students are and accept that students differ in important ways. The terms *differentiate* and *adapt* are used interchangeably in this chapter, as they are in many of the writings of Carol Ann Tomlinson, a well-known proponent of differentiated classrooms (e.g., 2003; Tomlinson et al., 2008; Tomlinson & Cunningham Eidson, 2003; Tomlinson & McTighe, 2006). Essentially, differentiating instruction means structuring a lesson at multiple levels and in such a way that each student has an opportunity to work at a moderately challenging, developmentally appropriate level. Differentiating teaching and assessment is the heart of inclusive education that honours diversity and strives for equity.

## Using the **ADAPT** Strategy to Analyze and Differentiate Teaching for Individuals and Groups

Curriculum tells teachers what to teach; differentiated instruction helps teachers decide how to teach it to a range of learners by using a number of teaching approaches. You can differentiate one, two, or all three of the following elements: the content (what the students are going to learn), the process (the activities), and the products (the accomplishments following a period of learning) (Tomlinson & Strickland, 2005). Chapter 1 introduced the five steps of **ADAPT**:

- Step 1: **A**ccounts of students' strengths and needs
- Step 2: **D**emands of the classroom
- Step 3: **A**daptations
- Step 4: **P**erspectives and consequences
- Step 5: **T**each and assess the match

Although our focus is on students with exceptionalities and others who may need differentiation, in both elementary and secondary school classrooms, ADAPT can be used with all learners.

### Step 1: Accounts of Students' Strengths and Needs

This first step requires that you know your students well. From the first day of school you should be familiar with the content of the confidential Ontario Student Record (OSR) of each exceptional student you teach. Usually the file contains the student's IEP, test reports, comments from previous teachers, and medical information that could be critical to the student's well-being (e.g., indication of allergies, epilepsy, or asthma). The IEP includes specific statements about strengths and needs, usually in three general areas: social, emotional, and behavioural; physical; and academic.

Social, emotional, and behavioural strengths can include engaging in conversation within collaborative groups and responding positively to suggestions. On the other hand, social, emotional, and behavioural needs could mean that a student requires significant instruction and support because he or she fights when unsupervised. Physical strengths and needs include motor skills, sight, and hearing.

**What do you think?**

Read Paul S. George's 2007 paper, A Rationale for Differentiating Instruction in the Regular Classroom, *Theory into Practice*, 44(3), pages 185–193). He argues that we differentiate because it is the right thing to do, because it honours diversity and equitable opportunity to learn in heterogeneous classrooms, and publicly funded heterogeneous classrooms are essential for the future of democracy. What do you think of his argument?

**Put into Practice**

View the following multimedia resources and discuss your understanding of differentiated classrooms with your peers:

Crévola, C. (2006). *Breakthrough: Redesigning classroom instruction to transform learning*, www.curriculum.org/LSA/files/LSAGuideBreakthrough.pdf.

Curriculum Services Canada. (2006). *Webcasts for educators: Differentiated instruction*, www.curriculum.org.

*READING rockets*, a national multimedia project funded for the Office of Special Education, U. S. Department of Education, to assist struggling readers and beginning readers, www.readingrockets.org.

**Cross-Reference**

Chapters 7 and 8 focus on ways you can create a classroom community and help all students to feel like they belong in the classroom.

Academic strengths and needs include the basic skills of reading, writing, mathematics, and learning strategies for test taking and problem solving. Tomlinson and Cunningham Eidson (2003) use the terms *readiness*, *interest*, and *learning profile* to describe these student characteristics—needs and strengths—that teachers must be familiar with if they are to attend successfully to differences. In all her writings, Tomlinson asserts that all tasks should be respectful of each learner.

## Step 2: Demands of the Classroom

Next consider the social, emotional, and behavioural demands of your classroom. Do students learn individually, work with peers, or do they do both? How long is the lecture portion of each lesson? Do you model positive interactions with all students? For physical demands, do you rely on an overhead or data projector, and can everyone see it clearly? The academic demands are manifested in things like the instructional materials you use (e.g., textbooks, computer programs), in your instructional approaches, and in your assessment methods. Direct instruction followed by guided and independent practice benefits students with learning disabilities, while open-ended assignments challenge gifted students. Tomlinson considers classroom demands under headings such as *focusing on the curriculum essentials* and *connecting assessment and instruction*.

## Step 3: Adaptations

In this step you compare a student's learning needs with the demands of the classroom and identify potential mismatches and differentiations (adaptations) that eliminate them. You can make adaptations—by planning and then carrying them out when teaching—in the fundamental organization and instruction that goes on in the classroom. To do so, you can either bypass a mismatch between student and curriculum demands or you can teach through the mismatch. Tomlinson emphasizes flexible grouping (as in the opening case studies) and adapting by flexible use of space, materials, time, and teacher contact to optimize learning for every student.

## Step 4: Perspectives and Consequences

Take time to reflect on each differentiation from many perspectives. What has your experience been with it? To bolster your self-efficacy, start small and build up to your highest aspirations. Expect glitches. Setbacks will likely occur and you will need to renew your efforts. Observe the exceptional students' experiences of differentiation. What is the class' view? How would parents view the differentiations that you used? And how would the community look on these adaptations? Next consider the consequences, intended and unintended, for the exceptional student—learning, drawbacks—and for others affected by the differentiation. Tomlinson emphasizes ongoing assessment so you can make adjustments as you teach and strive to provide the optimal level of challenge for every student.

## Step 5: Teach and Assess the Match

During and following the teaching, assess how well the differentiation overcame the mismatch between student strengths and needs and classroom demands. Persevere and give it time to be effective. Observe how engaged the student is, ask the student how she finds the changes, chart marks, analyze errors, and talk with parents.

**Put into Practice**

Informally ask parents, teachers, and students how they feel about differentiated instruction to meet the learning needs of exceptional students. What "hard questions" might you be asked by students without exceptionalities and their parents?

**Weblinks**

WEB RESOURCES FOR SPECIAL EDUCATION (2010) CONTAINS BRIIEF DESCRIPTIONS AND LINKS TO A RANGE OF TOPICS AND ISSUES (INCLUDING TEACHINING IN INCLUSIVE CLASSROOMS) www.eric.ed.gov

**Further Reading**

Carver, A., & Bailey, J. M. (2010). Unit pages: Differentiation for 200 students. *Science Scope, 33*(6), 12–17.

Fitzgerald, G., Koury, K., Mitchem, K. (2008). Research on computer-mediated instruction for students with high incidence disabilities. *Journal of Educational Computing Research, 38*(2), 201–233.

Haager, D., & Klingner, J.K. (2005). *Differentiating instruction in inclusive classrooms.* Boston, MA: Pearson Allyn & Bacon.

Karnes, F.A., & Bean, S.M. (Eds.). (2008). *Methods and materials for teaching the gifted* (3rd ed.). Waco, TX: Prufrock Press.

Ontario Expert Panel on Literacy and Numeracy. (2005). *Education for all.* Toronto, ON: Queen's Printer for Ontario.

Tomlinson, C.A., & Strickland, A.A. (2005). *Differentiation in practice: A resource guide for differentiating curriculum, grades 9–12.* Alexandria, VA: Association for Supervision and Curriculum Development.

Weblinks

STATISTICS CANADA: LEARNING RESOURCES FOR STUDENTS AND TEACHERS
www.statcan.gc.ca/edu/index-eng.htm

STATISTICS CANADA: LESSON PLANS FOR SECONDARY-LEVEL MATHEMATICS
www.statcan.gc.ca/kits-trousses/courses-cours/edu05_0019-eng.htm_0019-eng.htm

LESSON PLAN FOR "CANADA'S IMMIGRATION PATTERNS, 1955 TO PRESENT"
www.statcan.gc.ca/kits-trousses/immig1-eng.htm

Further Reading

On using Canadian statistics in the classroom:

Special Issue of *School Libraries in Canada*, 2002, *Vol. 22,* No. 1. (Contains 30 short articles on using statistics to teach in many curriculum areas and to challenge your students.)

What do you think?

Some provinces enable high school students to challenge for credit if they believe they have met "all the learning, process, interpersonal, participation objectives or outcomes or requirements of a course." See New Brunswick, www.gnb.ca/0000/publications/curric/challenge_for_credit.pdf

In Ontario, options include Advanced Placement courses, International Baccalaureate Programs, or taking courses at a local community college. Discuss with your peers the relative merits of these options as opposed to enriching and differentiating the grade-level curriculum.

# Choosing and Combining Strategies for Differentiating

The following three types of differentiations are especially effective as you plan how to teach exceptional students. They can be used individually or in combination.

## Teaching Around the Mismatch

Teaching-around strategies, sometimes called **bypass strategies** (Friend et al., 1998), allow students to succeed in the classroom using alternative means. They are helpful after teacher and student have tried concertedly for some time. To teach around a spelling disability, allow the student to use a spell checker; Braille bypasses sight to enable reading. Bypass strategies that enhance independence are usually preferable (e.g., a spell checker rather than a peer editor, although a peer editor may be a step towards independent use of a spell checker).

## Remediating or Accelerating to Overcome the Mismatch

A second strategy for overcoming a mismatch is intensive remediation or acceleration. Intensive **remediation** is designed to address basic skills or learning strategies that the student needs and that you believe the student can acquire. A resource teacher may do unison reading with a slow reader in grade 9 to help the student increase reading speed so he can comprehend his textbooks. You could instruct four students who have difficulty printing while the class writes daily journal entries. **Acceleration** is used to move academically advanced students into challenging learning. Two adolescents in your geography class are bored by your unit on immigration, well-prepared to take the unit test, and eager to meet this challenge; so you teach them to run a statistical program and analyze Statistics Canada data.

## Teaching Through the Mismatch

A third strategy is teaching through the mismatch. During the planning process you can make differentiations in the fundamental organization and instruction that goes on in the classroom. Try using these four steps (Collicott, 1994):

1. Identify the underlying concepts and learning outcomes of the lesson and differentiate these for exceptional students when necessary. (Why do I teach this?)
2. Identify the methods of presentation and differentiate these for exceptional students when necessary. (How do I teach this?)
3. Identify how students gain understanding of the concepts and differentiate these for exceptional students when necessary. (How do students learn this?)
4. Identify the means of student assessment and adapt these for exceptional students when necessary. (How do students show they have learned this?)

# What Differentiated Instruction Is Not

It is important that you acknowledge what differentiated instruction does *not* mean. It does not mean doing something different for each student in the class. And it does not mean disorganized and disorderly student activity, with everyone doing what they like. Differentiated instruction does not mean that you must always use groups, maintain the same groups over time, or isolate students who are experiencing difficulty learning. You can still engage in whole-class activities with all students taking part in the same activity. (See Ontario Ministry of Education, 2004, *Ontario leading math success, grades 7-12*, which addresses many of these issues: www.edu.gov.on.ca/eng/document/reports/numeracy/numeracyreport.pdf).

Sometimes exceptional students participate fully and sometimes partially. They may complete part of a task or a different task to achieve the same outcome (e.g., drawing instead of writing). The many aspects of the classroom that can be adapted are the focus of the next section.

# Analyzing Teaching: What You Can Adapt

In Chapter 1 we discussed three forms of adaptations: **accommodations** (specialized teaching and assessment strategies that do not alter the Ontario curriculum expectations for the grade); **modifications**, which refer to changes in grade-level expectations as well as teaching approaches; and **alternative expectations**, those that are not represented in the curriculum but are appropriate to the student's needs (such as orientation/mobility training or social skills not normally taught in the school context) (Ontario Ministry of Education, 2004).

When you use the ADAPT strategy to analyze and differentiate teaching, you will see many ways to make changes that meet student needs. For example, you can adapt the substance of your teaching (e.g., outcomes, content, cognitive complexity, authenticity, and interest of the task). Tomlinson (2003) refers frequently to **differentiating content**. Or you may find that it makes more sense to change the environment (e.g., seating). You may want to enhance student engagement by changing the method of instruction—through activity-based learning or by changing the form of practice. All these aspects of teaching are closely related and are often called **differentiating the process** (Tomlinson). You can also **differentiate the product of learning** (Tomlinson), which could be a report, debate, poster, brochure, model, etc.

Adams and Pierce (2003) describe teaching by **tiering**. They present the content at varying levels of complexity while using the same process for all students (e.g., grouping students at their current level of understanding). For younger students learning science, Adams and Pierce suggest one tier might investigate the kinds of objects a magnet can attract, while another tier at a more advanced stage of readiness might investigate whether the size of the magnet affects its strength. **Universal design for learning (UDL)** may inform the way we think about differentiation.

## Outcomes, Content, Cognitive Complexity, Authenticity, and Interest of Task

Outcomes and these other aspects of teaching are all related to the substance and intent of what is taught. As described in Chapter 1, in Ontario, alternative expectations involve changing learning outcomes to something radically different from those in the grade-level curriculum. This occurs when 14-year-old Adam, who has developmental disabilities, learns to make a sandwich with a educational assistant while

**Further Reading**

The Ontario documents, *Education for All* (Ontario Expert Panel on Literacy and Numeracy, 2005) and *Learning for All* (Draft, 2009) are designed to support teachers' efforts to incorporate the principles of Universal Design for Learning (UDL) to differentiate instruction. Other jurisdictions also assist their teachers with handbooks to guide them in adapting or differentiating teaching, such as *The Resource Book for Yukon Teachers* (2004–2005). British Columbia has developed a resource for orientation and mobility instruction (www.bced. gov.bc.ca/specialed/docs/fit. pdf), which includes learning outcomes and means of assessment for alternative programming. The Atlantic Provinces Special Education Authority has developed a resource, *Support for Students Who Are Deaf or Hard of Hearing in an Inclusive Setting* (www. apsea.ca), on assisting the student in speech-reading, as well as scaffolding adaptations to help the student follow class presentations and discussions.

How do the Ontario documents compare to those of other provinces?

# What Is Universal Design for Learning (UDL)?

The concept of universal design—briefly introduced in Chapter 1—originated in architectural studies, where considerations of physical access led to designs that incorporated assistive technologies and adaptations (e.g., curb cuts and automatic doors). One essential quality of universal design of physical space is that the adaptations allow access to those who have disabilities and also make it easier for everyone to use the space; e.g., ramps allow easier access when using a wheelchair or pushing a cart or a stroller.

Universal design for learning (UDL) uses innovative media technologies to make a curriculum that can respond to individual differences in learning and teaching. This means instructional materials and activities are designed to allow the learning goals to be achievable by individuals with wide differences in abilities to see, hear, speak, move, read, write, understand English, attend, organize, engage, and remember. UDL is achieved by means of flexible curricular materials and activities that provide alternatives for students with disparities in abilities and backgrounds. Examples of UDL include electronic versions of textbooks and other curricular materials, speaking spell checkers, accessible websites, captioned or narrated videos, talking dialogue boxes, voice recognition, picture menus, and word processors with word prediction. UDL, both print and electronic, provide teachers with the means to teach one flexible curriculum with variations to reach all students.

UDL does not eliminate the need for assistive technology (AT). Students with disabilities will continue to need AT devices, including wheelchairs, communication aids, and visual aids, to interact fully with their environment. Building accessibility into new technologies and new curricular materials will promote maximum inclusion of children with the widest range of functional capabilities.

## Three Essential Qualities of Universal Design for Learning

Most authors focus on three essential qualities of UDL:

1. Curriculum provides multiple or flexible means of representation
2. Curriculum provides multiple or flexible means of expression and performance
3. Curriculum provides multiple or flexible means of engagement

CAST (Center for Applied Special Technology) has been developing UDL for a number of years (www.cast.org/udl/index.html). The four steps of the PAL process developed by CAST are:

- setting goals;
- analyzing the current status of the curriculum and the classroom;
- applying UDL to lesson or unit development, and
- teaching the UDL lesson or unit (Meo, 2008).

## Websites About Universal Design and Curriculum Access

- BC Universal Design for Learning Project, www.setbc.org/setinfo/BCUDL
- Universal Design of Instruction, University of Washington, www.washington.edu/doit/Brochures/Academics/instruction.html
- National Center for Technology Intervention (US), http://nationaltechcenter.org
- American Youth Policy Forum, www.aypf.org/forumbriefs/2000/fb110300.htm
- National Early Childhood Technical Assistance Center, www.nectac.org/topics/atech/udl.asp

## Two Examples That Use Universal Design Principles

- WiggleWorks, an early literacy program from Scholastic, builds in design features that allow children with many different abilities and disabilities to learn together (http://teacher.scholastic.com/products/wiggleworks/index.htm).
- Encarta uses audio and video to make concepts clearer than text alone could do and uses captioning (http://encarta.msn.com).

## References

Meo, G. (2008). Curriculum planning for all learners: Applying universal deign for learning (UDL) to a high school reading comprehension plan. *Preventing School Failure, 52*(2), 21–30.

you and the rest of the class study the geography of your province. However, Sylvia, who is blind, has the geography curriculum at her grade level accommodated by using raised maps of the province and the guidance of a peer tutor. Modifying outcomes for a gifted student may mean including expectations from a higher grade level; for example, conducting a critical analysis of the declining role of landforms in demographic patterns of population and economics. Changes, whether minor or massive, are aligned with students' strengths and needs and based on classroom demands and will always ensure that the pupil learns.

**Cognitive complexity** refers to the cognitive demands made of the learner. When **authentic tasks** are presented to students in the form in which they occur in society, students usually find these tasks complex. A class staging a mock municipal election would research how to nominate municipal candidates, hold press conferences, produce brochures, and cast and count votes while learning about the issues. An exceptional student could work toward the goal of improving co-operation with peers (on his or her IEP) by becoming a member of a campaign team. A gifted student might be an ideal candidate to run for mayor. Such authentic tasks can provide concrete experiences of abstract ideas, such as democracy. Research suggests that gifted students may benefit from cognitively complex challenges because they develop deep sensitivities to issues and injustices at an early age (Hartsell, 2006).

**Interest** comprises an affective interaction between students and tasks. A frequent suggestion is for gifted students to follow their interests (e.g., Rakow, 2007; Renzulli et al., 2003). However, interest also plays an important role in engaging students who are not interested in learning for its own sake—often those with learning disabilities, ADHD, and other exceptionalities. For these students, developing curriculum around interests can produce focused attention and learning (Freeman et al., 2002; McPhail & Freeman, 2005; McPhail et al., 2004).

## Environment, Method of Presentation, Pace, and Quantity

**Environment** has to do with classroom climate and physical layout (see Chapter 7). High expectations accompanied by high support make for the best learning environments. Be alert to signs of discouragement and remind students of their accomplishments. You can also adapt the environment by changing seating, a useful strategy although rarely intense enough to make big changes in learning. Remove distractions, glare, and clutter to meet the needs of exceptional students. Consider keeping exceptional students near you so they can focus.

You can vary **method of presentation** to the advantage of your whole class like Ms. Ash did in the opening case study. Most average-achieving students, exceptional students, and English language learners benefit from being directly shown with clear explanations, models, guided practice, independent practice, and feedback in an array of subjects (Hogan & Forsten, 2007; Jones & Leahy, 2006; Olson & Land, 2007). Hands-on learning is often necessary for exceptional learners and helpful for other students. Remember you are not planning separate lessons but making adjustments to the lesson while planning it and teaching it.

**Pace** is the rate of presentation of new information or the rate of introduction of new skills. Often exceptional students need new skills to be introduced in small steps—and slowly—to ensure mastery, and they need concepts to be introduced slowly with opportunity and time to develop understanding before the next concept. This may mean setting priorities and deleting some concepts or skills for exceptional students, while gifted students may need the pace increased and the expectations raised. Strickland (2007) laid-out an "action tool" where teachers identify the unit goals the student has already mastered and the unit activities yet to be mastered. If the student is not participating in regular class activities, you would work out the enrichment or extension activities with the student. For example, "Chantal will work on her joint math and language arts project of writing a book for kindergartners about the joys of math" (p. 364), for which criteria should be developed.

@

**Weblinks**

ELECTIONS CANADA
www.elections.ca

HOW TO ORGANIZE AN ELECTION SIMULATION (IN CANADA, AT THE POLLS)
www.elections.ca (click on Young Voters)

**Further Reading**

On differentiation for gifted students:

Smith, K., & Weitz, M. (2003). Problem solving and gifted education: A differentiated fifth-grade fantasy unit. *Gifted Child Today, 26*(3), 56–57.

Van-Tassel-Baska, J., & Stambaugh, T. (2005). Challenges and possibilities for serving gifted learners in the regular classroom. *Theory into Practice, 44*(3), 211–217.

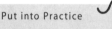

**Put into Practice**

Read at least two resources that focus on differentiating instruction and assessment for students with a specific exceptionality. Choose one from the list below and locate another source. Consider what, if anything, is unique about differentiating to meet the needs of a student with a specific exceptionality. Discuss with peers who have read other sources.

Bender, W. (2008). *Differentiated instruction for students with learning disabilities: Best teaching practices for general and special education.* Thousand Oaks, CA: Corwin Press.

Bowen, J.M. (2005). Classroom interventions for students with traumatic brain injuries. *Preventing School Failure, 49*(4), 34–41.

Broderick, A., Mehta-Parekh, & Reid, D. K. (2005). Differentiated instruction for disabled students in inclusive classrooms. *Theory into Practice, 44*(3), 194–202.

**Further Reading**

Joffe, V., Cain, K., & Maric, N. (2007). Comprehension problems in children with specific language impairment: Does mental imagery training help? *International Journal of Language and Communication Disorders, 42,* 648–664.

Prior, J., & Gerard, M. (2004). *Environmental print in the classroom: Meaningful connections for learning to read.* Newark, DE: International Reading Association.

## Student Engagement and Activities, Amount of Practice, and Form of Practice

Student **engagement** refers to the extent to which students embrace learning and classroom activities. Students who are disengaged from learning and from the social life of the classroom have little reason to go to school or to co-operate with those around them. A danger of poorly implemented inclusion is that students are only physically present in the classroom without being part of the community or engaged in learning. Students must be cognitively active to be engaged (Lutz et al., 2006; Kondor, 2007). Without providing choice and making a genuine effort to engage your students, you can expect behaviour problems and alienation (Bowen & Arsenault, 2008).

**Additional practice** is often critical to the learning of exceptional students. Brief reviews of key information or skills may help exceptional students' retention. Consider using colour-coded follow-up activities where blue paper may place triads at a centre in the classroom after they have completed the practice examples, yellow may require students to independently develop challenge questions, and the green may place students with you for review and practice. Change the colours so that green is not always the "easiest," change the groups so they don't become the stereotyped "buzzards, bluebirds and owls," and change the group that receives your attention. Adapting the **form of practice** means accepting oral or written practice, or whatever advances the students' learning.

## Scaffolding, Grouping, and Collaboration

**Scaffolding** is the support that may enable a student to exceed what he or she can do independently with the assistance of a peer or the teacher. **Zone of proximal development (ZPD)** refers to the learning the student is about to undertake that he or she can already understand with support (Vygotskty, 1986; 1996). Exceptional students often benefit from gradually decreasing scaffolding as they internalize what they first do in social situations, making **grouping** an important strategy in differentiated classrooms, along with collaborative and co-operative learning. Every resource on differentiating focuses on flexible grouping; for example, Gregory and Kuzmich (2004, p. 11) encourage teachers to use the TAPS strategy to decide on the size of group:

> **TAPS** for Adjustable Assignments:
>
> **T**otal group // **A**lone // **P**airs // **S**mall group

**Further Reading**

On cognitively complex issues, interest, and gifted students:

Balchin, T., Hymer, B., & Matthews, D. (Eds.). (2009). *The Rouledge international companion to gifted education.* New York, NY: Routledge Taylor & Francis Group.

Hartsell, B. (2006). Teaching toward compassion: Environmental values education for secondary students. *Journal of Secondary Gifted Education, 17,* 265–271.

von Karolyi, C. (2006). Grappling with complex global issues, issue awareness in young highly gifted children: "Do the claims hold up?" *Roeper Review, 28,* 167–174.

Pederson, K.S., & Kitano, M.K. (2006). Designing a multicultural literature unit for gifted learners. *Gifted Child Today, 29*(2), 38–49.

Reis, S. M., & Renzulli, J. S. (2009). Is there still a need for gifted education? An examination of current research. *Learning and Individual Differences,* doi.10.11.2009.

Renzulli, J.S., Gentry, M., & Reis, S. (2003). *Enrichment clusters: A practical plan for real-world, student-driven learning.* Mansfield, CT: Creative Learning Press.

# Differentiating Teaching of Listening, Reading, and Writing

## Building Listening Skills, Storytelling, and the Use of Environmental Print

We sometimes assume that our students know how to listen, but some exceptional students may lack this skill; other students may also benefit from activities that build listening skills. An effective strategy in elementary classrooms (Evans &

Strong, 1996) that can be adapted for secondary school classes in literature and content areas involves creating a brief narrative account that will interest your students. Remind them of three skills for *paying attention:*

- Look at the person reading or speaking
- Sit still
- Keep your hands in your lap.

Then focus on *listening skills* by explaining a purpose for listening:

- With younger students, show three pictures of an event in the story, such as the ending. Ask them to listen so they can choose the correct picture of the ending.
- With older students, replace the pictures with three brief sentences or passages. Ask them to listen so they can choose the passage that represents the viewpoint of a particular character, etc.

Older students who experienced difficulty listening were taught to produce mental images for sentences and stories, and improved their ability to recount those sentences and stories. (Joffe et al., 2007). Teach students to recount personal experiences and to listen to each other's accounts.

Environmental print refers to the common words and symbols of our environment which represent fast food restaurants, toy companies, carmakers, etc. (Prior & Gerard, 2004). With practice, children can recognize these familiar words in manuscript printing, as well as in symbols (Browne, 2007). Environmental print can also be used in teaching mathematics (e.g., Koellner & Wallace, 2007). Take advantage of environmental print by:

- encouraging cutting and pasting of symbols from magazines until the child can print the words in a personal journal;
- using manuscript print under the environmental print symbol to promote recognition of the printed form;
- posting printed signs around the classroom on the window, door, desk, etc.;
- posting children's names on their desks so the child with developmental disabilities can match names on books to names on desks and distribute books, etc.; and
- enlisting parents to help their children to use environmental print at home.

## Background to Differentiating Teaching of Reading

In April 2000 the National Reading Panel (NRP) in the United States released its research-based findings on teaching reading (www.nationalreadingpanel.org). Their thorough review of the vast literature on reading led them to focus on five components of teaching reading: **phonemic awareness, phonics, fluency, vocabulary,** and **comprehension.** Phonemic or phonological awareness is the awareness of and sensitivity to the smallest units within words—phonemes or sounds. Phonics stresses sound–symbol relationships, helping learners to match the letters of the alphabet to the already-known speech sounds. Fluency contributes to comprehension and involves children reading out loud with speed, accuracy, and proper expression. Vocabulary focuses on children understanding the meaning of words,

**Put into Practice**

Consider using three novels of varying levels of difficulty if that means that every student will engage with a book. Use listening stations with an audio book for students with LD. For content area text, consider using parallel texts where the same content is presented but at varying readability.

**Cross-Reference**

Chapter 7 focuses on classroom climate, community, and management—including strategies for creating an environment in which to ADAPT. It also includes a discussion of how to provide encouragement so that students do not lose heart.

Ryan and Deci's (2000) Theory of Self-Determination explains the importance of generating an affective interaction between students and tasks.

Ways to enhance social relations and use co-operative and collaborative learning are elaborated on in Chapter 8.

**Put into Practice**

Nancy Hutchinson taught a reading comprehension unit that included all of her curriculum goals (identifying the main idea and supporting details, reading captions, etc.) and was based on Saskatchewan's driver handbook. She recognized her students' struggle to read the content and capitalized on their interest in learning to drive to improve their comprehension. They all secured the coveted permit.

Consider how you can capitalize on student interest to enhance student learning in your classroom.

## Put into Practice

Drawing on the following materials, develop a plan for teaching phonemic awareness to all grade 1 students, with more regular practice for those at risk for learning disabilities.

Adams, M.J., Foorman, B.R., Lundberg, I., & Beeler, T. (2006). *Phonemic awareness in young children: A classroom curriculum.* Elsevier Australia.

Mraz, M., Padak, N., & Rasinski, T.V. (2007). *Evidence-based instruction in reading: A professional development guide to phonemic awareness.* Toronto, ON: Pearson Education Canada.

Rodriguez Perez, I. (2008). *Phonemic awareness: A step by step approach for success in early reading.* Blue Ridge Summit, PA: Rowman & Littlefield Education.

and reading comprehension is an active process of understanding that requires an intentional and thoughtful interaction between the reader and the text. Schools that have been continuously successful in teaching children to read use diverse approaches to reading instruction but include the five components described above (Denton et al., 2003). (See Walpole and McKenna, 2007, for a guide for primary teachers on differentiating reading instruction, using the components in the NRP report.)

## Adapting to Promote Learning to Read: Phonological Processing and Balanced Reading Programs

The past 20 years saw the so-called **reading wars**—controversies over whole language versus phonics emphases in early reading (Stanovich & Stanovich, 1995). Research indicates that the most critical factor beneath fluent word reading is the ability to recognize letters, spelling patterns, and whole words effortlessly and automatically on sight (Adams, 1990).

Research shows that the best way to develop early reading skills is with explicit instruction and teacher-directed strategy instruction, especially for at-risk children and children with learning disabilities (Stanovich, 1994; 2000). Researchers (e.g., Willows, 2002; Pressley, 2002; Pressley et al., 2002) suggest balancing explicit instruction of word-recognition skills (e.g., phonemic awareness) with meaningful reading activities (see also Grenawalt, 2004; Heydon et al., 2004/2005). See Figure 5.1 on teaching phonemic awareness. Phonemic awareness components involve:

- sensitivity to, and explicit awareness of, individual sounds in words;
- demands that children analyze or manipulate only sounds, not meaning; and
- early skills such as recognizing rhyming, and later skills such as segmenting the sounds in words and synthesizing the sounds in words.

## Weblinks

FOR PHONICS INFORMATION AND INSTRUCTIONAL MODULES:

A SITE FOR TEACHERS AND PARENTS THAT INCLUDES PRINTABLE RESOURCES, WEBLINKS, LITERACY GAMES AND ACTIVITIES
www.bbc.co.uk/schools/games

*PHONICS ONLINE* ANSWERS TEACHERS' QUESTIONS AND PROVIDES INSTRUCTIONAL MODULES. DIRECT INSTRUCTION IS RECOMMENDED FOR THE TEACHING OF PHONICS: STEPS INCLUDE SHOW, EXPLAIN, PRACTICE, ASSESS, AND TRANSFER.
http://reading.indiana.edu/phonics/d8/3directtrial.html

## FIGURE 5.1 TEACHING PHONEMIC AWARENESS

**Instructional Guidelines for Planning Phoneme Awareness Activities**

1. Identify the precise phonemic awareness task and select developmentally appropriate activities. Activities should be fun and exciting—play with sounds, don't "drill" them.

2. Use phoneme sounds (represented by / /) and not letter names when doing the activities. Remember that one sound may be represented by two or more letters; for example, only three sounds in the word *cheese*: /ch/–/ee/–/z/. Target specific sounds/words at first.

3. Continuant sounds (e.g., /m/, /s/, /l/) are easier to manipulate and hear than stop consonants (e.g., /t/, /g/, /p/). When introducing continuants, exaggerate by holding on to them: "rrrrring"; for stop consonants, use iteration (rapid repetition): "/k/–/k/–/k/–/k/–/k/atie."

4. When identifying sounds in different positions, the *initial* position is easiest, followed by the *final* position, with the *medial* position being most difficult (e.g., *top, pot, letter*).

5. When identifying or combining sound sequences, a CV pattern should be used before a VC pattern, followed by a CVC pattern (e.g., *pie, egg, red*).

Note: CV = consonant–vowel; VC = vowel–consonant; CVC = consonant–vowel–consonant.

Source: Edelen-Smith, P.J. (1997). How now brown cow: Phoneme awareness activities for collaborative classrooms. *Intervention in Clinic and School, 33*(2), 105. Used by permission.

## Teaching Phonics

Phonics, knowledge of individual letter names, is combined with phonemic awareness. The teaching of phonics should begin with the simple and regular forms and then move to the more complicated irregulars (Albert, 1994). Teach the more regular consonants like *buh* and *tuh* first, followed by the short vowels that appear in two-thirds of all English words. The *Jolly Phonics* program (Lloyd et al., 1998) is often used to ensure a systematic and engaging introduction of sounds through consonant digraphs (like *sh* in *ship*) and blends (like *bl* in *blends*), followed by long vowels and word patterns. Pattern books, rhymes, songs, and poems can help readers practise letter-sound relationships.

## Enhancing Fluency

Fluent readers recognize most words rapidly and accurately and can focus their attention on making sense of the text. Fluency develops through practice reading, especially reading familiar text. The strategy called repeated reading is particularly effective. Practising and then reading to an authentic audience is a good strategy with readers of all ages. Poor readers in grade 6 can read to buddies in kindergarten and grade 1 students can read to their parents and younger siblings. Madden and Sullivan (2008) provide exemplary lessons that help grade 4 to 6 readers achieve well-paced, expressive oral reading within a diverse classroom.

## Differentiating Reading to Learn: Using Textbooks by Adapting, Supplementing, and Bypassing

In the early primary grades, children learn to read. In the junior grades, children read to learn (Chall, 1979, 1983). In reading to learn, students must comprehend new text, relate new ideas to prior knowledge, and create an elaborate understanding. Inefficient readers often need prompting to attend to their relevant prior knowledge and relate it to their new learning, as well as requiring assistance with vocabulary and word recognition. Comprehension is purposeful and occurs before, during, and after reading.

The **scaffolded reading experience (SRE)** is designed for classes with students of varying abilities in reading to learn. It applies the steps of the ADAPT strategy, encouraging teachers to plan by considering the students, the reading selection, and the purpose of the reading. It includes **pre-reading activities** (e.g., activating prior knowledge, pre-teaching vocabulary), during-reading activities (e.g., shared and guided reading), and **post-reading activities** (e.g., discussion, writing, drama, artistic and nonverbal activities, re-teaching) (Graves & Braaten, 1996).

Textbooks can be supplemented with guest speakers, field trips, multimedia, trade books, newspapers, and hands-on activities. Grouping children with similar exceptionalities and assigning these activities to educational assistants are two ways that teachers who practice inclusion can ensure that these activities take place. Let gifted students challenge one another (Hong et al., 2006). To bypass the textbook, look for alternative texts that cover the same topics. Seek **high-interest, low-vocabulary books** for novel study and general reading.

**Further Reading**

On Differentiating Reading:

Effective Instruction for Adolescent Struggling Readers, www.centeroninstruction.org (choose special education).

Schumm, J.S. (2006). *Reading assessment and instruction for all learners.* New York, NY: Guilford Press.

Teaching All Students to Read in Elementary School: A Guide for Principals, www.centeroninstruction.org/files/Principals%20Guide%20Elementary.pdf.

Tyner, B., & Green, S.E. (2005). *Small-group reading instruction: A differentiated teaching model for intermediate readers, grades 3–8.* Newark, DE: International Reading Association.

Walpole, S., & McKenna, M.C. (2007). *Differentiated reading instruction: Strategies for the primary grades.* New York, NY: Guilford Press.

**Further Reading**

On resources that are high in interest and easy for exceptional students, reluctant readers, and ELL students to read:

Blasingame, J. (2007). Books for adolescents. *Journal of Adolescent & Adult Literacy, 50,* 686–686.

Fránquiz, M. (2008). Learning English with high-interest, low-vocabulary literature: Immigrant students in a high school new-arrival center. *English Leadership Quarterly, 30*(3), 5–8.

Geye, S., & Reynolds, J. (2008). *Orca soundings resource guide: Teen fiction for reluctant readers.* Victoria, BC: Orca Book Publishers.

Schatmeyer, K. (2007). Hooking struggling readers: Using books they can and want to read. *Illinois Reading Council Journal, 35*(1), 7–13.

Sullivan, E.T. (2002). *Reaching reluctant young adult readers: A handbook for librarians and teachers.* Lanham, MD: Scarecrow Press.

# Early Reading: A Delicate Balance

If you visit a kindergarten class in a school striving to develop a balanced reading program, you are likely to encounter the sights and sounds of children learning to read. For example, in Phyliss Trudeau's kindergarten class at Ridgewood Public School the children were following her lead to sound out and shape letters with their fingers when Jennifer Lewington visited to write a feature about the school for the *Globe* and *Mail* (1998). And if you visit a grade three class, you may encounter students reading a novel by Judy Blume, a favourite author for this age group, and eagerly responding to questions about the plot and the characters.

Schools striving to develop a balanced reading program usually combine systematic teaching of phonics and phonemic awareness with frequent reading of a wide range of books and other print materials of various kinds. Classrooms are likely to have a "word wall" for high-frequency words and to show the letters of the alphabet and their sounds prominently on the walls.

In 1998, when Jennifer Lewington reported on the reading program at Ridgewood School, she described Ridgewood as a school that took reading very seriously, and reported on the steady increase in their reading test scores. Their balanced approach to literacy included:

- teaching phonics systematically so students learned letter-sound combinations and word decoding;
- using rhymes and games to track phonemic awareness so students break "sand" into "s" and "and";
- integrating the use of a wide range of print resources so students could both choose their own books for independent reading and receive guidance from their teachers;

- using school-based and board-wide tests to identify student needs for additional teaching and practice with specific skills within reading, writing, and spelling;
- grouping students informally to challenge strong readers and to support readers encountering difficulties;
- partnering with parents to encourage reading at home;
- providing bags of books of appropriate difficulty for weekly home reading and logs for to record home reading;
- offering workshops and release time for teachers to work together to improve students' reading;
- committing school resources for reading improvement;
- requesting and honouring teachers' suggestions for making this balanced reading approach work.

Jennifer Lewington (1998) reported in her article that Mrs. Awde, a very experienced grade 1 teacher in Ridgewood Public School at the time, told her the most important part of this approach to reading was the focus on the individual child because it enables teachers to build on strengths and to help students overcome weaknesses. There are examples all over Canada of teachers using balanced reading approaches to ensure that students acquire phonemic awareness and phonics skills while also experiencing enjoyment and developing comprehension while learning to read. Like Mrs. Awde, these teachers want to help students build on strengths and overcome weaknesses.

To read more about this example of a balanced reading program, consult, Lewington, J. (1998). *Globe* and *Mail*, November 9, pp. C1, C7.

## Teaching Vocabulary and Comprehension Strategies

For many students it is enough to introduce new vocabulary and connect it to their existing language. For students with limited vocabulary, you will need to do more. A five-step approach can be used at the beginning, middle, and end of a unit (Carnine et al., 1990, 2003).

1. Choose a range of positive and negative examples to teach the new word or concept. For the concept of leisure, give examples of playing videogames, camping, playing soccer, etc. Non-examples might be working at a part-time job and running errands for your parents. Use six examples of the concept and at least two non-examples.

2. Use synonyms that the students already know. For *leisure*, you could use the word *play*. State the definition simply and clearly.

3. Model or point to positive and negative examples. For leisure, model telephoning a friend to arrange a gaming afternoon; point to pictures of people

@

camping. For non-examples, model going to work and point to pictures of people entering a factory, and so on.

4. Ask a series of yes/no questions to help students discriminate examples from non-examples. Ask how they know whether to say yes or no.

5. Find out whether students can discriminate this concept from others. Is *leisure* the same as rest? Different? Explore features that are sometimes present; e.g., leisure is sometimes done alone and sometimes done with friends.

Vocabulary development is important to reading and to understanding content. Similarly, in mathematics many students need direct teaching of vocabulary (Voytsekhovska, 2008). When vocabulary is taught explicitly, comprehension improves (Beck & McKeown, 1991, 2007; Klingner & Vaughn, 1998; VanDeWeghe, 2007).

Tobin and McInnes (2008) describes how two teachers successfully differentiated the teaching of reading (vocabulary and comprehension) in grade 2/3 classrooms. The two teachers used slightly different approaches to differentiate their instruction in language arts. Cynthia used guided reading and literacy centres, while Margot opted for book bundles and a menu of work products as a basis for differentiation.

## Enhancing Written Expression and Facilitating Note-Taking

To differentiate the writing of **narrative text**, use a series of scaffolded tasks. For those who write fluently and willingly, use only topic prompts. For students who cannot start with a topic prompt, introduce picture prompts and brainstorming about the pictures. Next time try only topic prompts, reintroducing picture prompts only for those who need them. For those who cannot begin from a picture prompt and brainstorming, add a **story-planning sheet** with the following prompts:

- Setting: where and when the story took place
- Main character: the person(s) at the centre of the problem or conflict
- Character clues: appearance, actions, dialogue, thoughts, others' comments
- Problem: conflicts
- Attempts: how the character tries to solve the problem
- Resolution: how the problem gets solved or does not get solved

Students can complete the prompts briefly on the story-planning sheet while brainstorming with a partner and later independently. Those who don't need a planning sheet can use a checklist of these prompts, with the addition of theme, to check that all essential elements are in their narratives. This approach can be adapted to scaffold student writing of notes from a text, lecture, discussion, or video. The principles are to provide no more scaffolding than students need and to gradually move students from peer and teacher support to independence with self-checking. Record daily the scaffolding that students use so you can prompt for more independence. If you copy each degree of scaffolding onto a different colour of paper, you can encourage students to move from yellow to green, etc., and see at a glance who is using each degree of scaffolding (see Lutz et al., 2007).

To differentiate the writing of **expository text** or **opinion essays**, teach the entire class to use a series of strategies. Then review the steps and scaffold strategy use for students with LD and others who find written expression difficult. Place a

**What do you think?**

Look for a source on teaching students to read and write. Consider the ideas of the author(s) and relate their ideas to what you have learned from experience about the connections between reading and writing in classrooms at the level at which you teach. Possible sources are:

Flint, A. S. (2008). *Literate lives: Teaching reading & writing in elementary classrooms.* Hoboken, NJ: Wiley.

Mather, N., Wendling, B. J., & Roberts, R. (2009). *Writing assessment and instruction for students with learning disabilities* (2nd ed.). San Francisco, CA: Jossey-Bass.

Meyerson, M. J. (2006). *Strategies for struggling readers and writers: Step by step* (2nd ed.). Upper Saddle River, NJ: Pearson Merrill Prentice Hall.

Moore, D.W. (2006). *Teaching adolescents who struggle with reading: Practical strategies.* Boston, MA: Allyn and Bacon.

Look for other sources and compare your ideas to the thinking of your peers.

poster on the wall. Give those who need it an individual copy of the strategy. Use **DARE** (Monroe & Troia, 2006) for planning the writing of an opinion essay:

**D**evelop a position statement.

**A**dd supporting arguments.

**R**eport and refute counterarguments.

**E**nd with a strong conclusion.

Many students who have difficulty expressing themselves in writing do not understand that revision is expected; some may even think it is cheating. For revising, you can try introducing the **SEARCH** strategy (Ellis & Friend, 1991):

**S**et goals (did I do that?).

**E**xamine the paper to see if it makes sense.

**A**sk if you said what you meant.

**R**eveal picky errors (e.g., sentences too long or too short?)

**C**opy over neatly.

**H**ave a last look for errors.

Have students work with a peer and model how to constructively ask each other tough questions about their writing. Create pairs carefully, especially pairs involving students with difficulty writing. Try a strategy that goes from small issues to large issues: **W**ords, **S**entences, **E**ssay, **C**ounterarguments, **SEARCH**:

Did I use descriptive **W**ords?

Were my **S**entences varied and clear?

Was my **E**ssay convincing?

Have I successfully refuted **C**ounterarguments?

Did I **SEARCH** thoroughly for all errors?

Finally, for reluctant writers, teach them how to engage in prompted self-regulation. Helpful are self-questions like, "What are the steps I follow by myself and with my partner?" or "What is the big issue for me in my writing today?" or a self-instruction, "I need to try hard to do my best today" (Monroe & Troia, 2006).

### CASE STUDY WHAT CAN BE DONE TO PROMOTE SOCIAL ACCEPTANCE FOR SALLY WHILE MAINTAINING DIFFERENTIATED INSTRUCTION?

Sally has always struggled with comprehending and interpreting what she reads. She no longer has an IEP, but she did have one for many years. In grade 11 English, the class is studying *Romeo and Juliet*. Yesterday the teacher, Yolanda Chiang, taught the class elements of Shakespeare's tragedies, and Sally is worried because she knows that she can't yet identify all those elements. Sally is relieved when Ms. Chiang divides the class into three groups. Two groups are given clear instructions, oral and written, and begin to compare the elements of tragedy in *Romeo and Juliet* to the elements of tragedy in *A Doll's House* by Ibsen, a play the class read a month earlier. Each of these two groups is to create a poster using words and drawings, showing the elements in each tragedy, providing examples, and making comparisons. Sally is part of a group of eight students who are working with Ms. Chiang to review the elements of Shakespeare's tragedies as seen in *Romeo and Juliet*. Many of these students have IEPs or, like Sally, had IEPs for many years. Ms. Chiang leads Sally's group in charting and providing examples of the elements (in words and drawings) from *Romeo and Juliet* and makes suggestions for illustrations. After Sally's

# Differentiating Teaching of Mathematics

In mathematics, adaptations reduce the mismatch between the student's strengths and needs and curriculum demands. Number sense is foundational for all mathematical learning, followed by fluency in computation and problem solving. Each aspect may need to be adapted.

## Number Sense

**Number sense** refers to an essential sense of what numbers mean, how to compare numbers, and how to see and count quantities. Most children acquire this conceptual structure informally through interactions with family and peers before kindergarten. Students with good number sense move effortlessly between quantities in the real world and mathematical expressions. Children who have not acquired this sense of numbers require formal instruction to do so (Jordan et al., 2007). Number sense may serve the same function for mathematics as phonological awareness serves for beginning reading—it appears to be essential for later competence. There is increasing evidence relating inadequate number sense to learning disabilities (Chard et al., 2008; Geary et al., 2000; Robinson et al., 2002).

Robbie Case (1998), who conducted research at the University of Toronto, and Sharon Griffin (Griffin & Case, 1997) developed an instructional program in number sense, called Rightstart, using three representational systems:

1.  conventional math symbols: digits and addition, subtraction, and equal signs;

2.  a thermometer that shows the number line in a clear vertical direction, so bigger is higher and smaller is lower; and

3.  a representational system that looks like the Candyland board game.

Students play games, comparing quantities and adding one number to another using the representational systems, with many opportunities to verbalize their understandings and problem-solving rationales (see Mascolo et al., 1998).

Many teachers use a **hundreds chart** to help students explore number sense. Vacc (1995) modified the hundreds chart to align its vocabulary and format with the vocabulary and methods used when manipulating numbers. It includes the numbers 0 to 99 and progresses from right to left (see Figure 5.2). Students can use the chart for numerical patterns, addition, subtraction, multiplication, division, and prime numbers. For example, to teach place value, say, "Cover the number that is two 'tens' and four 'ones.' Next cover five 'tens' and seven 'ones.'"

For numerical patterns say, "Begin with 0, count by 2s, placing a marker on each number counted. Describe the pattern you have made." Next you can add a prediction component for counting by 2s, 3s, etc. This is a systematic way to develop and enhance number sense.

**Further Reading**

To learn more about the Rightstart program for teaching number sense by Case and Griffin, please see:

Griffin, S. (2004). Building number sense with number worlds: A mathematics program for young children. *Early Childhood Research Quarterly, 19*(1), 173–180.

Griffin, S.A. (1997). Re-thinking the primary school math curriculum. *Issues in Education, 3*, 1–49.

Griffin, S. (2004). Teaching number sense. *Educational Leadership, 61*(5), 39–43.

Griffin, S.A., Case, R., & Siegler, R.S. (1994). Rightstart. In K. McGilly (Ed.), *Classroom Lessons: Integrating Cognitive Theory and Practice* (pp. 25–50). Cambridge, MA: MIT Press.

Mascolo, M.F., Kanner, B.G., & Griffin, S. (1998). Neo-Piagetian systems theory and the education of young children. *Early Child Development and Care, 40*, 31–52.

**What do you think?**

Why might this modified hundreds chart (see Figure 5.2) help children? Read and discuss with your peers:

Vacc, N.N. (1995). Gaining number sense through a restructured hundreds chart. *Teaching Exceptional Children, 28*(1), 50–55.

Naylor, M. (2006). From one to one hundred. *Teaching preK-8, 36*(5), 36–38.

Practical descriptions of five activities for different grade levels using the hundreds chart: chart tour (K–2); mystery number (grades 1–3); missing numbers (grades 1–3); multiple patterns (grades 3–5); and least common multiples (grades 5–8).

## FIGURE 5.2  REVISED HUNDREDS CHART

| 90 | 80 | 70 | 60 | 50 | 40 | 30 | 20 | 10 | 0 |
|----|----|----|----|----|----|----|----|----|----|
| 91 | 81 | 71 | 61 | 51 | 41 | 31 | 21 | 11 | 1 |
| 92 | 82 | 72 | 62 | 52 | 42 | 32 | 22 | 12 | 2 |
| 93 | 83 | 73 | 63 | 53 | 43 | 33 | 23 | 13 | 3 |
| 94 | 84 | 74 | 64 | 54 | 44 | 34 | 24 | 14 | 4 |
| 95 | 85 | 75 | 65 | 55 | 45 | 35 | 25 | 15 | 5 |
| 96 | 86 | 76 | 66 | 56 | 46 | 36 | 26 | 16 | 6 |
| 97 | 87 | 77 | 67 | 57 | 47 | 37 | 27 | 17 | 7 |
| 98 | 88 | 78 | 68 | 58 | 48 | 38 | 28 | 18 | 8 |
| 99 | 89 | 79 | 69 | 59 | 49 | 39 | 29 | 19 | 9 |

Source: Vacc, N.N. (1995). Gaining number sense through a restructured hundreds chart. *Teaching Exceptional Children, 28*(1), 51. Used by permission.

### Further Reading

Bloom, J.W. (2006). *Creating a classroom community of young scientists* (2nd ed.). New York, NY: Routledge.

Duschl, R.A., Schweinbruber, H.A., & Shouse, A.N. (2007). *Taking science to school: Learning and teaching science in grades K–8*. Washington, DC: National Academies Press.

Kurtts, S.A., Matthews, C.E., & Smallwood, T. (2009). (Dis)Solving the differences: A physical science lesson using universal design. *Intervention in School and Clinic, 44*(3), 151–159.

Horney, M.A., et al. (2009). Exploring the effects of digital note taking on student comprehension of science texts. *Journal of Special Education Technology, 24*(3), 45–61.

Moore, S.D., & Bintz, W.P. (2002). From Galileo to Snowflake Bentley: Using literature to teach inquiry in middle school science. *Science Scope, 26*(1), 10–14.

Ritz, W.C. (2007). *Head start on science: Encouraging a sense of wonder*. Arlington, VA: National Science Teachers' Association.

Steele, M.M. (2010). Helping students with learning disabilities succeed: teaching strategies can help students with learning disabilities improve their performance in the science classroom. *The Science Teacher, 75*(3), 38–42.

Taber, K.S. (2007). *Science education for gifted learners*. Abingdon, UK: Routledge.

Watson, S., & Johnson, L. (2007). Assistive technology in the inclusive science classroom. *The Science Teacher, 74*(3), 34–38.

Westphal, L.E. (2007). *Differentiating instruction with menus: Science*. Waco, TX: Prufrock Press.

## Computation

Often an effect of math learning disabilities is lack of fluency with **computation** and basic number facts. Teaching older students to use a calculator, a bypass strategy, is only justifiable after you have adapted teaching to increase number fact fluency.

When young children are counting the objects in two sets, do not immediately expect them to memorize number facts. Teach them to count on, by naming one number and counting on the other. Model this strategy using fingers, number lines, objects, or the 3 representational systems suggested by Griffin and Case. Teach the commutative principle by showing that 4 + 5 = 5 + 4. Encourage students to read number problems aloud and verbalize what they are thinking. Garnett (1992) suggests the order in which addition (and multiplication) facts should be learned. As students become more mature in their strategies, teach them to ask, "Do I just know this one?" and use retrieval strategies whenever possible. Press for speed with a few facts at a time. When students are not using retrieval strategies, encourage them to think out loud and discuss strategy use. Technology offers a means of adapting the teaching of multiplication. Irish (2002) used computer-assisted instruction and a multimedia software program (Memory Math) to teach students with learning disabilities the basic multiplication facts. The software utilizes keyword mnemonics.

## Problem Solving, Representation, Symbol Systems, and Application

Many exceptional students experience difficulty solving problems, a focus of recent curriculum reforms. Number sense and computational fluency are essential for problem solving. It is difficult to bypass number sense, while calculators can be used to bypass lack of computational fluency. Calculators can be of particular benefit for exceptional students for several reasons: students can focus on advanced concepts rather than number crunching (Antonijevic, 2007); calculations can be less tedious for exceptional learners (Steele, 2007); and real data sets can be used (Arnold, 2006). Overall, calculator use provides all students with practice and success in calculating ratios and solving proportion problems and increases student confidence, enthusiasm, and number sense (Moss & Grover, 2007).

Strategies to help students solve problems include using authentic problems, demonstrating concrete examples, and making the reasoning used to represent the problem visible to the student (see Overholt et al., 2008). Nancy Hutchinson, one of the textbook authors, developed a strategy to teach adolescents with learning disabilities to solve algebra word problems (Hutchinson, 1993). In this approach, students learned first to represent and then to solve word problems. The teacher models by thinking out loud using a set of self-questions, students engage in guided practice with an adult or a peer, and then engage in independent practice. Hutchinson (1997) used this approach to teach individuals, pairs, small groups, and finally whole classes.

*Self-Questions for Representing Algebra Word Problems*

1. Have I read and understood each sentence? Each word?

2. Have I got the whole picture, a representation, for this problem?

3. Have I written down my representation on the worksheet (goal; unknown[s]; known[s]; type of problem; equation)?

4. What should I look for in a new problem to see if it is the same kind of problem?

*Self-Questions for Solving Algebra Word Problems*

1. Have I written an equation?

2. Have I expanded the terms?

3. Have I written out the steps of my solution on the worksheet (collected like terms; isolated unknown[s]; solved for unknown[s]; checked my answer with the goal; highlighted my answer)?

4. What should I look for in a new problem to see if it is the same kind of problem?

Students complete each problem on a structured worksheet that matches the self-questions. In all seven studies Hutchinson conducted, students learned to solve the problems they were taught, could solve similar problems six weeks later, and transferred their problem solving to new kinds of problems.

Classroom teachers who differentiate teaching have developed many strategies to help diverse learners succeed in mathematics. Deb, a grade 4 teacher, enables students to represent their mathematical understanding using notebooks in which they use diagrams, graphs, and symbols to define mathematics words in their own ways and connect vocabulary to relevant situations (Lee & Herner-Patnode, 2007). Creating mathematics-oriented cartoons can provide visual and artistic opportunities for students who struggle with written or verbal strategies (Gay & White, 2002). Advanced organizers can help to make explicit connections between new concepts and previous learning, and can be used in any subject area (Preiss & Gayle, 2006).

# Differentiating Teaching in Content Areas: Science, Social Studies, Visual Arts, Music, Drama, and French

## Differentiating Science Teaching

The teaching of science for exceptional students can appear overwhelming. Issues of safety and supervision in the science laboratory (Chin, 1997; Conn, 2001) are intensified by the inclusion of exceptional students. Consider, for example, blind

**Further Reading**

Strebe, J.D. (2010). *Engaging mathematics students using cooperative learning.* Larchmont, NY: Eye on Education.

Flores, A. (2009). *Mathematics for every student. Responding to diversity, grades 9–12.* Reston, VA: National Council of Teachers of Mathematics.

Montague, M., & Jittendra, A.K. (2006). *Teaching mathematics to middle school students with learning difficulties.* Thousand Oaks, CA: Corwin Press.

Martin, H. (2007). *Active learning in the mathematics classroom, grades 5–8* (2nd ed.). Thousand Oaks, CA: Corwin Press.

Stone, R. (2007). *Best practices for teaching mathematics: What award-winning classroom teachers do.* Thousand Oaks, CA: Corwin Press.

Weblinks

SAFETY IN SCIENCE CLASSROOMS: WHAT RESEARCH AND BEST PRACTICE SAY
http://www.bio.txstate.edu/safety/Safety/safety1.pdf

THE MAY 2005 ISSUE OF AN ONLINE NEWSLETTER FOR TEACHERS FROM THE ALBERTA MINISTRY OF EDUCATION HAD AN UPDATE ON SAFETY IN SCIENCE CLASSROOMS:
www.education.alberta.ca/teachers/program/science/safety.aspx

**Weblinks**

SCIENCE WORLD
www.scienceworld.ca

TELUS WORLD OF SCIENCE EDMONTON
www.odyssium.com

TELUS WORLD OF SCIENCE CALGARY
www.calgaryscience.ca

SCIENCE NORTH
www.sciencenorth.ca

ONTARIO SCIENCE CENTRE
www.ontariosciencecentre.ca

DISCOVERY CENTRE
www.discoverycentre.ns.ca

PHYSLINK.COM (TEACHING RESOURCES
FOR PHYSICS AND ASTRONOMY)
www.physlink.com/Education

YES MAG (A CANADIAN MAGAZINE
FOR KIDS)
www.yesmag.bc.ca

SCIENCE TEACHERS ASSOCIATION
OF ONTARIO
www.stao.org

BC SCIENCE TEACHERS' ASSOCIATION
www.bcscta.ca

NATIONAL SCIENCE TEACHERS
ASSOCIATION
www.nsta.org

**Further Reading**

Chapman, C., & King, R. (2009). *Differentiated instructional strategies for writing in the content areas* (2nd ed.). Thousand Oaks, CA: Corwin Press.

Heydon, R. (2003). Literature circles as a differentiated instructional strategy for including ESL students in mainstream classrooms. *Canadian Modern Language Review, 59*(3), 463–475.

Lester, J. (2006). *Differentiating lessons using Bloom's taxonomy: Social studies.* Marion, IL: Pieces of Learning.

Westphal, L.E. (2007). *Differentiating instruction with menus: Social studies.* Waco, TX: Prufrock Press.

Zevin, J. (2007). *Social studies for the twenty-first century: Methods and materials for teaching in middle and secondary schools.* New York: Lawrence Erlbaum.

students and students with low vision, who require an orientation to the location of equipment and supplies and must be paired with a sighted peer; all members of the class must be reminded to return equipment to the same location. The visually impaired student can identify the contribution he or she can make to an activity after reading a Braille description of the activity or listening to an oral description. The student can time phases of an experiment on a Braille watch, make sound observations, or take readings on a Braille or talking thermometer. For students with low vision, a **CCTV** image magnifier can be set up so that experiments can be directly observed, and handouts can be copied at 129 or 156 percent. For blind students, a listing of the steps of the experiment in Braille and a "blow-by-blow" description by the teacher or a student will be necessary. Because few students have visual impairments, it is unlikely that your school laboratory will be stocked with the materials described here. Contact your district board office where the Blind/Low Vision Resource Teacher/Consultant could provide support. As well, W. Ross Macdonald School for the Blind in Brantford, Ontario, and Centre Jules-Leger, Ottawa, provide consultative services for pre-school and school-aged children up to the age of 21 years with blind or low vision and deaf-blindness who reside within the province.

There are many resources available to guide the science teaching of students who have visual impairment, hearing impairment, and physical disabilities (e.g., Riendl & Haworth, 1995; Weisgerber, 1993). Concrete suggestions appear in a paper on differentiating science teaching (Fetters et al., 2003). Hema's case study suggests how you might include a student with developmental disabilities in a science unit. Piggott (2002) describes ways to differentiate science teaching for students with disabilities and for students who are gifted, including an example of differentiating the teaching of electrolysis through enrichment and extension (reading extracts from Faraday's notebooks).

Because about half of exceptional students have learning disabilities, and because adaptations that help these students tend to be effective for all who read below grade level, consider the reading demands of your science text. The reading expected by science texts has increased over the past few decades. Look for texts with a lower reading level that provide parallel information or a website that is more accessible for poor readers. Other strategies include graphic organizers and study guides that help students pull the main ideas from complex text and see them in order, in a hierarchy, or connected to each other. Use real life examples and visual displays. Provide chapter notes for those who need them and summarize key concepts before and after students read each chapter (Steele, 2008). Homework assignments can be differentiated, too, by providing class time for students to begin homework so you can make sure they understand the assignment, breaking large tasks into parts and checking progress on each part.

## Differentiating Social Studies and Literature

**Reciprocal teaching** involves instructing students on teaching one another by taking turns leading discussions in small groups. Usually the teacher models how to lead the discussion and provides scaffolding for the groups as they begin. This teaching approach, developed by Anne Marie Palincsar and Ann Brown (1984; also see Palincsar & Herrenkohl, 2002; Deshler et al., 2007) has been used from kindergarten (Myers, 2005) to high school (Alfassi, 2004). Form groups of four or five students with one or two exceptional students in each group. Choose a different discussion leader for each group on a daily basis, beginning with a confident but patient student who will understand the process and model it well for peers. Students read a selection from their textbook (usually three to four pages). With younger students, you might ask them to stop after each paragraph. Each student receives a worksheet until the class is familiar with reciprocal teaching. On the worksheet, ask students to think of three good questions about what they have read. Prompt them to list the subheadings and three main points under each subheading. Then the group goes through the strategies of *questioning, summarizing, predicting,* and *clarifying.* For example, for the strategy of *questioning,* help the discussion leader to use *who, what, where, when,* and *why* questions to elicit key ideas. *Summarizing* involves the leader asking the others to provide a summary of the passage, beginning with the early highlights. After one student has answered, the discussion leader can ask others to add or to correct. *Clarifying* refers to asking questions "whenever we don't understand something." Emphasize that anyone who doesn't understand should ask a question. *Predicting* involves students in considering what comes next. Discussion of these predictions leads to increased comprehension.

Reciprocal teaching can benefit all students, including those with learning disabilities and reluctant readers (Meenakshi et al., 2007; Slater & Horstman, 2002), as well as individuals with intellectual disabilities (van den Bos et al., 2007). It can be applied in content areas beyond literature and social studies, including science (Herrenkohl, 2006) and math word problems (Van Garderen, 2004).

Differentiating teaching in any subject including social studies can be as simple as giving students choices in what they read, the tasks they complete, and the products they produce to demonstrate their learning. Kosky and Curtis (2008) integrated the arts into social studies units and found that what students appreciated most was being given choices in what and how they learned, which also increased motivation.

**Concept maps** and other explicit structures can help students understand the key relationships between the big ideas in social studies texts (Sturm & Rankin-Erickson, 2002). This flexible teaching approach, which can help to differentiate teaching, has been associated with increased knowledge retention not only in social studies, but in almost every area of teaching and learning, from economics to physics and biology (Nesbit & Adesope, 2006). The **problem-solution-effect** is one way to organize expository content: the problems that people or governments encounter might be linked to economic, health, autonomy, or human rights issues; the solutions people generate can be described as inventing, fighting, accommodating, tolerating, etc.; and the effects or outcomes could be new institutions, new problems, or changes in society.

## Differentiating Visual Art

Many view the arts as a great equalizer in education. Regardless of language and ability or disability, music, visual art, and drama are accessible to all. They argue that the arts are largely nonverbal and focus on creativity and self-expression, fundamental aspects of being human. Consider collaborations where feasible; for example, between ELL teachers and art teachers (Gregoire & Lupinetti, 2005) and collaborative projects in arts-based literacy (Cornett, 2006). A visual art program in which students work in small groups or individually on projects at an appropriate level of difficulty can be differentiated to allow full or partial participation in class activities. For

**Weblinks**

NATIONAL INSTITUTE OF ART AND DISABILITIES (SERVES ADULTS WITH DEVELOPMENTAL AND PHYSICAL DISABILITIES)
www.niadart.org

VSA ARTS (FOR PEOPLE WITH DISABILITIES TO LEARN THROUGH, PARTICIPATE IN, AND ENJOY THE ARTS)
www.vsarts.org

**Further Reading**

DeCoster, K., & Loots, G. (2004). Somewhere in between touch and vision: Art education for blind individuals. *The International Journal of Art & Design Education, 23,* 326–334.

Mason, C. V., & Steedly, K. M. (2006). Rubrics and an arts integration community of practice. *Teaching Exceptional Children, 39*(1), 36–43.

**Weblinks**

NATIONAL FILM BOARD (NFB) OF CANADA, SHAMELESS: THE ART OF DISABILITY
http://www.onf-nfb.gc.ca/eng/collection/film/?id=51620

KICKSTART DISABILITY, ARTS & CULTURE
www.kickstart-arts.ca

**What do you think?**

Some argue that exceptional students do not need or have time to learn music, visual art, French, etc. Construct both sides of this argument, referring to these resources:

Guay, D.M. (1995). The "Sunny Side of the Street": A supportive community for the inclusive art classroom. *Art Education*, 48, 51–56.

Kempe, A. (2004). *Drama education and special needs: A handbook for teachers in mainstream and special schools.* Cheltenham, Great Britain: Nelson Thornes.

Lapka, C. (2006). Students with disabilities in a high school band. 'We can do it!" *Music Education Journal*, 92(4), 54–59.

Mixon, K. (2005). Including exceptional students in your instrumental music program. *Teaching Music*, 13(3), 30–34.

Riley, M. (1997). Teaching French in a school for children with moderate learning difficulties. *British Journal of Special Education*, 24, 66–70.

students with physical, attentional, and other disabilities, teachers who successfully adapted visual art communicated regularly with resource teachers and other specialists, made rules and expectations explicit, and expected students to help one another (Guay, 1993). They gave clear instructions and used repetition, modelling, and motivational openings for each class. Overall, teachers need to keep in mind some of the fundamental principles of differentiating: teach to developmental needs, treat academic struggle as strength, provide multiple pathways to learning, give formative feedback, and "dare to be unconventional" (Wormeli, 2006a, p. 18).

## Differentiating Music

Music is often seen as a challenging area for exceptional students, especially those who are hard of hearing. Students who are deaf and hard-of-hearing can take part in music in elementary school classes if you teach all children to learn to sign the words while singing (Walczyk, 1993). Portable electronic keyboards can enable children to learn to play keyboard duets. McCord and Watts (2006) describe a number of ways to differentiate the instrumental music curriculum for exceptional students, such as making a videotape so students can see the music and a musician doing the fingering on an instrument like a saxophone at the same time. For students with cystic fibrosis and physical disabilities that affect breathing, stringed instruments would be a good choice (McCord and Fitzgerald, 2006). To read music, spaces can be highlighted with different colours and parts can be simplified whenever possible.

To differentiate the choral music curriculum for exceptional students and include exceptional students in a choral ensemble, plan ahead, write the rehearsal plan on the board, maintain consistency, and modify rehearsals so the routine considers the needs of specific exceptional students (Harwood, 2006; VanWeelden, 2001).

## Differentiating Drama

Drama includes many means of self-expression, including mime, monologue, tableau, and choral speaking, enabling teachers to negotiate the forms of assignments and self-expression with exceptional students. Adaptations include replacing body movement with facial expression and hand gestures for students in wheelchairs, allowing mime for non-verbal or shy students, and allowing students with learning disabilities to write and perform choral responses rather than monologues. Gifted students can negotiate open-ended assignments. The biggest challenge may be maintaining the attention of easily distracted exceptional students in the relatively unstructured drama classroom. Principles of classroom management and approaches for teaching students with ADHD may prove helpful. Wilhelm (2006) illustrates how drama is not only accessible through differentiation but also a motivator that helps to create a learning-to-life connection, especially for young adolescents.

## Differentiating the Teaching of French

"Differentiated instruction is often a necessity in the foreign language classroom, as mixed levels are not uncommon" (Educational website of PBS, www.pbs.org/teachers). Motivation is a key factor, especially when:

- students have language acquisition and literacy difficulties (e.g., learning disabilities);
- the target language has no personal meaning for the student;

**@**

**Weblinks**

COMMUNIQUÉ OF THE LOTE CENTER FOR EDUCATOR DEVELOPMENT IN AUSTIN, TEXAS
www.sedl.org/loteced/communique/n06.pdf

FRENCH IMMERSION IN MANITOBA: A HANDBOOK FOR SCHOOL LEADERS
www.edu.gov.mb.ca/k12/docs/fr_imm_handbook/chap_9.pdf

## FIGURE 5.3 SCAFFOLDING LEARNING AND MOTIVATION IN THE SECONDARY FRENCH CLASS

- Begin the year with a personal inventory sheet that includes students' interests, attitudes, likes, dislikes, parents' names, and telephone numbers; use all of these.
- Start with what students know: simple nouns, verbs, adjectives.
- Teach the key building blocks: conjugating each type of verb, one at a time, with a quiz to follow, so students have three strong quiz results at the start of term.

**Pre-Reading, Teaching, and Assessment of a Chapter in the Text**
- Build vocabulary understanding through activities and games.
- Explain context of first reading in English or second language so students can relate new knowledge to prior knowledge.
- Discuss the purpose, function, and construction of the grammar introduced in the chapter.
- Organize a paired treasure hunt of a grammar concept.
- Teach the grammar concept formally with cloze exercises or creation of examples.
- Give a written/oral assignment that features the grammar concept.
- Assess learning through projects, games, dialogues, listening tests, quizzes, exams, etc.

**Differentiations for Students with Disabilities**
- Comprehension checks by the teacher; guidance from peer tutor.
- Word cues on tests and quizzes.
- Open-text exam with a textbook guide to key topics (guide could be student created).

**Differentiations for Developmentally Advanced Students**
- Open-ended projects that allow them to be as creative as they can.
- A "bonus binder" for those who finish tasks early with challenging puzzles, crosswords, etc.
- Board games in French.

**Understanding the Learning Difficulties in French Class of Students with LD**
- Need for support and encouragement.
- The hardest part for them is understanding the comprehension questions.
- Teach students to use words from a question in the answer.
- Teach how to search for words that appear in a question in the assigned readings in the text.
- For writing, brainstorm sentence starters with the class so no one has a blank sheet.

Source: Developed by Nicole Lévesque, Barrie, Ontario. Used by permission.

**Further Reading**

On differentiating homework for exceptional students:

Brosvic, G.M., Dihoff, R.E., Epstein, M.L., & Cook, M.L. (2006). Feedback facilitates the acquisition and retention of numerical fact series by elementary school students with mathematics learning disabilities. *Psychological Record, 56*, 35–47.

Bryan, T., & Burstein, K. (2004). Improving homework completion and academic performance: Lessons from special education. *Theory into Practice, 43*(3), 213–219.

Cameron, L., & Bartel, L. (2009). The researchers are the homework! Perspectives of parents and teachers. *Education Canada, 49*(1), 48–51.

Hume, K. (2008). *Start where they are: Differentiating for success with the young adolescent.* Toronto, ON: Pearson Education Canada.

Mayer, K., & Kelley, M.L. (2007). Improving homework in adolescents with attention-deficit/hyperactivity disorder: Self vs. parent monitoring of homework behavior and study skills. *Child and Family Behavior Therapy, 39*(4), 25–42.

Myles, B.S., Ferguson, H., & Hagiwara, T. (2007). Using a personal digital assistant to improve the recording of homework assignments by an adolescent with Asperger syndrome. *Focus on Autism and Other Developmental Disabilities, 22*, 96–99.

Salend, S.J., Duhaney, L.M.G., Anderson, D.J., & Gottschalk, C. (2004). Using the internet to improve homework communication and completion. *Teaching Exceptional Children, 36*, 64–73.

- negative socio-political attitudes may be associated with the language; and
- students lack the basics from previous years' French classes.

Some strategies that may reduce the need for adaptations are an assertive behaviour management plan, 20-minute blocks of time for activities, and a variety of activities in which to use the four skill areas of reading, writing, speaking, and listening. Theisen (2002, www.sedl.org/loteced/communique/n06.pdf) provides many examples of differentiated instruction in the foreign language classroom. See Figure 5.3.

# Differentiating Homework

Research continues to show that completing homework is positively related to achievement for students in general (Chang et al., 2007; Trautwein, 2007). Most classroom teachers assign homework, and many report that students with learning

## FIGURE 5.4 GUIDELINES FOR HOMEWORK COMPLETION

The following guidelines are relevant for students with and without exceptionalities, and can be used to facilitate completion of homework by all students:

- Assign work that students already understand, rather than work they are likely to practise incorrectly; otherwise you will have to re-teach.
- Differentiate the amount of work assigned or time for completion as you do for in-class assignments. Make homework expectations realistic.
- Consider the IEPs of exceptional students and what is most essential for them to learn. Adapting homework does not mean being exempt.
- Do not make homework punitive. Motivate students to become more independent through imaginative homework assignments; for those who cannot complete the assignment independently, offer the option of working in pairs.
- Comment on homework occasionally so students feel that you value it. Give the message that it is worth students' effort to complete homework.
- Explain why you assign homework: consolidating classroom learning, increasing independent practice, in-depth understanding through longer-term projects, showing progress (young children reading books at home), etc.
- Use peer tutors, homework co-operative groups, or homework buddies, but develop some form of individual accountability.
- Develop predictable routines for homework early in the year, including a self-monitoring tracking system.
- Allow enough time in class for students to try the homework assigned so they can ask for help before the period ends and they leave.

### Put into Practice

Saskatchewan has a considerable history in integrating aboriginal perspectives into curricula (Saskatchewan Education, 1992, http://www.sasked.gov.sk.ca/docs/native10/S_L_Essentials.html#introduction) that includes how teachers can address students' cultural needs.

The Manitoba Department of Education document, *Integrating Aboriginal Perspectives into Curricula* (Manitoba Department of Education, 2003), also supports teachers in facilitating student understanding of Aboriginal perspectives and provides examples of projects to achieve this, such as an archaeology project, a trip to a fasting camp, a multimedia interactive drama performance workshop on Type 2 diabetes, and the sturgeon classroom project in senior science and math classes. For detailed descriptions see: www.edu.gov.mb.ca/k12/docs/policy/abpersp/index.html.

Review these documents in comparison with *The Teacher's Toolkit*. Consider ways that you could adapt your teaching to incorporate Aboriginal perspectives. Discuss with your peers.

disabilities and other exceptionalities experience difficulties completing homework (Bryan & Burstein, 2004). They may have difficulty focusing their attention, especially if they find the assignment difficult, and tend to show poor time management on long-term projects. A special issue of *Reading and Writing Quarterly* (2001, volume 17) focused on remedying the communication problems that make homework problematic (e.g., Polloway et al., 2001). Teachers can contribute to homework challenges if they do not make adaptations appropriate for exceptional students. Homework that is the same as that assigned to the rest of the class and is too difficult or time-consuming will compound learning challenges experienced by exceptional students (Bryan & Burstein, 2004). Ensure that students properly record assignments and have all necessary materials. (See Figure 5.4)

Families of exceptional students (e.g., Bryan & Burstein, 2004; Mayer & Kelley, 2007) and of students from cultural minorities (e.g., Brock et al., 2007; Sands et al., 2007) can effectively monitor and support their children's completion of homework with some direction from the school, making the benefits of homework accessible to students who need to optimize every opportunity to learn. Teachers can do their part by differentiating homework, making tasks meaningful and feasible for each student. Bryan and Burstein (2004) report that reinforcement, graphing, co-operative study teams, homework planners, and real-life assignments, along with parent involvement, have helped students to engage with and learn through homework. Hume (2008) reminds teachers that while feedback makes homework more effective, teachers can also ask students to self-assess and graph their improvement. Lead a class discussion on the homework and allow students choice in how they communicate their learning so every assignment is not the same.

# Adapting Teaching to Integrate Aboriginal Perspectives into Curricula

Ontario has recently introduced *The Teacher's Toolkit*, a collection of electronic resources from the Ministry of Education designed to assist elementary and secondary teachers in bringing Aboriginal perspectives into their classrooms (www.edu.gov. on.ca/eng/aboriginal/toolkit.html). The Toolkit includes two parts: (1) lists of the expectations in the revised curricula (2007) that contain Aboriginal perspectives and references to **Aboriginal cultures** and (2) teaching strategies related to the expectations that are directly applicable to classroom use. The Ministry describes *The Teacher's Toolkit* as a work in progress and additional teaching strategies continue to be added.

# Summary

This chapter has described how teachers can use the ADAPT strategy to analyze and adapt or differentiate teaching for exceptional learners, choosing from and combining numerous strategies. You can ADAPT many aspects of teaching, including substance (outcomes, content, cognitive complexity, authenticity, and task interest), or you can focus on changing the method of presentation, pace, and quantity for exceptional learners. Depending on the strengths and needs of exceptional students, it may be appropriate to ADAPT student engagement and activities, amount of practice, or the form of practice. Changing any of these aspects of teaching invariably affects other aspects because they are closely linked. Although homework may require adaptation, the goal of equity for exceptional students and their peers suggests that, as members of inclusive classrooms, exceptional students should have homework assignments just as their peers do.

# Key Terms

bypass strategies (p. 118)
remediation (p. 118)
acceleration (p. 118)
accommodations (p. 119)
modifications (p. 119)
alternative expectations (p. 119)
differentiating content (p. 119)
differentiating process (p. 119)
differentiating product of learning (p. 119)
tiering (p. 119)
Universal Design for Learning (EDL) (p. 119)

cognitive complexity (p. 121)
authentic tasks (p. 121)
interest (p. 121)
environment (p. 121)
method of presentation (p. 121)
pace (p. 121)
engagement (p. 122)
additional practice (p. 122)
form of practice (p. 122)
scaffolding (p. 122)
zone of proximal development (ZPD) (p. 122)
grouping (p. 122)

phonemic awareness (p. 123)
phonics (p. 123)
fluency (p. 123)
vocabulary (p. 123)
comprehension (p. 123)
reading wars (p. 124)
scaffolded reading experience (SRE) (p. 125)
pre-reading activities (p. 125)
post-reading activities (p. 125)
high-interest, low-vocabulary books (p. 125)
narrative text (p. 127)
story-planning sheet (p. 127)

# Challenges for Reviewing Chapter 5

1. How could you use the ADAPT strategy to analyze and differentiate teaching. What will be particularly challenging about this process? Particularly rewarding? How can teachers collaborate to enjoy the rewarding aspects while meeting the challenges?

2. Consider the principles that guide teachers in choosing and combining strategies for differentiating in the classroom. Discuss with both secondary and elementary teachers. Write a set of steps that you think will help you to differentiate your teaching. Compare them with the steps written by your peers. Why might they be different?

3. Choose one of the opening scenarios of this chapter and see how many of the aspects of teaching in your list can be differentiated to benefit the student in the scenario. How many of these are likely to also benefit other students?

4. Think about a student who might be in your one of your classes who is experiencing difficulty in a subject area and in completing homework. Describe the steps you would follow to differentiate your teaching and homework to meet the student's needs.

5. Return to the opening cases of Ms. Ash and Hema and answer the five questions that follow the cases.

# Chapter 6
## Adapting Assessment and Using Assessment to Differentiate Teaching

**Sasha is in grade 5 and has attention deficit disorder, as well as a learning disability in reading.** Sasha's teacher, Mr. Sinclair, has been differentiating teaching with the assistance of the resource teacher, and Sasha feels proud of being able to finish most assignments and understand what is being taught, especially in social studies and science. When Sasha receives his report card in October, he expects it to say he is doing well. He rips it open and sees low grades in every subject. Sasha doesn't understand. He asks the teacher, "Why do you say I'm doing good work and then give me Level 1, the lowest grade? I got 8 out of 10 on my science project." How can Mr. Sinclair explain to Sasha that his science project was only six pages long, while those of the other students were eight pages long, and that Sasha was allowed to replace some paragraphs with drawings? These adaptations were consistent with Sasha's IEP, which had provided clear guidance for Mr. Sinclair in differentiating teaching. Unfortunately the IEP contained vague information about how to adapt assessment and grading, and Mr. Sinclair had worried that Sasha would be crushed by his low marks.

**Belle has hearing loss and uses an FM system and speech-reading to learn in the secondary school classroom.** She has an IEP that guides her teachers at Oak Ridge Secondary School in differentiating teaching and adapting assessment. Belle's math teacher, Ms. Frost, knows that Belle tires easily and that although she is efficient at speech-reading, it only enables her to catch a fraction of what is said. Belle has math in the last period of the day. Ms. Frost uses a system of frequent oral tests to help students gauge their own learning and prepare for unit tests and term exams. Belle met with Ms. Frost after the first oral test to explain how difficult it was for her to understand the questions and to respond on paper quickly. The two of them reviewed Belle's IEP with the resource teacher. The decision was that Belle would take the tests and do her best, but that the oral quizzes would not contribute to Belle's final grade in the course. The weights of the other assessments—unit tests, homework completion, and term tests—would be increased. Belle felt that this was a fair resolution and was pleased that she could show Ms. Frost that she understood geometry and could use her graphing calculator effectively. However, she worried that other students who disliked the oral quizzes would think it was not fair for her to have different arrangements for calculating her grade.

### Learner Objectives

After you have read this chapter, you will be able to:

1. Describe how to use the ADAPT strategy to analyze and adapt assessment.

2. Describe large-scale assessment in Ontario and the accommodations used for exceptional students.

3. Explain how teachers can use classroom assessments to inform differentiated teaching.

4. Describe adaptations to classroom assessment, including tests, performance assessment, and portfolios.

5. Discuss adaptations and alternatives to report card marks.

1. What guidance do teachers need to adapt assessment for students who have disabilities that interfere with meeting the usual assessment expectations?

2. How can teachers match assessment to the differentiated teaching they are providing for exceptional students?

3. How can teachers prevent students like Sasha and Belle from giving up when effort and improved work are not recognized and rewarded?

4. Why might parents object if schools adapt assignments and then penalize the students after they do well on what they have been asked to do because their tasks have differed from those of their peers?

# Introduction

The subject of this chapter is adapting or differentiating assessment and using assessment data to differentiate teaching. **Assessment** refers to gathering information of many kinds about a student or a group of students using a variety of tools and techniques. **Large-scale assessment** refers to nationwide, province-wide, or district-wide efforts to provide information about student achievement, usually by means of paper-and-pencil tests. **Classroom assessment** refers to the day-to-day practices adopted by teachers to describe student learning, often through a variety of means, including portfolios, conferences with students, and paper-and-pencil tests. There is no judgment inherent in assessment; it is the act of describing student performance. **Testing** is one form of assessment, normally using a paper-and-pencil test (either designed by the teacher or commercially available) to gather information that describes a student's or group's level of performance. **Evaluation** involves making judgments and decisions, based on the assessment data, about a student or group of students. **Grading** is a symbolic representation of evaluation and **reporting** is the way in which evaluation results are communicated.

# Using the ADAPT Strategy for Assessment

You need strategies for adapting or differentiating assessment that are effective for exceptional students and efficient for you, and that become a regular part of your planning and teaching. You may remember that in Ontario three terms are used to refer to changes in students' expectations, instruction, and assessment:

1. Accommodations refer to ways we enable students to learn and to demonstrate learning which do not alter the provincial expectations for the grade.

2. Modifications are changes to the age-appropriate grade-level expectations (and teaching and assessment) that involve expectations from a different grade level.

3. Alternative expectations help students acquire knowledge and skills not represented in the Ontario curriculum.

You can use the ADAPT strategy introduced in Chapter 1 to differentiate assessment for learners with many exceptionalities, in elementary and secondary schools, for large-scale and classroom assessment. Chapter 5 included examples of using ADAPT for differentiating teaching. The ADAPT strategy has the following 5 steps:

- Step 1: **A**ccounts of students' strengths and needs
- Step 2: **D**emands of the classroom
- Step 3: **A**daptations
- Step 4: **P**erspectives and consequences
- Step 5: **T**each and assess the match

# Large-Scale Assessment and Exceptional Students in Ontario

In recent years educators have experienced pressure from governments, parents, and the general public for evidence to show how well schools are preparing students to compete

**Put into Practice**

Look for articles in local and national newspapers and magazines like *Maclean's* that reflect the recent demands for assessment to show that Ontario schools are delivering excellence. Discuss with your peers the ways that teachers can support one another and can work with families to reduce the feelings of pressure brought on by these demands.

in the global economy. Besides newspaper and magazine articles on this theme, there are international reports like *Education Indicators in Canada: An international Perspective* (2009, Canadian Education Statistics Council), which compares our academic achievement with countries in the Organization for Economic Cooperation and Development (OECD). Factors contributing to this pressure include increasing diversity and the changing role families play in education (Ben Jaafar & Anderson, 2007). It has been said that "What gets measured, how it gets measured, and how it is reported give a vivid accounting of what is seen as important" (Earl & Cousins, 1995, p. xi).

Until recently, schools in Canada demonstrated accountability by showing that they had developed programs for exceptional students, identified exceptional students, and written IEPs. However, following the release of the document, *Individual Education Plans: Standards for Development, Program Planning, and Implementation* (Ontario Ministry of Education, 2000a) schools received 14 standards to which IEPs must conform. These standards appear in Figure 6.1. Each standard is detailed under three headings: purpose, requirements, and compliance. Alberta also has *Standards for Special Education* (Alberta Learning, 2004) which focus on four topics: access, appropriateness, accountability, and appeals.

Demands for accountability are increasingly focusing on whether the process is producing the desired outcomes (Ben Jaafar & Anderson, 2007). Sonia Ben Jaafar (2006b) of the University of Toronto argues that Canada has a unique approach to accountability. She found that Ontario school leaders reported their beliefs were the key factor determining how they behaved in schools (Ben Jaafar, 2006a), while similar studies of principals in American schools showed they aligned their practices with state policies irrespective of their beliefs (Ladd & Zelli, 2002, 2003).

## FIGURE 6.1 STANDARDS FOR INDIVIDUAL EDUCATION PLANS IN ONTARIO

1. Reason for developing an IEP
2. Student profile
3. The student's strengths and needs
4. The special education program (current level of achievement, annual program goals, learning expectations)
5. Special education strategies, accommodations, and resources (teaching strategies and accommodations, human resources, individualized equipment)
6. Assessment, evaluation, and reporting (assessment methods and accommodations, evaluation and reporting of student achievement)
7. Provincial assessments (accommodations for participation in provincial assessments, exemptions from provincial assessments)
8. The transition plan
9. Parent/student consultation
10. Staff involvement in the development of the IEP
11. Information sources
12. Date of completion of the IEP
13. Implementation and monitoring
14. Review and updating.

———
Source: Information based on Ontario Ministry of Education. (2000a), *IEPs: Standards for Development, Program Planning, and Implementation.* Toronto: Ontario Ministry of Education.

# At the National Level

Although large-scale assessment plays a smaller role in education in Canada than in some other countries like the United States, every province has a large-scale assessment program and states that one purpose is system accountability (Klinger, DeLuca, & Miller, 2008). All provinces also participate in the Pan-Canadian Assessment Program (PCAP), administered by the Council of Ministers of Education, Canada (CMEC). PCAP assesses the performance of a sample of 13-year-olds in reading, mathematics, and science on a three-year cycle. Descriptions of the instruments and the reports of the provincial outcomes are available on the CMEC website (http://www.cmec.ca/Programs/assessment/pancan/Pages/default.aspx). Exceptional students drawn in the sample are encouraged to participate in PCAP, and on its Fact Sheet PCAP states that, "The students excused from participation [in the last administration] included those with highly limited abilities, those adversely affected by the test, those for whom appropriate modifications could not be made, and those whose parents requested it" (CMEC, 2009).

Students are entitled to the accommodations usually made for them in the classroom. "For example, students who normally had a scribe to write were permitted a scribe for these assessments. Students were given extra time to complete the assessments if they required it in the judgment of the school-based staff" (CMEC, 2003, p. 6). Some of the issues to consider when deciding what accommodations will make a large-scale assessment meaningful for an exceptional student appear in Figure 6.2.

## FIGURE 6.2 ADAPTING LARGE-SCALE ASSESSMENT FOR EXCEPTIONAL STUDENTS: ISSUES TO CONSIDER

**What is the role of the student's IEP?**

What accommodations for assessment are listed in the student's IEP?
What accommodations are used for classroom assessment, and are they appropriate for large-scale assessment?

**What accommodations are appropriate for this individual student given the nature of the large-scale test?**

How has the province, school board, school usually approached such accommodations?
What information is provided by the province or school board about conditions under which an exceptional student is exempted from large-scale assessment?
Where must the information about accommodations be recorded when the large-scale assessment is submitted?

**When should these adaptations be decided?**

How much time is needed to consult with the student, the parents, and all educators involved in the decisions?
How much planning and organizing is required to ensure the accommodations are ready?

**How are accommodations about setting decided?**

Can the student focus in the presence of thirty classmates?
Would preferential seating in the classroom be an adequate accommodation?
Would adaptive equipment be adequate to accommodate the student's needs (e.g., special lighting, pencil grip, keyboarding)?
Will the student likely distract classmates taking the large-scale assessment?
Are prompts required to focus the student's attention on the assessment?

## What do you think?

If Ontario policies require that large-scale assessment generally adopt the accommodations used in classroom assessment, what are the implications for you, the classroom teacher, and for the accommodations you are expected to make daily?

## What do you think?

In 2004 The Canadian Centre for Policy Alternatives (www.policyalternatives.ca) published *Passing the Test: The False Promise of Standardized Testing* (edited by Marita Moll), questioning the value of standardized testing in Canada. Do you think the issues emphasized in this book apply to exceptional students? For a different perspective, consult the book chapter by Diana Pullin (2005), "When One Size Does Not Fit All: The Special Challenges of Accountability Testing for Students with Disabilities," in *Uses and Misuses of Data for Educational Accountability and Improvement* (edited by J.L. Herman and E.H. Haertel, published by the National Society for the Study of Education).

## FIGURE 6.2 (*Continued*)

**How are accommodations about timing decided?**

Can the student work continuously for the length of the assessment?
Should the student have additional time to complete the assessment?
Should the student be given periodic supervised rest breaks during the assessment?
Does the student's regular medication affect the time of day when the assessment should be administered to the student?
Does the student's anxiety about a particular subject area suggest that that assessment should be administered last?

**How are accommodations of presentation decided?**

Can the student listen to and follow oral instructions?
Will an interpreter (sign language or oral interpreter) be needed for the student?
Will a Braille version of the assessment be required?
Will a large-print version of the assessment be required?
Will an audio version of the assessment be required?
Will it be necessary to provide a verbatim reading of the instructions and/or questions? (Interpretation of questions is usually not permitted.)

**How are accommodations to response format decided?**

Will it be necessary for the student to answer beside the question rather than in a response booklet?
Will the student require a computer to complete the response booklet?
Will it be necessary for responses to be audiotaped and transcribed?
Will other assistive devices or technologies be required (e.g., augmentative communication systems)?
Will verbatim scribing of responses be necessary?

---

Sources consulted: Thurlow, M.L., Elliott, J.L., & Ysseldyke, J.E. (2003). *Testing students with disabilities: Practical strategies for complying with district and state requirements* (2nd ed.). Thousand Oaks, CA: Sage; Education Quality and Accountability Office, Ontario. www. eqao.com/pdf_e/10/Sacg_pje_2010_web.pdf.

## Large-Scale Assessment in Ontario

The Ontario government established the Education Quality and Accountability Office (EQAO) in 1996 in response to the recommendations of Ontario's Royal Commission on Learning (1995) for "greater accountability and assurances of quality in the public education system." EQAO administers three large-scale assessment programs. On their website (http://www.eqao.com/), they describe the

## CASE STUDY ACCOMMODATIONS ON LARGE SCALE TESTS

Ryan's mother has come to Ben Krystol's classroom to ask that Ryan be given accommodations on the Grade 6 assessment this year. Ben is aware that Ryan was identified with a learning disability in the primary grades, but also knows that Ryan's parents have refused to allow Ryan to have any accommodations on day-to-day tests in the classroom this year. His mother is arguing that it would be unfair to ask Ryan to endure the stress associated with the Grade 6 test and she is aware that parents are to be involved in the decision about accommodations on EQAO tests. She won't listen when Ben suggests that Ryan can only have accommodations on EQAO tests that he has had on classroom assessments. After a heated exchange, Ben promises to arrange a meeting of himself, the principal, and Ryan's mother. Is Ryan entitled to accommodations? Is it fair to require the same accommodations on such different assessments as classroom quizzes and large-scale tests? Why?

Assessments of Reading, Writing, and Mathematics Primary Division (Grade 3) and Junior Division (Grade 6). These assessments provide both individual and system data on students' achievement. The Grade 9 Assessment of Mathematics provides individual and system data on students' achievement based on expectations in the Grade 9 mathematics curricula.

For each of these assessments, there is a guide for accommodations, special provisions, and exemptions. Students can receive accommodations on these tests provided that the accommodations are listed on their IEP and used for regular classroom summative assessment. The accommodations are to be decided:

- Based on the student's IEP
- For each student individually
- In consultation with the student, parent(s), and teacher(s)
- Based on regular classroom practice
- Prior to the assessment

The stated purpose of the third test, the Ontario Secondary School Literacy Test (OSSLT), is "to ensure that students have acquired the essential reading and writing skills." All students in Grade 10 who are working toward the Ontario Secondary School Diploma are required to write the OSSLT. Students who are unsuccessful on OSSLT may be eligible to fulfill the requirement through the Ontario Secondary School Literacy Course (www.edu.gov.on.ca/extra/eng/ppm/127.html).

The policy says, "The necessary accommodations must be made to ensure that students who are receiving special education programs and services and who have an Individual Education Plan (IEP) have a fair and equal opportunity to successfully complete the secondary school literacy test." The accommodations are to be consistent with those included in the student's IEP. The kinds of accommodations listed on the website are adjustments to:

- the environment in which the test is administered;
- the time allowed for the test;
- the format of the test (e.g., alternative forms of print); and
- the format of responses.

Students with special education needs who enroll in the OSSLC course can also receive the accommodations specified in their IEP. However, no modifications of the expectations are permitted. Some exceptional students (e.g., students with intellectual disabilities) may not be working toward the Ontario Secondary School Diploma and are not be required to complete the OSSLT or OSSLC.

## Comparison with the United States

In the United States, much has been written about including exceptional students in state and federal achievement tests in the era of No Child Left Behind (2001). These are called **"high-stakes" tests** because they influence whether students proceed to the next grade. Since 2000, exceptional students in the US have been expected to participate in district and state assessment, with or without accommodations, or by completing alternative assessments. Researchers suggest **alternative assessments** focus on authentic skills and experience in real-life environments (Salvia &

## FIGURE 6.3 ENSURING FAIRNESS AND VALIDITY

To ensure the fairness of standardized assessments and the validity of the results, answer these questions:

1. What test accommodations does the student need to demonstrate his or her knowledge without interference from his or her disability?
2. What test accommodations will not change the skill that the test items are assessing?
3. Has the student been provided with adequate opportunities to learn, practice, and apply the knowledge assessed by the test?
4. Has the student been provided with adequate opportunities to develop the necessary test-taking skills?
5. Has the student received adequate information about the testing process and the ways to express his or her needs during the assessment?
6. What accommodations does the student receive for classroom assessment (these should be identified in the IEP)?

Ysseldyke, 2007). Most states use portfolios as alternative assessments for students with severe intellectual disabilities (Cortiella, 2007).

In Canada, we do not offer alternative forms of assessment to students exempted from large-scale assessment. However, we have few high-stakes tests; even the OSSLT requirement can be met by some students by taking the OSSLC. Both Canadian and American policy-makers would do well to heed the cautions expressed by British researchers (e.g., Rustique-Forrester, 2005) about how increased demands for accountability have resulted in higher dropout rates for exceptional and at-risk students. Can educators ensure that large-scale assessments are administered fairly and produce valid results for exceptional students? Some questions to ask to ensure fairness and validity appear in Figure 6.3.

## Summary of Exceptional Students and Large-Scale Assessment in Canada

In summary, your students may be included in large-scale assessment (Klinger et al., 2008). Generally, exceptional students who have accommodations in their programs are included in large-scale assessment, and they receive the accommodations listed in their IEPs that they experience day to day in the classroom. Those students whose goals are considerably different from their peers and whose IEPs recommend alternative programs (estimated at less than 2 percent of the school population) are likely to be exempt from large-scale assessments. Being familiar with the IEPs of the students you teach will enable you to participate in decisions about the accommodations appropriate for your students on classroom assessments and large-scale assessments (Edgemon, Jablonski, & Lloyd, 2006).

# Classroom Assessment

## Changing Conceptions of Classroom Assessment

It is believed that teachers spend a quarter to a third of their professional time on assessment-related activities, and that effective assessment contributes to better learning for all students (Stiggins & Duke, 2008). In the past decade, researchers

# EDUCATIONAL PSYCHOLOGY

## Norm-Referenced and Criterion-Referenced Test Interpretation

Norm-referenced test interpretation is based on comparisons of a test-taker's performance with the performances of other people in a specified reference population (Frisbie, 2005). Items on norm-referenced tests are designed to ensure a distribution of scores, most often a normal distribution, which means it is not possible for all or even a majority of students to do well. In norm-referenced testing, a sample of people who have taken the test provides norms for interpreting an individual's score. Norms are scores that describe typical levels of performance for the norm group. By comparing an individual's raw score or number of items correct with the norms, we can interpret the individual's score as average, above average, or below average for that group. Sometimes the original sample serves as the comparison group. On large-scale assessment, the individual can be compared with all other grade 6 students in the province. However, the students within the district, school, or class can also serve as the norm group.

Typically norm-referenced tests contain questions that relate to a range of general objectives and are useful for obtaining a measure of overall achievement in an ability (like intelligence or phonemic awareness) or in a subject area (such as mathematics or reading). These tests may not provide helpful, diagnostic information about the learning accomplishments of an individual and are usually used to supplement information gathered by teachers and in-school teams. It is helpful to recognize the limitations of norm-referenced tests. The results are difficult to compare with a specific curriculum and, in fact, may be poorly matched to the curriculum in which you are most interested. They are rarely designed to measure psychomotor or affective objectives, and they tend to encourage competition and comparison of scores.

Criterion-referenced tests are tests that allow users to make score interpretations in relation to a functional performance level or a set standard of performance (Frisbie, 2005). They are sometimes called standards-based assessments. Usually they measure the degree of mastery of very specific objectives and are intended to provide indicators of student attainment of valued learning goals. Student performance may vary greatly, but there is no intent to deliberately spread student scores if all students have attained the goals. Typically one identifies how much students have learned thus far in relation to the goals of a specific curriculum without comparison with the results of other students.

You could set a standard such as four out of five correct for each type of mathematics problem taught in the recent unit as a criterion for students progressing to the next unit. Sometimes a standard of 100 percent is appropriate, for example, when we expect a professional (such as a surgeon) to get it right every time. This is one of the challenges of criterion-referenced assessment—setting the standard in a non-arbitrary fashion. For responding to this challenge, consult Berk (1986). While criterion-referenced tests are useful for assessing psychomotor and affective objectives, they may not prove helpful when ranking candidates or selecting the top few. As a classroom teacher, you should find criterion-referenced tests helpful when grouping students for instruction. Recent authors have argued that standards-based assessment enables more inclusive education; for a compilation of papers expressing this viewpoint, read Goodwin's *Assessment for Equity and Inclusion* (1997).

Self- or individual-referenced comparisons enable us to compare students with themselves and to make claims about their individual progress. For students who have alternative goals these may be very meaningful, especially in reporting their early progress toward goals that do not appear in the provincial curriculum.

Have you ever wondered what your students think about assessment? In a recent study, Dalbert, Scheidewind, and Saalbach (2007) asked secondary students in grades 7 to 12 for their ratings of the fairness of the three kinds of tests described above—norm-referenced, criterion-referenced, and self- or individual-referenced. The three kinds of grading were embedded in vignettes that the students judged. The students rated criterion-referenced as the fairest or most just, and individual-referenced was rated as almost just, while norm-referenced was rated as almost unjust. The authors recommend that when you are unable to use criterion-referenced assessment, you should carefully explain the rationale behind the application of other grading systems. This may be particularly applicable to exceptional students who often recognize that norm-referenced assessment is not really applicable to them.

### References

Berk, R.A. (1986). A consumer's guide to setting performance standards on criterion-referenced tests. *Review of Educational Research, 56,* 137–172.

Dalbert, C., Schneidewind, U., & Saalbach, A. (2007). Justice judgments concerning grading in school. *Contemporary Educational Psychology, 32,* 420–433.

Frisbie, D.A. (2005). Measurement 101: Some fundamentals revisited. *Educational Measurement: Issues and Practice, 24*(3), 21–28.

Goodwin, A.L. (Ed.). (1997). *Assessment for equity and inclusion.* New York: Routledge.

## FIGURE 6.4 QUESTIONS FOR TEACHERS TO ASK THEMSELVES WHEN PLANNING AND USING CLASSROOM ASSESSMENT TO INFORM TEACHING

**What are my students supposed to learn?**

Consider the curriculum, upcoming provincial tests, and community expectations.

**What have my students learned already?**

Use continuous evidence to consider the group as a whole, and each student's current place on the continuum of expected learning.

**What do my students still need to learn?**

Building on your answers to the previous questions, decide what you should focus on next.

**Which students need special services, accommodations, or modifications?**

Think about those individuals who are not meeting grade level expectations or who need to be taught differently.

**Have my students met the expectations?**

Compare their learning to grade expectations, and to expectations in their IEPs, for exceptional learners?

and educators have seen changing conceptions of **classroom assessment** and have considered the impact on all students.

The roles of schools and of assessment have evolved. In the past schools were often seen as sorting or ranking students based on their achievement. It was acceptable that some students learned and others didn't. In recent years, schools have committed to helping all students to learn, including students with disabilities. The changing role of schools has made it imperative that we rethink assessment (Stiggins, 2006).

At one time we relied on **norm-referenced** tests to compare students with their peers, while increasingly we rely on **criterion-referenced** tests. This involves comparing student performance to pre-set standards, asking who has met the standard, and then asking what we need to do to enable all students to meet the standard or to do the very best they can. The Theory and Research Box on page 147 elaborates on the differences between norm-referenced and criterion-referenced tests. Figure 6.4 provides questions to ask yourself when you are using classroom assessment to inform teaching.

In the past we used the terms **summative assessment** and **formative assessment**. Summative assessment referred to tests administered after learning was assumed to have taken place that were intended to provide parents and students with a summary of the students' learning and relative standing. This is increasingly called **assessment of learning**. Traditionally, formative assessment referred to assessment conducted during learning which was intended to promote learning and not simply judge whether students had learned. This is now called assessment *for* learning.

## Assessment *For* Learning

**Assessment for learning** is well matched to the demands of teaching in inclusive classrooms and is particularly helpful for differentiating teaching for exceptional learners and others who need tailored instruction. The emphasis is on creating descriptions that you can use in the next stage of teaching to differentiate learning for your students. "Assessment *for* learning happens in the middle of learning, often more than once, rather than at the end. It is interactive, with teachers providing assistance as part of the assessment. It helps teachers provide the feedback to scaffold next steps. And it depends on teachers' diagnostic skills to make it work" (Earl, 2003).

## Implications of Assessment for Learning for Student Confidence and Motivation

The changes that we are experiencing in assessment have implications for students' motivation, as well as for their learning. Albert Bandura (1994) argued that the experience of success can contribute to confidence, and described how individuals with a strong sense of self-efficacy are challenged by hard tasks rather than threatened, set goals for themselves, and persevere. "Such an efficacious outlook produces personal accomplishments, reduces stress and lowers vulnerability" (p. 9). We know that students judge themselves as learners and may give up on themselves if they fail repeatedly. Bandura explained that if individuals come to doubt their own abilities, "when faced with difficult tasks, they dwell on their personal deficiencies, on the obstacles they will encounter . . . rather than concentrate on how to perform successfully" (p. 7).

We use assessment to help students build a strong sense of academic self-efficacy by providing students with frequent information about how they are doing and differentiating our teaching based on that information. We can help all students, including exceptional students, to make progress and to recognize their progress.

Figure 6.5 includes a number of strategies that you may find helpful when using assessment *for* learning to make students a part of the assessment process.

### FIGURE 6.5 STRATEGIES FOR ASSESSMENT FOR LEARNING

**1. Helping Students to Understand What Good Work Looks Like and to Set Goals**

*Provide a vision of the learning target in language that students can understand;* For exceptional learners, adjust the language and explain individually

*Provide samples of student work along the route to the finished product;* For exceptional learners, make the steps appropriately smaller (or larger for gifted learners)

**2. Helping Students to Assess Their Progress**

*Provide specific descriptive feedback (anecdotal is preferable to numerical) so students know how to improve their work;* For exceptional learners, avoid overwhelming the student with too much feedback

*Teach students to provide descriptive feedback for themselves to improve their work;* For exceptional learners, help them to focus on their accomplishments

**3. Helping Students to Raise the Quality of Their Work**

*Draw students' attention to one key attribute of their work at a time, while reminding them that at the end, they will assemble all the pieces;* For exceptional learners, help them to focus on the most attainable change

*Teach students to reflect on changes in the quality of their work and on their enhanced abilities;* For exceptional learners, provide clear, concrete evidence of growth

Sources: Adapted from Chappuis, J. (2010). *The seven strategies of assessment FOR learning.* Portland, OR: ETS Assessment Training Institute; Stiggins, R. (2009). Assessment FOR learning in upper elementary grades. *Phi Delta Kappan, 90*(6), 419–421.

## TABLE 6.1 COMPARING ASSESSMENT OF, FOR, AND AS LEARNING

| | Assessment *of* Learning | Assessment *for* Learning | Assessment *as* Learning |
|---|---|---|---|
| Timing | After learning | Ongoing—before, during learning | During learning |
| Assessor | Teacher, school district | Teacher, gradually learner | Learner |
| Comparison | Other students | Standards, expectations | Personal goals |
| Major Uses | Judging placement, promotion | Making instructional decisions, providing learners with feedback about learning and with motivational support | Self-monitoring, self-regulation, autonomous learning |

Sources: Adapted from Stiggins, R. (2009). Assessment FOR learning in upper elementary grades. *Phi Delta Kappan, 90*(6), 419–421; Earl. L. (2003). Assessment of learning, for learning, and as learning. In L. Earl, *Assessment as learning: Using classroom assessment to maximize student learning.* Thousand Oaks, CA: Corwin Press.

### What do you think?

Use the ADAPT strategy to recommend accommodations to large-scale testing for one of the students—Sasha or Belle—described in the cases that open this chapter. Which steps of the ADAPT strategy are most relevant for adapting large-scale assessment? Why?

Each strategy includes information about how it can be made more effective for exceptional learners. Students need a clear, realistic target to aim for and work samples provide this target effectively. While students work toward these goals, provide continuous feedback which is descriptive and includes guidance about what to change and how to change it. Encourage students to self-assess and self-regulate—to describe what they have done well, what isn't so good, and why, and to set goals.

"Effective assessment empowers students to ask reflective questions and to consider a range of strategies for learning" (Earl, 2003, p. 44). Lorna Earl of University of Toronto explains that when students begin to self-regulate, we are moving into **assessment as learning**, the ultimate goal. Students link assessment and learning as "their own best assessors." Teachers in inclusive classrooms need to find a balance among the three approaches—assessment *of* learning, *for* learning, and *as* learning—because they all contribute to student learning. Table 6.1 compares these three forms of assessment.

### MAKING ASSESSMENT CONSISTENT WITH TEACHING

Assessment is most helpful when it is consistent, in content and form, with the learning outcomes that it is assessing (Roach et al., 2008). For example, if the purpose of a spelling activity is to help students spell common words in their journal writing, the assessment of that activity should reflect the words you teach and should ask students to produce those words in a context similar to that encountered in writing. Think about how you could differentiate assessment. Students who are strong in spelling could be expected to spell other words from the same word families as the taught words. Students who are not strong spellers may use and misspell simpler words in their journal writing, so they may learn and be assessed on simpler words. If the goal is to help students to be better editors of their written work, ask students to identify incorrectly spelled words. Because written work is usually in sentence format, teaching and assessing identification of incorrectly spelled words should probably involve sentences rather than lists of words.

### USING ASSESSMENT TO GAUGE STUDENT LEARNING AND TO DIFFERENTIATE TEACHING

Classroom assessment will help you differentiate your teaching. When you are planning instruction, assessment data can help you determine student needs in relation to specific outcomes: What does the group generally understand and show interest in? What do individual students understand and show interest in related to these objectives? By answering these questions, you can start a new instructional unit where the students are and work toward appropriately challenging outcomes. The assessments that inform you could include observations, test results, portfolios, and interviews. How can you streamline instruction and for which students? Who needs additional support and how can you provide it?

Assessment can guide you when you are in the midst of instruction: "constantly gather information to make decisions about when to move on, stop, or change direction" (Lambdin & Forseth, 1996, p. 298). You will be able to make in-process decisions about students' levels of mastery, misconceptions, insights, and needs (Moon, 2005). If only a few are not progressing well, assessment data will help you to provide scaffolding or differentiated teaching for those few. However, if most are not progressing well, you may need to make substantial instructional changes. Also consider students' interest in and engagement with the teaching. Such assessment *for* learning can consist of work samples, paper-and-pencil tests, and students' discussions and questions. You could form new student groups, change your pacing, or change the presentation and content for individuals or the class.

Assessment *of* learning tells you about student mastery of the content and can serve as preassessment for the next unit. You must discern to what extent each student has reached the outcomes, including exceptional students with IEP outcomes, while assessing the effectiveness of your teaching. You may decide to reteach concepts or, in the next unit, to supplement the text with audio for some students and have others write answers in individual words rather than sentences.

**Cross-Reference**

In Chapters 1 and 5, references were made to response to intervention (RTI) models that are beginning to appear in provincial documents and to be implemented in some school districts in Ontario

## Preparing Students and Parents for Equitable (but Not Necessarily the Same) Assessment

Sometimes you need to differentiate assessment. While most of the class writes a history test in forty-five minutes, Jacob (who has learning disabilities) writes the same test in 90 minutes in the resource room in accord with the accommodations in his IEP—more time in a quiet place. Bonita (who has intellectual disabilities and alternative learning goals) explains to a paraeducator how to travel to local sites of historic significance, working on two goals on her IEP—learning to travel independently by bus and planning and carrying out a conversation with an adult.

What do you say when students or parents ask why Jacob gets more time or Bonita has an oral test? From your first contact with students and parents, refer to your commitment to differentiating teaching and assessment to meet individual needs. Talk of students as individuals with varying strengths. Explain that including exceptional students in the classroom is the policy of the school, school district, and province. Use examples that make it easy for students and parents to see that this is about fairness. Blind students are taught in and receive tests in Braille. This does not disadvantage seeing students who don't need Braille. Similarly, research conducted in Canada shows that students without learning disabilities are not disadvantaged when their learning-disabled classmates receive appropriate accommodations on an assessment (e.g., Lesaux, Pearson & Siegel, 2006).

It is important that the way you assess your students is perceived as fair. And when you are differentiating assessment, the potential for being perceived as unfair

@

**Weblinks**

EXAMINE STUDY SKILLS AND STUDY GUIDES AT THE FOLLOWING SITES:

UNIVERSITY OF NORTHERN BRITISH COLUMBIA LEARNING SKILLS CENTRE
www.unbc.ca/lsc

TEENS HEALTH: TEST ANXIETY
http://kidshealth.org/teen/school_jobs/school/test_anxiety.html

TIPS ON GETTING TEENS TO DO THEIR HOMEWORK
http://parentingteens.about.com/cs/homeworkhelp/a/homeworktips.htm

TORONTO PUBLIC LIBRARY: HOMEWORK HELP FOR TEENS
http://ramp.torontopubliclibrary.ca/secondary/schoolstuff/one-content.jsp

STUDY GUIDES AND STRATEGIES
www.studygs.net

ELEMENTARY TEACHERS' FEDERATION OF ONTARIO STUDY GUIDES
www.nt.net/~torino/novels3.html

## FIGURE 6.6 WHAT MIDDLE SCHOOL AND HIGH SCHOOL STUDENTS EXPECT AS FAIR TREATMENT FROM EDUCATORS

**Interactional Fairness**

Neutrality or impartiality; everyone gets their turn and no one is favoured
Respectful treatment for everyone; teachers remain calm, discuss private matters in private
Consistent concern shown for everyone's well-being in the class; teachers care, listen, are available
Actions show integrity, e.g., consistency, truthfulness
Propriety; relationships are supportive but not too close, privacy is respected

**Fairness in Procedures**

Assessment that helps all students to learn as well as serving as a means of assigning grades
Clear expectations about attendance and concern about students' missed learning due to absence
Clear expectations about when students work together and when students work collaboratively
Opportunities for student voice to be heard about procedures including assessment

**Fairness in Outcomes**

Course grades that reflect what students believe they have learned and have earned
High expectations and support so all students can show what they know

**Further Reading**

Wormeli, R. (2006). *Fair isn't always equal: Assessing and grading in the differentiated classroom*. Portland, ME: Stenhouse Publishers.

Blaz, D. (2008). *Differentiated assessment for middle and high school classrooms*. Larchmont, NY: Eye on Education.

Ysseldyke, J., & Algozzine, B. (2006). *Effective assessment for students with special needs*. Thousand Oaks, CA: Corwin Press.

Salvia, J., Ysseldyke, J.E., & Bolt, S. (2007). *Assessment in special and inclusive education* (10th ed.). Boston: Houghton Mifflin Co.

is great. Students' thinking that what you are doing is unfair could undermine the trusting relationship you have developed with them.

**Fairness** is a complex concept. Sometimes we treat everyone equally—all children are treated with respect. Sometimes we treat children based on merit—the best singer gets the lead in the school musical. Sometimes we treat everyone equitably—they receive what they need, like differentiated assessment. If a student objects because Bonita has a different test, explain that this test is as hard for Bonita as theirs is for them. And make sure that this is the case.

Young children may find these issues difficult to comprehend because they have difficulty putting themselves in someone else's shoes. Welch (2000) suggests reflecting a student's feelings when the student says something is unfair, asking the student to write about their feelings, and discussing what they have written about their feelings individually. Be sensitive to the possibility the child is telling you they need acknowledgement for their accomplishments. Research suggests older students perceive three types of fairness and that the order of importance to students is: interactional fairness, procedural fairness, and fairness of outcomes (Lizzio, Wilson & Hadaway, 2007; Rodabaugh, 1996). These are described in Figure 6.6.

# Differentiating Classroom Assessment
## Adapting Learning Outcomes for Exceptional Students

This chapter contains many examples of differentiating learning outcomes for exceptional students. Wormeli (2006, pp. 57–58) describes **tiering assessments** for advanced students. He suggests you begin with the grade-level task and then raise or lower the challenge level. To increase complexity and challenge, ask students to manipulate information rather than echoing it, to extend the concept to other areas, to critique it against a set of standards, or to incorporate more facets.

Because exceptional students are included in regular classrooms, you are expected to differentiate your teaching and assessment for the class as a group and to meet the needs of exceptional learners as much as possible, but not to individualize all teaching and assessment. The learning outcomes for exceptional students are guided by the IEP. Thus, you need to consider what outcomes are appropriate for an exceptional student when you plan your teaching. These outcomes form the basis for the assessment following teaching, just as they do for students without exceptionalities. If Sasha, in the case study at the beginning of this chapter, is expected to produce less written work but work of a similar quality to his peers, then this outcome needs to be specified clearly. This differentiated outcome subsequently guides your assessment and grading of Sasha.

## Preparing Students for Classroom Tests

You can prepare all students, including exceptional students, for classroom tests. The strategies in Table 6.2 can be used with whole classes and then personalized for small groups and individual students who need more help preparing for classroom tests. These strategies can be used in any subject and are particularly helpful for teaching junior, intermediate, and senior students how to prepare independently.

## Adapting Classroom Tests During Test Construction

All students are likely to benefit from tests that are clearly written. However, some test items that will present no difficulties for most students may create problems for

**TABLE 6.2 SUGGESTIONS FOR PREPARING STUDENTS FOR CLASSROOM TESTS**

| | |
|---|---|
| Create study guides | Tell students what to study |
| | Could use an adapted webquest |
| | Help slow readers focus on important information |
| | Provide practice tests and feedback on how students did |
| | Arrange for tutoring by a peer, paraeducator, or resource teacher |
| | Organize study buddies or study groups |
| Help students analyze their previous tests | Go over previous tests so students can understand their mistakes |
| | Form groups and explain how to overcome their common errors |
| | Demonstrate correct procedures on overhead transparencies |
| Teach study skills | Use small group or whole class instruction |
| | Ask pairs to highlight what is most important in a passage |
| | Model how to remember the two most important highlighted parts |
| | Show which parts are most important and explain why |
| Develop chunking strategies and mnemonics | Help students group similar ideas and come up with memory aids |
| | For example, to remember the Great Lakes, think HOMES = Huron, Ontario, Michigan, Erie, Superior |
| Make concept maps | Provide a blank concept map with a few key words filled in |
| | After students fill it in, model yours and lead discussion |
| | Distribute copies of your concept map as a study aid |

## FIGURE 6.7 SUGGESTIONS FOR ADAPTING CLASSROOM TESTS DURING TEST CONSTRUCTION

**Suggestions for Adapting Objective Tests**

- Pretape the questions so that a non-reader or poor reader can work from a tape recorder.
- Present questions in a familiar format (the way they were taught).
- Alter the reading level by eliminating difficult words (you could write in an easier word with the same meaning above the difficult word).
- For fill-in questions, provide the possible answers at the bottom of the page.
- Use simple, direct statements in the stem of the question.
- Familiarize students with the format of the test by reviewing samples from previous tests.
- Use both oral and written directions (possibly with an example) for each section of a test.
- Consider an open-book test or allowing the use of a one-page summary.
- Make the print large enough to be read easily.
- Make the visual layout simple and clean.
- Underline, highlight, or bold key words.
- Arrange items in a logical sequence.
- Allow additional time for students who process or write slowly.
- Include or explain the marking scheme.

**Suggestions for Adapting Essay Tests**

- Use simple, direct phrases in the design of your essay questions.
- Underline, highlight, or bold key words in the questions.
- Suggest the number of key points that should be included and give the marking scheme.
- Provide a proofreading checklist.
- Provide an outline organization sheet.
- Alter the reading level by eliminating difficult words (you could write in an easier word with the same meaning above the difficult word).
- Allow additional time for students who process or write slowly.

———

Source: Adapted from Peel Board of Education (1990). *Looking at Assessment: More Than Just Marks*.

exceptional students; they may find the language and format confusing, need to use Braille or to have questions read to them. Figure 6.7 contains a number of suggestions for adapting a classroom test during its construction. Some of these could help all students and you may incorporate them into the test you distribute to the entire class, or you may make an adapted version for a number of students when you construct the original test. You can mark small changes that only apply to one or two students on the student's copy just before you distribute the test.

## Adapting Administration of Classroom Tests

What problems would you anticipate when exceptional students take classroom tests? Look to the IEP and your in-school team for guidance. For an objective or short-answer test, students could require additional time or fewer questions, oral administration, a scribe, interpretation of a question, a calculator for problem solving, relevant formulas or definitions, and other external memory aids. For an essay test, extended time or fewer required points in answers may be critical for those slow to process information. A quiet, distraction-free environment may be necessary. Spell-checking can improve the quality of written work. An open-book test may be appropriate to test use of knowledge rather than memory. If a student is to use a tape recorder, he or she should have been taught how to use one in test conditions.

Even a well-constructed test will fail to demonstrate the knowledge of exceptional students if it is administered inappropriately.

## Adapting Marking of Classroom Tests

Adapted scoring or marking of classroom tests should be guided by key information in students' IEPs and you may want to discuss the implications with your principal or the in-school team. When you mark objective tests or essay tests, students with disabilities in writing, spelling, or memory should not be penalized for spelling or grammatical errors. You could provide these students with an opportunity to edit their own work before you mark their tests, or you could ask them to indicate where they think they have made these types of errors. On essay tests, you may review written responses with students individually and allow students with writing disabilities to elaborate orally on their written responses. You could adapt the marking scheme; remember the case study of Belle at the beginning of this chapter? Because of her hearing loss, oral quizzes did not count toward her grade in mathematics. This serves as an example of the kind of reasonable adaptations that can be arranged. It may enhance self-awareness and self-advocacy to show exceptional students how they would have scored without and with the adapted scoring.

Recognize your own assumptions and views about marking classroom tests and then work collaboratively with colleagues who teach the exceptional students in your class. Research suggests that when teachers collaborated to develop personalized grading plans for exceptional students, everyone, including teachers, parents and students, found the process fairer and more effective than previous grading (Hong & Ehrensberger, 2007; Munk and Bursuck, 2001). Assess students frequently through a variety of means and make every effort to accurately convey achievement to parents and students. Give useful feedback that helps students to improve and remember that effective, informative classroom tests can increase students' self-efficacy and motivation (Segers, Gijbels, & Thurlings, 2008).

## Using Adapted Performance Assessments

**Performance assessment** refers to assessment activities that require students to perform tasks or generate their own responses. In studying municipal government, your grade 5 students may read local newspapers, attend a meeting of the municipal council, and invite a councillor to visit the classroom. If you assess what they have learned by asking them to write a letter about a community issue to a local politician, you will be using performance assessment. If you teach your grade 11 students in a career development and co-operative education course to answer interview questions by having them role-play interviewer and then interviewee, you can assess their interview skills while they are interviewed by an unfamiliar adult volunteer.

Characteristics of **authentic assessment**, according to Wiggins and McTighe (2005), are:

- performance on authentic, engaging, and important problems;
- performance on contextualized tasks that represent those expected in the adult world;
- real problems with a number of steps that require more than formulaic solutions; and
- tasks that demand students produce a quality product or performance.

**Put into Practice**

Consult a source on performance assessment, such as one of these:

Hibbard, K.M. (2000). *Performance-based learning and assessment in middle school science.* Larchmont, NY: Eye on Education, Inc.

Berman, S. (2008). *Performance-based learning.* Thousand Oaks, CA: Corwin Press.

Luongo-Orlando, K. (2003). *Authentic assessment: Designing performance-based tasks.* Markham, ON: Pembroke Publishers.

Develop a performance-based task and assessment and make adaptations for an exceptional student (whom you describe in one paragraph).

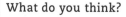

**What do you think?**

Read the following paper on researchers' understanding of authentic assessment and performance assessment, and debate with your peers whether the two terms represent the same concept or two distinct concepts.

Frey, B.B., & Schmitt, V.L. (2007). Coming to terms with classroom assessment. *Journal of Advanced Academics,* 18, 402–423.

## What do you think?

Read two sources on portfolio assessment. Then consult current documents and websites of the ministry of education in your province. What do you think of the use of portfolios in the assessment of learning of exceptional students?

Glor-Scheib, S., & Telthorster, H. (2006). Activate your student IEP team member using technology: How electronic portfolios can bring the student voice to life. *Teaching Exceptional Children Plus, 2*(3), Article 1.

Abrami, P.C., & Barrett, H. (2004). Directions for research and development on electronic portfolios. *Canadian Journal of Learning and Technology, 31*(3), 1–15.

Wade, A., Abrami, P.C., & Sclater, J. (2005). An electronic portfolio to support learning. *Canadian Journal of Learning and Technology, 31*(3), 33–50.

Zubizarreta, J. (2004). *The learning portfolio: Reflective practice for improving student learning.* Bolton, MS: Anker Pub.

Wesson, C.L., & King, R.P. (1996). Portfolio assessment and special education students. *Teaching Exceptional Children, 28*(2), 44–48.

Mahoney, J. (2002). *Power and portfolios: Best practices for high school classrooms.* Portsmouth, NH: Heineman.

Performance assessments enable students to show what they know. For example, Sasha has ADHD and reading disabilities and is in the grade 5 class that wrote letters to municipal politicians. Sasha drafted his letter on a computer, read it into a tape recorder, listened to it, and then reorganized the order of the paragraphs. By using a computer with a spell checker and a grammar checker, he corrected most of the errors and produced a quality product. Because he knows that he speaks better than he writes, Sasha telephoned city hall, made an appointment with the councillor representing his district, and hand-delivered his letter. Sasha demonstrated what he had learned about municipal government, and because he was highly motivated by this assessment, he made adaptations himself.

Sometimes students with disabilities miss the connections between assessments in school and the real-world contexts to which they apply. That is why Sasha's teacher ensured that the letter was written to an adult in the local power structure rather than simply to the teacher. Well-designed performance assessments can help students see these connections (Berman, 2008). However, this assessment required that the students learn how to write a persuasive letter, to provide specific examples that support an argument, and to sequence the parts of a letter. They needed plenty of practice before they embarked on the culminating task. At the same time Sasha's teacher recognized that if the process were not engaging, then it would become just another traditional test to exceptional students.

Students on modified programs can benefit from performance assessment. Bill, a non-verbal adolescent with autism, is learning to express his agreement and disagreement to unfamiliar adults so he can find employment or volunteer work. A performance assessment might require him to attend a meeting with the manager of a charity shop who needs a volunteer to sweep the floor and to unpack and sort donations. Bill will show the manager that he can communicate agreement and disagreement and can perform the assigned tasks. He practises the interview with a paraeducator, sweeps the classroom, and practises sorting a box of housewares daily. The paraeducator attends the workplace meeting with Bill and next term will accompany Bill to his two-hour-per-week on-the-job training at the charity shop. Performance assessments have great potential for assessing exceptional students in meaningful ways.

## Portfolios as Classroom Assessments for Exceptional Learners

**Portfolios** are collections of student work that show their achievements and their learning over time. They usually contain evidence of reflection and self-evaluation that contribute to students' valuing their work and themselves (British Columbia Ministry of Education, 2004). Electronic portfolios are described by Glor-Scheib and Telthorster (2006), and Harper, O'Connor, and Simpson (1999) suggest procedures like these for more conventional portfolios:

- *collect* in a container that is efficient for your classroom organization;
- *select* purposefully so the contents show students meeting outcomes and learning goals;
- *reflect*—students can write on cover sheets or sticky notes, or teacher and student can summarize a conference together; and

- *inspect*—teacher, student, and parents should consider the accomplishments in light of the outcomes and goals that were set (use this event to close the year or term's portfolio process).

Examples of content that might go into a portfolio in reading and writing (with adaptations for exceptional students in brackets) include:

- a log of books read with personal reactions (the personal reactions could be captioned drawings);
- an audio recording of the student reading (monthly recordings would show progress for early readers);
- representative responses to pre- and post-reading questions (could change gradually from multiple choice to fill in the blanks to written responses);
- a scrapbook of representative writing samples (increasing in length and complexity);
- notes from conferences with the teacher (ranging from a checklist to a paragraph)

Adaptations you may have to make include teaching exceptional students how to select and reflect on portfolio pieces, and offering more guidance in the organization of the information. If exceptional students cannot function independently in student-parent conferences, you may wish to be present and participate rather than being nearby and monitoring. Some portfolio assessments that have been used for students with alternative outcomes include a vocational résumé in grade 12, management of a student's own schedule, and engagement in hobbies. Portfolios provide a flexible, individualized approach to capture the learning outcomes of a heterogeneous group of students (Kleinert, Haig, Kearns, & Kennedy, 2000).

**Further Reading**

Read the following three papers on grading adaptations for exceptional students and discuss with your peers the most important issues that you think arise on this topic. How do the adaptations advanced by each of these papers differ? And how do the processes recommended for arriving at grading adaptations differ?

Munk, D.D., & Bursuck, W.D. (2004). Personalized grading plans: A systematic approach to making the grades of included students more accurate and meaningful? *Focus on Exceptional Children, 36*(9), 1–11.

Silva, M., Munk, D.D., & Bursuck, W.D. (2005). Grading adaptations for students with disabilities. *Intervention in School and Clinic, 41*(2), 87–98.

Salend, S.J. (2005). Report card models that support communication and differentiation of instruction. *Teaching Exceptional Children, 37*(4), 28–34.

## Adaptations and Alternatives to Report Card Marks

One of the most debated questions in education is how student learning should be reported, and even more contentious is the issue of how report grades should be adapted for exceptional students. We recognize that assessments must not discriminate against students with disabilities, and we do not want our grading practices to serve as disincentives to exceptional students like Sasha, described in one of the chapter-opening case studies. But we are aware, grades must speak to students, parents, teachers, and eventually to post-secondary institutions, and employers. What options do you have? Table 6.3 provides examples of grading

**TABLE 6.3 EXAMPLES OF GRADING ADAPTATIONS**

| Change Grading Criteria | Change to Letter and Number Grades | Use Alternatives to Letter and Number Grades |
|---|---|---|
| Vary grading weights | Add written comments | Use pass–fail grades |
| Modify curricular expectations | Add student activity logs | Use competency checklists |
| Grade on the basis of improvement | Add information from portfolios and/or performance-based assessments | Use contracts and modified syllabi |

Source: Friend, M., Bursuck, W., & Hutchinson, N.L. (1998). *Including exceptional students: A practical guide for classroom teachers.* Scarborough: Allyn and Bacon Canada, p. 359. Reprinted with permission.

adaptations that could be used for exceptional students—across a wide range of exceptionalities and needs, from mild to severe. It is important to know the policies for your jurisdiction, so you understand which of these options are acceptable in your school. We review the options and then the current policies in Ontario.

The first of these options is **changing grading criteria**. Belle's case at the beginning of this chapter demonstrates how you can vary grading weights so students are not disadvantaged by an impossible task. Adapting curricular expectations must build on the IEP, and then it is critical to assess what is expected for the exceptional student (Silva et al., 2005). If you expect Linda, a student with developmental disabilities, to learn to discuss the historical sites in the community, then assess her on this outcome with a high mark for excellence or a low mark for poor performance. **Grading contracts** or **modified course syllabi** *may* enable you to give students credit for attendance, promptness, effort, co-operative behaviour, and improvement (Munk & Bursuck, 2004), especially if these are consistent with outcomes in their IEPs. Ensure that the student and parents are aware of the criteria. You can also grade on students' performance on prioritized content and assignments. Suppose there are two topics in the unit, and you believe the topic on biography is much more important than the work on poetry. You could give an exceptional student 66 percent of the grade on the biography topic and 33 percent on poetry, instead of treating the two topics as if they are of the same value (Silva et al., 2005).

**Changes to letter and number grades** may mean clarifying with a comment that explains the reading level of the books used in language arts or explaining that Billy is using the grade 3 math text although he is in grade 5. A summary of student activities constitutes a **student activity log**. This may be particularly beneficial in reporting progress for students on alternative programs. You may be able to include a summary that describes the key accomplishments shown in the portfolio.

Much has been written on these issues in recent years by researchers (e.g., Jung & Guskey, 2007) and in the popular press (Rushowy, *Toronto Star*, October 13, 2009). Curriculum Services Canada provides podcasts on its website, including "Rethinking Classroom Assessment with Purpose in Mind," Lorna Earl, (http://www.curriculum.org/secretariat/april27.shtml). Consistent with the emphasis on this challenging issue, in 2010, Ontario is in the midst of changing its policies and procedures on assessment, evaluation, and reporting. The guides to the provincial report cards that are still available on the Ministry of Education website were developed in 1998 for grades 1 to 8 and in 1999 for grades 9 to 12 (http://www.edu.gov.on.ca/eng/document/forms/report/1998/report98.html). In 2008, *Growing Success, Assessment, Evaluation, and Reporting: Improving Student Learning* (Ontario Ministry of Education, 2008) was disseminated with the claim that it would enable educators in Ontario "to better support students with specific needs" including "students who receive special education services and programs" (p. 2). Consistent with previous documents, it includes the principle, "accommodate the needs of students with special education needs, consistent with the strategies outlined in their Individual Education Plan." Table 6.4 outlines Ontario's report card policies for students with special education needs.

Whatever forms of grading adaptation you use, you must ensure they are consistent with the policies and procedures that govern your work and acceptable to your in-school administrators. Be prepared to explain them to the student and parents and collaborate with others who teach the exceptional student (see Farenga &

**TABLE 6.4 ONTARIO REPORT CARD POLICIES FOR STUDENTS WITH IEPS IN ELEMENTARY AND SECONDARY SCHOOL**

| Student's IEP | Elementary |
|---|---|
| Student with an IEP receives only accommodations for a subject/strand | Not necessary or advisable to check the IEP box on the student's report card |
| Student with an IEP has modified expectations, which vary from the expectations of the regular program for the grade, but are based on the Ontario Curriculum, Grades 1-8 | Check the IEP Box when it applies to a particular subject or strand. The following Statement must appear in the Strengths/Weaknesses/Next Steps section: "The grade/mark for this strand/subject is based on achievement of the expectations in the IEP, which vary from the Grade __ expectations." |
| Student has an IEP and expectations are alternatives to the curriculum expectations | An alternative format may be used to record achievement (e.g., the evaluation section of the IEP) |

| Student's IEP | Secondary |
|---|---|
| Student with an IEP receives only accommodations for a course | Not necessary or advisable to check the IEP box on the student's report card |
| Student with an IEP has some learning expectations for a course that are modified from the curriculum expectations, but the student is working toward a credit for the course | Check the IEP Box |
| Student with an IEP has learning expectations modified to such an extent that the principal deems a credit will not be granted for the course | Check the IEP Box<br><br>The following statement must be included in he Comments section (with comments about the student's achievement): "This percentage grade is based on achievement of the expectations specified in the IEP, which differ significantly from the curriculum expectations for the course." |
| Student has an IEP and expectations are alternatives to the curriculum expectations | Check the IEP Box<br><br>The following statement must be included in the Comments section (with comments about the student's achievement): "This percentage grade is based on achievement of the expectations specified in the IEP, which differ significantly from the curriculum expectations for the course"<br><br>Or an alternative format may be used to record achievement (e.g., the evaluation section of the IEP) |

Sources: Based on information in: Ontario Ministry of Education. (2008). *Growing success*. Toronto: Ministry of Education; Ontario Ministry of Education. (1998, 1999). *Guide to the provincial report card (Grades 1-8/Grades 9-12)*. Toronto: Ontario Ministry of Education.

Joyce, 2000; Silva et al., 2005). In all you do, think about how you would want a teacher to report on the progress of your exceptional child (if you were the parent of such a child); hold yourself to the standards you would expect of others.

# Summary

This chapter focused on using assessment to inform differentiated instruction and on a contentious issue in exceptional education: adapting assessment to report fairly the learning of exceptional students. All teaching and assessment of exceptional students should be guided by the annual outcomes listed in their IEPs and by the descriptions of strengths and needs. We reviewed here how to use the ADAPT strategy to analyze assessment. The chapter then described large-scale assessment in Ontario and the adaptations used for exceptional students. This was followed by descriptions of how teachers conduct classroom assessment and use it to inform differentiation. There were descriptions of classroom assessment, including tests, performance assessment, and portfolios, and one final topic on adaptations and alternatives to report card marks.

# Key Terms

assessment (p. 141)

large-scale assessment (p. 141)

classroom assessment (p. 141)

testing (p. 141)

evaluation (p. 141)

grading (p. 141)

reporting (p. 141)

high-stakes test (p. 145)

alternative assessments (p. 145)

norm-referenced (p. 148)

criterion-referenced (p. 148)

summative assessment (p. 148)

formative assessment (p. 148)

assessment of learning (p. 148)

assessment for learning (p. 148)

assessment as learning (p. 150)

fairness (p. 152)

tiering assessment (p. 152)

performance assessment (p. 155)

authentic assessment (p. 155)

portfolios (p. 156)

changing grading criteria (p. 158)

grading contracts (p. 158)

modified course syllabi (p. 158)

changes to letter and number grades (p. 158)

student activity log (p. 158)

# Challenges for Reviewing Chapter 6

1.  Discuss with your peers how you could use the ADAPT strategy to analyze and adapt assessment. Why is it not enough to differentiate instruction without differentiating assessment?

2.  Read the brief descriptions of Sasha and Belle at the beginning of this chapter. Focus on one of these students. This student is in your class and large-scale assessment will be conducted at your grade level this year. Review the relevant sections of this chapter. Describe how you will decide what accommodations will be appropriate for this student.

3.  Write a brief scenario for a class at a grade level you teach that includes at least one gifted student and one student with a disability; describe the students briefly. Describe how you would conduct assessment so it would inform differentiated teaching. Think about tiered teaching and other forms of differentiation. Compare your ideas with those of your peers who teach at different levels, and look for commonalities across grade levels.

4.  Use the scenario you created for question #3. Assume the role of one member of an in-school team for one of the exceptional students in the scenario. Ask a peer to assume one of the other roles on the team. Discuss adaptations to classroom assessment and to reporting report card grades, for the student in your scenario, that you would make to ensure assessment was meaningful.

5.  Return to the opening cases of Sasha and Belle and answer the four questions that that follow the cases.

# Chapter 7
## Climate, Community, and Classroom Management

**Mandy has been at Bayside since September.** She is in Ms. Turner's grade 6 class. Ms. Turner tells visitors to her classroom how Mandy invited another student who has few close friends to play basketball in the schoolyard. This act of kindness assumes significance when you know the rest of the story. If you had visited Mandy's grade 5 class at another school the previous June, you might have seen Mandy scream at her teacher, punch another student, or storm out of the classroom. It was terrible for Mandy and for her previous teacher. What has changed? Mandy moved to a small school with a caring and involved principal and to Ms. Turner's classroom. Ms. Turner is described as an exemplary teacher—every year children hope they will be in her class. Pre-service teachers love interning with her. They say, "All the kids treat each other so well. There is never any bullying. She won't have it. Everyone belongs." Mandy says, "I like Ms. Turner. She always says 'good morning' to me and makes me feel important. I don't want her to be disappointed in me. So I try my best. She never lets anyone hurt me and I don't have to hurt anyone back." At her last school, Mandy had been identified as having a behaviour exceptionality. Her principal thought that she needed a fresh start where the students and teachers were unaware of her reputation, with a teacher known for valuing and respecting every student—a teacher like Ms. Turner.

**Jacob is in grade 10.** He has cerebral palsy and a learning disability. He uses arm crutches to move around the school. To keep his energy up, Jacob has permission to eat healthy snacks in class. Recently he has been bringing chocolate bars and candy to his history class and has become very popular by handing out treats. Mr. Chan knows he will have to tackle this threat to his orderly classroom. Every day when the grade 10 students enter class, they find a "challenge" on their desks and have four minutes to determine, with a partner, which historical figure made the quoted statement. Recently some students have been too busy seeking a treat from Jacob to find solutions to the challenge. Mr. Chan does not approve of bribery, but he has noticed that more students talk with Jacob and invite him to join their groups for collaborative activities. Perhaps talking with the resource teacher who tutors Jacob will help Mr. Chan develop a response to the actions of Jacob and his classmates.

1. Under what circumstances could Mandy and Jacob be considered a challenge to the climate, organization, and management of their inclusive classrooms?

2. How can teachers develop classrooms that feel like communities, where all students are respected?

## Learner Objectives

After you have read this chapter, you will be able to:

1. Identify and describe the key elements of creating a classroom community.

2. Describe developing an inclusive climate: physical layout and norms for interaction.

3. Identify and describe the major parts of negotiating and enforcing classroom rules and procedures.

4. Describe the major components of managing behaviour in an inclusive classroom and explain how they can be adapted to meet the needs of exceptional students.

3. How can teachers discuss their approaches to classroom management with their classes and later refer to these discussions when responding to students who challenge order and learning in the classroom?

4. Whom might teachers like Ms. Turner and Mr. Chan turn to for assistance in teaching students to change their actions in the classroom?

5. How can Mr. Chan enable Jacob to eat a healthy snack when he needs it and to maintain his improved peer relations, while preventing bribery and chaos in the classroom?

# Introduction

Mandy and Jacob are two of the approximately 300000 exceptional and special needs students in Ontario schools, which means you will meet challenges like those described above. This chapter will introduce you to ways to create a positive and inclusive classroom climate and ways to manage your classroom with the goal of creating a community where diversity is encouraged and all students feel their contributions are valued.

# Creating a Community

You know to expect diversity in any Ontario classroom. You will be teaching students with a wide array of exceptionalities and health conditions. Your classes may include Aboriginal students and others with a multiplicity of cultural and ethnic heritages. Building community is a deliberate process that requires attention over a period of time. Many provinces, Ontario included, have recently renewed their commitment to this process. As well, initiatives on safe schools strategies, like Ontario's (www.edu.gov.on.ca/eng/safeschools/publications.html), have been developed as a response to the threat of school violence. Although the juvenile homicide rate has declined since the mid-1990s, the media attention given to school violence and school shootings has made the problem seem large. It is much more likely that students will be bullied (National Center for Educational Statistics, 2007). Schools and their surrounding neighbourhoods must work together to ensure that, when at school, students experience community, feel safe, and receive the social and emotional support they need.

**Community** involves a sense of belonging, of the group's concern for each individual, of individual responsibility for the good of the group, and of appreciation for shared experiences (Noddings, 1996). The Working Forum on Inclusive Schools (1994) documented successful inclusive schools in Canada and the United States and found these schools were characterized by a common vision; problem-solving teams; parents, teachers, students, and others working as partners; time for planning and collaboration; warm relationships; little jargon; and flexible scheduling. We can apply these characteristics to the classroom to understand community dynamics.

## Common Vision and Problem-Solving Teams

You can involve your students in setting classroom rules and the consequences for not following these rules. Don't assume the consequences will be obvious to students; research suggests that even gifted students benefit from having the consequences of their actions explained clearly (Kaplan, 2008). Students have many ideas about what classrooms can and should be like and energy to work toward their own goals (Berry, 2006). To this end, provide leadership and a structure for productive class discussion, and model behaviour that includes everyone. Emphasize the importance of **climate**, the feeling created when we treat each other respectfully.

Problem-solving teams can teach students to handle real-world problems and create a sense of belonging. In elementary classrooms, this problem solving could be applied to devising efficient ways to ensure that all students have computer time or deciding on a realistic timeline and budget for studying pond ecology in the community. In secondary settings, student committees might orchestrate classroom

### Further Reading

Review the following provincial documents and compare them to the Ontario initiative. Consider similarities and differences.

*Ontario's equity and inclusive education strategy: Realizing the promise of diversity* (2009).

*Caring and Respectful Schools: Ensuring Student Well-Being* in Saskatchewan (2004).

British Columbia's *Safe, Caring and Orderly Schools, a Guide* (2008).

Newfoundland and Labrador's *Safe and Caring Schools Policy* (2006).

### Weblinks

INCREASINGLY, PROVINCIAL AND TERRITORIAL INITIATIVES FOCUS ON ENHANCING THE SENSE OF SAFETY IN SCHOOLS, IN PART AS A RESPONSE TO THE THREAT OF SCHOOL VIOLENCE, THE YOUTH JUSTICE POLICY DIVISION OF JUSTICE CANADA HAS PREPARED A COMPREHENSIVE REVIEW ON SAFE SCHOOLS AND YOUTH JUSTICE.

*BRIEFING BOOK ON INNOVATIVE CANADIAN INITIATIVES, ACTIVITIES AND REPORTS, RELATED TO SAFE SCHOOLS AND YOUTH JUSTICE*

www.safehealthyschools.org/whatsnew/initiatives.htm

### Cross-Reference

Chapter 1 focuses on the general context for inclusion in Canadian society, while Chapter 8 examines social relations between students and how to enhance the inclusion of diverse students.

debates or forums or invite community leaders to help stage a simulated election. Consider using problem-solving teams to recommend possible solutions to classroom challenges.

## Parents, Teachers, and Students as Partners

Many resources are available on the subject of team building. Some focus on parents and extended families as partners and on culturally responsive parental involvement (e.g., Goodwin & King, 2002). All students, even secondary students, are more successful in school when their parents are involved in their education (Jeynes, 2007). Consider sending letters to parents early in the year, as well as meeting to talk about their priorities for their children's learning. You could invite a parent to observe his or her child or adolescent, who is disrupting the class, to devise joint approaches for home and school (Krogness, 1995). Student-led parent-teacher conferences and using students as peer negotiators or peacemakers are other options (Fine, Lacey, & Baer, 1995). Whatever strategies you choose, focus on creating an equitable community (Levin, 2004) with high-quality communication among all partners (Capuzzi & Gross, 2004; Faltis, 2007).

## Time for Collaboration and Joint Planning

Put into Practice

Read about creating an inclusive climate. Develop an approach you might use from the first day of school:

Wood, J.W. (2009). *Practical strategies for the inclusive classroom.* Upper Saddle River, NJ: Merrill/Pearson.

Larivee, B. (2008). *Authentic classroom management: Creating a learning community and building reflective practice.* Boston: Allyn & Bacon.

Sapon-Shevin, M. (2007). *Widening the circle: The power of inclusive classrooms.* Boston: Beacon Press.

Hensley, M., Powell, W., Lamke, S., & Hartman, S. (2007). *The well-managed classroom: Strategies to create a productive and cooperative social climate in your learning community.* Omaha, NE: Boys Town Press.

Brownlie, F., Feniak, C., & Schnellert, L. (2006). *Student diversity: Classroom strategies to meet the learning needs of all students.* Markham, ON: Pembroke Publishers.

Schedule time for your students to learn and practise collaboration and joint planning. Include learning outcomes listed in your curricula, such as effective oral communication, planning and co-operating, and development of self-awareness. Include these when you do your long-range planning and be prepared to explain their role in creating community. Ms. Turner, in one of the opening cases, spends significant time with her grade 6 class during the initial weeks of the school year teaching her students what she expects of them and helping them to collaborate. She is confident that she can easily catch up to the other classes, in the academic realm, in late September and early October since she will spend less time on management issues throughout the rest of the school year. Vicki Gill, an award-winning teacher, agrees: "I spend a great deal of time in the first week creating a sense of community, generating excitement for the curriculum, and setting up classroom expectations" (2007). Her goals for that week are to have each student feel validated and to understand what is problematic behaviour and what the attendant consequences are.

## Caring Relationships

Research documents how teachers begin to create safe and productive environments for diverse student populations on the first day of school through **culturally responsive classroom management (CRCM)** (Bondy et al., 2007; Weinstein et al., 2004). CRCM is characterized by teachers developing a respectful, caring, and personal relationship with each student in addition to building a learning community with an emotional climate where students can take risks, laugh, and trust one another as well as their teacher. Bondy's study (2007) describes three teachers who introduced themselves to their students on the first day in a way that communicated genuine interest in them. They also shared personal information about themselves, their hobbies, and families. They used "getting to know you" activities and communicated core lessons about the importance of respect and kindness, e.g., "We don't laugh at anyone in here. You can feel very secure in this classroom." (p. 336).

## Clear Language and Flexible Scheduling

Model clear use of language that is understood by all. Communication should be tactful so parents don't feel they are being "talked down to." If you use a classroom website, maintain other means of communication as well for families that do not have computer access. Use familiar language and referents with your students. The effective teachers in Bondy's study (2007) who demonstrated culturally responsive classroom management used words and expressions that were familiar to the students and were used by their cultural group. These teachers also made references to popular culture. They gave straightforward directives that were explicit and used no jargon. One teacher said on the first day of school, "This is how it's going to work this morning. People will come in and I will have to go to the door to welcome them to the class. You will wait quietly. You can work on your favourites worksheet" (p. 344). Although the teachers were warm and funny, there was no question that they meant what they said. Consider your use of time, making schedules as flexible as possible so students can work with volunteers and each other at strategic times. Building community should complement, rather than replace, the mandated curriculum and should enhance collaborative learning.

**Further Reading**

On creating community in the classroom:

Brophy, J., Alleman, J., & Knighton, B. (2010). *A learning community in the primary classroom.* New York: Routledge.

Barnard, R., & Torres-Guzmán (Eds.). (2009). *Creating classroom communities of learning: International case studies and perspectives.* Bristol, UK: Multicultural Matters.

Obenchain, K.M., & Abernathy, T.V. (2003). Twenty ways to build community and empower students. *Intervention in School and Clinic, 39*(1), 55–60.

Capuzzi, D., & Gross, D. (Eds.). (2004). *Youth at risk: A prevention resource for counselors, teachers, and parents* (4th ed.). Alexandria, VA: American Counseling Association.

Gill, V. (2007). *The ten students you'll meet in your classroom: Classroom management tips for middle and high school teachers.* Thousand Oaks, CA: Corwin Press.

# Developing an Inclusive Climate

The **physical space** can be inviting and inclusive for all students, including exceptional students, as well as work efficiently for learning. Classroom norms for interaction and discussion can also contribute to an inclusive climate.

## Making the Physical Space Efficient, Inviting, and Accessible

The social environment you are creating should be supported by a physical arrangement that allows students to talk and collaborate for part of each day or part of each period; it should also allow for learning in a whole-class setting and individually (Charles & Charles, 2004; Hadjioannou, 2007). Consider furniture (including desks for the students and yourself), audiovisual equipment, visual aids (such as bulletin boards), and any extra items you bring (such as plants). Think proactively about the physical needs of exceptional students, such as Jacob in the opening case, for space, adapted desks, computers, and other specialized equipment.

### ARRANGING FOR EFFICIENCY AND ACCESSIBILITY

There may be exceptional students who need a predictable physical layout because of visual impairments and students who need wide aisles to manoeuvre their wheelchairs. Your goals should be to keep pathways clear to permit orderly movement, keep distractions to a minimum, and make efficient use of the available space.

After your teaching is under way and patterns of use of time and space emerge, make a floor plan showing the size and location of built-in features. You might want to make scale representations of the furniture. Ask yourself the following questions:

- What learning spaces, for small and large activities, are available?
- Which spaces do students use frequently? Occasionally? Rarely?

- What are the crowded areas?
- Which spaces are the pathways for movement?
- Which spaces are used for quiet activities? Which for noisy activities?

Use this information to rearrange the room to support the learning activities you value and to make access as easy for exceptional students as it is for everyone else. Overall, think about high traffic areas, sightlines, location of and access to teaching materials, and seating arrangements (see Evertson & Emmer, 2008).

### ARRANGING AN INVITING CLASSROOM

Ask yourself how the physical set-up of your classroom can make each student feel that he or she is a valued member of your classroom. Students are more likely to be engaged if they think their teachers are positive and sensitive (Rimm-Kaufman, et al., 2005). For ELL students, post a sign in their first language. For a student like Jacob, who has a physical disability, it might be a poster that includes someone in a wheelchair or using arm crutches. For students with learning difficulties, help them to know exactly what is expected, so write an agenda on the board or on chart paper to make the day predictable. For preliterate students, use picture symbols like a book to show story time. For a preliterate student in a literate class, tape a daily schedule in symbols to his desk to help avoid embarrassment. Students with behaviour disabilities or ADHD may also benefit from a schedule taped to their desks.

What do you think?

What are your criteria for seating plans? How do you assess their relative effectiveness? How often do you rearrange seating arrangements? Why? Discuss with a peer and ask for input on your plans and vice versa.

Make good use of bulletin boards. Use inspirational posters. Generate interest in an upcoming unit by connecting the topic to current events or popular culture. Post student work or seasonal art. Change displays frequently, post classroom rules (see next section), and ask for suggestions to enhance bulletin boards. Use colour, but avoid distracting students. Post a welcome message. As one Aboriginal student commented, "Last year, I had . . . a history teacher, and I walked into the room and I saw that on his walls were pictures of Native American people. And I think, 'Okay, I'm going to like this guy'" (Pewewardy & Hammer, 2003).

Desktops and tabletops should be clean and the room free of clutter. The appearance of order and organization in the physical environment communicates that you expect students to behave in an organized way. Place relevant materials at a level where a student in a wheelchair can reach them independently. Look at the classroom from the perspective of the students and of a parent who comes to visit, as well as from your own perspective. Ensure that it is inviting.

## Teaching Norms for Classroom Interaction and Learning

Teaching **norms for classroom interaction** and learning is complex. First, be a model of effective communication and respectful interactions with students. Establish norms for discussion and lead discussions effectively.

### MODELLING COMMUNICATION AND LEADING DISCUSSION

You are responsible for making it safe for people to share ideas and for affirming them as part of the community. This means teaching students to engage in **give-and-take dialogues**. When leading such brainstorming sessions, listen to all ideas, ask students to "tell us more" if their ideas are not clear, write all suggestions briefly on chart paper, and encourage a range of solutions. Don't evaluate during

Weblinks

CHECK OUT THESE SITES DESIGNED TO INFORM PARENTS AND HELP THEM DEAL WITH THEIR ADOLESCENTS. YOU MAY FIND VALUABLE INFORMATION, AND YOU WILL CERTAINLY BE BETTER INFORMED ABOUT HOW PARENTS MAY BE APPROACHING ISSUES OF APPROPRIATE BEHAVIOUR IN THEIR ADOLESCENTS. YOUR STUDENTS. MANY OF THESE SITES HAVE INFORMATION ON CHILDREN AS WELL.

CANADIAN PARENTS.COM: TWEENS AND TEENS
www.canadianparents.com/tweens-and-teens

INTERNET ARCHIVE: EDUCATIONAL FILM FROM THE 1950S ON DISCIPLINING ADOLESCENTS
www.archive.org/details/discipline_during_adolescence

ABOUT.COM: PARENTING OF ADOLESCENTS
http://parentingteens.about.com/od/disciplin1

AMERICAN ACADEMY OF CHILD & ADOLESCENT PSYCHIATRY
http://www.aacap.org/page.ww?name=Facts+for+Families&section=Facts for Families

this stage. Expect to make constant decisions about issues, such as when to let "wrong" answers and values that you do not want to promote go uncorrected in the service of promoting give-and-take. Stop before everyone tires of the discussion, acknowledge the group's accomplishments in specific terms, and suggest what the class will do to complete the task. Make "discussion rules" one of the earliest topics for discussion.

## ESTABLISHING NORMS FOR DISCUSSION

The Tribes program is proactive in teaching discussion and community participation (Gibbs, 2001, 2006). The two groupings in Tribes are the community circle (all members of the class) and the small groups or tribes that are introduced gradually. For secondary school students, you can refer to whole-class discussion and small-group discussion and use the Tribes approach flexibly. During the introductory session introduce the signal you will use to get attention. Tribes recommends raising your hand, but some teachers flick the lights, play a few notes on the piano, or start rhythmic clapping and invite everyone to join in. Explain that at this **signal**, everyone stops talking and raises his or her hand, etc. With young students, practise the signal. Tell older students that if they are not successful on the first few occasions, you will practise the signal with them.

Tribes begins with the whole group or **community circle**. There are over a hundred activities with detailed lesson plans, many of which are appropriate to the community circle. For younger students, you might start with "Five Tribles" (faces ranging from very sad to joyous), in which you ask everyone to report how they feel today. For adolescents, "Bumper Sticker" might be an appropriate introductory activity. One of the earliest discussions should be about what is needed to feel safe in a group. From this discussion, settle on a maximum of four or five statements. Gibbs (2001, 2006) suggests the four **community agreements**:

- attentive listening;
- appreciation—no put-downs;
- right to pass and right to participate; and
- mutual respect.

Talking circles embody an Aboriginal approach to experiential learning that stimulates awareness of and respect for individual differences as well as facilitating group cohesion (Running Wolf & Rickard, 2003; Triplett & Hunter, 2005). They incorporate traditions from various First Nations, including the Iroquois Confederacy council meetings, such as handing a feather around the circle to the person who will speak next. This could help students to listen to one another and could ensure that only one person speaks at a time. Anne Hunter, an elementary teacher, uses Talking Circles on Mondays because students are eager to share their weekend stories.

## TEACHING AND PRACTISING CLASSROOM NORMS

The skills for working together need to be taught and practised regularly. Attentive listening can be practiced with activities in paraphrasing and reflecting the feelings of the speaker. You can make these skills explicit. For example, discuss and come to agreement on what listening looks like (e.g., eyes looking, leaning forward), sounds like (one person talking at a time, sounds of "good ideas"), and feels

### What do you think?

The *right to pass* means that students have the right to choose the extent to which they will participate in a group activity that requires sharing personal information. Is it sound to allow students to pass when discussing personal feelings or information? How can you ensure that this privilege is not abused? What reading informs your thinking on this issue?

### Further Reading

For more information on engaging in give-and-take dialogues, consult:

Everston, C.M., & Emmer, E.T. (2009). *Classroom management for elementary teachers.* Upper Saddle River, NJ: Pearson.

Levin, D. (2003). *Teaching young children in violent times: Building a peaceable classroom.* Cambridge, MA: Educators for Social Responsibility.

Charles, C.M., & Charles, M.G. (2004). *Classroom management for middle-grades teachers.* Boston: Pearson Allyn & Bacon.

Emmer, E.T., & Everetson, C.M. (2008). *Classroom management for middle and high school teachers.* Boston: Allyn & Bacon.

**Weblinks**

SAFE SCHOOLS AND YOUTH JUSTICE: BRIEFING BOOK ON INNOVATIVE CANADIAN INITIATIVES, ACTIVITIES AND REPORTS (COUNCIL OF MINISTERS OF EDUCATION)
www.safehealthyschools.org/whatsnew/initiatives.htm

ARTICLES DEFINING RESTORATIVE JUSTICE, BRIEFING PAPERS, AND AN INTERNATIONAL PERSPECTIVE ON RESTORATIVE JUSTICE
www.restorativejustice.org/

ONTARIO SAFE SCHOOLS ACTION TEAM REPORT, "SHAPING A CULTURE OF RESPECT IN OUR SCHOOLS: PROMOTING SAFE AND HEALTHY RELATIONSHIPS
www.edu.gov.on.ca/eng/teachers/RespectCulture.pdf

ONTARIO SAFE SCHOOLS PUBLICATIONS
www.edu.gov.on.ca/eng/safeschools/publications.html

THE LEAGUE OF PEACEFUL SCHOOLS
www.leagueofpeacefulschools.ednet.ns.ca/

**Further Reading**

On classroom management:

Emmer, E.T., & Evertson, C.M. (2008). *Classroom management for secondary teachers*, 7th ed. Boston: Allyn and Bacon.

Vitto, J.M. (2003). *Relationship-driven classroom management.* Thousand Oaks, CA: Corwin Press.

*Khalsa, S.S. (2007). Teaching discipline and self-respect: Effective strategies, anecdotes, and lessons for successful classroom management strategies.* Thousand Oaks, CA: Corwin Press.

Jones, V., & Jones, L. (2004). *Comprehensive classroom management: Creating communities of support and solving problems.* Boston: Pearson Education.

like (people care, "I'm being heard"). Post the four community agreements in a prominent place. Affirm students when you see them upholding the agreements, and refer to the agreements when you notice infringements. These agreements are normative and shape classroom interventions.

# Negotiating and Enforcing Classroom Rules and Procedures

Rules and procedures enable the classroom to function smoothly and predictably. After negotiating and teaching rules and procedures, you must monitor students to ensure these are followed. Consistent application of consequences is critical.

## Negotiating Rules

What classroom rules do you intend to establish? Rules help create a sense of order and predictability and enable you to be proactive in preventing difficulties. Teachers who are effective at managing their classrooms engage in community building and communicate the message that they care but also have well-defined rules (e.g., Bondy et al., 2007). Effective classroom **rules** are brief and specific, positively worded, clearly understood by students, and consistent with school rules. Bondy's study of three effective teachers who used culturally responsive classroom management showed how they recognized that definitions of appropriate classroom behaviour are culturally defined and incorporated knowledge of their students' cultural backgrounds, which helped each of them to be an authoritative teacher but not authoritarian (Bondy et al., 2007). Each introduced rules and procedures within the first two hours of school, but, as the fifth grade teacher said, "It will probably take about two weeks, so I'm going to keep going over rules and consequences" (p. 338).

Although there is disagreement on this issue, with research supporting both sides (see DiClementi & Handelsman, 2005; Emmer & Evertson, 2008; Lewis & Burman, 2006), we recommend involving the students in the discussion about rules rather than deciding the rules alone. Consider asking students to think of reasons for having rules and reasons for dispensing with rules, and ask what kind of class they want to have. In small groups, have students suggest three rules they think are important. Provide a general model—short, clear, and positively stated— such as "Respect and be polite to all people." Have each group, in turn, come up with a rule not previously stated. Continue eliciting suggestions until nothing further emerges. To prevent key issues being overlooked, you could take a turn. After writing the suggestions on the board, group them into roughly three to five specific but broad rules and use other student suggestions as examples of the rules, such as be respectful of people and property, listen quietly while others are speaking, and be polite and helpful. Write the rules on a poster and mount it. The standard to aim for is that student conduct is the same when you are in the classroom and when you step out briefly.

## Key Aspects of Teaching Rules

Three key aspects of teaching rules are demonstration, practice, and feedback (Marshall, 2005; Martin, Sugarman, & McNamara, 2001). First, describe and then demonstrate the desired behaviours. Be specific. If students may talk to one another in quiet voices while working in small groups, then use a quiet voice when you ask a student to speak quietly. Give feedback about the volume; if it was too loud, repeat the procedure. With adolescents, engage in teaching the rules with sensitivity to their age; perhaps ask each group to teach a rule to the class. Second, rehearsal means asking students to show that they understand. Younger students may need to practise standing up to a bully. Never have a student enact the role of the bully, because that amounts to you teaching someone to be a bully. Rather, ask students to imagine seeing a bully push their friend. Then have them practise asking the bully to stop and helping their friend report the incident to an adult (including asking the adult when they can expect a report on action taken). Again, feedback is important.

When rules are violated, take the student aside and say privately, for instance, "I heard you call John an unpleasant name. Next time that happens, I will call your name, and you will stand beside the door until I discuss this with you. I will not tolerate bullying. We agreed that we would not treat one another that way. Do you understand what I'm saying? Do you need to practise following the rules?"

## Establishing Procedures

Teachers usually develop classroom procedures for areas of classroom space, seat work and teacher-led activities, transitions into and out of the room, and small-group activities. **Classroom procedures** are efficient ways of moving everyone through the day or the period that are consistent with your goals for the classroom. Make the connection between rules and procedures. Teach the most critical procedures first, introduce them as the need arises during the first few days, and introduce only as many in a day as the class can handle. Procedures that enable a productive and focused opening of class, like Mr. Chan's "challenge" at the outset of the period, help to set a positive tone, focus the students, and transition into the lesson (see case at opening of this chapter).

## Monitoring Student Actions

**Monitoring** involves being alert and responsive to student action and learning. When you present information to the class, position yourself so you can see every student's face. Move around the classroom so you come close to all students. Ensure that a student who speech-reads can see your face straight on: you will not be able to move around the classroom while presenting. Scan the whole class; some teachers tend to focus on the middle front rows, but you should be aware of the reactions of students on the periphery. Some teachers use response cards to monitor the responses and understanding of all students—students can write on a response card or hold up a preprinted response card (Randolph, 2007). Others use "thumbs-up" or "thumbs-down" and, more recently, clickers.

If you teach one small group while other groups are working independently, position yourself so you can see all the students. Move around the room between working with one group and the next group. Ask if anyone has a question that could not be answered by a classmate. If there is a question, tell the students you will give a brief reply, name a peer to whom the student with the question should direct any further questions, and then call for the next small group to assemble. While you are engaged with a small group, keep monitoring.

Put into Practice

Interview an experienced principal or teacher about how they maintain consistency in applying consequences and still retain the flexibility they need to treat exceptional students equitably. Ask how they talk with students about consistency and flexibility.

Weblinks

SAFE AND CARING SCHOOLS AND COMMUNITIES: BULLYING AND VIOLENCE PREVENTION, CHARACTER EDUCATION, CONFLICT MANAGEMENT, AND RESPECTING DIVERSITY (RESOURCES AND ELABORATIONS OF EARLIER BOOK BY BENNETT AND SMILANICH [1994])
www.sacsc.ca/index.html

LEARNING RESOURCES CENTRE OF THE GOVERNMENT OF ALBERTA
www.lrc.education.gov.ab.ca/pro/default.html

COOL QUOTES FOR TEENS
http://quotations.about.com/cs/inspirationquotes/a/Teens1.htm

BC'S PARTNERSHIP FOR RESPONSIBLE GAMBLING (FOCUS ON YOUTH GAMBLING)
www.bcresponsiblegambling.ca/problem/youth5.html

ADOLESCENT PEER CULTURE: PARENTS' ROLE
www.answers.com/topic/adolescent-peer-culture-parents-role

When all students are working on independent assignments, circulate and check each individual's progress. Avoid prolonged discussion with one student that interferes with alert monitoring. Remind students that they should ask you for help only after they have tried to obtain the assistance of a peer. Some teachers adopt, "Ask three before me." If a student requires sustained assistance, the two of you should move to a location from which you can monitor the entire class.

After introducing a new lesson and students have begun independent seat-work, check on exceptional students to ensure that they understand the instructions. Keep checking when they move to the next example. Quietly and individually ask the students experiencing difficulty to join you for reteaching at an area from which you can monitor the rest of the class, what Bender (2008) calls "tearing away." To prevent these invitations from being seen as punishment, ask the advanced students to join you at the reteaching area for challenge activities after they have completed the assigned work. Ensure that all students can work with you in this area.

Monitor student work by collecting assignments frequently, even if you have asked students to check their own work in class. Write brief comments so students see you have read their work, and keep your mark book current. Patterns will emerge of students who do not attempt assignments, leave assignments incomplete, or complete work only with assistance. Set quarter-way and halfway **checkpoints** for longer assignments or projects. Use checklists for students to self-monitor and write brief, specific, and encouraging feedback on the checklist. Conference with students who need guidance or **scaffolding** (support that can gradually be removed) to ensure that the adapted outcomes of exceptional students are appropriate.

### Applying Consequences Consistently

**Consistency** and equity should be discussed together to eliminate any misunderstanding. Be consistent in your expectations from day to day and apply consequences consistently. For example, if you say students must move to the door and await a conversation with you for being disrespectful to a peer, then apply this consequence to all students. Obvious inconsistencies confuse students about what is acceptable behaviour, and students may test you to find the limits.

However, there are occasions when circumstances justify making exceptions. Consider the student who was ill between when the assignment was set and the halfway checkpoint. Enlist the student's participation in setting a new timeline which will increase the likelihood he or she will stay on schedule. Students with IEPs, ELL students, and those at risk for other reasons may need adapted outcomes, differentiated instruction, and more scaffolding. Lead discussions that help students value diversity and understand that fairness does not necessarily mean sameness.

# Managing Behaviour in the Inclusive Classroom

Managing student behaviour contributes to learning in the inclusive classroom. We focus on increasing appropriate behaviour, decreasing undesirable behaviour, and enhancing self-management. This section ends by briefly discussing positive behavioural supports and considering harsh and inappropriate punishments.

# Increasing Appropriate Behaviour

In effective classrooms, teachers and students respect and trust each other and students are engaged in learning. To increase appropriate behaviour, give positive attention to the behaviour you want to maintain or increase, what Lindberg and Swick (2006) call common sense classroom management. Provide verbal cues, prompts, and praise to indicate the behaviour you expect. And recognize social and academic achievement and qualities unique to individual students. Effective teachers who increase students' appropriate behaviour have **"invisible" classroom management** techniques (Bennett & Smilanich, 1994, www.sacsc.ca). (See Focus on Schools).

Don Jacobs (also known as Four Arrows) suggests that we need to shift our attention to "virtue awareness" when trying to increase positive participation and "decrease negative behaviours that prevent [Aboriginal] children from contributing to healthy and peaceful classroom environments" (2003, p. 2). Core virtues include courage, generosity, humility, honesty, fortitude, and patience. The goal is for children to seek inner meaning and to explore their experiences in terms of these core values. To do so would enable all students to be active participants in moral decisions and to take greater responsibility for increasing virtuous actions.

All district school boards in Ontario now include character education programs in all schools, both elementary and secondary. Following a discussion paper in 2006 and province-wide consultations in 2007, programs were implemented in 2008. Previously individual school boards decided whether to initiate such programs. The framework document, *Finding Common Ground: Character Development in Ontario Schools, K–12* (2008), describes the focus of the Character Development Initiative as requiring "high expectations for all students in learning, academic achievement and citizenship and character development" (p. 4). It must be a whole-school initiative that actively promotes positive values, attitudes, and behaviours within a learning culture that is inclusive, respectful, safe, and caring.

### CATCH 'EM BEING GOOD

**Catch 'em being good** is a strategy that was developed many years ago and is exemplified in the Focus on Schools box. When a student's behaviour is consistent with expectations, you acknowledge and praise or reward the behaviour. Sometimes students misbehave simply because you have not communicated effectively what is unacceptable. Catching one student being good lets all the others know what you expect and value. However, with adolescents, speaking to them privately about their positive behaviour can be more effective. Speaking privately to ELL students can help you to discern the extent to which they have understood your comments.

### THE GOOD BEHAVIOUR GAME

Another more formal, if somewhat more controversial, version of the same strategy is the **good behaviour game**. Developed over 30 years ago (Barrish, Saunders, & Wolff, 1969), teachers still find it effective (Babyak, Luze, & Kamps, 2000). Tell students that you will award points to teams within the class for positive behaviours; then describe these behaviours clearly. Points might be awarded for returning materials to their proper places after an activity or for successful completion of a group work task. Select only a couple of positive behaviours at a time and post them at the front of the classroom to remind all teams. Set a time period during the

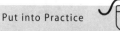

**What do you think?**

How does teaching awareness of core values differ from other approaches to promoting appropriate behaviour? With a peer, discuss how you might teach core values throughout the curriculum, and the benefits and disadvantages of this approach for Aboriginal and non-Aboriginal students.

**Put into Practice**

Review the document, *Character Development in Action K–12, Successful Practices in Ontario Schools* (2008). It is a compilation of successful practices from school boards throughout the province that were used in the implementation of the Ontario Character Development Initiative. Compare your school's initiative with those highlighted in the document. Do you see room for improvement? How could you proceed?

**What do you think?**

Consider why there is controversy about The Good Behaviour Game. What is your position on using a reward system like this one? Discuss your views with a colleague who teaches the same grade or subject. If you have tried a similar reward system in your own teaching, assess its relative effectiveness.

# A School that Focuses on Respect and on Catching Students Being Good

The story told here, briefly, is one you can read in much more detail in Sandra Dean's book, *Hearts and Minds: A Public School Miracle* which was published in 2000 by Penguin Books Canada. When she was the principal of South Simcoe Public School in Oshawa, Sandra Dean set out to recreate the village environment she had experienced in her childhood in Trinidad. When she began at South Simcoe, this school had very low results on board-wide tests in math and reading and writing. But within five years, the school had attained high test results and had won a national award from the Conference Board of Canada for excellence.

What Sandra Dean did to recreate the caring feeling of her childhood village is easy to describe but challenging to implement. Some of the elements included teachers' standing at their classroom doors, welcoming students, and calling them by name and business people from the community coming into the school to read to children. Flowers were planted in the schoolyard. Teachers telephoned parents regularly to give them good news about their children. At the centre of this approach was a concerted focus on values including respect and interdependence. Students were given a "respect ticket" each time they showed respect and did something that was considered good behaviour. These tickets could be cashed in for gifts. The largest gift was an opportunity to attend a dinner served by teachers and community leaders including the community's chief of police.

Sandra Dean's premise was that for children to show respect at school, they had to feel respected at school. She encouraged teachers to create a welcoming tone, and asked them to refrain from yelling at students. The expression, "Shut up!" was not to be used in the school. The school had a Respect Tree and every child who received 75 or more respect tickets had his or her picture put on the tree. Children would often stand at the front of the classroom and explain how they had received a respect ticket at recess for picking up an errant ball, for example, and returning it to those playing with it instead of kicking it away. Sometimes the goal for the week was written on the blackboard, which might be, "I will walk respectfully in the halls."

While all schools expect respect, what made South Simcoe School different was the way respect was explicitly taught, not just expected. Teachers found the shift in thinking meant that instead of looking for things that were going wrong, they were looking for ways to support children so things were going right. They were always on the lookout to catch students being god. This started with small things like students pushing in their chairs at the end of the day, building toward students gaining a strong sense of self and of respect for themselves. The word respect was used frequently in this school. And students were praised for doing right—which made them shine.

You can learn more about the program at South Simcoe Public School by reading Sandra Dean's book, *Hearts and Minds: A Public School Miracle* [Toronto: Penguin Books Canada, 2000].) It was also described in "The three Rs plus respect equals results" The *Globe and Mail*. October 10, p. A9 by S. Fine.

day when the game will be played. For a secondary school class, it could be the first 20 minutes of the period. Let the students know every time you see an appropriate behaviour and tally a point. At the end of the day or period, post the points. As a variation, set a target for all groups to reach and provide a reward as long as all teams reach the minimum. Choose a reward that is meaningful for students of that age and for that class. Some teachers use a strategy like this early in the year and then only during the most stressful periods of the school year, such as before winter break.

### REWARD SYSTEMS

In the past, **reward systems** were widely used in special education programs that served students with emotional and behaviour disabilities. They are much less common in today's inclusive classrooms, with their growing emphasis on intrinsic motivation and teaching students to regulate their own behaviour. Point systems have been criticized because they encourage students to gain rewards without teaching them to appreciate the academic and social learning they perform to receive awards. As well, they may discourage teachers from looking for the causes of misbehaviour or learning difficulties (Henley, 2006). Teacher attention and encouragement may be the most powerful rewards that have few drawbacks.

While teacher praise and attention are powerful influences on student performance, classrooms are busy places (Wolford, Heward, & Alber, 2001). As a consequence, children may have trouble receiving positive attention and praise may be offered infrequently. A five-step strategy for teaching exceptional students to "recruit" their teachers' attention in a positive way follows:

- **C**omplete your work;
- **L**ook it over for mistakes;
- **A**sk yourself if the teacher is available;
- **S**ignal the teacher and ask her/him to look at your work; and
- **S**ay "Thank you" (Alber & Heward, 1997).

The steps are easy to remember using the acronym **CLASS**.

Students will need opportunities to practise and to receive feedback on how they are doing. Although some students need individual teaching to learn the strategy, research has shown positive results for students with learning disabilities and with intellectual disabilities in recruiting praise, and in student learning with attendant increases in the amount of praise delivered by teachers (Wolford et al., 2001).

### ENCOURAGEMENT

Some researchers suggest encouragement is a healthier way for teachers to support and increase appropriate behaviour than praise (e.g., Larivee, 2006). **Encouragement** refers to giving courage or spurring someone on, and it can be particularly helpful in alleviating the discouragement that exceptional students can feel when challenged to participate and learn in inclusive classrooms. Effective encouragement is specific, personal, embedded in trusting relationships, and available to all, not just those who are achieving. Teachers who encourage know their students well, give credit to others, and remember how good acknowledgement feels (Kouzes & Posner, 2007; McIntyre, Kyle, & Moore, 2006).

## Decreasing Undesirable Behaviour

Your attempts to make everyone feel included and to increase positive behaviour will not be enough for some students. An alternative approach is to focus on decreasing undesirable behaviours and helping students replace them with desirable actions. Often we assume that students know what to do and are simply refusing to do it. This is not always the case. Try using the steps of the ADAPT strategy described in Chapter 1 and minimal interventions or low-key responses. When a student exhibits problem behaviour, refer to the classroom rules that were established and identify which rule is being violated. This can be done with a pre-arranged gesture or signal, by using humour (with good judgment), or by verbally confronting the student (but in private). Try to identify environmental factors that could be altered, such as seating. Consider using a quick tension- or energy-releasing activity.

### LOW-KEY INTERVENTIONS

Effective teachers appear to respond to misbehaviour at a moment's notice; however, they actually anticipate and act or **pro-act** almost before the behaviour occurs

**Further Reading**

Learn about the root causes of anger and specific methods for responding in the classroom:

Plummer, D.M. (2008). *Anger management games for children.* Philadelphia, PA: Jessica Kingsley Publishers.

Flick, G.L. (2004). *Coping with anger: Complete anger management program, grades 6–12.* Hoboken, NJ: John Wiley & Sons.

Galey, P. (2004). *Keep cool! Strategies for managing anger at school.* Markham, ON: Pembroke Pub.

Leseho, D., & Howard-Rose, D. (2005). *Anger in the classroom: A practical guide.* Calgary: Detsileg Enterprises.

Larson, J. (2002). *Helping school-children cope with anger: a cognitive-behavioral intervention.* New York: Guilford Press.

**Cross-Reference**

While this chapter focuses primarily on creating an inclusive classroom climate that is well-managed and welcoming for exceptional students, Chapter 8 places much more emphasis on schoolwide approaches. For an example, see Rosenberg, M., & Jackman, L. (2003). Development, implementation, and sustainability of comprehensive school-wide behaviour management systems. *Intervention in School and Clinic, 39*(1), 10–21.

## FIGURE 7.1 LOW-KEY PROACTIVE RESPONSES TO DECREASE UNDESIRABLE BEHAVIOUR

**Proximity:** Move toward a misbehaving student immediately, but not so close that the student feels physically threatened. Usually there is no verbal exchange.

**Touch:** Check your school's policy. A quick, light, non-threatening touch to the shoulder without eye contact or verbal exchange shows that you are aware and care.

**The look:** As soon as attention-seeking begins, quickly and silently communicate to a student that the behaviour is inappropriate. This is not a glare.

**Student's name:** Use this positively to make the student feel included just before misbehaviour or as soon as misbehaviour occurs. Use a kind tone, not a nagging one. Don't overuse.

**Gesture:** Communicate expected behaviour, e.g., forefinger on the mouth to say "shhh" or a shake of the head to say "no." Ensure your meaning is understood by ELL students.

**The pause:** At the beginning of instructions, if a few are not listening, pause obviously. Combine with moving toward them, catching their gazes, and gesturing for quiet.

**Ignore:** Use with caution. Ignoring is best when the student's behaviour does not interfere with teaching or learning. If two students misbehave together, ignoring will be ineffective. Don't show agitation or the students will have won the attention they are seeking.

**Signal to begin/signal for attention:** Wait until you have their attention. Make signal age-appropriate: a flick of the lights or rhythmic hand clapping. One elementary school teacher called out a word ("baseball") and the students gave a choral response ("Blue Jays"); the students chose a new word and response each week (Bennett & Smilanich, 1994).

**Deal with the problem, not the student:** Quietly remove the object a student is tapping on the desk. Say, "Book, please," and extend your hand to the students arguing over it. Say it as if you expect compliance. If they do not, they have escalated the situation beyond a low-key proaction.

(Henley, 2006). Such **low-key interventions** or minimal actions do not disrupt the flow of the class. They de-escalate rather than raise the stakes, and they communicate to the students that you are "with it" and that they cannot get away with anything. Over time, effective teachers develop a repertoire and match their "proaction" to the action they anticipate, remembering that overusing a proaction will result in loss of effectiveness. (See Figure 7.1.)

## THEORY AND RESEARCH HIGHLIGHTS FROM

## EDUCATIONAL PSYCHOLOGY

## Motivation and Rewards

Motivation is often described as intrinsic or extrinsic. Intrinsic refers to a person engaging in a task or behaviour who develops internally satisfying consequences during or after his or her actions. Examples include acquisition of knowledge, task completion, and sense of mastery. Extrinsic refers to a person engaging in a task or behaviour to reach satisfying consequences outside oneself during or after actions. Token systems, social approval, and tangible objects are examples.

Arguments against using extrinsic rewards include concerns about children not engaging in learning for its own sake and fearing that children who receive external rewards will come to depend on and expect these rewards (Witzel & Mercer, 2003). Extrinsic rewards are easily overused, are ineffective at teaching students how to regulate their behaviour, and may not generalize beyond the classroom.

Arguments in favour of using extrinsic rewards include recognizing that not all students are intrinsically motivated to manage their own behaviour. Grolnick and Ryan (1990) found that students with learning disabilities had less internal control for academic work than their classmates without disabilities. Cameron and Pierce's (1994) meta-analysis on 100 studies involving rewards found that participants receiving tangible rewards reported higher intrinsic motivation than non-rewarded participants. When students received contingent verbal praise, they demonstrated significantly higher motivation (measured by time on task and by attitude) than those who did not receive praise. They concluded that rewards, tangible and verbal, increase positive behaviour and learning while students are being rewarded and do not interfere with intrinsic motivation for low-interest activities.

Two aspects of Cameron and Pierce's findings may be key to understanding the role of extrinsic motivation and rewards: first, that extrinsic rewards did not interfere with motivation for low-interest activities; and second, that pairing an external reward with information, in the form of verbal praise, was most effective.

Student interest in the activity is important to understanding rewards and motivation. A specific theory of motivation, self-determination theory (SDT) (Deci & Ryan, 1985; 1992), identifies three motivational needs to be self-determining: competence (feeling effective), autonomy (feeling of acting in accord with one's sense of self), and relatedness (feeling connected to others). SDT postulates a continuum of motivation ranging from amotivation through four degrees of decreasing external motivation to intrinsic motivation where one engages in a task for the pure joy and inherent satisfaction derived from doing the task (Ryan & Deci, 2000).

When activities, including many school activities, are not intrinsically motivating; people are not likely to engage in them willingly or fully without some external motivation. To move along the continuum toward intrinsic motivation, people need to experience competence, autonomy, and relatedness. According to SDT, the more that students feel effective at school tasks, feel they have chosen to engage in the tasks, and feel they belong in the classroom, the more likely they are to engage in school tasks for their own sake. External rewards may keep students at uninteresting tasks long enough to develop feelings of competence, autonomy, and relatedness.

Conversely, a classic study by Greene and Lepper (1974) found that giving preschoolers extrinsic rewards for drawing, an inherently interesting task for these children, led to decreased interest in drawing unless rewards were offered. Deci, Koestner, and Ryan's (1999) meta-analysis of 128 studies found the same outcome. Thus rewards may be appropriate for increasing student motivation for tasks that students find uninteresting or very difficult. But the function of rewards should be to move students along the continuum.

*How* a reward is delivered matters. Teacher praise can focus students' attention on the value and relevance of the task as well as inform students' self-perceptions. This information may be particularly important for exceptional students who look to others for guidance and reassurance.

Avoid overuse of external rewards. Look for opportunities to pair informational feedback and praise with rewards, but only for tasks that are not intrinsically motivating. Enhancing feelings of competence, autonomy, and belongingness—by teaching well, giving students choices, and creating a positive classroom climate—can support intrinsic motivation.

## References

Cameron, J., & Pierce, W.D. (1994). Reinforcement, reward, and intrinsic motivation: A meta-analysis. *Review of Educational Research, 64,* 363–423.

Deci, E.L., & Ryan, R.M. (1985). *Intrinsic motivation and self-determination in human behavior.* New York: Plenum Press.

Deci, E.L., Koestner, R., & Ryan, R.M. (1999). A meta-analytic review of experiments examining the effects of extrinsic rewards on intrinsic motivation. *Psychological Bulletin, 125,* 627–668.

Deci, E.L., & Ryan, R.M. (1992). The initiation and regulation of intrinsically motivated learning and achievement. In A. Boggiano & T. Pittman (Eds.), *Achievement and motivation: A social developmental perspective* (pp. 9–36). Cambridge, UK: Cambridge University Press.

Greene, D., & Lepper, M.R. (1974). Effects of extrinsic rewards on children's subsequent intrinsic interest. *Child Development, 45,* 1141–1145.

Grolnick, W.S., & Ryan, R.M. (1990). Self-perceptions, motivations, and adjustments in children with learning disabilities: A multiple group comparison study. *Journal of Learning Disabilities, 23,* 177–184.

Ryan, R.M., & Deci, E.L. (2000). Self-determination theory and the facilitation of intrinsic motivation. *American Psychologist, 55,* 68–78.

Witzel, B.S., & Mercer, C.D. (2003). Using rewards to teach students with disabilities. *Remedial and Special Education, 24,* 88–96.

## Cross-Reference

In Chapters 3 and 4 you read descriptions of many exceptionalities. For which exceptionalities do you think a time out might be suitable? For which personal characteristics might it be a bad match?

## Put into Practice

Video self-modeling is a technique to decrease inappropriate behaviour, especially for exceptional children with autism. Two elements are required for children to function as their own models: audiovisual technology that allows them to view themselves and the ability to change their behaviour so that they can function or appear to function beyond their present level (see Graetz et al., 2006). Buggey (2007) describes using this self-monitoring strategy to motivate students with reading disabilities who were discouraged by their inadequate reading. Do you see possibilities for applying this approach to your own practice?

## Further Reading

Consult resources on connecting behaviour intervention plans to IEPs:

Murdock, S.G., O'Neill, R.E., & Cunningham, E. (2005). A comparison of results and acceptability of functional behavioral assessment procedures with a group of middle school students with emotional/ behavioral disorders (E/BD). *Journal of Behavioral Education, 14*(1), 5–18.

Buck, G.H., Polloway, E.A., Kirkpatrick, M.A., Patton, J., & Fad, K.M. (2000). Developing behaviour intervention plans: A sequential approach. *Intervention in School and Clinic, 36*(1), 3–9.

Bateman, B., & Golly, A. (2003). *Why Johnny doesn't behave: Twenty tips for measurable BIPs.* Verona, WI: Attainment Company, Inc.

### TIME OUT: A CONTROVERSIAL STRATEGY

Inappropriate behaviour at times requires more than a low-key response. A **verbal reprimand** may be necessary if a behaviour continues. "If reprimands are to be used, the most effective ones are those that are immediate, unemotional, brief, and backed up with a time-out or loss of privileges" (Roberts et al., 1997, p. 81). A **time out** is the temporary removal of a student from classroom activities because of his or her disruptive behaviour. As a consequence for inappropriate behaviour, it should be pre-planned, as part of a student's IEP or behavioural plan, and used sparingly only when less restrictive interventions have not been successful, with the exception of unexpected behaviours that jeopardize the safety of other students and of teachers (*Guidelines for Using Timeout in Schools*, 2002; http://education .alberta.ca/media/547960/timeout_oct_2002.pdf). Before using a time out, an in-school team should explain to the student and parents the serious misbehaviours for which time out will be used and the reasons for doing so. Alternative strategies for teaching students to quickly and calmly disengage from disruptive behaviours include redirecting students' attention (see Grskovic et al., 2004).

### GIVING THE CHOICE TO BEHAVE APPROPRIATELY

Sometimes you want to provide a student or pair of students with a choice to behave appropriately. For example, offer two students who are discussing hockey rather than geography the choice of working quietly together on mapping or having their seats changed until the end of the unit. Do not offer any choice that you are unwilling to apply. One of Nancy Hutchinson's favourite choices when students are playing with toys, hair accessories, etc., is "In your pocket or mine—you choose." These choices are not ultimatums. They can end problem behaviour without escalating conflict. Often they involve **natural consequences**. Keep your sense of humour; a laugh and a second chance are better than prosecuting, especially for small infractions.

### HOLDING PATTERN

Sometimes you need to put a student in a **holding pattern**. Some teachers arrange to have a misbehaving student wait in an office. A simpler approach is to have the student stand beside the door in the classroom, unless the rest of the class could be disrupted. In that case, have the student stand immediately outside the door until you are available to talk to the pupil. Keep the time brief and ensure the student's safety. If these talks are rare and heartfelt, they are likely to be taken seriously.

## Enhancing Self-Management

The goal of this chapter is that your class conduct themselves the same way whether you are in the classroom or have stepped out into the hall. Similarly, you want to help individual students develop self-control or self-management.

### PROBLEM-SOLVING APPROACHES

Some educators develop a **problem-solving approach** that asks a student to answer a set of questions after engaging in unacceptable behaviour. The questions usually ask the students what they think the problem was, what they did to contribute to the problem, how they can make amends, and how they can prevent the problem from recurring. Sometimes the student and the teacher sign the form. What makes this an effective strategy is the follow-through, in which the adult and the student decide "who is going to do what" about the situation and work together to resolve it.

## INFORMAL CONFERENCES

Improving self-management is not easy for students. Be prepared to provide moral support, encouragement, regular checks on progress, praise when you observe the student being good, and additional informal, positive chats. Steps for an **informal conference** (Bennett & Smilanich, 1994):

- Greet the student to set a positive tone.
- Define the problem clearly. Be sure there is agreement before proceeding.
- Generate solutions together, so you solve the problem mutually.
- Choose the best solution(s) together (and perhaps prioritize the other solutions); agree on what each of you will do to implement the solution.
- Ensure that you have a shared understanding of the solution(s).
- End positively by thanking the student.

If the problem continues, warn the student that a formal contract is the next step.

## CONTRACTS

With a young child, a **contract** can be about a matter as straightforward as hanging his or her coat on a hook when the youngster comes into the classroom instead of throwing it on the floor. This reflects the principle of starting with a series of easily and quickly met agreements that provide immediate evidence of success and provide you with a way to give genuine praise (privately or publicly).

After two easy and successful contracts, you can move to your real objective: having the student start the day and get to her desk without touching another student or having a verbal disagreement. Begin the day by praising the student, building on this success to tackle unacceptable behaviours that sabotage learning throughout the day. Younger children may tell their classmates about their contract. Hutchinson has had success with adolescents whose contracts were private and individualized. Word the contract simply (not like a legal document), ensure that it states what both you and the student agree to do, with dates for checking progress, and specify the positive reward and the consequence for failure to live up to the agreement.

## SELF-MONITORING

**Self-monitoring** is another strategy for transferring responsibility to the student. It is particularly applicable for students who are off-task and require help focusing attention. Students observe and collect data on their own behaviour (e.g., Peterson et al., 2006). They need an understanding of the behaviour they are to monitor, an easy recording system, and a reward. In the beginning, you should monitor closely and then give increasing responsibility to the student. Explain in advance: "Put a check on your tracking sheet when I say, 'Let's keep track,'" or "Put a check at the end of every page." A simple self-monitoring card can be taped to the student's desk; the student makes a check mark at each signal or at the end of each task, etc. After some successful self-monitoring, you could use checklists taped to the desk or to sticky-note reminders. Exceptional adolescents can be taught to use self-monitoring cards taped inside their notebooks to help them focus their attention. (See Figure 7.2)

### Further Reading (and Viewing)

There are many multimedia resources to supplement the information in this chapter. View two and discuss them with peers who have viewed other resources.

*The art and science of teaching* [videorecording]. (2008). Alexandria, VA: Association for Supervision and Curriculum Development.

Kronow, E.L. (2008). *The teacher's guide to success: Teaching effectively in today's classrooms* [multimedia]. Boston: Pearson Allyn & Bacon.

*A practical approach to classroom management and discipline, grades 6-12* [videorecording]. (2007). Bellevue, WA: Bureau of Education and Research.

*A practical guide to classroom management and discipline, grades 3-6* [videorecording] (2006). Bellevue, WA: Bureau of Education and Research.

*Classroom management that works* [videokit]. (2004). Alexandria, VA: ASCD.

### Further Reading

Carr, E.G., Horner, R.H., Turnbull, A.P., et al. (2000). *Positive behavior support for people with developmental disabilities: A research synthesis.* Washington, DC: American Association on Mental Retardation.

Ganz, J.B. (2008). Self-monitoring across age and ability levels: Teaching students to implement their own positive behavioral interventions. *Preventing School Failure, 53*(1), 39–48.

Farmer, T.W., & Xie, H. (2007). Aggression and school social dynamics: The good, the bad, and the ordinary. *Journal of School Psychology, 45*(5), 461–478.

## Further Reading

Research on positive behavioural supports (PBS) and the questions it raises:

Curtis, R., Van Horne, J.W., Robertson, P., & Karvonen, M. (2010). Outcomes of a school-wide positive behavioral support program. *Professional School Counselling, 13*(3), 159–164.

Sugai, G., & Horner, R.R. (2006). A promising approach for expanding and sustaining school-wide positive behavior support. *School Psychology Review, 35*(2), 243–259.

Warren, J.S., et al. (2006). School-wide positive behavior support: Addressing behavior problems that impede student learning. *Educational Psychology Review, 18,* 187–198.

Carr, E.G. (2006). SWPBS: The greatest good for the greatest number, or the needs of the majority trump the needs of the minority? *Research and Practice for Persons with Severe Disabilities, 31,* 54–56.

Lassen, S.R., Steele, M.N., & Sailor, W. (2006). The relationship of school-wide positive behavior support to academic achievement in an urban middle school. *Psychology in the Schools, 43,* 701–712.

Franzen, K., & Kamps, D. (2008). The utilization and effects of positive behavior support on an urban school playground. *Journal of Positive Behavior Interventions, 10*(3), 150–161.

Morrison, J.Q., & Jones, K M. (2007). The effects of positive peer reporting as a class-wide positive behavior support. *Journal of Behavioral Education, 16,* 111–124.

Taylor-Greene, S.J., & Kartub, D.T. (2000). Durable implementation of school-wide behavior support, the high five program. *Journal of Positive Behavior, 2*(4), 233–235.

## FIGURE 7.2 IMPLEMENTING A COGNITIVE BEHAVIOUR MANAGEMENT PROGRAM

Cognitive behaviour modification (CBM) is a broad term describing many specific techniques that teach self-control. All work by increasing a student's awareness of cognitive processes and knowledge of how behaviour affects learning.

CBM interventions require student evaluation of performance rather than teacher evaluation. This means that they are practical for busy teachers and parents.

Self-instruction is one technique that helps students to regulate their own behaviours—social and academic. It uses self-statements to help students recall the steps required to solve academic or social problems, such as rushing through assigned work, lack of focus on assigned work, talking out of turn , and eating or giving food to others in the classroom. Initially, students say the steps aloud to a teacher or parent, then to a peer or themselves, then they say the steps covertly.

The actions a teacher and student follow include:

1. They agree on a problem—social or academic—that is getting in the way of learning.
2. The teacher makes a cue card to prompt the student to use the steps of self-instruction.
3. The teacher models using the self-instruction steps to solve a problem.
4. The student practises using the self-instruction steps aloud with the teacher.
5. The student practises with a peer and then alone, using the steps to solve the problem.
6. The teacher arranges booster practice regularly to review the strategy with the student, using verbal rehearsal, as well as practising in familiar and new situations.
7. The teacher and the student decide on a signal for the teacher to use to let the student know when to use the steps. Use of the signal is then phased out since the student should do the monitoring. For the SNAP strategy, snapping fingers may be a good signal.

**Sample Cue Card to Tape to a Student's Desk or Book**

SNAP out of it!

See my problem.

Name my best plan.

Act on my best plan.

Pat myself on the back. I solved my problem!

Source of SNAP strategy: Hutchinson, N.L. (2004). Teaching exceptional children and adolescents: A Canadian casebook (2nd ed.). Toronto: Allyn and Bacon. Used by permission of Pearson Education Canada.

## Positive Behavioural Supports and Classroom Management

**Positive behavioural supports** (PBS) and interventions focus on the fixing of poor contexts that have been documented to be the source of problem behaviours. (See Heineman, Dunlap, & Kincaid, 2005, for a review of the literature on PBS.) The emphasis is on altering the environment before problem behaviour occurs or teaching appropriate behaviours as a strategy for eliminating the need for problem behaviours to be exhibited. Change should be systemic, build on students' strengths, and improve the quality and predictability of events in school, in the community, and at home. The intent is to make problem behaviours ineffective and to provide students with ways to reach their goals without resorting to inappropriate behaviours. Intensive supports, including functional assessments, are necessary for a small number of students with severe behavioural or cognitive disabilities.

## CASE STUDY HOW CAN ASHLEY BECOME MORE SELF-REGULATING AND GAIN SELF-ESTEEM?

Ashley is in grade 5. She has been identified by a psychoeducational assessment as having a learning disability and attention deficit disorder. She is neither disruptive nor does she misbehave. Because she is quiet and unassuming, she "flies under the radar" in a complex class where almost half of the students have IEPs, many of whom are obstreperous boys. She is, however, highly distractible, rarely completes assigned tasks, and has a poor sense of self. The only subject where she experiences success is visual art. How would you go about implementing a cognitive behaviour management program that would support her and develop her self-esteem while also allowing her to experience some academic success? Specify your recommendations and identify your rationale for each recommendation.

PBS is an assessment-based approach for preventing problems and promoting prosocial behaviour. It is especially well-suited to helping students with behaviour disorders to adapt their behaviour to the regular classroom. PBS is now often implemented at three levels—schoolwide, classroom, and individual student. Essentially, one determines the aspects of the environment associated with or contributing to behaviour by documenting circumstances when behaviour occurs and the outcomes that it might enable students to obtain or avoid. Schoolwide programs are intended to establish a safe, positive climate for all students, but they do help students with behavioural exceptionalities in particular because they create predictable school environments. At the classroom level, PBS systems are used to create environments where students engage in work and disruptions are minimized. At the individual level, PBS provides a problem-solving process for students who do not respond to the first two levels: schoolwide and classroom. Some teachers use daily behaviour report cards to record individual students' behaviour and progress within PBS (see Chafouleas et al., 2005; Chafouleas et al., 2006).

## Harsh Punishments and Inappropriate Punishments

There are harsh punishments, such as suspension and expulsion, and there are inappropriate forms, such as corporal punishment and academic tasks. **Punishment** is usually defined as an unpleasant consequence aimed at reducing the likelihood of inappropriate behaviour. It is expected to work because it causes pain. Punishment can control misbehaviour, but by itself it will not teach desirable behaviour (Good & Brophy, 2002). Harsh punishment also alienates students from you and tends to destroy the goodwill necessary to effect behavioural change.

### SUSPENSIONS AND EXPULSIONS

Suspension and expulsion are drastic measures, so try every other possible avenue first. **Suspension** means temporary removal from the classroom (for a day or more), while **expulsion** means permanent removal. Suspension and expulsion are not effective for teaching students or for changing their behaviour for many reasons, such as:

- The student misses the content you are teaching.
- The student does not receive assistance from school personnel.

Put into Practice

Develop a tracking sheet for self-monitoring to be used by a student in grade 3 or a student in grade 10 who is trying to increase his or her focus in your class. Seek models in books and journals. For example, Dawn Reithaug (1998b), a BC educator, has developed a book of forms and guidelines for making clear behaviour plans.

Reithaug, D. (1998b). *Orchestrating positive and practical behavior plans.* West Vancouver: Stirling Head Enterprises.

What do you think?

Debate with your peers whether *harsh* and *inappropriate* are always apt descriptors for the punishments described in this chapter. Defend the position opposite to what you believe. Why is this exercise valuable for an educator?

Put into Practice

The literature is extensive on using self-management and self-monitoring to enhance the attention, participation, and learning of students with a range of exceptionalities. Choose three papers from this list. Develop a strategy to help Mandy or Jacob (opening cases) to be more successful in an inclusive classroom.

Children with LD, speech and language exceptionalities, or EBD: Hoff, K.E., & Doepke, K.J. (2006). Increasing on-task behavior in the classroom: Extension of self-monitoring strategies. *Psychology in the Schools, 43,* 211–221.

**Put into Practice** 🖱️

Children with ADHD:

Reid, R., Trout, A.L., & Schwartz, M. (2005). Self-regulation interventions for children with attention deficit/ hyperactivity disorder. *Exceptional Children, 71*, 361–377.

Adolescents with ADHD:

Gureasko-Moore, S., DuPaul, G.J., & White, G.P. (2006). The effects of self-management in general education classrooms on the organizational skills of adolescents with ADHD. *Behavior Modification, 30*, 159–183.

Children and adolescents with EBD:

Mooney, P., et al. (2005). A review of self-management interventions targeting academic outcomes for students with emotional and behavior disorders. *Journal of Behavioral Education, 14*, 203–221.

Desbien, N., & Royer, E. (2003). Peer groups and behavior problems: a study of school-based intervention for children with EBD. *Emotional and Behavioral Difficulties, 8*, 120–139.

- Those who want to be out of school are rewarded.

- Some students who have been suspended or expelled come to school to "hang out," and school officials have little authority over them.

- As a general rule, behaviour does not improve as a result of suspensions or expulsions. (McQueen, 1992)

The exception to these drawbacks may be in-school suspension: a student is expected to attend school, complete assigned work, spend the day in a suspension room under supervision, and stay away from peers and social interactions. Flanagain's (2007) research on students' views of in-school and out-of-school suspensions found that out-of-school suspensions did not act as a deterrent, often antagonizing relations of students with teachers and administrators. In-school suspensions were viewed somewhat more positively, but students needed to receive support for their difficulties during the suspension.

### CORPORAL PUNISHMENT AND USING ACADEMIC TASKS AS PUNISHMENT

In Canada it is unacceptable to strike a student or threaten to strike a student. Corporal punishment has been banned in public and private schools since 2004. Every province had provincial bans prior to 2004 except Ontario, Alberta, and Saskatchewan. Corporal punishment violates students' rights and is ineffective in changing behaviour (Robinson et al., 2005). Whenever teachers blame and punish the whole class for the misdeeds of a few, they endanger the students' trust and respect that was so hard-earned (Thornberg, 2006). Beware of assigning "lines" or mathematics problems as punishment. The contradictory message sent by assigning **academic tasks as punishment** only makes our job more difficult. However, requiring students to complete work missed due to absence is defensible. Optimally we want our classes so well-taught and interesting that students hate to miss anything. The challenge with having exceptional students included in every class is that each of their differentiated programs also has to be so worthwhile that they want to be in class.

# Summary

It is important that classrooms in inclusive schools provide a sense of community so all members feel accepted and valued. Many elements contribute to developing an inclusive classroom climate, including the physical layout and the norms of classroom interaction. Teachers negotiate and enforce classroom rules and procedures to ensure that all students, including exceptional students, find the classroom predictable and safe. Managing behaviour in an inclusive classroom requires strategies for increasing appropriate behaviour, decreasing unacceptable behaviour, and enhancing self-management.

# Key Terms

community (p. 163)
climate (p. 163)
culturally responsive classroom management (CRCM) (p. 164)
Physical space (p. 165)
norms for classroom interaction (p. 166)
give-and-take-dialogues (p. 166)
signal (p. 167)
community circle (p. 167)
community agreements (p. 167)
rules (p. 168)
classroom procedures (p. 169)
monitoring (p. 169)

checkpoints (p. 170)
scaffolding (p. 170)
consistency (p. 170)
"invisible" classroom management (p. 171)
catch 'em being good (p. 171)
good behaviour game (p. 171)
reward systems (p. 172)
encouragement (p. 173)
pro-act (p. 173)
low-key interventions (p. 174)
verbal reprimand (p. 176)
time out (p. 176)
natural consequences (p. 176)

holding pattern (p. 176)
problem-solving approach (p. 176)
informal conference (p. 177)
contract (p. 177)
self-monitoring (p. 177)
positive behavioural supports (p. 178)
punishment (p. 179)
suspension (p. 179)
expulsion (p. 179)
academic tasks as punishment (p. 180)

# Challenges for Reviewing Chapter 7

1. Consider how teachers go about creating a classroom community in an elementary or secondary classroom. What priority tasks would you undertake before the beginning of the school year, for the first day of school, and during the first week of school? Compare your list with peers who teach in the other panel and identify common and differing elements. Are the differences due to panel demands, your respective teaching philosophies, or other reasons?

2. What is an inclusive classroom climate? How would you assess the relative importance of the physical layout to an inclusive climate? The relative importance of the social environment and norms for interaction?

3. Prepare a series of lesson plans for negotiating and enforcing classroom rules and procedures. Take into account the age and grade level of the students you teach. Exchange plans with a peer and provide feedback.

4. Write a brief scenario that includes some of the greatest challenges to your teaching and management in a classroom with a student like Mandy (in the opening case), who has a history of losing her temper. Identify the major adaptations you would make in your plan for managing the classroom. How would you establish and maintain a positive relationship with Mandy.

5. You are a member of the in-school team in Jacob's school (opening case). Assume the role of one team member. The team includes Jacob's history teacher, two other teachers, the learning program support teacher, the principal. Develop a systematic approach for curbing the problems that are emerging—without spoiling Jacob's improving relationship with his classmates. Provide a rationale. Consider role playing the scenario with your peers.

6. Return to the opening cases of Mandy and Jacob and answer the five questions that follow the cases.

# Chapter 8
## Enhancing Social Relations

### Learner Objectives

After you have read this chapter, you will be able to:

1. Discuss the ways in which social development and social acceptance of exceptional learners are central to inclusion.

2. Describe the role of friendship in the development of exceptional individuals.

3. Discuss elementary and secondary schools as social environments, including Ontario initiatives for safe schools and approaches to preventing bullying.

4. Use the ADAPT strategy to analyze the social demands of the classroom and select collaborative and co-operative teaching strategies.

5. Discuss the role of the community in enhancing social relations.

**Val started grade 1 in September with the children who had been in her kindergarten class and had attended preschool with her.** Val participated in an early intervention program, was always encouraged to explore her environment, and is quite adventuresome once she is familiar with her surroundings. Because Val is blind, she does not play much on the equipment in the playground. Some days she asks the teacher on playground supervision to help her get onto a swing, but at recess she usually invites a classmate to stand with her under a tree or to sit with her on a bench. One day, Val's teacher reminds the other children to play games at recess that include Val. Peter and Yamun pipe up that they like to play catch and that Val cannot play "because she can't see the ball." Peter says, "It just wouldn't be safe." On the way out to the playground later in the day, Yamun tells the teacher, "It's kind of boring spending recess with Val. She can't do much. And I don't like when she doesn't look at me. Why does she look at my ear when I'm talking to her?"

**Lynn rushes into the resource room with her friend Suparna.** These two grade 11 students are almost inseparable. Lynn and Suparna both have learning disabilities. They participate together on the school cheerleading squad, and when the two aren't together they are talking on the phone. Lynn has severe difficulties with written expression, and she has brought her latest English assignment to the resource room so she can edit it with a peer tutor from grade 12. When I ask Lynn how her day is going, she replies, "Great!" The girls part, promising to meet in the locker room after school. Suparna goes to her history class and Lynn sits down with her peer tutor. Not many people know how severe Lynn's learning disability is—other than her closest friends, her peer tutor, her classroom teachers, and me. As Lynn's resource room teacher and counsellor, I know how hard it is for her to complete her written assignments without "blowing her cover." Lynn leaves class rather than read aloud in front of her peers, works hard with me and with her peer tutor to edit all written work before she submits it, and writes her tests in the resource room where it is quiet and she has extra time. When you ask Lynn why she comes to school, she will tell you, "To be with my friends!"

1. How would you describe the peer relations of Val and Lynn?

2. What should teachers be expected to do to meet the social and friendship needs of students like Val and Lynn?

3. How might the social characteristics and social relations of these students and other exceptional learners affect their learning in inclusive classrooms?

4. What teaching strategies are likely to help exceptional students be part of the social and academic life of the classroom?

5. What school and community resources can a teacher draw on to enhance the social relations of students like Lynn and Val?

**Further Reading**

Examples of books and articles available on topics like social relations and friendship:

Rubin, K.H., Bukuwski, W.M., & Laursen, B. (Eds.). (2009). *Handbook of peer interactions, relationships, and groups.* New York: Guilford Press.

Diamond, K.E. (2002). The development of social competence in children with disabilities. In P. Smith & C. Hart (Eds.), *Blackwell handbook of childhood social development* (pp. 570–587). Malden, MA: Blackwell.

Cotterell, J. (2007). *Social networks in youth and adolescence* (2nd ed.). New York: Routledge/Taylor & Francis.

Rillotta, F., & Nettelbeck, T. (2007). Effects of an awareness program on attitudes of students without an intellectual disability towards persons with an intellectual disability. *Journal of Intellectual and Developmental Disability, 32,* 19–27.

Burgess, K.B., Wojslawowicz, J.C., Rubin, K.H., Rose-Krasnor, L., & Booth-Laforce, C. (2006). Social information processing coping strategies of shy/withdrawn and aggressive children: Does friendship matter? *Child Development, 77*(2), 371–383.

Karten, T.J. (2005). *Inclusion strategies that work! Research-based methods for the classroom.* Thousand Oaks, CA: Corwin Press. (Contains teaching ideas for a disability awareness program.)

**Cross-Reference**

In describing the first two steps in the ADAPT strategy, Chapter 1 emphasizes students' social, emotional, and behavioural strengths and needs, as well as the social, emotional, and behavioural demands of the classroom.

# Introduction

The focus of this chapter is the **social relationships** of exceptional learners in inclusive classrooms. Friendships are among the most important and the most complex of our social relationships. "Friendships provide a safety or comfort zone for self-exploration and the consideration of new roles and goals" (Azmitia, Ittel, & Radmacher, 2005, p. 23). Hartup (2006) argues that within children's social networks, darker relationships coexist with brighter ones, and important developmental outcomes are associated with both. In this chapter we think about our role in fostering the friendships, social acceptance, and full participation, what Haring (1991) described as "social integration," that are necessary if inclusion is to be more than a placement (e.g., Hutchinson, Freeman, & Steiner-Bell, 2002; Webster & Carter, 2007).

Recent research informs us of the perspectives of youth with disabilities (e.g., Steiner Bell, 2005), of gifted youth (e.g., Gross, 2006; Masden, 2005), and of students without disabilities on friendship and on belonging (e.g., McDougall et al., 2004). Many approaches that are used extensively in schools foster social interactions and are recommended to teachers; such as co-operative learning, collaborative learning, small groups, activity centres, etc. You can use the ADAPT strategy to analyze the social demands of your classroom organization and of tasks and compare these demands to student strengths and needs. This chapter provides examples of some of the options for the social structure of learning, with examples drawn from many current Canadian resources and Ontario Ministry of Education policies and documents The role of the community in social development is explored.

## The Importance of Social Development and Social Acceptance to Inclusion

Chapter 1 describes how participating in all facets of Canadian society, including educational institutions, is a fundamental right of all Canadians. If inclusion means full and valued participation in the life of the classroom, then we need to understand how **social competence** of exceptional students, **social acceptance** by peers, and **friendships** contribute to equity and inclusion. Social competence involves being able to engage in age-appropriate social cognitions and actions (Diamond, 2007; Frostad & Pijl, 2007), while social acceptance refers to the consensual liking or disliking that is directed by the group toward the individual (Hamm & Faircloth, 2005; Harter, 2006). Friendships are close relationships characterized by reciprocity and commitment between individuals who see themselves as equals (Hartup, 2006). In the next two sections, we focus on the perspectives of exceptional students on their peer relations and on the perspectives of their peers on social relations with exceptional students.

## Perspectives of Exceptional Students on Their Peer Relations

What do exceptional students think about their relationships, friendships, and feelings of belonging with their classmates? Only recently have researchers begun to focus on the voices of exceptional students on this issue. Despite variability in their reports, the importance of feeling connected with peers, with and without disabilities, seems to be a dominant theme. For example, Tom, an adolescent with Asperger syndrome, described his best friend: "He helps me figure out things that

I really like; if I'm afraid of something, he helps me get over my fear" (Howard, Cohn, & Orsmond, 2006, p. 622). Similarly, adolescents who attended intense programs for gifted and talented youth reported that the greatest benefits were their "interesting peers" (McHugh, 2006, p. 182) and the friendships they formed with them and the feelings of belonging they developed.

"Friends are what gets me through school I guess you could say. They're always there to support me . . ., so they're very important." These are the words of Lynn, the grade 11 student with LD introduced in the second case study at the beginning of this chapter. Lynn attends the same Ontario secondary school as Matt, a grade 11 student with LD and ADHD. Matt, however, said, "Ah, just sometimes I just don't know how to relate to a lot of the people anymore. . . . It's not very important I don't think. . . . Maybe they just don't like me or, you know, they find me annoying" (Lévesque, 1997). Where Lynn is a popular cheerleader with close friends, Matt is socially isolated and cannot find anyone to listen to him talk about his favourite computer game. Buhrmester (1998; Underwood & Buhrmester, 2007) developed a theory of adolescent friendship characterized by four elements of **interpersonal competence**: initiating and sustaining conversation, initiating plans to spend time with friends outside school, disclosing personal thoughts and empathy, and managing conflict effectively. In interviews and observations, Nicole Lévesque (1997) of Queen's University found that Lynn demonstrated these four competencies, while all four posed a challenge for Matt. Lynn's story is uplifting and illustrates how some exceptional students thrive academically, socially, and personally in supportive environments. Matt, in contrast, stands alone in the halls, is unable to have a reciprocal conversation, and reports nothing positive about returning to school after the winter break.

In the past decade a number of studies have given voice to students with physical disabilities. Lucy, who was in a wheelchair, attended a mainstream secondary school: "On my first day at the school it was scary because I was worried if I was going to make friends or not. But I made friends straight away" (Curtin & Clark, 2005, p. 205). Lucy wanted to be as independent as possible: "I want to do a lot for myself" (p. 205). Lucy felt she was accepted by her friends in spite of the actions of some of her teachers. One teacher would say, "Come on quickly," when Lucy had difficulty writing as fast as her peers. (p. 205).

In contrast, Marilyn, another student in a wheelchair, described a teacher who told the class about Marilyn, her disability and her wheelchair, and explained that Marilyn would be a full member of the class. Marilyn suggests, "The key to inclusion is making people without disability feel comfortable with disability, [but also helping them] accept that they have got a responsibility to help remove the barriers" (Ballard & McDonald, 1999, p. 102). Marilyn's and Lucy's insights highlight how important it is for teachers to promote social relations for all students, including exceptional learners.

## Perspectives of Peers on Social Relations with Exceptional Classmates

The research reports a range of **peer perspectives** on relationships with students with disabilities. Figure 8.1 describes research findings on these perspectives.

Case studies that provide the perspectives of students with and without disabilities on their social relations (e.g., Ainscow, Booth, & Dyson, 1999; Hall & McGregor, 2000) are helpful for suggestions to promote social status and social interactions of exceptional children and adolescents.

### Further Reading

*Discover Together: A Disability Awareness Resource* (kit). Department of the Secretary of State of Canada. ($35.00 binder.) (Six units examining different exceptionalities, to raise awareness about the competencies of people with disabilities. Recommended for grades K–8. Adapt the recommendations for developing a (dis)ability awareness program appropriate for a secondary school environment. Consider a film festival.)

Safran, S.P. (2000). Using movies to teach students about disabilities. *Teaching Exceptional Children, 32*(3), 44–47.

Ivory, P. (1997), Disabilities in he media: The movies. *Quest, 4*(4), www.mda.org/publications/ Quest/q44movies.html.

### Weblinks

FILMS INVOLVING DISABILITIES (UK): INCLUDES INFORMATION ABOUT OVER 2500 FILMS AND IS DIRECTED TOWARD EDUCATORS
www.disabilityfilmstripod.com

AMAZON.COM (US), MOVIES ABOUT PEOPLE WITH DISABILITIES: INCLUDES QUOTATIONS FROM CHARACTERS IN THE FILMS
www.amazon.com/Movies- about-People-with- Disabilities/lm/ 295R795C0Y6NT

EXTENSIVE ANNOTATED LISTING OF PHYSICAL AND MENTAL DISABILITIES IN THE MOVIES.
www.lib.berkeley.edu/MRC/ disabilitiesbib.html

## FIGURE 8.1 WHAT DO CLASSMATES THINK OF THEIR PEERS WITH DISABILITIES?

**Inclusion of blind students**

In an interview study (MacCuspie, 1996) that reflects the case study of Val, classmates described their friendships with blind elementary school students as based on helping rather than on shared interests or fun activities, which characterized their relations with non-disabled friends.

Blind classmates could not safely play catch or tag; lack of eye contact made young, non-disabled children uncomfortable; some did not understand that blind children had no sight, but thought that they could just see less clearly.

Recommendation: Teachers must be forthcoming about the nature of the disability and explain why a blind child is unable to maintain eye contact.

**Low status of children and adolescents with disabilities in regular classrooms**

Many studies have reported that children and adolescents with disabilities tend to have low social status in regular classrooms (e.g., Hall & Strickett, 2002; Frostad & Pijl, 2007). In studies of social status based on sociometric rating—namely, whether classmates would choose these students as best friends or as playmates—Judith Wiener of the University of Toronto and Nancy Heath of McGill University reported low social status of Canadian children with learning disabilities and emotional and behavioural disorders (e.g., Bloom, Karagiannakis, Toste, Heath, & Konstantinopoulos., 2007; Wiener & Tardif, 2004).

A large study of the social networks of 400 children from grades 2 through 5 included 17 focal children with autism or Asperger syndrome. Findings showed the focal children experienced lower social status, companionship, and reciprocity than their normally developing peers (Chamberlain, Kasari, & Rotheram-Fuller, 2007).

**Factors contributing to more positive attitudes of students toward classmates with a disability.**

A study of high school students in Ontario reported the attitudes of almost 2,000 grade 9 students toward their peers with disabilities. The majority of students (61 percent) held positive attitudes; 21 per cent held attitudes ranging from slightly below neutral to very negative (McDougall et al., 2004). When students perceived that the school encouraged learning for all students rather than competition among students, their views of peers with disabilities were more positive. As well, positive relationships between teachers and students and positive student relationships were associated with more positive attitudes. Having a friend or classmate with a disability contributed to more positive attitudes.

A study of 80 children with a range of disabilities used quantitative and qualitative methods to identify child characteristics that could contribute to low social status. The researchers found that socially accepted children tended to have disabilities that were less likely to affect social problem solving and emotional regulation. Children who were socially rejected had disabilities that were more likely to affect social competence (Odom et al., 2006).

As teachers, you can promote the social status of exceptional students in your classrooms by fostering the perception of these students as valued classmates and by teaching so everyone experiences the benefits of being included. Try to make your students comfortable with what disability involves and minimize students' sense of disabilities as foreign and exotic. Provide information and eliminate any mystery about the exceptionality. Ensure that exceptional students are treated as everyone else would be.

Parents may express their concern to you about their exceptional child's socialization with other children. Suggestions about ways to promote social interactions of their children with disabilities could include:

- For young children, taking an active role in initiating play opportunities with neighbouring families so children without disabilities can feel comfortable alongside the exceptional child.

- Encouraging long-term friendships, given that they appear to provide considerable benefits to exceptional students.

- Indicating that similar benefits accrue from connections with extended family outside of school and providing opportunities for these relationships to develop.

Figure 8.2 can help you to plan a **(dis)ability awareness program** for your classroom or school. There are several well-established programs that can serve as models and many resources that detail how to go about promoting disability awareness.

Figure 8.3 provides suggestions for parents (or teachers) to help children or adolescents with severe disabilities to develop skills for interacting with peers and handling emotions. The next section describes the importance of friendship to development and elaborates on why teachers and parents should make the effort to foster such friendships.

**Cross-Reference**

You may want to revisit Chapter 7 and think about the suggestions for teachers to develop a positive classroom climate that would foster interaction among all students, including exceptional learners.

## FIGURE 8.2 (DIS)ABILITY AWARENESS PROGRAMS

**Purposes of Disability Awareness Programs:**

To foster greater understanding of people with disabilities

To increase students' knowledge about specific disabilities.

To increase students' sensitivity toward individuals with disabilities.

Develop a program that reflects your local school needs. Invite parents of children with disabilities, older students with disabilities, and adults with disabilities to take part in the planning and in the program. Following are some resources that you may wish to consult:

**Family Village. Disability Awareness.**

www.familyvillage.wisc.edu/general/disability-awareness.html

**Center for Disability Information and Referral (Indiana University)**

www.iidc.indiana.edu/index.php?pageId=34

**Kids' Corner: Have you ever wondered what it's like to have a disability?**

www.iidc.indiana.edu/cedir/kidsweb

**EasterSealsNewBrunswick**

Disability Awareness Training CD-ROM.

http://easterseals.nb.ca/prog_datcd.php

**DAWN Ontario (DisAbled Women's Network Ontario). Interacting with People with DisAbilities: An Etiquette Hand-book.**

http://dawn.thot.net/Etiquette.html

(Originally developed by the University of Arkansas, 2002)

**Variety Village**

Provides integrated sports and lifeskills programs for youth with disabilities. Although headquartered in Toronto, programming can be provided across Ontario.
www.varietyontario.ca/village/index.htm

Foley, J.T., Tindall, D., Lieberman, L., & Kim, S.-Y. (2007). How to develop disability awareness using the sport education model. *Journal of Physical Education, Recreation and Dance*, Nov/Dec.

Rillotta, F., & Nettelbeck, T. (2007). Effects of an awareness program on attitudes of students without an intellectual disability towards persons with an intellectual disability. *Journal of Intellectual and Developmental Disability, 32,* 19–27.

Department of the Secretary of State of Canada. *Discover together: A disability awareness resource (kit).* (A teaching kit with six units to raise awareness about the competencies of people with disabilities. Recommended for grades K–8.)

Kirch, S.A., Bargerhuff, M.E., Cowan, H., & Wheatly, M. (2007). Reflections of educators in pursuit of inclusive science. *Journal of Science Teacher Education, 18,* 663–692. (Describes a program for enhancing disability awareness of teachers.)

**Weblinks**

ABOUT ADOLESCENTS AND PEER RELATIONS:

FOCUS ADOLESCENT SERVICES
http://focusas.com/PeerInfluence.html

FRIENDSHIPS—HELPING YOUR CHILD THROUGH EARLY ADOLESCENCE (US DEPARTMENT OF EDUCATION)
www.ed.gov/parents/academic/help/adolescence/part9.html

## FIGURE 8.3 STRATEGIES FOR PARENTS (AND TEACHERS) TO TEACH SOCIAL SKILLS FOR PEER INTERACTIONS

### Incidental Teaching

This strategy means taking advantage of "teachable moments." During naturally occurring situations, parents (or teachers) remind or show children how to use social skills.

### Example

Fiona is playing at Maggie's house. Fiona and Maggie reach for the green crayon at the same time. Maggie's mother takes this opportunity to remind Maggie to share, saying, "Maybe you can let Fiona use the green crayon now, and you can use the blue one until she is finished. Then you can use the green crayon. Remember: Fiona is our guest."

### Analyzing an Incident

This strategy involves a parent (or teacher) in guiding a child through an analysis of what went wrong after a child has lost his or her temper or handled a social situation poorly. It usually helps to allow the child to cool down first.

### Example

Marc was watching a video in the family room with two boys from his class. His father was reading the paper in the next room. When Marc did not understand what was happening in the plot of the movie, he started asking the other boys why the robbers were returning the money. When they didn't explain, Marc asked again and again. The other two boys became annoyed and decided to go home. Marc ejected the video and threw it across the room. Marc was sent to his room to cool down. When he returned to the family room, his father asked him, "What did you do?" "What happened next?" "Was this a good outcome?" "What will you do next time?" Marc's suggestion was to ask the other boys if he could stop the video, ask them to explain what the robbers were doing and why, then turn the video on again as soon as he understood.

### Coaching Emotional Responses

This strategy describes parents (or teachers) leading children through steps to become more emotionally aware. It involves listening and being aware of the emotion, naming the emotion, and planning what to do next time.

### Example

Vema tells her mother how another girl embarrassed her at school. Her mother asks Vema to explain what happened and how she felt. The girl had said she did not want Vema on her softball team because Vema's leg brace made her run too slowly. Vema's mother helped Vema find words to express her feelings. Her mother related an experience that she had, explained that this is called embarrassment, and reminded Vema that all people feel embarrassment at times. Vema's mother talked about what was not acceptable—throwing the softball bat or the ball at the girl. Then she and Vema discussed acceptable solutions. Vema laughed. "I will try to remember to suggest what you said—that they have a designated runner for me. Because I can hit the ball. But she's right: I am a slow runner."

Adapted from:

Elksnin, L.K., & Elksnin, N. (2001). *Assessment and instruction of social skills*. Mahwah, NJ: Lawrence Erlbaum Associates.

Coombs-Richardson, R., & Meisgeier, C.H. (2004). *Connecting with others: Lessons for teaching social and emotional competence*. Champaign IL: Research Press.

Vernon, A. (1998). *The Passport Program: A journey through emotional, social, cognitive, and self-development*. Champaign, IL: Research Press. (3 volumes: grades 1–5, 6–8, 9–12.)

Northfield, S., & Sherman, A. (2004). Acceptance and community building in schools through increased dialogue and discussion. *Children and Society, 18*, 291–298.

# The Role of Friendship in the Development of Exceptional Individuals

Social competence and social acceptance are important for all children and adolescents. Friendship has been called "the most human relationship" (Bukowski & Sippola, 2005, p. 91). Social skills and competencies are acquired in both close friendships and general peer group relationships. Intimacy skills are more likely to develop in friendships and skills like leadership and feelings of inclusion are more likely to develop in peer relations.

Research suggests that children and adolescents with poor peer adjustment are at greater risk for criminality and dropping out of school (e.g., Bukowski, Rubin, & Parker, 2004). Social skills are also increasingly important to successful participation in the workplace (Conference Board of Canada, 2003; Hutchinson et al., 2008). Researchers have shown that social co-operation also contributes to cognitive development. Vygotsky (1978, p. 163) wrote that "social relations . . . underlie all higher functions and their relationships." He argued that all learning is first carried out between the individual and others in the environment. In these social interactions, the individual gradually internalizes what he or she has been doing, saying, and thinking. Speech and dialogue are thought to be important mediators of internalization (Ostad & Sorenson, 2007; Trent, Artiles, & Englert, 1998). Dialogues that lead to developmental change involve finely tuned coordinations between the child and another person, and occur within the **zone of proximal development** between the child's independent problem solving and what the child can do with adult guidance or in collaboration with more capable peers. The most effective partnerships are thought to be two individuals who differ from one another in expertise, although two novices can contribute to each other's learning of problem solving.

Do children co-operate better with friends than with non-friends? When children do school tasks with friends, they interact more, pay more attention to equity rules, and discuss mutually beneficial outcomes more (e.g., Hartup, Daiute, Zajac, & Sholl, 1995; Zajac & Hartup, 1997). We have heard adolescents working co-operatively say, "Once you've worked in a group, you would never want to just learn alone" (Hutchinson, Freeman, & Quick, 1996). When children write stories collaboratively, their stories are more advanced than if they were written individually (Vass, 2002). These findings suggest that the benefits of learning co-operatively may be enhanced by learning with friends.

However, the issue may be more complex than previously thought. In a large, well-designed study, Kutnick and Kington (2005) reported that girls' friendship pairings performed at the highest levels while boys' friendship pairings performed at the lowest levels. The students were working on science reasoning tasks. Perhaps the friendship pairings of boys did not remain on task, which we know is essential when students are learning together.

Children and adolescents whose ability to express themselves is limited to individual words or nods are likely to be disadvantaged in cognitive development and learning. There are limited opportunities for the reciprocity that characterizes friendships and involves sharing and self-disclosure.

## What do you think?

Exceptional children who have not learned to socialize, who are not socially accepted in the classroom, or who do not have friends may be disadvantaged cognitively. Think of exceptional students like Matt, who described himself as friendless, or Val, in the opening case study, who did not have anyone to play with at recess. These individuals have few opportunities to improve their interaction skills and become better at learning with their peers Why do you think that cooperation beetween friends is well suited to cognitive development?

**Cross-Reference**

Chapter 2 includes a section on educational assistants and their roles in educating students with exceptionalities. You may remember that the issue was raised of educational assistants sometimes coming between children with disabilites and their classmates. How might that situation contribute to the level of social competence and social acceptance of exceptional students? What can you do to ensure that exceptional students benefit from the actions of educational assistants and are not socially disadvantaged?

# Elementary and Secondary Schools as Social Environments

Schools are highly social environments in which students spend the day working and playing with their classmates. Classic studies (e.g., Bryan, 1991; Vaughn, 1991) and recent research (e.g., Northfield & Sherman, 2004; Hutchinson et al., 2004) suggest that it is important to enhance both the social competence of youth with exceptionalities and their social acceptance by peers because neither alone is sufficient. Teachers must create a context where co-operation, community, and peer support thrive. This means informal teaching of social competence and acceptance of diversity with the entire class and making your thinking apparent to students (Northfield & Sherman, 2004).

## Informal Teaching: Climate and Role Models

Teachers create positive and inclusive climates in their classrooms by showing respect for all members of the class, making all students feel that their presence counts, and interacting with all students in ways that communicate caring and acceptance. This includes: avoiding teasing and sarcasm (McIntosh & Vaughn, 1993), communicating high expectations, and supporting students to reach them (Urdan & Schoenfelder, 2006). When there are difficulties, you can respond by "seizing the moment" and negotiating with the group.

## Facilitating Friendships

You may feel that it is beyond your responsibilities as a teacher to facilitate friendships among your students. However, facilitating friendships may make the classroom a better place for everyone, including you. Figure 8.4 shows some of the steps that you can take.

Intensive programs may require the participation of a resource teacher, occupational therapist, or social worker, but many teaching strategies serve as friendship interventions. These teaching strategies include "getting-to-know-you activities early in the year and literature with friendship themes. Use modelling, guided practice, and independent practice to teach social skills so students can conduct themselves appropriately in your classroom, in assembly, or on a field trip.

**Further Reading**

To enhance the friendship and conversational skills of students with many of the exceptionalities described in Chapters 3 and 4, research has been conducted and programs developed. For example:

- Children with attention deficit hyperactivity disorders (DuPaul & Weyandt, 2006);
- Children and adolescents with autism (Palmen, Didden, & Arts, 2008; Stichter et al., 2007);
- Children with Asperger syndrome (Crooke, Hendrix, & Rachman, 2008);
- Youth with Williams syndrome (Klein-Tasman, & Albano, 2007);
- Children with physical disabilities (Bennett & Hay, 2007; Clarke & Wilkinson, 2008);
- Young children with a range of disabilities (Terpstra & Tamura, 2008).
- Children with fetal alcohol spectrum disorders (Laugeson, Paley, Schonfeld, Carpenter, Frankl, & O'Connoe, 2007).

### FIGURE 8.4  WHAT CAN YOU DO?

- During the early years at school, you can provide a structured and supervised social program that can help children practise relationships.

- In middle childhood, it helps to provide activities that encourage prosocial interaction during unstructured times of the day when some children may be excluded. At this age, children choose friends on the basis of personality and interests and friendships become increasingly stable. Boys may form gangs, while girls tend to form small intimate groups.

- During preadolescence, helping and confiding replace playing and many students need assistance with conversational skills. Involving students in co-operative and collaborative activities throughout these elementary and middle school years gives you an opportunity to teach social skills as part of regular curriculum activities (Dion, Fuchs, & Fuchs, 2005; Kutnick, Ota, & Berdondini, 2008).

- During adolescence, friendships are about trust, intimacy, and the sharing of deeply personal thoughts. These close friendships are complemented by membership in larger groups identified by taste in music, clothing styles, and vernacular expressions.

For students who have behaviour problems or are lonely, set friendship goals. With young children, ask whom they would like to get to know. With older students, you may be able to set goals for participation in an extracurricular activity or group. Teach students to handle rejection by considering what they should say if the peer they approach turns them down. Structure social times like recess and lunch periods by forming groups that include isolated students. Create peer buddy programs, ask socially able students to include a shy child in their conversation. Ensure that adult presence does not interfere in fledgling conversations or friendships.

## THEORY AND RESEARCH HIGHLIGHTS FROM

## EDUCATIONAL PSYCHOLOGY

# The Construct of Friendship

There have been calls recently for friendship research to return to its conceptual roots and focus on clarifying the construct and on revealing the dynamics of friendship, positive and negative (Bukowski & Sippola, 2005). Many researchers have suggested that friendship has both a deep structure and a surface structure (Hartup & Stevens, 1997). By deep structure, they mean friendship's essence or meaning—mutuality and reciprocity. Surface structure refers to the social exchanges within the reciprocal, companionable relationship, but when these exchanges are fraught with difficulty, friendship can create our greatest problems and anxieties (Bukowski, Adams, & Santo, 2006).

Some writers in special education have observed that friendship seems to be harder for exceptional adolescents than for children or adults (Steiner-Bell, 2004). At every age there are preoccupying concerns to which people must attend. In early childhood, friendships meet the need for equality-based exchange relationships (Brett & Willard, 2002), and adolescence is characterized by concerns with self-clarification, self-validation, and obtaining assistance to cope (Buhrmester & Prager, 1995). These concerns shape the surface structure of friendship and its social exchanges; for example, young children play beside or with one another, often more focused on the play than on themselves. Adolescents "hang out," self-disclose, engage in supportive problem solving, and seek self-defining activities with friends (Buhrmester, 1998). Buhrmester argues that four interpersonal competencies follow from these developmental concerns that are essential for dyadic friendships during the adolescent years:

(a) initiating and sustaining conversation;

(b) making plans to spend time together;

(c) self-disclosing personal thoughts and providing emotional support; and

(d) working through conflicts.

Friends are most often of a similar age and preoccupied with similar developmental issues. This may not be the case when exceptional adolescents are cognitively or socially less mature, or more mature, than their non-disabled peers That friends wrestle with common issues suggests that adolescents need at least one supportive peer.

There appear to be different "cultures" or contexts for male and female relations during adolescence (Tannen, 1990). Interactions between female adolescents focus on building interpersonal connections. However, recent research shows that females are also more likely to engage in co-rumination, repeatedly focusing on problems and dwelling on negative affect, and this disclosure process has been related to depression in adolescent females (Rose, 2002; Rose, Schwartz, & Carlson, 2005). This suggests that not all close adolescent-female friendships have positive effects.

Interactions between adolescent males focus more on agentic concerns and less on communal ones. They have been described as "side-by-side" interactions because they focus on doing things together, mainly sports and competitive games (Wright, 1982). Their supportive discussions often focus on the accomplishments of sports teams and individuals. Such interactions may meet needs for achievement, recognition, and power. Close male-adolescent friendships can also produce negative effects. At-risk boys reinforce the deviant behaviours of friends (Dishion, McCord, & Poulin, 1999). The more friends laugh at deviant behaviour, the more it increases over time.

Case studies like those developed by Steiner-Bell may help us to combine what we know about disabilities with recent work on the psychological construct of friendship to enhance the social relations of exceptional adolescents. While friendship can effect healthy development, it can also contribute to psychopathology (Bukowski

*(Box continued on next page)*

et al., 2006). There is potential for darker aspects of friendship in research with exceptional populations (Hartrup, 2006).

## References

Brett, B., & Willard, W.W. (2002). The origins of reciprocity and social exchange in friendships. *New Directions for Child and Adolescent Development, 95,* 27–40.

Buhrmester, D. (1998). Need fulfilment, interpersonal competence, and the developmental contexts of early adolescent friendship. In W.M. Bukowski, A.F. Newcomb, & W.W. Hartup (Eds.), *The company they keep: Friendship in childhood and adolescence,* 2nd ed., (pp. 158–185). New York: Cambridge University Press.

Buhrmester, D., & Prager, K. (1995). Patterns and functions of self-disclosure during childhood and adolescence. In K.J. Rotenberg (Ed.), *Disclosure processes in children and adolescents,* (pp. 10–46). New York: Cambridge University Press.

Bukowski, W.M., Adams, R.E., & Santo, J.B. (2006). Recent advances in the study of development, social and personal experience, and psychopathology. *International Journal of Behavioral Development, 30,* 26–30.

Bukowski, W.M., & Sippola, L.K. (2005). Friendship and development: Putting the most human relationship in its place. *New Directions for Child and Adolescent Development, 109,* 91–97.

Dishion, T. J., Nelson, S.E., & Bukkick, B. (2004). Premature adolescence autonomy: Parent adisengagement and deviant process in the amplification of problem behavior. *Journal of Adolescence, 27,* 515–530.

Hartrup, W.W. (2006). Relationships in early and middle childhood. In A.L. Vangelist & D. Perlman (Eds.). *The Cambridge handbook of personal relationships* (pp. 177–190). New York: Cambridge University Press.

Hartup, W.W., & Stevens, N. (1997). Friendship and adaptation in the life course. *Psychological Bulletin, 121,* 355–370.

Rose, A.J. (2002). Co-rumination in the friendships of girls and boys. *Child Development,* 73, 1830–1843.

Rose, A.J., Schwrtz, R.A., & Carlson, W. (2005). *An observational assessment of co-rumination in the friendships of girls and boys.* A paper presented at the Society for Research in Child Development, Atlanta, GA.

Steiner-Bell, K. (2004). *Social understanding in the friendships of persons with a developmental syndrome.* Unpublished doctoral thesis, Queen's University, Kingston, Ontario.

Tannen, D. (1990). Gender differences in topical coherence: Creating involvement in best friends' talk. *Discourse Processes, 13,* 73–90.

Wright, P.H. (1982). Men's friendships, women's friendships and the alleged inferiority of the latter. *Sex Roles, 8,* 1–20.

**Put into Practice**

The Ontario Ministry of Education recommends that all students be given the Kids Help Phone telephone number. How would you go about making your students aware of the purpose of the Kids Help Phone and providing them with the number? The number is **1-800-668-6868**.

## Safe Schools Strategy

The Ontario Ministry of Education has undertaken several initiatives as part of a concerted approach to making all schools safer. The *Ontario Schools Code of Conduct* (2000) was superseded in June, 2007, with the passing of Bill 212, the Education Amendment Act (*Progressive Discipline and School Safety*). The Act came into effect in February, 2008, and applies province-wide. Revisions to the Provincial Code of Conduct included new policies and procedures related to hate propaganda and other forms of behaviour motivated by hate or bias. The policy and procedures for suspension and expulsion were revised. These included consideration of mitigating factors before students are suspended or expelled and responding to inappropriate behaviour in the most appropriate way, rather than automatic suspensions and expulsions. Bullying was added to the list of infractions that can lead to suspension. As well, district school boards were required to provide programs to students on long-term suspension or expulsion so they can continue their education and access services, e.g., anger management and career counselling. All schools were also required to develop and implement a school-wide progressive discipline policy (www.edu.gov.on.ca/eng/safeschools/discipline.pdf) that takes a whole-school approach, using a continuum of interventions, supports, and consequences to deal with inappropriate student behaviours and building upon strategies that advance positive student behaviour and character development. Every school has had to establish a safe school team. Members of the team include the principal and at least one student, parent, teacher, support staff member, and community partner.

As part of the Safe Schools Strategy, a fact sheet on bullying prevention was developed for parents, *Making Ontario Schools Safer: What Parents Need to Know*. (www.edu.gov.on.ca/eng/safeschools/pdfs/saferSchools.pdf). This addressed the meaning of progressive discipline, specified what a code of conduct is, explained school-wide bullying prevention programs, identified responses to inappropriate behaviour, and detailed suspension and expulsion policies and procedures. The Ministry also created an extensive Registry of Bullying Prevention Programs available to schools and organizations (www.edu.gov.on.ca/eng/teachers/bullyprevention/registry.html). It has also partnered with Kids Help Phone which offers anonymous support 24/7 to bullying victims, bystanders, and bullies themselves.

Ontario has become the first province in Canada to require all school staff to report any serious student incidents—including bullying—to the principal (www.edu.gov.on.ca/eng/safeschools/KeepKidSafeSchool.pdf). In addition, anyone working directly with students must respond to incidents that could impact negatively on the school climate, e.g., vandalism, graffiti, and racist or sexist comments. This report and response measure came into effect on February 1, 2010, as part of the Education Amendment Act (*Keeping Our Kids Safe at School*, 2009). This legislation was in response to the recommendations in the Safe Schools Action Team Report, *Shaping a Culture of Respect in Our Schools: Promoting Safe and Healthy Relationships* (2008) (www.edu.gov.on.ca/eng/teachers/RespectCulture.pdf)

Another recommendation arising from the report focused on school climate suggested that schools conduct a climate assessment to determine school needs and to develop bullying prevention programs. Sample climate surveys about equity, inclusive education, and bullying/harassment for students, staff, and parents are available (www.edu.gov.on.ca/eng/teachers/climate.html).

## Schoolwide Approaches and Teachers' Roles

In Chapter 7 we focused on ways in which you can create a classroom community and a positive climate for learning with your students. The social climate of the school contributes to the social climate of your classroom. Important aspects of the social environment in a school can be influenced by **schoolwide approaches**.

### CODE OF CONDUCT

Although there is a provincial Code of Conduct, (www.edu.gov.on.ca/eng/document/brochure/conduct/conduct.html), district school boards can continue to require principals to develop additional **codes of conduct** that are designed particularly for their schools. These must be consistent with the provincial Code of Conduct and clearly indicate what is acceptable and unacceptable behaviour for all members of the elementary or secondary school community (e.g. parents, students, staff, visitors, and volunteers). The Rainbow District School Board Code of Conduct (www.rainbowschools.ca/students/discipline.php), for example, details guiding principles, roles and responsibilities of the school community, standards of behaviour, respect-civility-and responsible citizenship, safety, and suspension and expulsion in accordance with the provincial Code of Conduct. Principals are expected to consult their school council and seek input from all members of the school community. The local codes of conduct must be disseminated to all members of the school community.

**What do you think?**

While many researchers have advocated involving students in all aspects of generating a code of conduct to achieve a safer and more positive school climate, others have argued that codes of conduct marginalize those who do not conform easily and are intended to produce docile citizens and workers. Read the following papers by Paula Denton of the University of Massachusetts and Rebecca Raby of Brock University to decide what you think.

Denton, P. (2003). Shared rule-making in practice: The Jefferson committee at Kingston High School. *American Secondary Education*, 31(3), 66–96.

Raby, R. (2005). Polite, well-dressed and on time: Secondary school conduct codes and the production of docile citizens. *Canadian Review of Sociology and Anthropology*, 42, 71–91.

Read recent sources on cyberbullying and what can be done about it. See below. Then discuss the issue with your peers. Break into work groups to develop a workshop, based on readings and on experience, for a specific group affected by cyberbullying (e.g., parents, parents of exceptional students, administrators, children, adolescents, elementary or secondary teachers). Share your approaches. Try out your workshop and make changes in light of the feedback you receive.

Examples of sources:

Misha, F., Saini, M., Solomon, S. (2009). Ongoing and online: Childen and youth's perceptions of cyberbyllying. *Children and Youth Services Review, 31*(2), 1222–1228.

Hinduja, S., & Ratchin, J. (2009). *Bullying beyond the schoolyard: Preventing and responding to cyberbullying.* Thousand Oaks, CA: Corwin.

Urbansksi, J., & Pernuth, S. (2009). *The truth about bullying: What educators and parents must know and do.* Lanham, MD: Rowman & Littlefield Education.

Baute, N. (December 22, 2009). Enemies lurk on friendly Facebook: Social networking sites fall prey to cyberbullies who steal identiites. *Toronto Star.*

Put into Practice

Develop a code of conduct for your classroom. Make two lesson plans for introducing the code and two for reviewing it with your class.

York Region District School Board has a *Safe and Supportive Schools* brochure that requires the signature of both students and their parents/guardians (www.yrdsb.edu.on.ca/pdfs/w/innovation/safeschools/YRDSBSafeSchools.pdf). While a code of conduct should involve the entire school community, it is only one strategy to improve the social environment of a school. To engage in **moral leadership**, educational leaders must lead by example and focus their attention on activities that enhance the sense of community within the school, and create rituals and traditions that symbolically represent the values and culture of the school community.

## Schoolwide Behaviour Management Systems

**Schoolwide behaviour management systems** are comprehensive approaches to managing behaviour throughout a school (Colvin, 2007). They are process-based models in which collaborative teams of teachers, administrators, parents, and students work together to obtain consensus.

### PREVENTING BULLYING

Research suggests that students who are harassed and bullied are more likely to exhibit aggression and antisocial behaviour that might interfere with their participation in social learning activities with peers (Rusby et al., 2005). Data from the Canadian National Longitudinal Survey of Children and Youth found that students who reported being bullied at school were more likely to obtain low levels of achievement (Beran, Hughes, & Lupart, 2008).

"**Bullying** is a form of abuse at the hands of peers that can take different forms at different ages" (Craig, Pepler, & Blais, 2007, p. 465). These forms include physical, emotional, verbal, and cyberbullying. **Cyberbullying** is a form of psychological cruelty perpetrated virtually, and refers to threats, insults, and demeaning messages spread through the internet or by cell phone. The proliferation of social networking sites in conjunction with texting has provided new opportunities for bullying to occur. While cyberthreats and cyberbullying usually take place away from school grounds, they have repercussions for our schools and students, and we cannot ignore their potential for destroying students' safety and well-being 24 hours a day, in school and out of school (Mason, 2008; Willard, 2007). Bullying begins in elementary school, increases during the middle school years, and usually decreases in secondary school (Beale & Hall, 2007).

Children and youth with exceptionalities are at increased risk of being marginalized and are more vulnerable to victimization by peers who have higher status and more social power (Cummings, Pepler, Mishna, & Craig, 2006; Luciano & Savage, 2007). And a recent interview study suggests that, while Canadian teachers recognize and respond to physical bullying, they find it much more difficult to recognize and intervene in cases of indirect bullying (Mishna et al., 2005). Beran (2006) reported, in another Canadian study, that students' and teachers' reports of what constitutes bullying are not highly correlated. These studies remind us how challenging dealing with bullying can be for educators.

Olweus' (2003) extensive research on bullying shows that, to minimize bullying, school environments must be characterized by:

- warmth, positive interest, and involvement from adults;
- firm limits on unacceptable behaviour;

# Anti-Bullying and Anti-Violence Programs

There are many websites available to help you and your school tackle bullying on a schoolwide basis. Most of these Canadian sites also provide links to other international sites.

**London (Ontario) Family Court Clinic:**

www.lfcc.on.ca/bully.htm

This site contains extensive information about bullying for parents and teachers. The highly readable information is an excerpt from the second edition of A.S.A.P.: A School-based Anti-violence Program that is available from the London Family Court Clinic. It has a video and 65 lessons.

**PREVnet:**

www.prevnet.ca

This combined research and practice website focuses on promoting relationships and eliminating violence. Based at Queen's University and York University, it involves many of the leading researchers in Canada in the field of bullying and a wide range of organizations and agencies.

**Olweus Bullying Prevention Program:**

www.clemson.edu/olweus

This is the North American website for the most researched anti-bullying program, developed by Dan Olweus of Norway.

**Bullying.org (children at Banded Peak School in Bragg Creek, Alberta, and their teacher, William Belsey):**

www.bullying.org

This site was started after the shooting at W.R. Myers High School in Taber, Alberta, when stories emerged that the accused had been bullied. A group of grade 1 to 8 students who met to provide peer support grew into www.bullying.org which attempts to help young people help each other. Not only can you and your students learn by visiting this site, but you might be inspired to commit to an online project that would ensure that your students internalize and live the lessons you are learning together.

**Stop Cyberbullying:**

www.cyberbullying.ca

This site was started by the developers of www.bullying.org, Bill Belsey and his students. It contains practical suggestions about combatting cyberbullying, including lobbying the telecommunications industry about the problem.

---

- consistent application of non-punitive, non-physical sanctions for unacceptable behaviour or violations of rules;
- adults who act as authorities and positive role models; and
- coaching students to include all classmates in activities, supporting victims, reporting incidents, and taking part in role-playing to practise leadership and citizenship.

Wendy Craig of Queen's University and Debra Pepler of York University lead the Canadian Initiative for the Prevention of Bullying (http://prevnet.ca). Their longitudinal research has found that many of the 10 percent of youths who persistently bully through adolescence have troubled relationships with their parents and friends, and consistently use power and aggression to control and distress others (Craig, Pepler, Murphy, & McCuaig-Edge, 2010; Pepler & Craig, 2008; Pepler, Jiang, Craig, & Connolly, 2008). They suggest that intervention strategies need to involve the wider community, including parents and other adults, and must help children and adolescents to intervene effectively. Bullies, as well as victims, require support and relationship problems require relationship solutions. Peplar (www.arts.yorku.ca/lamarsh) reports that teachers respond only about 10 percent of the time. Children need consistent teacher response, and opportunities to role-play proactive and prosocial responses to bullying. (See Figure 8.5 for strategies to help students respond to bullying.) Figure 8.6 introduces a strategy called ABC—TELL NOW, to help students of all ages with intellectual disabilities, to learn how to report incidents of cyberbullying.

**Further Reading**

Colvin, G. (2009). *Managing non-compliance and defiance in the classroom: A road map for teachers, specialists, and behavior support teams.* Thousand Oaks, CA: Corwin Press.

Haynes, C.C. (2009). Schools of conscience. *Educational Leadership, 66*(8), 6–13.

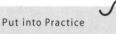

**Put into Practice**

Look at the Olweus Bullying Prevention Program at www.clemson.edu/olweus. It includes teacher guides, booklets, and videos. Are there features of the Olweus Program that might be incorporated into your classroom? into your school?

### Further Reading

These two papers focus on two different approaches to helping children cope with harassment and bullying. Newman develops a framework for understanding effective and ineffective help seeking by children. Merrell and colleagues review the research on effectiveness of school bullying intervention programs.

Merrell, K.W., Gueldner, B.A., Ross, S.W., & Isava, D.M. (2008). How effective are school bullying intervention programs? A meta-analysis of intervention research. *School Psychology Quarterly, 23*(1), 26–42.

Newman, R.S. (2008). Adaptive and nonadaptive help seeking with peer harassment: An integrative perspective of coping and self-regulation. *Educational Psychologist, 43*, 1–15.

## FIGURE 8.5 HELPING STUDENTS RESPOND TO BULLYING

- Help students to recognize when they should seek adult intervention.
- Encourage children and adolescents to come forward and report bullying and cyberbullying early, before the emotional effects become too great.
- Be aware of the signs of bullying and support those who experience bullying. Avoidance, including avoiding school, may be a sign that a child is being bullied. Watch for students who experience stomach aches, headaches, and depressive symptoms or who are victims of exclusion, including virtual exclusion.
- Monitor exchanges between more powerful and less powerful students closely. You need to be aware of unusual pairings of students. Remember that bullying can be physical, verbal, emotional, or virtual. Be vigilant. The longer bullying goes on, the harder it will be to put an end to it.
- Watch for signs of responses to bullying. Girls are more likely to use relationship skills to try to deal with bullying, while boys are more likely to resort to violence or retaliation.
- Provide children and youth who are bullied with effective strategies. Help them to recognize healthy and unhealthy relationships (even friends can engage in bullying) and encourage students to report bullying immediately.
- Help those who are bullied to walk away. Help students to practise their replies to things that they may be teased or bullied about (unusual name, glasses, hearing aid, etc.) so they can give the impression it doesn't bother them. And encourage students to report bullying immediately.
- Create a positive social climate in which all are valued, teach students your expectations, and respond to bullying and cyberbullying consistently and in accord with the protocol about which students have been informed.

> Developed after reading: Stones, R. (2005). *Don't pick on me: How to handle bullying* (3rd ed.). Markham, ON: Pembroke Publishers. Craig, W., Pepler, D., & Blais, J. (2007) Responding to bullying: What works? *School Psychology International, 28*, 465–477. Beale, A.V., & Hall, K.R. (2007). *Cyberbullying: What school administrators (and parents) can do. Clearing House, 81*(1), 8–12.

Most bullying incidents occur out of the sight of teachers and adult volunteers. Increasing supervision, along with other schoolwide components, contributes to reducing bullying. Other approaches include peer tutoring and co-operative and collaborative teaching in the classroom.

## FIGURE 8.6 TEACHING STUDENTS A STRATEGY FOR REPORTING CYBERBULLYING

This strategy, ABC—TELL NOW, teaches students who don't know how to report bullying to recognize what is happening to them and to report it to an adult. Students with intellectual disabilities, of any age, should be taught to use to use their ABCs to TELL NOW.

Post the strategy in the classroom in large print, review it frequently, and teach older pupils to support children and students with intellectual disabilities in using the strategy.

**Sample Poster to Hang in the Classroom**

> **ABC**—TELL NOW
>
> **A**m I hurt?
>
> **B**y computer or cell phone?
>
> '**C**ause it was mean?
>
> **T**ELL an adult NOW

# Using the ADAPT Strategy to Analyze Social Demands in the Classroom: Peer Teaching and Collaborative Learning

You can use the ADAPT strategy to analyze the social demands of classroom organization and tasks and compare these demands with student strengths and needs. There may be opportunities for students to learn from one another through peer teaching, as well as through collaborative and co-operative learning.

## Peer Teaching

**Peer teaching,** which has a long history, can take many forms and goes by a number of names, including peer tutoring, peer-assisted learning, and peer-mediated instruction (for a review of its history, see Topping, 2005). Essentially it involves peers as teaching partners. It can be especially effective when second-language students translate for one another. Fuchs and Fuchs (2005) paired high- and low-achieving readers throughout the elementary grades, and showed how peer-mediated instruction enhanced students' reading outcomes. They remind readers that a small number of children, about 10 percent, did not respond even to their most successful peer-mediated instruction, suggesting the need for more intensive, individualized interventions for a small number of students, as discussed in Chapter 1.

Overall, reviews have shown that social and self-concept outcomes are positively correlated with academic outcomes (Ginsburg-Block, Rohrbeck, & Fantuzzo, 2006) and that peer tutoring is effective for younger learners and for students with mild disabilities in secondary settings (e.g., Stenhoff & Lignugaris/Kraft, 2007).

## Using Co-Operative and Collaborative Learning to Meet Academic and Social Goals

Integrating social skills enhancement into the ongoing curriculum within the classroom requires sufficient opportunities to practise these skills in a supportive environment (Hutchinson, Freeman, & Berg, 2004). **Collaborative learning** methods include co-operative learning and problem solving in pairs and groups and usually involve students of varying abilities and skills, that is, heterogeneous groupings rather than homogeneous groupings. The essence of collaboration is the construction of shared meanings for conversations, concepts, and experiences (Palincsar & Herrenkohl, 2002). Collaborative learning methods have been successful in improving academic performance of students of varying ages, grades, subjects, and abilities (see Gillies, Ashman, & Terwel, 2007). During collaborative learning, students tend to reproduce teacher discourse and to meet the expectations communicated by the teacher (Webb, Nemer, & Ing, 2006). Therefore you need to model verbalizing your thinking, asking questions, and providing explanations if you want your students to do the same.

The major benefits of collaborative learning for exceptional students include improved self-esteem, a safe learning environment, and better classroom success rates and products (Jenkins, Antil, Wayne, & Vadasy, 2003). The primary modification for exceptional students is selecting suitable partners for them.

### Further Reading

Gillies, R.M., Ashman, A., & Terwel, J. (Eds.). (2007). *The teacher's role in implementing cooperative learning in the classroom.* New York: Springer. (This edited volume provides an overview of the research and underlying theory as well as practical illustrations drawn from the author's research on how teachers can use co-operative and collaborative learning.)

Udvari-Solner, A., & Kluth, P. (2007). *Joyful learning: Active and collaborative learning in inclusive classrooms.* Thousand Oaks, CA: Corwin Press. (Presents techniques for using differentiation, active learning, and collaborative learning at the elementary and secondary levels. Includes reproducible handouts.)

O'Donnell, A.M., Hmelo-Silver, C.E., Erkens, G. (Eds.). (2005). *Collaborative learning, reasoning, and technology.* Mahwah, NJ: Erlbaum. (Presents research on using technology to support learning and reasoning in collaborative contexts.)

Statham, L. (2008). *Counting them in: Isolated bilingual learners in school.* Miami: Stylus Pub. (Focuses on using a variety of approaches, including co-operative learning, to teach isolated English language learners.)

Coelho, E. (2004). *Adding English: A guide to teaching in multilingual classrooms.* Don Mills, ON: Pippin Pub. Co. (A Canadian resource for meeting the needs of culturally diverse students.)

Sonnier-York, C., & Stanford (2002). Learning to co-operate: A teacher's perspective. *Teaching Exceptional Children, 34*(6), 40–44. (A helpful description of how one teacher learned to use co-operative learning.)

**Put into Practice**

Review the ADAPT strategy in Chapter 1. Use it to devise a peer teaching approach to promote social development, social acceptance, and academic learning of an exceptional student.

## Further Reading

Coelho, E., & Winer, L. (2000). *All sides of the issue: Photocopiable activities for cooperative jigsaw groups* (2nd ed.). Burlingame, CA: Alta Book Center. (Canadian source includes blackline masters.)

Gillies, R.M. (2007). *Cooperative learning: Integrating theory and practice.* Thousand Oaks, CA: Sage. (Contains planning guides and scripts that would be helpful for both in-service and pre-service teachers.)

Jacobs, G.M., Power, M.A., & Loh, W. (2002). *The teacher's sourcebook for cooperative learning: Practical techniques, basic principles, and frequently asked questions.* Thousand Oaks, CA: Corwin Press. (Valuable resource for lesson planning and classroom management.)

*@*

## Weblinks

SASKATOON SCHOOL DIVISION, INSTRUCTIONAL STRATEGIES ONLINE (INCLUDES A SELF-GUIDED TUTORIAL ON CO-OPERATIVE LEARNING)
http://olc.spsd.sk.ca/DE/PD/instr/strats/coop/index.html

THE COOPERATIVE LEARNING NETWORK, SHERIDAN COLLEGE
www-acad.sheridanc.on.ca/scls/coop/cooplrn.htm

JIGSAW CLASSROOM: A COOPERATIVE LEARNING TECHNIQUE
www.jigsaw.org

THE COOPERATIVE LEARNING CENTER AT THE UNIVERSITY OF MINNESOTA
www.cehd.umn.edu/research/highlights/coop-learning/

DALHOUSIE UNIVERSITY: WHAT IS COOPERATIVE LEARNING?
http://learningandteaching.dal.ca/taguide/WhatisCooperativeLearning.html

# Planning for Formal Teaching of Collaboration

Choose a collaborative strategy when you intend to promote positive peer support, social acceptance, and social competence—especially when the knowledge can be best learned through the contributions of many learners. There are many examples of lesson plans for collaborative learning (e.g., Udvari-Solner, & Kluth, 2007; Villa, Nevin, & Thousand, 2007). There are also excellent models of planning collaborative teaching for classes that include students with special needs (Villa, Nevin, & Thousand, 2007).

### TTYPA

A simple method to use during a lecture, film, or reading is called **TTYPA**, or "turn to your partner and . . ." The teacher stops and tells the students to "Turn to your partner and . . . introduce yourself . . . or describe a time when you. . . . Then switch roles" (Bellanca & Fogarty, 2003). With seatwork tasks, one partner describes the instructions and the second partner describes the first two steps. Such interdependence is good preparation for more complex collaborative activities.

### PAIRED PARTNERS: THINK ALOUD

In **Partners Thinking Aloud,** you model thinking aloud and ensure that the students understand what is expected of them (Bellanca & Fogarty, 2003). One student is the problem solver and the other the monitor. The problem solver thinks aloud throughout the task, and the monitor cues the "self-talk" of the solver by asking questions such as, "What is your goal?" "Does this make sense?" "Why?" Then they switch roles. This approach can be adapted to teach exceptional learners:

- Owen and Fuchs (2002) taught math to grade 3 students with learning disabilities;
- Clapper et al. (2002) taught reading comprehension to at-risk secondary school students;
- Xu et al. (2005) used pairs to increase socialization between ESL students and native speakers of English in grade 2 classrooms.

### CO-OPERATIVE LEARNING

**Co-operative learning** has been used extensively to promote interdependence in classrooms of typical and exceptional students. "Cooperative Learning is a relationship in a group of students that requires five necessary elements: positive interdependence (a sense of sink or swim together), individual accountability (each of us has to contribute and learn), interpersonal skills (communication, trust, leadership, decision making, and conflict resolution), face-to-face promotive interaction, and processing (reflecting on how well the team is functioning and how to function even better)" (Johnson & Johnson, www.co-operation.org). Co-operative learning strategies that incorporate individual accountability and group rewards are more likely to improve the achievement of students with disabilities (Nyman, McMaster & Fuchs, 2002).

The **jigsaw** strategy (also known as "expert groups") is a structured cooperative learning approach with a four-step structure:

Step 1 Students form a "home" group.

Step 2 Each student is assigned a number, colour, or letter. The topic overview is presented.

Step 3 Students now move to form an "expert group" with other students who have same number or colour, or letter. Each "expert group" works on one part of the larger topic.

Step 4 When time is up, the experts regroup with their original home groups. Each expert now teaches the skills or content learned in his or her subtopic to the home group.

Because all members contribute something to the topic, everybody has an opportunity to be an expert. Each team member learns skills or content from the others; therefore, team members must depend on one another to complete the overall tasks. Evaluation is based on both individual performance and an overall team effort mark.

## Teaching Students to Collaborate

How can you learn to use co-operative learning strategies successfully? Begin with simple, short activities that provide frequent occasions for participation. Try participation in pairs through TTYPA and Think Aloud pairs and progress to short co-operative learning activities such as group work on a five-minute mystery. For the most important social skills (such as giving everyone a chance to talk, listening actively, and providing explanations), students need practice, effective role models, and help to persist in the face of deterrents. (See Cohen, 1998; Cohen et al., 2004, for examples of activities and games.)

## Challenges to Collaborative Learning

Collaborative learning can be challenging to implement. Being aware of these challenges may help you to overcome them. Figure 8.7 shows some of the challenges you may encounter that can compromise collaborative learning outcomes.

Exceptional students and gifted students in inclusive classrooms are more likely to experience these drawbacks than are their peers. You may have to provide alternative evaluation criteria and modified or adapted goals and activities for some students with special needs. To promote group responsibility and individual accountability when assessing students in groups, you could have your students learn material in a group and perform it alone. You can also assess group performances through group products (e.g., case discussions, dramatic or musical productions, and group investigations) (Johnson & Johnson, 2004). Peer assessment is great for immediate and detailed formative feedback, and self-assessment helps students to set their own goals and monitor their progress toward these goals, our ultimate aim as educators.

Focus on the needs of exceptional students when creating groups. Gifted students can benefit from being placed with gifted peers, where they can challenge

Put into Practice

Read the following article and develop an intervention using direct instruction to improve the social skills of an exceptional student so the student can better participate in collaborative learning:

Johns, B.H., Crowley, P., & Guetzloe, E. (2005). The central role of teaching social skills. *Focus on Exceptional Children, 37*(8), 1–8.

Read the following and make a plan for supplementing the direct instruction for this student with other strategies (e.g., using children's or adolescent literature to teach social skills and to establish friendships).

Church, K., Gottschalk, C.M., & Leddy, J.N. (2003). 20 ways to enhance social and friendship skills. *Intervention in School and Clinic, 38,* 307–310.

## FIGURE 8.7 CHALLENGES TO CO-OPERATIVE LEARNING

- Peers may find it difficult to be sufficiently clear and explicit for exceptional learners to succeed.
- There can be unfair evaluation outcomes when all students receive the same grade but not all students have contributed equally.
- Gifted students may be disadvantaged if they know all of the content before the unit begins and are still expected to complete the same tasks as their peers .
- On occasion, a student may become dependent on the more able members of the group.

**Further Reading**

Children with autism and Asperger syndrome experience particular challenges because lack of social competence is at the heart of their disability (Chapter 4 contains a section on characteristics of students with autism and Asperger syndrome). The following three sources focus specifically on enhancing the social competence and social acceptance of these students:

Boutot, E.A. (2007). Fitting in: Tips for promoting acceptance and friendships for students with autism spectrum disorders in inclusive classrooms. *Intervention in School and Clinic, 42*, 156–161.

Webb, B.J., Miller, S.P., Pierce, T.B., Strawser, S., & Jones, W.P. (2004). Effects of social skill instruction for high-functioning adolescents with autism spectrum disorders. *Focus on Autism and Other Developmental Disabilities, 19*, 53–62.

Grandin, T. (2008). *The way I see it: A personal look at autism and Asperger's*. Arlington, TX: Future Horizons. (An insider's view. into the real issues of autism faced by parents, teachers, and individuals on the spectrum. Helpful do's and don'ts, practical strategies, and try-it-now topics based on Grandin's experiences.)

one another and pursue advanced tasks (Winebrenner, 2007). If they are far ahead of the rest of the class, they may be too impatient to be supportive and good models for the lowest achievers. Use heterogeneous groups as much as possible. Usually students who are academically competent (not necessarily gifted), socially competent, and patient make the best partners or group members for exceptional students.

Secondary school teachers often find it challenging to adopt collaborative learning when they feel pressure to "cover the curriculum." Many teachers report that the gains in motivation, reasoning, and self-directedness more than compensate for the time required to teach students to work collaboratively (e.g., Bellanca & Fogarty, 2003). Additional pressure can be felt by you and your upper-year students who may be competing for entry to post-secondary education and scholarships. Some adolescents show a low tolerance for diversity (Cobia & Carney, 2002) and become frustrated by group members who contribute less than their share.

Although there are considerable challenges, there are also benefits in social development and social acceptance when you use collaborative teaching approaches in the classroom. In addition, look to the community for additional opportunities to enhance social relations of exceptional students.

## CASE STUDY  WHAT CAN BE DONE TO PROMOTE SOCIAL COMPETENCE AND SOCIAL ACCEPTANCE FOR SAM?

Sam is in grade 5 and had been identified in grade 3 as gifted. At that time, he was also diagnosed with ADHD. In class discussions Sam rarely raised his hand and his rapid-fire answers continually seemed to erupt. No one wanted their desk to be next to Sam's because he fidgeted, poked the back of the student who sat in front of him, and was rarely quiet during seatwork activities, making disparaging comments about his classmates who worked less quickly than he did. He had no sense of personal space and seemed not to understand what his peers meant when they said, "Get out of my face, Sam." At recess and lunch he was avoided by his classmates. There was no one in the class whom he would call his friend, yet he did not appear to be bothered or upset by this; he seemed oblivious. What can his teacher do to enhance Sam's social competence and social acceptance?

# The Community and Social Relations

**Community-referenced learning** refers to two approaches to using the community to enhance social relations. The first is to bring the community into the school, and the second is to take the students into the community. Community education is based on the beliefs that a school is a fundamental part of the community where everyone has a voice in shaping the school and the community culture is a fundamental part of the social and academic life of the school (Decker & Decker, 2000; Decker et al., 2005; Saskatchewan Learning, 2001, 2004).

Community-referenced learning involves using the community as a classroom. This can be done informally or through a formal program. Community integration activities, such as recreation programs with spaces for exceptional youth provide you and your students with goals to work toward, special events to share, and evidence of the progress you are making toward inclusion in the community. Consider using educational assistants and volunteers to accompany small groups of students to events or activities when it is not feasible for the whole class to take part. Formal community-referenced learning includes work experiences, research teams, and

**Weblinks**

HOAGIES' GIFTED EDUCATION PAGE
www.hoagiesgifted.org/
play_partner.htm

CHILDREN'S LITERATURE WEB GUIDE
www.acs.ucalgary.ca/~dkbrown/
index.html

Consider the challenges when gifted students feel more comfortable with older friends. Look for other websites, books, and articles that focus on enhancing the social relations and friendships of children and adolescents who are gifted.

service learning. Research teams are heterogeneous groups of students using the community as the place to do research such as conducting interviews, making observations, or exploring artifacts. Kluth (2000) describes a group of three students from a grade 7 home economics class going into the community to shop. Two of the students practiced comparative shopping while learning mathematics and nutrition skills. For a third student with disabilities, the weekly trip provided life skills experiences such as traveling by city bus and grocery shopping. Setting goals based on the learning needs of all students can foster social co-operation and social development, using learning-in-community contexts.

# Summary

Social development and social acceptance are critical to inclusion because they refer to exceptional students' ability to take part in the social and academic life of the classroom and to be accepted by classmates. Both exceptional students and their peers without disabilities have expressed an array of views on inclusion and on the social processes that accompany it. Friendship is probably much more important to learning than we have previously understood. It appears that working collaboratively with friends enables children to learn from the challenges their friends present to their ideas. Both elementary and secondary schools are social environments, and schoolwide approaches can ensure that schools are inviting and safe for all students. As a teacher, you can analyze social demands and choose a wide range of collaborative and social approaches to learning as well as use the community to enhance social relations.

# Key Terms

social relationships (p. 184)
social competence (p. 184)
social acceptance (p. 184)
friendships (p. 184)
interpersonal competence
(p. 185)
peer perspectives (p. 185)
(dis)ability awareness program
(p. 187)

zone of proximal development
(p. 189)
schoolwide approaches (p. 193)
code of conduct (p. 193)
moral leadership (p. 194)
schoolwide behaviour management
system (p. 194)
bullying (p. 194)
cyberbullying (p. 194)

peer teaching (p. 197)
collaborative learning (p. 197)
TTYPA (p. 199)
Partners Thinking Aloud
(p. 198)
co-operative learning (p. 198)
jigsaw (p. 198)
community-referenced learning
(p. 200)

# Challenges for Reviewing Chapter 8

1.  Why are social development and social acceptance of exceptional learners so important to the inclusion of these students? What role can the elementary or secondary teacher play to promote their social development and social acceptance?

2. Identify the role of friendship in the lives of students with and without exceptionalities, and particularly, in their lives at school. Why should you be aware of the role of friendship for exceptional learners' development?

3. Create a fuller description of Val, the blind grade 1 student described in the case at the beginning of this chapter and, using the ADAPT strategy, analyze the social demands of math class and of recess for this student. Which collaborative and co-operative teaching strategies could assist you?

4. Lynn, the young woman with learning disabilities in the opening case, is in your secondary class. Using the ADAPT strategy, analyze the social demands your typical lesson imposes on her. Which collaborative and co-operative teaching strategies would be most helpful?

5. Describe what you would do at the beginning of the school year so the exceptional students in your class benefit from community-referenced learning? Why does inclusion make it necessary for us to think about the role of the community in enhancing social relations?

6. Answer the five questions that follow the opening cases of Val and Lynn.

# Conclusion

## Meeting the Challenges
## and Looking Ahead

> My first day of teaching finally arrived and I embarked on a completely foreign adventure. . . . I was scared, excited, and (in hindsight) idealistic. The truth is I continue to operate with this mixed bag of emotions, but underneath it all, I love it!
>
> Christa Armstrong (1997, p. 67)

## Succeeding as a Teacher

This conclusion is not about exceptional children and adolescents. It is about you. It is about how you can thrive as a teacher. The word *thriving* conjures up accomplishment, satisfaction, and prosperity. Teachers enter the profession with high expectations, a vision of the future, and a mission to educate children and adolescents. Years of research, including studies by Alan King (e.g., King, Warren, & Peart, 1988; King & Peart, 1990) of Queen's University, suggest that effective and rewarding teaching is most apt to be accomplished by optimistic and self-confident teachers (see also Cochran-Smith, 2006; Cockburn & Haydn, 2004; McEwan, 2002). A positive outlook and the support of colleagues and administrators are also needed to succeed (Center for Comprehensive School Reform and Improvement, 2007; Gratch, 1998; Johnson & Kardos, 2008).

Teachers cite many rewarding aspects of their work that contribute to their positive outlook. In an Ontario study, teachers reported that the three most satisfying aspects of teaching involved their relationships with their students. These were (a) experiencing good rapport and relationships with young people; (b) recognizing that students are suddenly understanding or enjoying their lessons; and (c) seeing student success, achievement, and satisfaction. These rewards of teaching reflect the reasons that many teachers give for choosing their profession: "I enjoy children" and "I love history and really want to pass my love of learning on to others." The next most frequently mentioned reward was interacting with and receiving support from colleagues (King et al., 1988). The same themes persist in interview studies of teachers (e.g., King & Peart, 1992; Moore Johnson & The Project on the Next Generation of Teachers, 2004). We encourage you to consider what you need to thrive as an educator. When you listen to colleagues who thrive on teaching, what do you hear?

# Being a Change Agent

Like many other professions, teaching in the current era is caught in the throes of massive and continual change. Some teachers find themselves looking back rather than looking ahead and fighting a rearguard action to maintain the profession as they have known it. Michael Fullan (2001; Levin & Fullan, 2008) of the University of Toronto describes how change has been introduced in Canadian schools without regard for the impact it has on teachers' daily lives. Almost all change, even when we embrace the innovation, results in feelings of loss and grief (Browning, 2008). Change also makes teachers feel incompetent (or less competent than when they were doing what they knew well) and creates confusion and conflict. Unless each of these issues is matched with an appropriate response, change is unlikely to succeed (Hargreaves, 2004; Levin & Fullan, 2008; Sarason, 2002), even when we want to improve our practice.

"Teachers vastly underestimate their power to change things" (Sarason, 1993, p. 6). In a perceptive analysis of what it takes to be a change agent, Donna Patterson (1996) of the University of Regina suggests that teachers focus on self-care, political astuteness, planning, effective conflict resolution, and humour. Collegial relationships and a culture that encourages teachers to learn together empower them to become agents of change (Dearman & Alber, 2005; Lovett & Gilmore, 2003; Valverde, 2008).

# Handling Stress

Most teachers thrive on the challenges of the profession. However, for others, the rewards of personal satisfaction and sense of accomplishment do not last. Many of these teachers choose to leave the profession and most often cite stress or burnout as the reason. In the past few decades, the helping professions in many countries have experienced this loss of talented and capable members. Over twenty-five years ago, Bryan Hiebert of the University of Calgary summarized the research on teacher stress in Canada (Hiebert, 1985). Canadian teachers referred most often to work overload (or pace of work) and student discipline problems or challenges in interacting with students whose lives were complex. Across all the studies, representing all parts of the country, the problems usually seemed to involve some form of personal interaction or time-management concerns. These issues persist as seen in Jennifer Lawson's (University of Manitoba) recent study on women administrators in high-poverty community schools (2008). Since Hiebert's report in 1985 the pressures on Canadian classroom teachers have, if anything, increased with the growing diversity in Canadian classrooms, including the inclusion of exceptional students in regular classrooms (Dei, 2003; Edmunds, 1998; Fullan, 2001; Hutchinson, 2007). As we have seen, inclusion and increasing diversity can involve many of the factors that contribute to teaching being rewarding (e.g., satisfaction in seeing students "get it," collaboration with colleagues) or being stressful (increased workload, discipline problems, lack of administrative support) (Dearman & Alber, 2005; Grayson & Alvarez, 2008).

Hiebert (1985) also reported that the studies showed that Canadian teachers did not have a large repertoire of strategies aimed specifically at coping with stress. Cochran-Smith (2006) argued that teachers who stay in the profession deal effectively with the pressures because they love teaching and their students, see teaching as hope and possibility because they feel they make a difference for their students, and continue to be passionate about their own learning as well as others' learning. These characteristics were apparent in Lawson's (2008) interviews with women leaders in schools in high-poverty communities. What is stress, and how can you, as a teacher, cope well with this challenge? One of the most widely cited perspectives on teacher burnout describes three dimensions—emotional exhaustion (which may underlie the other two), depersonalization, and feelings of low personal accomplishment. Listen to Maria describe to her support group what she found when she returned to her grade 5 class after recess on the afternoon of October 19:

> I am soooo frustrated. I was late getting to my room yesterday because I had separated four students who were fighting on the playground. I felt my blood pressure soar when I yelled at them, avoided taking any random punches, and led them to the principal's office—only to find the office empty. I couldn't leave them alone, on the verge of tearing each other apart, could I? So I worried about the fights that might be breaking out in my class. And fretted that someone might pick on Josh, who has childhood rheumatoid arthritis and is frail and vulnerable. After what seemed like an eternity, the principal's secretary came strolling down the hall. When I asked her where the principal was, she laughed and pointed toward my room. How could I have forgotten? He was in my room waiting to observe me teaching.
>
> In the excitement, it had slipped my mind completely. All I could think of then was, "What an idiot he will think I am! I knew I should have asked someone to switch recess duty with me. Why did no one volunteer? They knew I had an observation." By then I was angry with the whole staff! I was so nervous that my hands were wet, my throat was dry, and my mind was blank. I always feel inadequate when I am evaluated. Especially when it is the first evaluation—I can't seem to stay calm, even though I have taught for five years. I asked myself, "What was the lesson I planned to teach?" I had to look in my daybook to jog my memory; the lesson involved a complex explanation, hands-on practice, and follow-up written practice in adding fractions. Why did I not choose something simpler? I must have been trying to show off and impress him with my up-to-date methods. I fumbled my way through the explanation, forgot to do the hands-on activity, and had to explain the written activity about a thousand times–to almost every student individually! By the time my principal left, my stomach was almost sick. I dread receiving the evaluation. Even I think I should be fired.

Maria went on to explain to the members of her group that she had just moved to this downtown school a couple of months ago in September when her partner was transferred to the city from a small town. She found that the teachers were not as friendly as in her previous school, and the children fought all the time in the school-yard, "like gang warfare." Maria's husband was rarely home because of his new job, and her preschool children hated the new daycare, begging every morning to go to Sue's, the home of their previous child minder. Maria concluded, "I'm so stressed!"

To try to take control of the situation, Maria had called the number on a poster the first day it was tacked onto the bulletin board in the staff room. The poster said

Feel stressed? Need support?
New group starting September 30 at Eastside Teachers' Centre.
Call today!

That is why Maria told eight strangers about her most frustrating day at work.

## Focusing on Your Well-Being

Recently, researchers have studied the stress of large numbers of teachers in Britain and North America. They suggest that stress is triggered and sustained by

## FIGURE C-1 STEPS FOR TEACHERS IN COPING WITH STRESS

1. Identify and acknowledge the causes of stress in your life.
   (a) Professional causes of stress
   (b) Personal causes of stress
2. Identify your feelings and your emotional reactions to these feelings.
3. Become aware of the unmet needs behind your feelings.
   (a) Emotional-physical needs
   (b) Psycho-social needs
   (c) Personal-intellectual needs
4. Learn stress-reduction strategies.
   (a) Identify what you can and cannot change.
   (b) Change your beliefs and actions in situations you can control.
   (c) Choose your reaction to situations you cannot control (you can control your reaction).
   (d) Use assertive communication to say no in a constructive way.
   (e) Use relaxation techniques.
   (f) Take charge of your physical health through nutrition, sleep, and exercise.
   (g) Seek social support.

the cognitive processes we choose to use when we perceive a threat, is affected by the emotions we experience, and affects our health (Grayson & Alvarez, 2008; Wood & McCarthy, 2002). This means that stress affects all our being. We make decisions about how we will cope with a threat. When our coping mechanisms are successful, distress is minimized—and we may even feel a positive type of stress (eustress). However, when our coping mechanisms are not adequate, we experience negative emotions and feel threatened. Our immune system can be affected, resulting in illness. While this all sounds menacing, there are many suggestions to assist teachers in handling their stressors and in learning new coping mechanisms (Nagel & Brown, 2003; Wood & McCarthy, 2002; see Figure C-1).

In the *Professional Health* program (Gold & Roth, 2004), problem solving is the focus and personal and professional needs are the content. Teachers are urged to go beyond stress management and focus on their underlying problems and needs. We may also need psychological support to grow over the long term and to develop professional health. Otherwise, we could be continuously engaged in stress management when what we need is to gain self-control. Gold and Roth report that teachers begin to withdraw after they feel isolated from their colleagues. Ways for teachers to come out of their isolation are: visit other teachers' classrooms, arrange exchanges, join the local association of science teachers, or find a support group like the one Maria found.

While teaching offers the promise of intellectual stimulation, it is easy for us to become buried in paperwork and spend the evenings marking, rather than reading about innovative teaching approaches or attending stimulating cultural events. However, discovering new ideas and learning innovative techniques contribute to our personal-intellectual needs. For example, Gold and Roth (2004) encourage teachers to embrace intellectual challenges so they can thrive at work: enrol in professional development or graduate courses, take out a subscription to a concert series, or learn to play a musical instrument. Rena Upitis, dean of education at Queen's University from 1995 to 2000, always advised teacher candidates and colleagues to learn something new every school year. Upitis argues that not only is this intellectually stimulating, but it also allows teachers to become novices and renew empathy for their students who are not experts in everything that is taught in the classroom.

## FIGURE C-2 LIFE STORY: HELPED HUNDREDS OF YOUNGSTERS

Benny Sheardown: Father, husband, guidance counsellor, athlete. Born in Whitehorse in 1944. Died of cancer in Calgary aged 55. Cathy Sheardown wasn't surprised by the number of people who paid tribute to her late husband Ben. It was the tenor of it all that caught her off-guard.

More than 1 000 people attended the guidance counsellor's memorial service in Whitehorse, and Ms. Sheardown could easily decorate a huge wall with cards and letters from admirers and friends from all over the Yukon and well beyond its borders. "They feel that he was really there when nobody else could be or cared to be. He felt everybody deserved a second, third and fourth chance depending on the story," said Ms. Sheardown.

Benjamin Clarke Sheardown was born in the Yukon, spent his life there and affected the lives of many, especially young people to whom he devoted so much time. After graduating from the University of Alaska in Fairbanks, the father of two returned to the Yukon and became a gym teacher in 1972. Later on, as a guidance counsellor, he heard more than a few stories of broken homes and suicidal youth.

"He affected a ton of people in different ways, never, ever taking the credit and letting [the kids] almost believe it was their idea," said Ms. Sheardown.

After his death, local newspapers ran letters to the editor from as far away as Mexico City, from people who credited him with shaping their lives, and, in some cases, saving their lives. "I'm getting numerous cards in the mail that start out, 'You don't know me but . . .' and they're telling me, 'If it wasn't for Mr. Sheardown I would never have become who I am or never been able to do what I've done, I certainly wouldn't have gone through school,'" said Ms. Sheardown.

Last year, Mr. Sheardown was inducted into the Yukon Sports Hall of Fame. It was an award he almost refused to accept, thinking it was out of pity for a man with a terminal illness. But after talking to family and friends, he concluded that the award was as much a tribute to those who helped him accomplish great things in his lifetime as it was to him. A planned sports multiplex in Whitehorse might even be named after him. He always pursued a healthy lifestyle. He played hockey (helping the Yukon to win gold in the Arctic Winter Games in 1972) and basketball. He also took part in running, biking, swimming and Nordic skiing. In winter, he was often seen riding his bike or taking his dog Tacumsa on long walks through downtown trails. On the front of his memorial-service pamphlet, he's photographed with Tacumsa in the shadow of a hilltop called the King's Throne near Kathleen Lake, a pristine area on the cusp of Kluane National Park. He's wearing mismatched cross-country skis and, according to a childhood friend, couldn't care less.

Jim Perry knew Mr. Sheardown from the age of 10, when he moved to Whitehorse from Ireland. "He took me under his wing. He reached out to this little immigrant boy and we became lifelong friends," said Mr. Perry, who made the trip from Abbotsford, BC, to Whitehorse to speak at the memorial service. "This memorial was a true indication of the kind of support and the number of lives he touched. Ben left a huge footprint on many hearts." Mr. Perry said he always lived life fully and brought the best out of other people.

———

Source: Carlucci, M. (1999). Life story: Helped hundreds of youngsters. *The Globe and Mail*, August 3, p. A17. Reprinted with permission.

# The Last Word

This book has examined the many facets of teaching and including exceptional children and adolescents in our classrooms—so they may take their places in Canadian society. The kind of teacher many of us aspire to be is one who touches the lives of children or adolescents and who leaves a mark. To this end, Benny Sheardown should have the last word (Figure C-2). We wish we had known him.

# Glossary

## A

**Aboriginal cultures** Aboriginal peoples are nations, that is, political and cultural groups with values and lifeways distinct from those of other Canadians.

**academic tasks as punishment** The practice of assigning students additional homework or lines to write as a punishment.

**acceleration** An approach for educating gifted students that allows them to move through the curriculum in an area of strength at an accelerated pace or to work at the next grade level.

**accommodations** Changes to how a student is taught, including such things as teaching strategies, supports, and alternate formats, when the outcomes are consistent with the student's grade placement.

**acquired brain injury (ABI)** See *traumatic brain injury (TBI)*.

**ADAPT** A systematic strategy for adapting teaching to include exceptional learners consisting of five steps: **A**ccounts of students' strengths and needs; **D**emands of the classroom; **A**daptations; **P**erspectives and consequences; **T**each and assess the match.

**adapted program** An exceptional student's program that retains the learning outcomes of the prescribed curriculum but provides adaptations so that the student can participate, including alternate formats, instructional strategies, and assessment procedures.

**adaptive skills** Areas of participation in the life of the community in which individuals with development disabilities may be delayed: communication, home living, community use, health and safety, leisure, self-care, social skills, self-direction, functional academics, work.

**additional practice** Providing more opportunities for exceptional learners to practise what has been taught and to develop full understanding of ideas, procedures, etc.

**ADHD, Predominantly Inattentive** More characteristics of inattention than of hyperactivity-impulsivity are exhibited. Characteristics include ignoring details, careless errors, trouble staying on task while working or playing.

**ADHD, Predominantly Hyperactive-Impulsive** More characteristics of hyperactivity-impulsivity than of inattention are exhibited. Characteristics include fidgeting and squirming, moving constantly, blurting out answers, difficulty waiting for one's turn.

**ADHD, Combined Type** Many characteristics of both inattention and hyperactivity-impulsivity are displayed

**advocate** A person who represents or champions the cause of another.

**aggression** Bold, direct action that is intended to hurt someone else or take property; unprovoked attack.

**alcohol-related neurodevelopmental disorder (ARND)** (formerly called fetal alcohol effects FAE) A lifelong birth defect due to prenatal exposure to alcohol without facial or growth abnormalities; however, learning and behaviour deficits are enduring.

**allergen-free alternative** Refers to the practice of creating an alternative activity or snack that is safe for students with allergies so they can participate in class activities and excursions.

**allergy** An abnormal reaction to a normal substance (e.g., peanuts).

**alternative learning expectations** Related to the development of skills deemed essential to learning in areas not represented in the curriculum policy documents.

**alternative assessments** Assessments that focus on authentic skills and experience in real-life environments, for example, portfolios, in contrast to traditional testing formats.

**American Association on Intellectual and Developmental Disabilities (AIDD)** (formerly the American Association on Mental Retardation AAMR) Promotes progressive policies, sound research, effective practices and universal human rights for people with intellectual and developmental disabilities.

**American Sign Language (ASL)** A manual language system that has its own rule-governed syntactic system.

**amniocentesis** A test of the fluid surrounding a fetus to check for many kinds of abnormalities.

**amplification** The process of enhancing sound, usually through the use of hearing aids or FM (frequency modulation) systems.

**anaphylactic shock** See *anaphylaxis*.

**anaphylaxis** A sudden, severe allergic reaction that causes breathing difficulties; death can occur within minutes unless an injection is administered.

**antidepressants** Medications for managing attention deficit/hyperactivity disorder.

**articulation** Word and sound production.

**Asperger syndrome** Severe and sustained impairment in social interaction with restricted, repetitive patterns of behaviour, interests, and activities, with no significant delays in language acquisition or cognitive development.

**assessment** Data collection, gathering information of many kinds about a student or a group of students, using a variety of tools and techniques.

**assessment *as* learning** Assessment that is the ultimate goal where students are able to be reflective and self-regulating, linking their own learning and self-assessment.

**assessment *for* learning** Assessment that is well matched to the demands of teaching in inclusive classrooms and is particularly helpful for differentiating teaching for exceptional learners and others who need tailored instruction. This takes place during learning and is interactive, with teachers providing assistance as part of the assessment (formerly called formative assessment).

**assessment *of* learning** Tests administered after learning was assumed to have taken place that were intended to provide parents and students with a summary of the students' learning and relative standing (formerly called summative assessment).

**assistive technology** An item, piece of equipment, or product system that is used to maintain or improve the functional capabilities of individuals with disabilities.

**asthma** Obstructed airways that hinder the flow of air in and out of the lungs; an attack is characterized by persistent wheezing, tightness in the chest, and excess phlegm, and can be life threatening.

**at risk** More likely to develop special needs due to poverty and other social conditions, including sexual and physical abuse, exposure to drugs, etc.

**Attention Deficit/Hyperactivity Disorder (AD/HD)** A persistent pattern of inattention and impulsiveness that may be accompanied by hyperactivity and that hinders social, academic, and vocational expectations.

**augmentative and alternative communication (AAC)** Communication systems used to augment speech or as an alternative to speech, thereby supplementing or replacing speech and written communication for students with communication disorders.

**authentic assessment** Assessment on tasks that are engaging, contextualized, and represent those expected in the adult world.

**authentic tasks** Learning activities close to real-world tasks, usually involving problems that are engaging, contextualized, and represent those expected in the adult world.

**autism** Limited development in communication and social interaction, and a severe delay in intellectual, emotional, and behavioural development.

**Autism Spectrum Disorders (ASDs)** All of the disorders that are considered ASDs are characterized by varying degrees of impairment in three areas: communication skills, social interactions, and repetitive and stereotyped patterns of behaviour. The five disorders in the autism spectrum are autism, Asperger syndrome (AS), Rett syndrome, childhood disintegrative disorder, and pervasive developmental disorder not otherwise specified (PDD-NOS).

## B

**behaviour ratings** Scales on which student behaviour is evaluated for frequency and intensity of symptoms.

**behavioural or emotional exceptionalities** Usually characterized by dysfunctional relationships at home and/or school and at least one of aggression, negative psychological states, and social problems.

**blindness** Characterized by loss of sight and use of auditory and tactile sources of information to replace sight.

**Braille** A system of raised dots that can be read by touch by persons who are blind.

**bullying** A pattern of actions that involves an imbalance of power, a victim who is upset, and a bully who is cool and in control and who shows a lack of compassion; can take many forms, including physical, emotional, and verbal.

**bypass strategies** Teaching and learning approaches that allow students to gain access to practise, or demonstrate, learning of the curriculum in alternative ways.

## C

**cancer** A malignant tumour or growth of body cells.

**career development** Growing understanding of changing roles and responsibilities, including adult responsibilities, roles, and the nature and meaning of work.

**carrel** A private space for working, which can be a booth made out of wood or from a cardboard crate that once held a large appliance.

**case coordinator** Person responsible for ensuring that the various services required by an exceptional student are coordinated; sometimes parents assume this role.

**catch 'em being good** A strategy developed many years ago in which teachers monitor students and acknowledge and reward behaviour that is consistent with expectations.

**CCTV** Closed-circuit television system consisting of a digital camera and display so that anything placed in front of the camera is magnified on the display to allow visually impaired people to see things that are far away—such as a demonstration at the front of a classroom—or read a book or look at a photograph.

**cerebral palsy (CP)** A group of disorders impairing body movement and muscle coordination as a result of an interference in messages between the brain and the body.

**changes to letter and number grades** Clarifying with a comment to indicate that a student may be using a textbook that is below the actual grade level of the class or to explain the reading level of books used in language arts.

**changing grading criteria** Varying grading weights so exceptional students are not disadvantaged by an impossible task; for example, students who are hard of hearing do not have part of their grade determined by their inability to hear during pop quizzes.

**Charter of Rights and Freedoms** Legislation that protects the rights of all Canadians and, in particular, Canadians who are members of minority groups, including people with disabilities.

**checkpoints** Checklists for students to complete at quarter- and halfway points of long-term assignments to show progress and receive feedback.

**chromosomal abnormalities** Chromosomes contain genes with the chemical codes that direct cell function; aberrant chromosomes are those with abnormal numbers or structures.

**chronic health condition** A qualified medical practitioner has certified that a student requires medical procedures, excluding administration of medication only, to ensure the health and safety of the student while in school or requires ongoing special education interventions due to the student's limited school attendance or because the condition adversely affects the student's educational performance.

**chronic health impairment** See *chronic health condition*.

**chronic medical disorder** See *chronic health condition*.

**chunking strategies** Ways of grouping information; used for remembering important lists.

**classroom assessment** Day-to-day practices adopted by teachers to describe student learning through portfolios, conferences with students, paper and pencil tests, etc.

**classroom procedures** Efficient ways of moving all members of a class through the day or the period that are consistent with the teacher's goals and follow from the rules (e.g., transitions and distribution of materials).

**climate** The general feeling created in a classroom; positive classroom climate usually is thought to develop when people treat each other with respect.

**code of conduct** Brief guidelines that clearly identify school rules and acceptable student behaviours and contain consequences.

**cognitive abilities** Processes and knowledge, including vocabulary, verbal fluency, retention, generalizing, making abstractions, organizing, and planning.

**cognitive-behaviour management (CBM)** Programs that teach students how to use cognition to control their own behaviour by using self-talk and self-instruction.

**cognitive complexity** The cognitive demands made of the learner by teaching and learning in the classroom.

**cognitive strategies** Plans and processes designed to accomplish learning or solve problems.

**collaboration** Teachers and other professionals learning from each other's experiences and working in teams where all members feel that their contributions are valued.

**collaborative learning** Teaching approaches that include co-operative learning and problem solving in pairs and groups and that usually involve student groups of varying abilities and skills, that is, heterogeneous groupings.

**community** A group of people who have shared interests and who mutually pursue the common good.

**community agreements** Four guidelines for students to use in developing a sense of community in the classroom: attentive listening, appreciation/no put-downs, the right to pass when given an opportunity to speak, and mutual respect (*Tribes*, Gibbs, 2001).

**community-based** Education that focuses on relating what is learned in school to what occurs in the community; often learning takes place in the community as well as in the school.

**community circle** The gathering of all students in a class in a large circle where each student is given an opportunity to present himself or herself in a structured way and to reflect on what is happening in his or her world (*Tribes*, Gibbs, 2001).

**community-referenced learning** Refers to using the community as a classroom. This can be conducted informally or through a formal program.

**components of an IEP** The seven sections that usually comprise an IEP are present level of functioning, long-term goals, short-term goals, instructional strategies and materials, dates for review, identification of participants (including parents) and their responsibilities, and evaluation procedures.

**comprehension** Reading comprehension is an active process of understanding that requires an intentional and thoughtful interaction between the reader and the text.

**computation** Mathematical skill and understanding in using the four basic operations to combine numbers.

**concept maps** Graphic organizers that show relationships among concepts as well as essential characteristics of the concepts.

**concrete-to-representational-to-abstract (CRA)** A sequence of instruction that takes students through Concrete hands-on instruction with manipulative objects, then through pictorial Representations of these manipulatives, to learning through Abstract notation including operational symbols.

**consistency** In classroom management, maintaining the same expectations from day to day and applying the same consequences when students fail to meet expectations while honouring adaptations for exceptional students.

**contract** A behaviour management technique involving a written agreement that states what the teacher and the student agree to do, and specifies the positive rewards and the consequences for failing to live up to the agreement.

**co-operative learning** A teaching approach that involves students in learning with peers in small groups, taking roles, and working interdependently.

**corporal punishment** Punishing a student for misbehaving by striking the student or threatening to strike the student.

**creativity** Demonstrated by students' contributing ideas, transforming and combining ideas, asking questions, and being curious.

**criterion-referenced** Data in which a student's work is compared to expected outcomes.

**cueing** A method of directing students' attention to specific aspects of the learning environment.

**culturally responsive classroom management (CRCM)** Management that is characterized by teachers developing a respectful, caring, and personal relations with each student in addition to building a learning community with an emotional climate where students are supported to take risks and to trust one another, as well as their teacher.

**cyberbullying** Psychological cruelty that is perpetuated virtually by threats, insults, and demeaning messages spread through the Internet or by cell phone.

**cystic fibrosis (CF)** Increasingly severe respiratory problems and extreme difficulty in digesting nutrients from food.

## D

**deaf** Characterized by hearing loss that interferes with the acquisition and maintenance of the auditory skills necessary to develop speech and oral language and causes one to use visual sources of information to replace hearing.

**Deaf community** Many deaf adults describe themselves as a cultural minority and use the term *deaf* to designate cultural group membership; the common language is American Sign Language (ASL).

**depression** A pervasive mood of unhappiness accompanied by long-term difficulties in sleeping, feelings of worthlessness, and inability to experience pleasure.

**developmental disabilities** The development of cognitive abilities and adaptive behaviours at a much slower rate than normal, which results in significant limitations in these areas severe levels.

**developmentally advanced** See *gifted*.

**diabetes** A condition in which the pancreas fails to produce a sufficient amount of the hormone insulin for proper sugar absorption in the body, which may place restrictions on physical activity.

**diabetes emergency kits** A ration package containing juice, raisins, or dextrose, often carried by an individual with diabetes and sometimes kept in a central location in a school to be used by students with diabetes in an emergency.

**differentiated instruction** Instruction that is student-centred to address specific skills and difficulties and is based on student differences in interests, learning profile, and level of functioning; guiding principles include respectful tasks, flexible grouping, and ongoing assessment and adjustment.

**differentiating content** The process of adapting what is being taught and making the subject matter accessible for every student.

**differentiating process** The provision of appropriate activities that will promote the development of students' potential; such as, by making changes to instructional methods or to the environment.

**differentiating the product of learning** The design of assignments that allow students to demonstrate their understanding and apply what they have learned in meaningful, satisfying, and engaging ways.

**(dis)ability awareness programs** Programs developed to foster greater understanding of people with disabilities, to increase students' knowledge about specific disabilities, and to increase students' sensitivity toward individuals with disabilities.

**discipline code** See *code of conduct*.

**discrepancy** A controversial method of identifying a learning disability by establishing a difference between ability (usually measured by an intelligence test) and achievement in one or more of the following areas: reading, writing, language acquisition, mathematics, reasoning, or listening.

**domains** Areas, such as overall intellect, leadership, creativity, or the arts, where gifted students excel.

**double-deficit hypothesis** deficits in both phonemic awareness and rapid naming.

**Down syndrome** A genetic defect causing limitations in physical and cognitive development; physically, children with Down syndrome have low muscle tone and a generalized looseness of the ligaments.

**Duchenne muscular dystrophy (DMD)** A musculoskeletal condition with marked physical degeneration that occurs during the school years.

**dyscalculia** Learning disabilities in arithmetic, especially calculations.

**dysgraphia** Learning disabilities in writing.

**dyslexia** Learning disabilities in reading.

## E

**echolalia** Speech that is an immediate imitation of that of some other speaker.

**educational assistants** Paraprofessionals assigned to work with one or more exceptional students in a classroom, while other times they are assigned to support a teacher's work with the entire class while monitoring the exceptional students and offering them assistance at key moments.

**encouragement** Giving courage or spurring someone on which can be particularly helpful in alleviating the discouragement experienced by exceptional students when challenged to participate and learn in inclusive classrooms.

**enforcing a rule** In teaching classroom rules, enforcement usually follows demonstration and practice and refers to the follow-up and feedback provided by teachers to commend students when they follow the rules and to ensure that consequences are applied when students fail to follow the rules.

**engagement** The extent to which students embrace learning and throw themselves into the activities of the classroom.

**environment** Context of learning, composed of both classroom climate and physical layout.

**enzyme supplements** Medication taken by a person with cystic fibrosis before a meal or snack to replace pancreatic enzymes that the body does not produce and that are essential to digestion.

**epilepsy** A neurological disorder that occasionally produces brief disturbances in normal electrical functions of the brain that lead to sudden, brief seizures that vary in nature and intensity from person to person.

**epinephrine** Adrenalin; administered in the event of an anaphylactic allergic reaction; can be life saving.

**EPIPEN®** Brand name of an easily administered form of adrenalin often carried by children who have allergies and anaphylactic reactions.

**equal participation** The United Nations' (1993) *Standard Rules on the Equalization of Opportunities for Persons with Disabilities* targeted eight areas for equal participation in the local community, including education, health, employment, and social services.

**equality rights** In Canada, the equality rights that apply to education are contained in section 15(1) of the Charter: "Every individual is equal before and under the law and has a right to the equal protection and equal benefit of the law without discrimination based on race, national or ethnic origin, colour, religion, sex, age, or mental or physical disability."

**evaluation** Making decisions based on the assessment data that have been gathered about a student or group of students; on an IEP, this refers to procedures the in-school team will use to demonstrate accountability by showing that the student is making reasonable progress.

**exceptional students** Learners who are gifted as well as students with disabilities; used interchangeably with terms like *students with special needs* to describe students in need of special education programs.

**expository text** Content-area text with the purpose of providing information, in contrast to narrative text which tells a story.

**expulsion** Permanent removal of a student from the classroom as a consequence of the student behaving inappropriately, violating the code of conduct, etc.

## F

**feedback** Specific information for students about what they are doing correctly and incorrectly.

**fetal alcohol spectrum disorders (FASD)** A lifelong birth defect characterized by physical and physiological abnormalities due to prenatal exposure to alcohol causing delays in development, central nervous dysfunction, learning problems, with possible facial abnormalities.

**fetal alcohol syndrome (FAS)** Physical and physiological abnormalities due to prenatal exposure to alcohol. A lifelong birth defect with growth deficiency in height and weight, facial abnormalities including small eyes, and brain impairment.

**fluency** Contributes to comprehension and refers to children reading out loud with speed, accuracy, and proper expression.

**form of practice** Allowing students to engage in oral or written practice or another form of practice that advances their learning; can be ADAPTed for exceptional students.

**formal assessment** Assessment using standardized tests; these could include an intelligence test, behaviour observation checklists, vision, hearing or language assessments, and medical tests.

**formative assessment** Assessment conducted during learning which was intended to promote learning and not simply judge whether students had learned, presently referred to as assessment for learning.

**frequency modulation (FM) systems** With a classroom FM system, the carrier wave is transmitted through the air by frequency modulation from a teacher-worn microphone to a student-worn FM receiver; students with hearing impairments can hear the teacher clearly from any location in the classroom.

**friendships** Close relationships characterized by reciprocity, that is, give and take, and by commitment between individuals who see themselves as equals.

**functional curriculum** Outcomes for a student are based on life skills, such as shopping, banking, and cooking.

## G

**generalized seizures** Epileptic seizures that involve the whole brain.

**genetic screening** Identification of the risk of a couple having a child with a condition caused by chromosomal abnormalities.

**gifted** Exceptionally high abilities in one or several areas, including specific academic subjects, overall intellect, leadership, creativity, or the arts.

**give-and-take dialogues** Problem-solving discussions in which all students feel they can advance ideas, be heard, comment on others' ideas, and feel that the classroom is a safe place.

**good behaviour game** A strategy for reducing disruptive behaviour and promoting positive behaviour in the classroom in which students work on teams to earn points for appropriate behaviour toward a reward.

**grading** Symbolic representation of evaluation or judgments based on assessment data, often in the form of letter grades, percentages, or performance levels.

**grading contract** An agreement between teacher and student on the basis for awarding a grade; may include giving exceptional students credit for attendance, promptness, effort, and co-operative behaviour.

**grouping** The practice of deliberately placing students in learning or working groups; used extensively in co-operative and collaborative learning approaches.

**guided practice** Scaffolded practice in which students are prompted to use each step of a strategy; enables exceptional students to learn the strategy.

## H

**hard of hearing** Partial hearing loss that interferes with the acquisition and maintenance of the auditory skills necessary to develop speech and oral language; use visual sources of information to supplement or replace hearing.

**head injury** See *traumatic brain injury (TBI)*.

**hearing aids** Systems that amplify all sounds, worn in the ear.

**hearing status** Description of one's ability to hear; used to describe the parents of children who are deaf.

**high blood sugar (hyperglycemia)** An abnormally high amount of sugar in the bloodstream; usually associated with diabetes.

**high-incidence exceptionalities** Frequently occurring exceptionalities, including giftedness, learning disabilities, attention deficit/hyperactivity disorder, communication exceptionalities, behaviour exceptionalities, and mild developmental disabilities.

**high-interest low-vocabulary books** Written materials designed to interest and engage students while using simple vocabulary and uncomplicated sentence structures.

**high-stakes tests** Tests that influence whether students proceed to the next grade or graduate.

**high task commitment** Found in students who work hard and need little external motivation, especially in areas that interest them.

**holding pattern** A strategy teachers use when they have a misbehaving student wait (in the office, at the side of the classroom, immediately outside the door) until the teacher is available to meet and talk with the student.

**hundreds chart** A chart containing the numbers from 1 to 100 or 0 to 99 in rows and columns; used to help students learn the meaning of place value and relationships among numbers.

**hydrocephalus** A condition characterized by an excessive accumulation of cerebrospinal fluid in the brain due to an obstruction of its flow.

**hyperactivity** Characterized by fidgeting, squirming, moving constantly, talking excessively, and finding it challenging to play or work quietly.

**hypersensitivity** The tendency to be extremely sensitive to sensory stimuli, such as touch and to engage in unusual behaviour to obtain a particular sensory stimulation.

## I

**Identification, Placement, and Review Committee (IPRC)** In Ontario, this committee, consisting of the teacher, special educators, administrators, and parents, meets to consider whether a child is exceptional and recommends a placement prior to the IEP meeting.

**immune system** The mechanism that enables a body to resist infections, toxins, etc., owing to the presence of specific antibodies or sensitized white blood cells.

**impulsivity** Characteristics include blurting out answers before the teacher has finished asking a question, not waiting for one's turn, and interrupting other students.

**inattentiveness** Characterized by ignoring details, making careless errors, having trouble concentrating and staying on task while working or playing.

**inclusion** The social value and policy that persons with disabilities are entitled to full participation in all aspects of Canadian society, including education.

**increase students' appropriate behaviour** Giving positive attention to the student behaviour one wants to maintain or increase; praising students publicly or privately and providing specific feedback.

**independent practice** Students practising on their own; choosing, using, and monitoring strategies.

**Individual Education Plan (IEP)** A written plan developed for an exceptional student that describes the adaptations, modifications, and services to be provided.

**inflammation** A localized physical condition with heat, swelling, and pain.

**informal assessment** Testing carried out by the classroom teacher or the resource teacher that provides information about an exceptional student's current level of functioning.

**informal conference** A behaviour management technique in which a teacher and student meet to define the problem clearly, generate solutions together, and agree on what each will do to implement the solution.

**information processing** The human mind's activity of taking in, storing, and using information.

**in-school team** A solution-finding group whose purpose is to provide a forum for dialogue by parents, teachers, and other professionals about the needs of students.

**instructional strategies, materials, and services** A section of the IEP that usually describes the adaptations to teaching and modifications to curriculum as well as other efforts made to provide an appropriate education for an exceptional student.

**insulin** Pancreatic secretion that transports glucose from the bloodstream to the cells.

**insulin injections** Shots, often self-administered, of the pancreatic secretion that transports glucose from the bloodstream to the cells.

**integration** A term used in the 1970s and 1980s that referred to moving exceptional students from segregated settings into classrooms in the mainstream, with the emphasis on physical integration or placement rather than on learning or participating.

**intellectual disabilities** Have to do with an individual's functioning within the community and that person's limitations in both intelligence and adaptive skills.

**intelligence** Ability or abilities to acquire and use knowledge for solving problems and adapting to the world.

**interest** An affective interaction between students and tasks.

**interpersonal competence** The abilities needed for friendships, including initiating and sustaining conversation, initiating plans to spend time with friends outside of school, disclosing personal thoughts and empathy, and managing conflict effectively.

**"invisible" classroom management** Techniques used by teachers to increase students' appropriate behaviour so that they rarely have to draw attention to inappropriate behaviour.

## J

**jigsaw strategy** A collaborative learning approach in which students leave home groups to study in expert groups and later teach what they have learned to their home groups.

**juvenile arthritis (JA)** A chronic arthritic condition with continuous inflammation of one or more joints, stiffness, pain, and possible involvement of the eyes.

## L

**language impairment** Language is disordered when a student has impairment in expressive or receptive language.

**large-scale assessment** Nationwide, province-wide, or district-wide efforts to provide information about student achievement, usually by means of paper and pencil tests.

**learned helplessness** The expectation, based on previous experiences with a lack of control, that all one's efforts will lead to failure.

**learning disabilities (LD)** Dysfunctions in processing information that may occur in reading (dyslexia), writing, or arithmetic calculations; often defined as a discrepancy between ability and achievement despite average or above-average intelligence.

**learning strategies** Techniques or principles that enable a student to learn to solve problems, read, communicate, and organize independently.

**leukemia** A type of cancer that forms in the bone marrow, causing abnormal white blood cell development.

**limited range of motion** An inability to move affected limbs and grasp a pencil with swollen fingers that is seen in children with juvenile arthritis, for example.

**low blood sugar (hypoglycemia)** The condition in which there is an abnormally low amount of sugar in the bloodstream; a complication of diabetes.

**lower reading level materials** Text materials that parallel the required or recommended text but are written at a lower reading level and are more accessible to those reading below grade level.

**low-incidence exceptionalities** Any of the less common exceptionalities, including severe developmental disabilities, hearing impairment, visual impairments, autism, and Asperger syndrome.

**low-key interventions** Minimal actions taken by teachers to respond to minor misbehaviours so that the teachers' actions do not disrupt the flow of the class and to de-escalate rather than raise the stakes.

**low vision** A condition of partial impairment of sight or vision that even with correction affects educational performance adversely.

## M

**mainstreaming** A term used in the 1970s and 1980s that referred to moving exceptional students from segregated settings into classrooms in the mainstream when they could meet traditional academic expectations or when those expectations were not relevant.

**manipulatives** Learning materials children can handle to aid learning, such as counters when adding in arithmetic.

**MedicAlert**® An identification bracelet worn by individuals with medical conditions that can help you make fast decisions in an emergency.

**metacognition** Knowledge about our own thinking.

**method of presentation** The means used to communicate information to students, including oral, visual, video-recorded demonstration, live demonstration, and hands-on techniques.

**mnemonics** Impose an order on information to be remembered using poems, rhymes, jingles, funny sayings, or images. For example, to remember the names, in order, of the five largest cities in Canada, use Teachers Make Very Odd Exams, for Toronto, Montreal, Vancouver, Ottawa, and Edmonton.

**mode of presentation** See *method of presentation*.

**model strategy use** Explain carefully, by thinking aloud, your thinking patterns, how to decide when to use a strategy, and how to do each step.

**modifications** Changes made to the content of the learning expectations, making them substantially different from the prescribed curriculum for the student's grade placement, and specifically selected to meet the exceptional student's needs in accordance with the IEP.

**modified course syllabus** A document, perhaps produced by the IEP team, that states specific learning expectations, grading criteria, and other changes made in a course for an exceptional student.

**monitoring** The process of the teacher being alert and responsive to student action as part of classroom management.

**moral leadership** Leading by example with a focus on activities that enhance the sense of community within a school and create rituals and traditions that symbolically represent the values and culture of the school community.

**muscular dystrophy (MD)** A group of muscle disorders characterized by progressive weakness and wasting away of the voluntary muscles that control body movement.

**musculoskeletal conditions** Chronic health conditions that affect the muscles and the skeleton and that can affect all aspects of a student's life (e.g., muscular dystrophy and juvenile arthritis).

# N

**narrative text** Written expression that is intended to tell a story.

**natural consequences** Punishment in which a student suffers the logical outcome of a misbehaviour (e.g., a student removing pencil marks from a desk after writing on the desk).

**nebulizer** An aerosol machine that connects to a mask that fits over the mouth and nose to administer medication to persons with asthma.

**needs** Areas in which an exceptional student has relatively weak abilities and skills that need to be developed or bypassed in his or her education by drawing on or compensating with areas of relative strength; schools often focus on academic, social/emotional, and behavioural needs in preparing a student's IEP.

**negative psychological states** Often seen in students with behavioural and emotional exceptionalities; include anxiety, depression, and stress-related disorders.

**neighbourhood schools** A policy of educating exceptional students in regular classrooms in neighbourhood or local schools or at least making these the first placement option considered, in consultation with families.

**nervous system impairment** Results of damage or dysfunction of the brain or spinal cord that may have occurred before, during, or after birth; examples of exceptionalities are cerebral palsy, spina bifida, epilepsy, Tourette syndrome, brain injury, and fetal alcohol syndrome.

**neurological dysfunction** See *nervous system impairment*.

**normalization** The concept that all persons, regardless of disability, should live and learn in environments as close to normal as possible.

**norm-referenced** Data in which a student's work is compared to the work of other students who are comparable in age or grade.

**norms for classroom interaction** Expectations and rules about how students will initiate interactions with and respond to one another: effective communication and respectful interaction in conversation and discussion.

**number sense** Essential sense of what numbers mean, how to compare numbers, and how to see and count quantities in the world around us.

# O

**opinion essays** A form of writing where personal opinion is expressed through a position statement and subsequently supported by arguments that justify the position taken, including the presentation of counterarguments that are refuted.

**outcomes** Learning that is expected of students, often expressed as short-term and long-term goals.

# P

**pace** The rate of presentation of new information or rate of introduction of new skills.

**parent–teacher conferences** Formal meetings of parents and teachers at regular intervals during the school year and more frequent informal discussions that can build a productive partnership.

**partial seizures** Epileptic seizures that involve one area of the brain; there may be strange sensations, possibly accompanied by inappropriate movements, such as plucking at clothes or books, smacking the lips, or aimless wandering but without complete consciousness being lost.

**partial fetal alcohol syndrome (PFAS)** Less obvious and seemingly milder than fetal alcohol syndrome with few or no facial abnormalities; however, learning and behaviour deficits are enduring.

**Partners Thinking Aloud** A collaborative learning activity in which students work in pairs, alternating roles of teacher and learner with the learner thinking aloud and the teacher offering prompts and feedback; can be used for guided practice.

**peer perspectives** The views of classmates on their relationships with children and adolescents with disabilities, in the literature on social relationships of exceptional children.

**peer teaching** See *peer tutoring*.

**peer tutoring** A teaching approach that involves peers as teaching partners.

**performance assessment** Assessment that provides opportunities for students to demonstrate directly their ability to combine and use their knowledge, skills, and habits of mind.

**perseveration** Repeating an activity.

**Personal Program Plan (PPP)** The form that the IEP takes in some provinces (e.g., Saskatchewan).

**personalization** Classroom routines and practices that put the learner at the centre, with assessment and instruction tailored to students' particular learning and motivational needs.

**phonemic awareness** Sensitivity to and explicit awareness of individual sounds that make up words, which demands that children analyze or manipulate the sounds (includes early skills such as recognizing rhyming and later skills such as segmenting the sounds in words and synthesizing the sounds in words).

**phonics** Stresses sound–symbol relationships, helping learners to match the letters of the alphabet to the already known speech sounds.

**physical disabilities** A range of conditions restricting physical movement or motor abilities as a result of nervous system impairment, musculoskeletal conditions, or chronic medical disorders.

**physical space** The physical layout and areas of a classroom that can make it inviting, accessible, and efficient (including arrangement of furniture, audiovisual equipment, visual aids, etc.).

**positive behavioural supports** An approach to dealing with problem behaviours that focuses on the remediation of deficient contexts documented to be the source of the problems, with the emphasis on altering the environment before a problem behaviour occurs or teaching appropriate behaviours as a strategy for eliminating the need for problem behaviours to be exhibited.

**portfolio** A collection of the student's work in an area showing growth, self-reflection, and achievement.

**post-reading activities** Activities following individual, paired, or group reading of an assigned piece of text; usually include application of what has been read and a review of learning by the teacher

**precision** The provision of instruction that is precise to the level of readiness and the learning needs of the individual student, linking assessment for learning with differentiating teaching and learning activities.

**prenatal exposure to alcohol** Maternal use of alcohol during pregnancy.

**pre-reading activities** Activities that occur prior to individual, paired, or group reading of an assigned piece of text and usually include an introduction to the topic and the vocabulary and a preview of the text by the teacher.

**pre-referral intervention** Actions taken by a teacher, possibly with the aid of a resource teacher, after the teacher has voiced concerns about a student and before the student has been referred for formal assessment.

**pre-referral process** An informal assessment of a student's learning strengths and needs, often in collaboration with a resource teacher, prior to a formal referral.

**pre-teaching** The technique of preparing exceptional students, frequently used with students who are deaf or hard of hearing, by teaching them the vocabulary and concepts prior to introducing new material to the entire class.

**preventers** Anti-inflammatory drugs taken regularly to prevent and treat inflammation in persons with asthma.

**principles of fairness** Fairness does not necessarily mean sameness; this can be a difficult concept for young children to understand and for adolescents to accept.

**pro-act** The actions of teachers effective at classroom management who appear to respond to misbehaviour at a moment's notice; they actually anticipate and act almost before the behaviour occurs (Bennett & Smilanich, 1994).

**problem–solution–effect** A text structure used to organize expository content that emphasizes that the problems encountered might be linked to issues, and that the solutions people generate can have broad effects, such as new institutions, new problems, or changes in society.

**problem-solving approach** A behaviour management technique in which the teacher asks students questions about what they think the problem was, what they did to contribute to the problem, how they can make amends, and how they can prevent the problem from recurring, and then the teacher follows up.

**professional learning** Learning that contributes to teachers' professional development through professional learning communities (PLCs) within a culture of collaboration.

**progress monitoring** Ongoing monitoring of student progress to inform instructional decision-making; a specific form receiving recent attention is responsiveness to intervention (RTI) which sequentially increases the intensity and duration of instruction.

**prosocial behaviours** Behaviours that exemplify the relations of an individual's emotional needs to the social environment.

**psychostimulant medications** Drugs used to treat AD/HD, most commonly Ritalin and Dexedrine, which may have side effects.

**puffer** A small device that delivers medication in a pre-measured amount to persons with asthma; sometimes called an inhaler.

**punishment** A response or consequence aimed at decreasing the likelihood of an inappropriate behaviour.

# R

**rapid naming** Identifying and saying aloud rows of repeated letters, numbers, colours, or objects as quickly as possible; used with young children as a predictor of reading performance.

**reading comprehension** Reading skill involving understanding the meaning of what has been read.

**reading wars** Controversies over the whole language versus phonics emphases in teaching early reading (see Stanovich & Stanovich, 1995).

**reciprocal teaching** A teaching approach that involves enabling students to teach one another by taking turns leading discussion in small groups; usually the teacher models how to lead the discussion and provides scaffolding for the groups as they begin.

**referring teacher** A classroom teacher who recognizes that a student may need an adapted or modified program, implements pre-referral interventions, and then refers the student to the in-school team for problem solving and possibly an individual assessment and an IEP.

**reinforcers** Consequences that cause a behaviour to increase.

**relievers** Rescue medications to relax the muscles of the airways and provide quick relief of breathing problems for persons with asthma.

**remediation** Intensive instruction, to address basic skills in an area in which a student has needs, that can be carried out with an individual or a small group in the classroom or in a resource room.

**remission** Temporary disappearance of the symptoms of a health condition or disease.

**reporting** The way in which evaluation results are communicated, including individual student report cards, which can be computer generated or written by teachers.

**resource teacher** A special educator who supports teachers and exceptional students, usually by consulting with teachers and offering some direct services to exceptional students, either in the classroom or in the resource room; can have many titles, including learning assistance teacher, learning program teacher, tutor, and curriculum resource teacher.

**responsiveness to intervention (RTI)** A form of progress monitoring that is usually focused on primary students. It involves tiered instruction where struggling students receive more intense instruction, either in small groups or one-on-one, that is of longer duration than instruction which occurs in the regular classroom.

**reward systems** Teachers give students as a group or as individuals, tokens or points in a systematic way for appropriate behaviour or work.

**right to pass** Students having the right to choose the extent to which they will participate in a group activity that requires sharing personal information; teachers acknowledge a pass by saying, "That is fine," and offer a second chance for those who passed (used in community circle; *Tribes*, Gibbs, 2001).

**rules** Expressions of what can and cannot be done in the classroom that are brief and specific, positively worded, and clearly understood by students.

# S

**Scaffolded Reading Experience (SRE)** Designed for classes with students of varying abilities in reading, it involves teachers in ADAPTing the three steps of pre-reading, reading, and post-reading activities by providing varying degrees of support so all students can learn.

**scaffolding** Support for learning and problem solving; can be clues, reminders, encouragement, breaking the problem into parts, or anything that enables a student to grow in independence as a learner.

**school connectedness** School and classroom environments that engage students through relationships and create a sense of belonging; dependent on teachers' holding high, manageable expectations of academic success and on students' perceiving they are supported by their teachers within a safe school environment.

**schoolwide approach** A program that is adopted, implemented, and enforced throughout a school; for example, a code of conduct or anti-bullying policy that is applied in every part of the school.

**schoolwide behaviour management system** A comprehensive whole school approach to managing behaviour where collaborative teams of teachers, administrators, parents, and students work together to obtain consensus.

**seizures** Brief bursts of electrical activity in the brain.

**self-advocacy** An individual's ability to effectively communicate, convey, negotiate, or assert his or her own interests, desires, needs, and rights.

**self-awareness** Knowing about oneself; developing a picture of the kind of person one is.

**self-care** The personal care activities that maintain hygiene and health.

**self-concept** Our perceptions about ourselves.

**self-determination** The abilities, motivation, and volition that enable people to define goals for themselves and to take and sustain the initiative to reach those goals.

**self-monitoring** A strategy in which students are taught to check whether they have performed targeted behaviours.

**self-referenced** Data that compare a student's progress to where that student started from, regardless of whether that starting point is ahead of, even with, or behind others in the class; often the most appropriate form of data for students on modified programs.

**self-regulation** Learners proactively monitoring, directing, and regulating their behaviour to achieve self-set goals of acquiring knowledge and expanding expertise, with the emphasis on autonomy and control by the individual.

**severe developmental disabilities** Includes those previously considered to have moderate, severe, or profound disabilities, spanning a range of abilities from those who can acquire academic skills to those who require assistance with self-care.

**shunt** A mechanism installed to drain the fluid that builds up with hydrocephalus, for reabsorption in individuals with spina bifida.

**signal** The means used by teachers to obtain and maintain the attention of students, including flicking the lights, raising a hand, rhythmic clapping or speaking, or even blowing a whistle in the gymnasium; usually taught to classes at the beginning of term.

**simple absence seizure (petit mal)** This generalized seizure occurs in children; they stare or daydream for 5 to 15 seconds and there may be small muscle movements in the face, the eyes may roll up or to one side, and the child may be confused about the seconds "missed."

**SMART goals** Specific, Measurable, Achievable, Relevant, and Time limited goals for Individual Education Plans (IEPs) that describe what the student will do, how and when the student will do it, and what the time frame will be for achieving it.

**social acceptance** The response and evaluation by peers of students' social behaviours, including approving of their behaviours, considering them to be members of the group, and including them in social and learning activities.

**social competence** See *social development*.

**social development** The ability to implement developmentally appropriate social behaviours that enhance one's interpersonal relationships without causing harm to anyone.

**social inclusion** The value system that holds that all students are entitled to equitable access to learning, achievement, and the pursuit of excellence in all aspects of their education; incorporates basic values that promote participation, friendship, and interaction.

**social problems** Risk factors often experienced by students with emotional and behavioural exceptionalities, including delinquency, substance abuse, and neglect.

**social relationships** Friendships, peer relations, and romantic relationships that change with development; for example, by middle childhood, children choose friends on the basis of personality and interests and friendships become increasingly stable.

**social skills difficulties** A controversial aspect of learning disabilities, not present in all students with LD; for example, teachers report that *most* students with LD experience social skills difficulties and peers report that *many* have low social status; however, only a *few* children with LD report low social self-concept.

**social status** A rating of a child's or adolescent's popularity with their classmates, that is, how well they are liked.

**social stories** Describe a situation from the perspective of a student, direct the student to do the appropriate behaviour, and are in the first person; developed by Gray (2002) for children with autism.

**sociometric rating** A system of collecting data by asking children to indicate which classmates they would choose as best friends, to play with, etc., and which they would not choose; enables researchers to develop ratings of popularity or social status for individual students.

**special education** Programs or services designed to accommodate students whose educational needs cannot adequately be met through the use of regular curriculum and services only.

**spectrum of autistic disorders** Refers to the range of characteristics and degrees of severity displayed by individuals with autism.

**speech-activated** Describes equipment that responds to the human voice, usually computer equipment used by individuals with visual impairments.

**speech and language exceptionalities** Problems encountered in the oral production of language and/or impairment in the use or comprehension of spoken language that interfere with communication.

**speech impairment** Speech is disordered when it deviates so far from the speech of other people that it calls attention to itself, interferes with communication, or causes the speaker or listeners distress.

**speech-reading** The skill of understanding speech by watching the lips and face; sometimes called lip-reading.

**spina bifida** A condition developed prenatally that disturbs proper development of the vertebrae or spinal cord and results in varying degrees of damage to the spinal cord and nervous system.

**stimulant medications** A class of medication (e.g. Ritalin) commonly used as treatment for ADHD.

**story-planning sheet** Scaffolding to help students create narrative text that includes prompts, such as: setting, main character, character clues, problem, attempts to solve the problem, and resolution.

**strengths** Areas in which an exceptional student has relatively strong abilities and skills on which to draw in compensating or learning in areas of relative weakness; schools often focus on academic, social/emotional, and behavioural strengths in preparing a student's IEP.

**structure** Predictability and organization in learning activities that enables exceptional students to feel safe and focus on learning.

**student activity log** A summary of student activities that may be particularly beneficial in reporting progress for students on modified programs because it can include a summary of key accomplishments shown in the portfolio or performance-based assessments.

**students with special needs** See *exceptional students*.

**study guides** Learning aids that tell students what to study for a test and can enable them to be more efficient in their preparation; they include outlines, abstracts, and questions that emphasize important information in texts.

**study skills** The actions students take to prepare for tests that usually involve reviewing notes and texts.

**summative assessment** Tests administered after learning was assumed to have taken place that were intended to provide parents and students with a summary of the students' learning and relative standing, presently referred to as assessment of learning.

**suspension** Temporary removal of a student from the classroom (for a day or more) as a consequence of the student behaving inappropriately, violating the code of conduct, etc.

# T

**taped books** A technique of reading books onto audiotape so they can be used by persons who are print-disabled, usually people who are blind or have learning disabilities in the area of reading (dyslexia).

**task commitment** The degree to which students set their own goals, embrace challenges, and show perseverance.

**testing** A form of assessment, normally using a paper and pencil test (either designed by the teacher or commercially available) to gather information that describes a student's or a group's level of performance.

**theory of mind** The notion that others think, feel, and know; Baron-Cohen (1995) hypothesized that people with autism do not have a theory of mind.

**thinking aloud** Teachers or peers can make the invisible visible by verbalizing their thoughts and showing students how to use a strategy, solve a problem, etc.

**think-pair-share** A collaborative activity in which the teacher poses a problem, students think and jot down their thoughts, pair with a classmate to discuss the question, and a few students share the thoughts of their pair with the class.

**tics** Involuntary, rapid, sudden muscular movements; uncontrollable vocal sounds; and inappropriate words (seen in Tourette syndrome).

**tiering** Presenting content at varying levels of complexity while using the same process for all students; for example, grouping students based on their current level of understanding.

**tiering assessments** Beginning with a grade-level task and raising or lowering the challenge level to accommodate exceptional students accordingly.

**time out** Punishment in which a student is removed from opportunities for reward as a consequence for inappropriate behaviour.

**tonic-clonic (grand mal) seizure** In this generalized seizure, the individual sometimes gives a sharp cry before falling to the floor, the muscles stiffen, then begin to jerk rhythmically, and there may be loss of bladder control, some breathing difficulty, and saliva may gather at the mouth.

**Tourette syndrome** A neurological disorder involving motor tics and uncontrollable vocal sounds or inappropriate words that are often accompanied by obsessions and hyperactivity.

**transition plan** A formal, written plan that some provinces require, for students with an IEP, to ensure that preparation for post-secondary endeavours begins early in the high school years.

**traumatic brain injury (TBI)** Damage to brain tissue as a result of a blow to the head or an accident that can cause physical difficulties (e.g., paralysis) and cognitive problems (e.g., memory loss).

**TTYPA** A collaborative learning activity in which a teacher stops and tells the students to "turn to your partner and . . . introduce yourself . . . or describe a time when you . . ." Then the students switch roles.

**Twinject ®** Brand name of an easily administered epinephrine injection for the emergency treatment of those with severe allergies, including anaphylactic reactions.

# U

**universal design for learning** The design of instructional materials and activities that allows the learning goals to be achievable by individuals with wide differences in their abilities to see, hear, speak, move, etc. by means of flexible curricular materials and activities designed to include alternatives for students with diversity in abilities and backgrounds.

# V

**verbal reprimand** Punishment in which a student is reminded of the classroom rules; the most effective reprimands are immediate, unemotional, brief, and backed up with a time out or loss of privileges.

**vision teacher** A special educator who teaches or tutors students who are blind or have impaired vision.

**visual impairment** Disability characterized by partial or complete loss of sight and use of auditory and tactile sources of information to supplement or replace sight.

**vocabulary** The kind and level of language used in oral and written expression to communicate meaning to students; can also refer to the kind and level of language used in oral and written expression by students.

**voice synthesizer** Converts information typed or scanned into a computer into speech.

## W

**wheezing** Breathing with an audible chesty, whistling sound; a symptom of an asthma episode.

## Z

**zone of proximal development (ZPD)** Distance between a child's development as shown in independent problem solving and the level of potential development as determined through problem solving with adult guidance or collaboration with more capable peers; from the work of Vygotsky.

# References

Adams, M. J. (1990). *Beginning to read: Thinking and learning about print.* Cambridge, MA: MIT Press.

Adams, C. M., & Pierce, R. L. (2003). Teaching by tiering. *Science and Children*, 30–34.

Ainscow, M., Booth, T., & Dyson, A. (1999). Inclusion and exclusion in schools: Listening to some hidden voices. In K. Ballard (Ed.), *Inclusive education: International voices on disability and justice* (pp.139–151). London, UK: Falmer Press.

Alber, S. R., & Heward, W. L. (1997). Recruit it or lose it: Teaching students to recruit contingent teacher attention. *Intervention in School and Clinic, 5,* 275–282.

Albert, E. (1994). *Phonics for learning how to read.* (ERIC Reproduction Document No. ED 370078)

Alberta Education. (2004). *Standards for special education.* Edmonton, AB: Alberta Learning.

Alberta Education. (2006). *Focusing on success: Teaching students with attention deficit/hyperactivity disorder.* Edmonton: Alberta Education. Retrieved from http://education.alberta.ca/admin/special/resources/adhd.aspx.

Alfassi, M. (2004). Reading to learn: Effects of combined strategy instruction on high school students. *Journal of Educational Research, 9*(4), 171–184.

Allard, E.R., & Williams, D.F. (2008). Listeners' perceptions of speech and language disorders. *Journal of Communication Disorders, 41*(2), 108–123.

American Psychiatric Association (APA). (2000/2004). *Diagnostic and statistical manual of mental disorders* (4th ed., DSM-IV-TR). Washington, DC: APA.

Anderson, K.M. (2007). Differentiating instruction to include all students. *Preventing School Failure, 51*(3), 49–54.

Anderson, L. W. (2003). *Classroom assessment: Enhancing the quality of teacher decision making.* Mahwah, NJ: L. Erlbaum Associates.

Antonijevic, R. (2007). *Usage of computers and calculators and students' achievement: Results from TIMSS 2003.* Online Submission, ERIC ED497737.

Arnold, S. (2006). Investigating functions using real-world data. *Australian Senior Mathematics Journal, 20*(1), 44–47.

Arthritis Foundation JA Alliance. www.arthritis.org/ja-school-success.php#5.

Assouline, S. G., Nicpon, M. F., & Whiteman, C. (2010). Cognitive and psychosocial characteristics of gifted students with written language disability. *Gifted Child Today, 54*(2), 102–115.

Atlantic Provinces Special Education Authority (2001a). *Resource booklet on educational interpreting.* Halifax: Atlantic Provinces Special Education Authority. Retrieved from www.apsea.ca/download/rbei.pdf.

Austin, V. L. (2003). Pharmacological interventions for students with ADD. *Intervention in School and Clinic, 38,* 289–296.

Azmitia, M., Ittel, A., & Radmacher, K. (2005). Narratives of friendship and self in adolescence. In N. Way & J. V. Hamm (Eds.), The experience of close friendships in adolescence. *New Directions for Child and Adolescent Development, 107* (pp. 23–39). San Francisco: Jossey-Bass.

Babyak, A. E., Luze, G. J., & Kamps, D. M. (2000). The good student game: Behavior management for diverse classrooms. *Intervention in School and Clinic, 35,* 216–223.

Bach, M. (2002). *Social inclusion as solidarity: Rethinking the child rights agenda.* Toronto: Laidlaw Foundation Working Paper Series.

Baker, S., Gersten, R., & Scanlon, D. (2002). Procedural facilitators and cognitive strategies: Tools for unraveling the mysteries of comprehension and the writing process, and for providing meaningful access to the general curriculum. *Learning Disabilities Research and Practice, 17,* 65–77.

Bakermans-Kranenburg, M. J., Ijzendoorn, M. H. V., Pijlman, F. T. A., Mesman, J., & Juffer, F. (2010). Experimental evidence for differential susceptibility: Dopamine D4 Receptor Polymorphism (DRD4 VNTR) moderates intervention effects on toddlers' externalizing behavior in a randomized controlled trial. *Developmental Psychology, 44*(1), 293–300.

Balaban, T., Hyde, N., & Colantonio, A. (2009). The effects of traumatic brain injury during adolescence on career plans and outcomes. *Physical & Occupational Therapy in Pediatrics, 29*(4), 367–383.

Ballard, K., & McDonald, T. (1999). Disability inclusion and exclusion: Some insider accounts and interpretations. In K. Ballard (Ed.), *Inclusive education: International voices on disability and justice* (pp. 97–115). London, UK: Falmer Press.

Bandura, A. (1994). *Self-efficacy in changing societies.* New York: Cambridge University Press.

Barger, R. H. (2009). Gifted, talented, and high achieving. *Teaching Children Mathematics, 16*(3), 154–161.

Barkley, R. (1997). *AD/HD and the nature of self-control.* New York: Guilford Press.

Baron-Cohen, S. (1995). *Mindblindness.* Cambridge, MA: MIT Press.

Barrish, H. H., Saunders, M., & Wolf, M. M. (1969). Good behavior game: Effects of individual contingencies for group consequences on disruptive behavior in a classroom. *Journal of Applied Behavior Analysis, 2,* 119–124.

Baxter, S., Brookes, C., Bianchi, K., Rashid, K., & Hay, Fiona (2009). Speech and language therapists and teachers working together: Exploring the issues. *Child Language Teaching and Therapy, 25*(2), 215–234.

Beale, A. V., & Hall, K. R. (2007). Cyberbullying: What school administrators (and parents) can do. *Clearing House, 81*(1), 8–12.

Beck, I. L., & McKeown, M. G. (1991). Conditions of vocabulary acquisition. In R. Barr, M. Kamil, P. Mosenthal, & P. D. Pearson (Eds.), *Handbook of reading research* (Vol. 2, pp. 789–814). New York: Longman.

Beck, I. L., & McKeown, M. G. (2007). Increasing young low-income children's oral vocabulary repertoires through rich and focused instruction. *Elementary School Journal, 107,* 251–273.

Beitchman et al. (2008). Models and determinants of vocabulary growth from kindergarten to adulthood. *Journal of Child Psychology and Psychiatry, 49*(6), 626–634.

Bellanca, J., & Fogarty, R. (2003). *Blueprints for achievement in the cooperative classroom.* Thousand Oaks, CA: Corwin Press.

Ben Jaafar, S. (2006a). *Educational accountability: Differences in policy and practice.* Paper presented at the International Congress for School Effectiveness and Improvement annual conference, Ft Lauderdale, Florida.

Ben Jaafar, S. (2006b). From performance-based to inquiry-based accountability. *Brock Education, 16,* 62–77.

Ben Jaafar, S., & Anderson, S. (2007). Policy trends and tensions in accountability for educational management and services in Canada. *Alberta Journal of Educational Research, 53*(2), 207–228.

Bender, W. N. (2008). *Differentiating instruction for students with learning disabilities: Best teaching practices for general and special educators* (2nd ed.). Thousand Oaks, CA: Corwin Press.

Bennett, B., & Smilanich, P. (1994). *Classroom management: A thinking and caring approach.* Toronto: Bookation. Retrieved from www.sacsc.ca/.

Bennett, S., Weber, K., & Dworet, D. (2008). *Special education in Ontario schools* (6th ed.). St David's, ON: Highland Press.

Beran, T.N. (2006). A construct validity study of bullying. *Alberta Journal of Educational Research, 52,* 241–250.

Beran, T.N., Hughes, G., & Lupart, J. (2008). A model of achievement and bullying: Analyses of the Canadian National Longitudinal Survey of Children and Youth data. *Educational Research, 50,* 25–39.

Berg, D. H. (2006). *Role of processing speed and working memory in children's mental addition.* Unpublished doctoral thesis, Queen's University, Kingston, Ontario, Canada.

Berg, D.H. (2008). Working memory and arithmetic calculation in children: The contributory roles of processing speed, short-term memory, and reading. *Journal of Experimental Child Psychology, 99*(4), 288–308.

Berlak, A., & Berlak, H. (1989). *Dilemmas of schooling: Teaching and social change* (2nd ed.). New York: Routledge.

Berman, S. (2008). *Performance-based learning: Aligning experiential tasks and assessment to increase learning.* Thousand Oaks, CA: Corwin Press.

Berry, R. A. W. (2006). Inclusion, power and community: Teachers and students interpret the language of community in an inclusion classroom. *American Educational Research Journal, 43,* 489–529.

Bethell, C. D., Read, D., Blumberg, S. J., & Newacheck, P. W. (2008). What is the prevalence of children with special health care needs? Toward an understanding of variations in findings and methods across three national surveys. *Maternal and Child Health Journal, 12,* 1–14.

Billiard, P. (2009). Another look at attention deficit hyperactivity disorder. *The Delta Kappa Gamma Bulletin, 75*(2), 30–32.

Bloom, E. L., Karagiannakis, A., Toste, J. R., Heath, N. L., & Konstantinopoulos, E. (2007). Severity of academic achievement and social skills deficits. *Canadian Journal of Education, 30,* 911–930.

Bondy, A. S., & Frost, L. A. (1994). The picture exchange communication system. *Focus on Autism and Other Developmental Disabilities, 9*(3), 1–19.

Bondy, E., Ross, D. D., Gallingane, C., & Hambacher, E. (2007). Creating environments of success and resilience: Culturally responsive classroom management and more. *Urban Education, 42,* 326–348.

Bouk, E. (2009). Functional curriculum models for secondary students with mild mental impairment. *Education and Training in Developmental Disabilities, 44*(4), 435–443.

Boutot, E. A. (2009). Using "I Will" cards and social coaches to improve social behaviors of students with Asperger syndrome. *Intervention in School and Clinic, 44,* 276–281.

Bowen, G.M., & Arsenault, N. (2008). It's all about choice. *Science Teacher, 75*(2), 34–37.

Boyle, J. R. (2008). Reading strategies for students with mild disabilities. *Intervention in school and clinic, 44*(1), 3–9.

Boyle, J. M., McCartney, E., O'Hare, A., & Forbes, J. (2009). Direct versus indirect and individual versus group modes of language therapy for children with primary language impairment: Principal outcomes

from a randomized controlled trial and economic evaluation. *International Journal of Language & Communication Disorders, 44*(6), 826–846.

Bray, M. A., Kehle, T. J., Grigerick, S. E., Loftus, S., & Nicholson, H. (2008). Children with asthma: Assessment and treatment in school settings. *Psychology in the Schools, 45,* 63–73.

Brislin, D. C. (2008). Reaching for independence: Counseling implications for youth with spina bifida. *Journal of Counseling and Development, 86,* 34–38.

British Columbia Ministry of Education. (1996). *Awareness of chronic health conditions: What the teacher needs to know.* Victoria: Queen's Printer for British Columbia.

British Columbia Ministry of Education. (2010). *Students with intellectual disabilities: A resource guide for teachers.* Retrieved from www.bced.gov.bc.ca/specialed/sid.

British Columbia Ministry of Education. (2004). *Provincial student assessment program.* Victoria: Queen's Printer for British Columbia.

British Columbia Special Education Branch. (2008). *Special education services: A manual of policies, procedures, and guidelines.* Victoria: Queen's Printer for British Columbia [www.bced.gov.bc.ca/specialed/ppandg/toc.html].

Brock, C. H., Lapp, D., Flood, J., Fisher, D., & Keomghee, T. H. (2007). Does homework matter? An investigation of teacher perceptions about homework practices for children from nondominant backgrounds. *Urban Education, 42,* 349–372.

Brookfield, S.D. (1995). *Becoming a critically reflective teacher.* San Francisco: Jossey-Bass.

Browne, A. (2007). *Teaching and learning communication, language and literacy.* Thousand Oaks, CA: Sage/Paul Chapman Pub.

Bryan, L.C., & Gast, D. L. (2000). Teaching on-task and on-schedule behaviors to high-functioning children with autism via picture activity schedules. *Journal of Autism and Developmental Disorders, 30*(6), 553–567.

Bryan, T. (1991). Social problems and learning disabilities. In B. Y. L. Wong (Ed.), *Learning about learning disabilities* (pp. 195–229). San Diego, CA: Academic.

Bryan, T., & Burstein, K. (2004). Improving homework completion and academic performance: Lessons from special education. *Theory Into Practice, 43*(3), 213–219.

Buhrmester, D. (1998). Need fulfillment, interpersonal competence, and the developmental contexts of early adolescent friendship. In W. M. Bukowski, A. F. Newcomb, & W. W. Hartup (Eds.), *The company they keep: Friendship in childhood and adolescence* (pp. 158–185). New York: Cambridge University Press.

Bukowski, W.M., Rubin, K.H., & Parker, J.G. (2004). Social competence: Childhood and adolescence. In N.J. Smelser, & P.B. Baltes (Eds) *International encyclopedia of the social and behavioral sciences* (pp. 14258–14264). Elsevier: St. Louis, MO.

Bukowski, W.M., & Sippola, L.K. (2005). Friendship and development: Putting the most human relationship in its place. *New Directions for Child and Adolescent Development, 109,* 91–97.

Bullock, L. M., Gable, R. A., & Mohr, J. D. (2005). Traumatic brain injury: A challenge for educators. *Preventing School Failure, 49*(4), 6–10.

Burd, L. J. (2007). Interventions in FASD: We must do better. *Child: Care, Health and Development, 33,* 398–400.

Burge, P., Ouellette-Kuntz, H., Box, H., & Hutchinson, N. L. (2008, December 3). A quarter century of inclusive education for children with intellectual disabilities in Ontario: Public perceptions. *Canadian Journal of Educational Administration and Policy, 87.* Retrieved from www.umanitoba.ca/publications/cjeap/currentissues.html.

Burge, P., Ouellette-Kuntz, H., & Lysaght, R. (2007). Public views on employment of people with intellectual disabilities. *Journal of Vocational Rehabilitation, 26*(1), 29–37.

Calculator, S. N. (2009). Augmentative and alternative communication (AAC) and inclusive education for students with the most severe disabilities. *International Journal of Inclusive Education, 13*(1), 93–113.

Campbell, D. S., Serff, P., & Williams, D. (1994). *Breakaway company.* Toronto: Trifolium Publishing.

Canadian Association of the Deaf. *Definition of "deaf".* Retrieved from www.cad.ca/en/issues/definition_of_deaf.asp.

Canadian Education Statistics Council. (2009). *Education indicators in Canada: An international perspective.* Ottawa, ON: Statistics Canada. Retrieved from www.statcan.gc.ca/bsolc/olc-cel/olc-cel?catno= 81-604-x&lang=eng.

Canitano, R., & Vivanti, G. (2007). Tics and Tourette syndrome in autism spectrum disorders. *Autism, 11,* 19–28.

Canney, C., & Byrne, A. (2006). Evaluating circle time as a support to social skills development: Reflections on a journey in school-based research. *British Journal of Special Education, 33*(1), 19–24.

Cantwell, D. P. (1996). Attention deficit disorder: A review of the past 10 years. *Journal of the American Academy of Child and Adolescent Psychiatry, 34,* 1262–1271.

Capuzzi, D. & Gross, D. (Eds.) (2004). *Youth at risk: A prevention resource for counselors, teachers, and parents* (4th ed.). Alexandria, VA: American Counseling Association.

Carnine, D., Silbert, J., & Kameenui, E. (1990). *Direct instruction reading.* Columbus, OH: Merrill.

Carnine, D. W., Kameenui, E. J., Silbert, J., & Tarver, S. G. (2003). *Direct instruction reading* (4th ed.). Rutherford, NJ: Prentice Hall.

Cederlund, M., Hagberg, B., & Gillberg, C. (2010). Asperger syndrome in adolescent and young adult males. Interview self- and parent assessment of social, emotional, and cognitive problems. *Research in Developmental Disabilities, 31*(2), 287–298.

Center for Comprehensive School Reform and Improvement. (2007, December). *Improving teacher retention with supportive workplace conditions: Newsletter.* Washington, DC: Center for Comprehensive School Reform and Improvement.

Chafouleas, S. M., McDougal, J. L., Riley-Tillman, T. C., Panahon, C. J., & Hilt, A. M. (2005). What do daily behavior report cards (DBRCs) measure? An initial comparison of DBRCs with direct observation for off-task behavior. *Psychology in the Schools, 42,* 669–676.

Chafouleas, S. M., Riley-Tillman, T. C., & Sassu, K. A. (2006). Acceptability and reported use of daily behavior report cards among teachers. *Journal of Positive Behavior Interventions, 8,* 174–182.

Chall, J. S. (1979). The great debate: Ten years later, with a modest proposal for reading stages. In L. B. Resnick & P. A. Weaver (Eds.), *Theory and practice of early reading* (Vol. 1, pp. 29–55). Hillsdale, NJ: Lawrence Erlbaum Associates.

Chall, J. S. (1983). *Stages of reading development.* New York: McGraw Hill.

Chamberlain, B., Kasari, C., & Rotheram-Fuller, E. (2007). Involvement or isolation? The social networks of children with autism in regular classrooms. *Journal of Autism and Developmental Disorders, 37,* 230–242.

Chang, M., Singh, K., & Mo, Y. (2007). Science engagement and science achievement: Longitudinal models using NELS data. *Educational Research and Evaluation, 13,* 349–371.

Chard, D. J., Baker, S. K., Clarke, B., Jungjohann, K., Davis, K., & Smolkowski, K. (2008). Preventing ealy mathematics difficulties: The feasibility of a rigorous kindergarten mathematics curriculum. *Learning Disability Quarterly, 31,* 11–20.

Charles, C. M., & Charles, M. G. (2004). *Classroom management for middle-grade teachers.* Boston: Pearson Allyn & Bacon.

Chesson, R., Chisholm, D., & Zaw, W. (2004). Counseling children with chronic physical illness. *Patient Education and Counseling, 55,* 331–338.

Chin, P., & Members of the STAO Safety Committee (1997). Teaching science safely in the ESL classroom. *Crucible, 27*(1), 24–25.

Chin, P., Munby, H., Hutchinson, N. L., & Steiner-Bell, K. (2000). Meeting academic goals: Post-secondary students' intentions for participating in high school co-operative education programs. *Journal of Vocational Educational Research, 25,* 126–154.

Christner, B., & Dieker, L. A. (2008). Tourette syndrome: A collaborative approach focused on empowering students, families, and teachers. *Teaching Exceptional Children, 40*(5), 44–51.

Chung, K.K., & Tam, Y.H.(2005). Effects of cognitive-based instruction on mathematical problem solving by learners with mild intellectual disabilities. *Journal of Intellectual and Developmental Disability, 30*(4), 207–216.

Clapper, A., Bremer, C., & Kachgal, M. (2002). *Never too late: Approaches to reading instruction for secondary school students with disabilities.* Minneapolis, MN: National Center on Secondary Education and Transition. (ERIC Document Reproduction Service No. ED 466913).

Clarke, M., & Wilkinson, R. (2008). Interactions between children with cerebral palsy and their peers 2: Understanding initiated VOCA-mediated turns. *Augmentative and Alternative Communication, 24,* 3–15.

Cobia, D. C., & Carney, J. S. (2002). Creating a culture of tolerance in schools: Everyday actions to prevent hate-motivated violent incidents. *Journal of School Violence, 1,* 87–103.

Cochran-Smith, M. (2006). *Stayers, leavers, and dreamers: Why people teach and why they stay: The Barbara Biber Lecture.* New York: Bank Street College of Education. Retrieved at www.accessmylibrary.com/article-1G1-124793845/stayers-leavers-lovers-and.html.

Cockburn, A., & Haydn, T. (2004). *Recruiting and retaining teachers: Understanding why teachers teach.* London: RoutledgeFalmer.

Cohen, E.(1998). Designing groupwork: Strategies for the heterogeneous classroom (2nd ed.). New York: Teachers College Press.

Cohen, E. Brody, C.M., & Sapon-Shevin, M. (2004). *Teaching cooperative learning: The challenge for teacher education.* Albany, NY: State University of New York Press.

Colangelo, N., & Assouline, S.G. (2005). Accelerating gifted children. *Principal, 84*(5), 62.

Collicott, J. (1994, Winter). Multi-level instruction: A guide for teachers. *Keeping in Touch* (Quarterly Newsletter of CEC Canada).

Colvin, G. (2007). *Seven steps for developing a proactive schoolwide discipline plan: A guide for principals and leadership teams.* Thousand Oaks, CA: Corwin Press.

Conduct Problems Prevention Research Group. (2010). The effects of a multiyear universal social–emotional learning program: The role of student and school characteristics. *Journal of Consulting and Clinical Psychology, 78*(2), 156–168.

Conference Board of Canada. (2003). *Innovation skills profile.* Ottawa, ON: Conference Board of Canada.

Conn, K. (2001). Supporting special students. *Science Teacher, 68*(3), 32–35.

Cornett, C. E. (2006). Center stage: Arts-based read-alouds. *The Reading Teacher, 60,* 234–240.

Cortiella, C. (2007). *Learning opportunities for your child through alternate assessments: Alternate assessments based on modified academic achievement standards.* National Center on Educational Outcomes, University of Minnesota.

Council of Ministers of Education of Canada. (2009). *Pan-Canadian assessment program for 13-year-olds (PCAP-13 2007): Fact sheet.* Toronto, ON: Council of Ministers of Education of Canada.

Craig, W., Pepler, D., & Blais, J. (2007). Responding to bullying: What works? *School Psychology International, 28,* 465–477.

Craig, W.M., Pepler, D.J., Murphy, A., McCuaig-Edge, H. (2010). What works in bullying prevention? In E. M. Vernberg & B. K. Biggs (Eds.), *Preventing and treating bullying and victimization* (pp. 215–241). New York: Oxford University Press.

Crawford, T. (2005, June 10). Lost in transition. *Toronto Star.*

Cross. T. L. (2002). Competing with the myths about the social and emotional development of gifted students. *Gifted Child Today, 25*(3), 44–45 & 65.

CTV. (2007). *A convenient diagnosis.* Produced by Sarah Stevens.

Cuccaro, C., & Geitner, G. (2007). Lunch and recess: The "eye of the storm": Using targeted interventions for students with behavioral problems. *Teaching Exceptional Children Plus, 3*(4). Retrieved at http://escholarship.bc.edu/education/tecplus/vol3/iss4/art2.

Cummings, J. G., Pepler, D. J., Mishna, F., & Craig, W. (2006). Bullying and victimization among students with exceptionalities. *Exceptionality Education Canada, 16,* 193–222.

Cunningham, A. E., & Stanovich, K. E. (1997). Early reading acquisition and its relation to reading experience and ability 10 years later. *Developmental Psychology, 33,* 934–945.

Curriculum Services Canada. Rethinking Classroom Assessment with Purpose in Mind. [podcast] Retrieved at www.curriculum.org/secretariat/april27.shtml.

Curtin, M., & Clark, G. (2005). Listening to young people with physical disabilities' experiences of education. *International Journal of Disability, Development and Education, 52,* 195–214.

Cystic Fibrosis. Teachers guide to CF. *A teacher's guide to cystic fibrosis.* Retrieved from www.cysticfibrosis.ca/assets/files/pdf/Teachers_Guide_to_cystic_fibrosisE.pdf.

Dalton, C. A. (2010). *Listening to students with mild and moderate hearing loss: Learning and social-emotional needs in educational contexts.* Unpublished master's thesis, Queen's University, Kingston, Ontario, Canada.

Dearman, C. C., & Alber S. R. (2005). The changing face of education: Teachers cope with challenges through collaboration and reflective study. *Reading Teacher, 58,* 634–640.

Decker, L. E., & Decker, V. A. (2000). *Engaging families and communities: Pathways to educational success.* Fairfax, VA: National Community Education Association.

Decker, L. E., Decker, V. A., Townsend, T., & Neal, L. L. (2005). Community education: Global perspectives for developing comprehensive integrated human and community services. *World Leisure Journal, 47*(2), 23–30.

Dei, G. J. S. (2003). *Anti-racism education: Theory and practice.* Black Point, NS: Fernwood.

Delisle, J. R., & Galbraith, J. (2004). *When gifted kids don't have all the answers: How to meet their social and emotional needs.* Minneapolis, MN: Free Spirit Publishing.

Denton, C. A., Foreman, B. R., & Mathes, P. O. (2003). Schools that beat the odds: Implications for reading instruction. *Remedial and Special Education, 24,* 258–261.

DePaepe, P., Garrison-Kane, L., & Doelling, J. (2002). Supporting students with health needs in schools: An overview of selected health conditions. *Focus on Exceptional Children, 35*(1), 1–24.

Deshler, D., Palincsar, A.S., Biancarosa, G., & Nair, M. (2007). *Informed choices for struggling adolescent readers: A research-based guide to instructional programs and practices.* Newark, DE: International Reading Association.

Dever, R. B. (1990). Defining mental retardation from an instructional perspective. *Mental Retardation, 28,* 147–153.

Dewey, J. (1916). *Democracy and education: An introduction to the philosophy of education.* New York: Macmillan.

Diamond, K. E. (2007). The development of social competence in children with disabilities. In P. Smith & C. Hart (Eds.), *Blackwell handbook of childhood social development* (pp. 570–587). Malden, MA: Blackwell.

DiClementi, J. D., & Handelman, M. M. (2005). Empowering students: Class-generated course rules. *Teaching of Psychology, 32,* 18–21.

DiGiorgio, C. (2004). A learning experience: Case study of an integrated resource teacher. *Westminster Studies in Education, 27,* 189–205.

Dion, E., Fuchs, D., & Fuchs, L. (2005). Differential effects of peer-assisted learning strategies on students' social preference and friendship making. *Behavioral Disorders, 30,* 421–429.

Dods, J. C. (2010). *The educational experience of youth who have lived through trauma: Learning from students' stories.* Unpublished master's thesis, Queen's University, Kingston, Ontario, Canada.

Dods, J., Hutchinson, N. L., & Dalton, C. (2009). *Supporting the mental health needs of students in high school: A review of the literature prepared for the MISA Professional Network Centre.* Unpublished report, Faculty of Education, Queen's University, Kingston, Ontario, Canada.

Dodwell, K., & Bavin, E.L. (2008). Children with specific language impairment: An investigation of their narratives and memory. *International Journal of Language and Communication Disorders, 43*(2), 201–218.

Douglas, D. (2004). Self-advocacy: Encouraging students to become partners in differentiation. *Roeper Review, 26*(4), 223–228.

Downing, J. E., & Peckingham-Hardin, K. D. (2007). Inclusive education: What makes it a good education for students with moderate to severe disabilities? *Research & Practice for Persons with Severe Disabilities, 32,* 16–30.

Dunn, L. (1968). Special education for the mildly retarded: Is much of it justifiable? *Exceptional Children, 35,* 5–22.

DuPaul, G.J., & Stoner, G.D. (2003). *ADHD in the schools: Assessment and intervention.* New York: Guilford Press.

DuPaul, G. J., & Weyandt, L.L. (2006). School-based intervention for children with attention deficit hyperactivity disorder: Effects on academic, social, and behavioral functioning. *International Journal of Disability, Development and Education, 53,* 161–176.

Duquette, C. (1992). Integrating mildly and moderately handicapped children: What goes on in a successful school? *Exceptionality Education Canada, 2*(1&2), 139–153.

Dworet, D., & Rathgeber, A. (1998). Confusion reigns: Definitions of behaviour exceptionalities in Canada. *Exceptionality Education Canada, 8*(1), 3–19.

Earl, L. (2003). Assessment of learning, for learning, and as learning. *In Assessment as learning: Using classroom assessment to maximise student learning* (pp. 34–47). Thousand Oaks, CA: Corwin Press.

Earl, L., & Cousins, J. B. (1995). *Classroom assessment: Changing the face, facing the change.* Toronto, ON: Ontario Public School Teachers Federation.

Eaton V. Brant (County) Board of Education (1995), 22O.R. (3d) 1 (C.A.).

Edgemon, E. A., Jablonski, B. R., & Lloyd, J. W. (2006). Large-scale assessments: A teacher's guide to making decisions about accommodations. *Teaching Exceptional Children, 38*(3), 6–11.

Edmunds, A. (1998). Classroom teachers are not prepared for the inclusive classroom. *Exceptionality Education Canada, 8*(2), 27–40.

Edmunds, A. (1999). Acquiring learning strategies. *Teaching Exceptional Children, 31*(4), 69–73.

Education Quality Accountability Office. (2009). *Guide for accommodations, special provisions and exemptions: Support for students with special education needs and English language learners.* Toronto, ON: Queen's Printer for Ontario. Retrieved from www.eqao.com.

Edwards, K. L. (2000). *"They can be successful too!" Inclusive practices of secondary school science teachers.* Unpublished master's thesis, Faculty of Education, Queen's University, Kingston, ON.

Ehri, L. C., Nunes, S. R., Stahl, S. A., & Willows., D. M. (2001). Systematic phonics instruction helps students to learn to read. *Review of Educational Research, 71,* 393–447.

Eisenman, L. T. (2007). Social networks and careers of young adults with intellectual disabilities. *Intellectual and Developmental Disabilities, 453*(3), 199–208.

Elementary Teachers' Federation of Ontario. (2007). *Special education handbook.* Toronto, ON: Elementary Teachers' Federation of Ontario.

Ellis, E. S., & Friend, P. (1991). Adolescents with learning disabilities. In B. Y. L. Wong (Ed.), *Learning about learning disabilities* (pp. 505–561). San Diego, CA: Academic Press.

Emmer, E. T., & Everton, C. M. (2008). *Classroom management for middle and high school teachers.* Boston: Allyn & Bacon.

Erkolahti, R., & Ilonen, T. (2005). Academic achievement and the self-image of adolescents with diabetes mellitus type-1 and rheumatoid arthritis. *Journal of Youth and Adolescence, 34,* 199–205.

Evans, D. D., & Strong, C. J. (1996). What's the story? Attending, listening, telling in middle school. *Teaching Exceptional Children, 28*(3), 58–61.

Everston, C. M., & Emmer, E. T. (2008). *Classroom management for elementary teachers.* Boston: Allyn & Bacon.

Fagella-Luby, M., Schumaker, J. S., & Deshler, D. D. (2007). Embedded learning strategy instruction: Story-structure pedagogy in heterogeneous secondary literature classes. *Learning Disability Quarterly, 30*(2), 131–147.

Faggella-Luby, M. N., & Deshler, D. D. (2008). Reading comprehension in adolescents with LD: What we know; what we need to learn. *Learning Disabilities Research & Practice, 23*(2), 70–78.

Faltis, C. J. (2007). *Joinfostering: Teaching and learning in multi culture education.* Oxford, UK: Pearson.

Farenga, S., & Joyce, B. (2000). Preparing for parents' questions. *Science Scope, 23*(6), 12–14.

Fetters, M., Pickard, D. M., & Pyle, E. (2003). Making science accessible: Strategies to meet the needs of a diverse student population. *Science Scope, 26*(5), 26–29.

Fenstermacher, K., Olympia, D., & Sheridan, S. M. (2006). Effectiveness of a computer-facilitated interactive social skills training program for boys with attention deficit hyperactivity disorder. *School Psychology Quarterly, 21*(2), 197–224.

Fiese, B. H., Everhart, R. S., & Wildenger, L. (2009). Wheezing, sleeping, and worrying: The hidden risks of asthma and obesity in school-age children. *Psychology in the Schools, 46*(8), 728–738.

Fine, E. S., Lacey, A., & Baer, J. (1995). *Children as peacemakers.* Portsmouth, NH: Heineman.

Flanagain, W. C. (2007). *A survey: The negative aspects of in and out of school suspensions and alternatives that promote academic achievement.* (ERIC Document Reproduction Service No. ED 499538).

Fletcher, J.M., Lyon, G.R., Fuchs, L.S., & Barnes, M.A. (2007). *Learning disabilities: From identification to intervention.* New York: Guilford Press.

Forbes, J. (2008). Knowledge transformations: Examining the knowledge needed in teacher and speech and language therapist co-work. *Educational Review, 60*(2), 141–154.

Forness, S. R., Swanson, J. M., Cantwell, D. P., Guthrie, D., & Sena, R. (1992). Response to stimulant medication across six measures of school-related performance in children with ADHD and disruptive behavior. *Behavioral Disorders, 18,* 42–53.

Forster, E. M., & Holbrook, M. C. (2005). Implications of paraprofessional support for students with visual impairments. *RE:view: Rehabilitation Education for Blindness and Visual Impairment, 36,* 155–170.

Foster, J., & Matthews, D. (2006). *Troubling times: How parents and teachers can help children understand and confront adversity.* Retrieved from www.sengifted.org/articles_social/FosterMatthews_Troubling-Times.shtml.

Freeman, J. G., McPhail, J. C., & Berndt, J. A. (2002). Sixth graders' views of activities that do and do not help them learn. *Elementary School Journal, 102,* 335–347.

Friend, M., Bursuck, W., & Hutchinson, N.L. (1998). *Including exceptional students: A practical guide for classroom teachers, Canadian edition.* Scarborough, ON: Allyn & Bacon.

Frostad, P., & Pijl, S. J. (2007). Does being friendly help in making friends? The relation between the social position and social skills of pupils with special needs in mainstream education. *European Journal of Special Needs Education, 22,* 15–30.

Fuchs, D., & Fuchs, L. S. (2005). Peer-assisted learning strategies: Promoting word recognition, fluency, sand reading comprehension in young children. *Journal of Special Education, 39,* 34–44.

Fuchs, L.S., & Fuchs, D. (2007). A model for implementing responsiveness to intervention. *Teaching Exceptional Children, 39*(5), 14–20.

Fullan, M. (2001). *The new meaning of educational change* (3rd ed.). New York: Teachers College Press.

Gable, R. A., Hendrickson, J. M, Tonelsom, S. W., & Acker, R. V. (2002). Integrating academic and non-academic instruction for students with emotional/behavioral disorders. *Education and Treatment of Children, 25,* 459–475.

Garnefski, N., Koopman, H., Kraaij, V., & ten Cate, R. (2009). Brief report: Cognitive emotion regulation strategies and psychological adjustment in adolescents with a chronic disease. *Journal of Adolescents, 32*(2), 449–454.

Garnett, K. (1992). Developing fluency with basic number facts: Intervention for studentswith learning disabilities. *Learning Disabilities: Research and Practice, 7,* 210–216.

Gay, A. S., & White, S. H. (2002). Teaching vocabulary to communicate mathematically. *Middle School Journal, 34*(2), 33–38.

Gayle, B.M., Allen, M., Preiss, R.W., & Burrell, N. (2006). *Classroom communication and instructional processes: Advances through meta-analysis*. Mahwah, NJ: Lawrence Erlbaum.

Geary, D. C., Harmson, C. O., & Hoard, M. K. (2000). Numerical and arithmetical cognition: A longitudinal study of processing and concept deficits in children with learning disability. *Journal of Experimental Child Psychology, 77*, 236–263.

Geddes, K. A. (2010). Using tiered assignments to engage learners in advanced placement physics. *Gifted Child Today, 33*(1), 32–40.

Gentry, M., Peters, S.J., & Mann, R.L. (2007). Differences between general and talented students' perceptions of their career and technical education experiences compared to their traditional high school experiences. *Journal of Advanced Academics, 18*(3), 372–401.

Giangreco, M. F., Smith, C.S., & Pinckney, E. (2006). Addressing the paraprofessional dilemma in an inclusive school: A program description. *Research and Practice for Persons with Severe Disabilities, 31*, 215–229.

Gibbs, J. (2001). *Tribes: A new way of learning and being together*. Windsor, CA: CenterSource Systems.

Gibbs, J. (2006). *Reaching all by creating tribes learning communities*. Windsor, CA: Center Source.

Gill, V. (2007). *The ten students you'll meet in your classroom: Classroom management tips for middle and high school teachers*. Thousand Oaks, CA: Corwin Press.

Gillies, R.M., Ashman, A., & Terwel, J. (Eds.). (2007). *The teacher's role in implementing cooperative learning in the classroom*. New York: Springer.

Ginsburg-Block, M. D., Rohrbeck, C. A., & Fantuzzo, J. W. (2006). A meta-analytic review of social, self-concept, and behavioral outcomes of peer-assisted learning. *Journal of Educational Psychology, 98*, 732–749.

Glor-Scheib, S., & Telthorster, H. (2006). Activate your student IEP team member using technology: How electronic portfolios can bring the student voice to life. *Teaching Exceptional Children Plus, 2*(3), Article 1.

Goddard, K. (2009). *Social skill training interventions for students with Asperger syndrome*. Unpublished master's project, Queen's University, Kingston, Ontario, Canada.

Gold, Y. & Roth, R. A. (1993). *Teachers managing stress and preventing burnout: The professional health solution*. London: Falmer.

Gomes & Smith (2007, March/April). Responding to school health crises. *Leadership*, 28–29, 46.

Good, T., & Brophy, J. (2002). *Looking in classrooms* (9th ed.). New York: Harper & Row.

Goodman, A. (2008). Student-led, teacher-supported conference: Improving communication across an urban school district. *Middle School Journal, 39*(3), 48–54.

Goodwin, A. K., & King, S. H. (2002). *Culturally responsive parental involvement*. New York: AACTE Publications.

Government of Canada. (1982). *The Charter of Rights and Freedoms*. Ottawa: Minister of Supply and Services. Retrieved from www.efc.ca/pages/law/charter/charter.text.html.

Government of Ontario. (1990). *Education Act*. Toronto: Queen's Printer for Ontario. Retrieved from www.e-laws.gov.on.ca/html/statutes/english/elaws_statutes_90e02_e.htm.

Government of Ontario. (2001). *Ontarians with Disabilities Act*. Toronto: Queen's Printer for Ontario. Retrieved from www.e-laws.gov.on.ca/html/statutes/english/elaws_statutes_01o32_e.htm.

Government of Ontario. (2005). *Accessibility for Ontarians with Disabilities Act*. Toronto: Queen's Printer for Ontario. Retrieved from www.search.e-laws.gov.on.ca/en/isysquery/1bf6c383-9f0c-4445-8f9f-3fdc35deb06f/1/doc/?search=browseStatutes&context=#hit1.

Graham-Day, K.J., Gardner, R., & Hsin, Y-W. (2010). Increasing on-task behaviors of high school students with attention deficit hyper-activity disorder: Is it enough? *Education and Treatment of Children, 33*(3), 205–221.

Gratch, A. (1998). *Growing teaching professionals: Lessons taught by first year teachers*. Paper presented at the annual conference on Qualitative Research in Education, Athens, GA.

Graves, M. F., & Braaten, S. (1996). Scaffolded reading experiences: Bridges to success. *Preventing School Failure, 40*, 169–173.

Gray, C., (2002). *My social story book*. London: Jessica Kingsley Publishers.

Grayson, J.L., & Alvarez, H.K. (2008). School climate factors relating to teacher burnout: A mediator model. *Teaching and Teacher Education, 24*(5), 1349–1363.

Gregoire, M. A., & Lupinetti, J. (2005). Support diversity through the arts. *Kappa Delta Pi Record, 41*(4), 159–163.

Gregory, G. H., & Kuzmich, L. (2004). *Data driven differentiation in the standards-based classroom*. Thousand Oaks, CA: Corwin Press.

Grenawalt, V. (2004). Going beyond the debate: Using technology and instruction for a balanced reading program. *Teacher Librarian, 32*(2), 12–16.

Gresham, F. M. (2002). Teaching social skills to high risk children and youth: Preventive and remedial strategies. In M.R. Schinn, H. M. Walker, & G. Stoner (Eds.), *Interventions for academic and behavior problems II: Preventative and remedial approaches* (2nd ed., pp. 403–432). Washington, DC: National Association of School Psychologists.

Griffin, S., & Case, R. (1997). Re-thinking the primary school math curriculum: An approach based on cognitive science. *Issues in Education, 3*, 1–49.

Groom, B., & Rose, R. (2005). Supporting the inclusion of pupils with social, emotional and behavioural difficulties in the primary school: The role of teaching assistants. *Journal of Research in Special Education Needs, 5*, 20–30.

Gross, M. U. M. (2006). Exceptionally gifted children: Long-term outcomes of academic acceleration and non-acceleration. *Journal for the Education of the Gifted, 29*, 404–429.

Grskovic, J. A., Hall, A. M., Montgomery, D. J., Vargas, A. U., Zentall, S. S., & Belfiore, P. J. (2004). Reducing time-out assignments for students with emotional/behavioral disorders in a self-contained classroom. *Journal of Behavioral Education, 13*, 25–36.

Guay, D. M. (1993). Cross-site analysis of teaching practices: Visual art education with students experiencing disabilities. *Studies in Art Education, 34*, 233–243.

Haager, D., & Klingner, J. (2005). *Differentiating instruction in inclusive classrooms: The special educator's guide*. Boston: Pearson Education.

Hadjioannou, X. (2007). Bringing the background to the foreground: What do classroom environments that support authentic discussion look like? *American Educational Research Journal, 44*, 370–399.

Hall, L. J., & McGregor, J. A. (2000). A follow-up study of the peer relationships of children with disabilities in an inclusive school. *Journal of Special Education, 34*, 114–126.

Hall, L. J., & Strickett, T. (2002). Peer relationships of pre-adolescent students with disabilities who attend a separate school. *Mental Retardation and Developmental Disabilities, 37*, 399–409.

Hamm, J. V., & Faircloth. B. S. (2005). The role of friendship in adolescents' sense of school belonging. In N. Way & J. V. Hamm (Eds.), The experience of close friendships in adolescence. *New Directions for Child and Adolescent Development, 107* (pp. 61–78). San Francisco: Jossey-Bass.

Hannah, C. L., & Shore, B. M. (2008). Twice-exceptional students' use of metacognitive skills on a comprehension monitoring task. *Gifted Child Quarterly, 52*(1), 3–18.

Hanvey, L. (2003). *Social inclusion research in Canada: Children and youth.* Ottawa, ON: Canadian Council on Social Development. Retrieved from www.ccsd.ca/events/inclusion/papers/hanvey.pdf.

Hargreaves, A. (2004). Inclusive and exclusive educational change: Emotional responses of teachers and implications for leadership. *School Leadership and Management, 24,* 287–309.

Hargrove, K. (2005). What makes a "good" teacher "great" in the classroom? *Gifted Child Today, 28*(1), 30–31.

Haring, T. G. (1991). Social relationships. In L. H. Meyer, C. A. Peck, & L. Brown (Eds.), *Critical issues in the lives of people with severe disabilities* (pp. 195–217). Baltimore: Paul H. Brookes.

Harper, M., O'Connor, K., & Simpson, M. (1999). *Quality assessment: Fitting the pieces together.* Toronto: Ontario Secondary School Teachers Federation.

Harter, S. (2006). Where do we go from here? In M. H. Kernis (Ed.), *Self-esteem issues and answers: A sourcebook of current perspectives* (pp. 430–438). New York: Psychology Press.

Hartmann, T. (1995). *ADD success stories: A guide to fulfillment for families with attention deficit disorder.* Grass Valley, CA: Underwood Books.

Hartsell, B. (2006). Teaching toward compassion: Environmental values education for secondary students. *Journal of Secondary Gifted Education, 17,* 265–271.

Hartup, W.W. (1993). Adolescents and their friends. In B. Laursen (Ed.). *Close friendships in adolescence* (Vol. 60, pp.3–22). San Francisco: Jossey-Bass.

Hartup, W.W. (2006). Relationships in early and middle childhood. In A.L. Vangelisti & D. Perlman (Eds.), *The Cambridge handbook of personal relationships* (pp. 177–190). New York: Cambridge University Press.

Hartup, W.W., Daiute, C., Zajac, R., & Sholl, W. (1995). *Collaboration in creative writing by friends and nonfriends.* Unpublished manuscript, Harvard University.

Harwood, J. (2006). You can't be in my choir if you can't stand up: One journey towards inclusion. *Music Education Research, 8*(3), 407–416.

Hawley, C. A. (2004). Behaviour and school performance after brain injury. *Brain Injury, 18,* 645–659.

Heacox, D. (2002). *Differentiating instruction in the regular classroom: How to reach and teach all learners, grades 3–12.* Minneapolis, MN: Free Spirit Publishing.

Heller, K. W., Mezei, P. J., & Avant, M. J. T. (2009). Meeting the assistive technology needs of students with Duchenne Muscular Dystrophy. *Journal of Special Education Technology, 23*(4). Retrieved from www.tamced.org/jset-index/meeting-the-assistive-technology-needs-of-students-with-duchenne-muscular-systrophy.

Henley, M. (2006). *Classroom management: A proactive approach.* Upper Saddle River, NJ: Pearson Merrill Prentice Hall.

Herrenkohl, L. R. (2006). Intellectual role taking: Supporting discussion in heterogeneous elementary science classes. *Theory into Practice, 45*(1), 47–54.

Heydon, R., Hibbert, K., & Iannacci, L. (2004/2005). Strategies to support balanced literacy approaches in pre- and inservice teacher education. *Journal of Adolescent and Adult Literacy, 48*(4), 312–319.

Hiebert, B. (1985). *Stress and teachers: The Canadian scene.* Toronto: Canadian Education Association.

Hieneman, M., Dunlap, G., & Kincaid, D. (2005). Positive support strategies for students with behavioral disorders in general education settings. *Psychology in the Schools, 42,* 779–794.

Hinton, V.J., De Vivo, D.C., Fee, R., Goldstein, E., & Stern, Y. (2004). Investigation of poor academic achievement in children with Duchenne muscular dystrophy. *Learning Disabilities Research and Practice, 19,* 146–154.

Hogan, B., & Forsten, C. (2007). *8-step model drawing: Singapore's best problem-solving math strategies.* Peterborough, NH: Crystal Springs Books.

Hong, B., & Ehrensberger, W. (2007). Assessing the mathematical skills of students with disabilities. *Preventing School Failure, 52*(1), 41–47.

Hong, E., Greene, M.T., & Higgins, K. (2006). Instructional practices of teachers in general education and gifted resource rooms. *Gifted Child Quarterly, 50*(2), 91–103.

Howard, B., Cohn, E., & Orsmond, G.I. (2006). Understanding and negotiating friendships: Perspectives from an adolescent with Asperger syndrome. *Autism, 10,* 619–627.

Hoza, B. et al. (2005). What aspects of peer relationships are impaired in children with attention-deficit/hyperactivity disorder? *Journal of Consulting and Clinical Psychology, 73*(3), 411–423.

Hume, K. (2008). *Start where they are: Differentiating for success with the young adolescent.* Toronto: Pearson Education Canada.

Hurlington, K. (2010). *Bolstering resilience in students: Teachers as protective factors* (Research Monograph 25). Toronto, ON: The Literacy and Numeracy Secretariat, Ontario Ministry of Education.

Hutchinson, N.L. (1993). Effects of cognitive strategy instruction on algebra problem solving of adolescents with learning disabilities. *Learning Disability Quarterly, 16,* 34–63.

Hutchinson, N.L. (1997). Creating an inclusive classroom with young adolescents in an urban school. *Exceptionality Education Canada, 6*(3&4), 51–67.

Hutchinson, N.L. (2007). *Inclusion of exceptional learners in Canadian schools: A practical handbook for teachers* (2nd ed.). Toronto: Pearson Prentice Hall.

Hutchinson, N.L., & Freeman, J.G. (1994). *Pathways.* Scarborough, ON: ITP Nelson Canada.

Hutchinson, N.L., Freeman, J.G., & Berg, D.H. (2004). Social competence of adolescents with learning disabilities: Interventions and issues. In B. Y. L. Wong (Ed.), *Learning about learning disabilities* (pp. 415–448, 3rd ed.). New York: Academic Press.

Hutchinson, N. L., Freeman, J. G., & Quick, V. E. (1996). Group counseling intervention for solving problems on the job. *Journal of Employment Counseling, 33*(1), 2–19.

Hutchinson, N.L., Freeman, J.G., & Steiner Bell, K. (2002). Children and adolescents with learning disabilities: Case studies of social relations in inclusive classrooms. In B.Y.L. Wong & M. Donahue (Eds.), *The social dimensions of learning disabilities* (pp. 189–214). Mahwah, NJ: Lawrence Erlbaum Associates.

Hutchinson, N.L., Versnel, J., Chin, P., & Munby, H. (2008). Negotiating accommodations so that work-based education facilitates career development for youth with disabilities. *Work: A Journal of Prevention, Assessment & Rehabilitation, 30,* 123–136.

Hutzal, C. E., Wright, F. V., Stephens, S., Schneiderman-Walker, J., & Feldman, B. M. (2009). *Physical & Occupational Therapy in Pediatrics, 26*(4), 409–425.

Irish, C. (2002). Using peg- and keyword mnemonics and computer-assisted instruction to enhance basic multiplication performance in elementary students with learning and cognitive disabilities. *Journal of Special Education Technology, 17,* 29–40.

Jacobs, D. (2003). *Shifting attention from "discipline problems" to "virtue awareness" in Amerian Indian and Alaska Native education.* ERIC Digest (ERIC Document Reproduction Service No. ED 480732).

Janssen, M.J., Riksen-Walreven, J.M., VanDijk, J.P.M., Ruijssenaars, W., & Vlaskamp, C. (2007). Team interaction coaching with educators of adolescents who are deaf-blind: Applying the diagnostic intervention model. *Journal of Visual Impairment and Blindness, 101,* 677–689.

Janus, M., Lefort, J., Cameron, R., & Kopechanski, L. (2007). Starting kindergarten: Transition issues for children with special needs. *Canadian Journal of Education, 30,* 628–647.

Jenkins, J.C., Antil, L.R., Wayne, S.R., & Vadasy, P.F. (2003). How cooperative learning works for special education and remedial students. *Exceptional Children, 69,* 279–292.

Jenkinson, J., Hyde, T., & Ahmad, S. (2002). *Occupational therapy approaches for secondary special needs: Practical classroom strategies.* Independence, KY: Taylor & Francis.

Jeynes, W. H. (2007). The relationship between parental involvement and urban secondary school student academic achievement. *Urban Education, 42,* 82–110.

Joffe, V. L., Cain, K., & Maric, N. (2007). Comprehension problems in children with specific language impairment: Does mental imagery training help? *International Journal of Language and Communication Disorders, 42,* 648–664.

Johnson, C. J., Beitchman, J. H., & Brownite, E. B. (2010). Twenty-year follow-up of children with and without speech-language impairments: Family, educational, occupational, and quality of life outcomes. *American Journal of Speech-Language Pathology, 10*(1), 51–65.

Johnson, D. W., & Johnson, R. T. (2004). *Assessing students in groups: Promoting group responsibility and individual accountability.* Thousand Oaks, CA: Corwin Press.

Johnston, T., & Kirby, J. R. (2006). The contribution of naming speed to the simple view of reading. *Reading and Writing: An interdisciplinary Journal, 19*(4), 339–361.

Jones, J., & Leahy, S. (2006). Developing strategic readers. *Science and Children, 44*(3), 30–34.

Jones, M. G., Minogue, J., Oppewal, T., Cook, M.P., & Broadwell, B. (2006). Visualizing without vision at the microscale: Students with visual impairments explore cells with touch. *Journal of Science Education and Technology, 15,* 345–351.

Jordan, A., & Stanovich, P. (1998). *Exemplary teaching in inclusive classrooms.* Paper presented at the annual meeting of the American Educational Research Association, San Diego, CA.

Jordan, A., & Stanovich, P. (2004). The beliefs and practices of Canadian teachers about including students with special education needs in their regular elementary classrooms. *Exceptionality Education Canada, 14*(2&3), 25–46.

Jordan, N. C., Kaplan, D., Locuniak, M.N., & Ramineni, C. (2007). Predicting first-grade math achievement from developmental number sense trajectories. *Learning Disabilities Research and Practice, 22,* 36–46.

Jung, L. A. & Guskey, T. R. (2007).Standards-based grading and reporting: A model for special education. *Teaching Exceptional Children, 40*(2), 48–53.

Kamps, D., Kravits, T., Rauch, J., Kamps, J. L., & Chung, N. (2000). A prevention program for students with or at risk for ED: Moderating effects of variation in treatment and classroom structure. *Journal of Emotional and Behavioral Disorders, 8*(3), 141–154.

Kanevsky, L., & McGrimmond, L. (2008, June). *A survey of acceleration practices in Canada.* Paper presented at the annual meeting of the Canadian Society for the Study of Education, Vancouver, BC.

Kaplan, S.N. (2008). Curriculum consequence: If you learn this, then . . . *Gifted Child Today, 31,* 41–42.

Katzir, T., Young-Suk, K., Wolf, M., Morris., R., & Lovett, M. (2008). The varieties of pathways to dysfluent reading. *Journal of Learning Disabilities, 41*(1), 47–66.

Kern, L., Bambara, L., & Fogt, J. (2002). Class-wide curricular modification to improve the behaviour of students with emotional or behavioral disorders. *Behavioral Disorders, 27,* 317–326.

Kidder, R. M. (2009). Why don't you tell the teacher? *Education Canada, 49*(1), 35.

King, A. J. C., & Peart, M. J. (1990) *The good school: Strategies for making secondary schools effective.* Toronto: Education Services Committee (Research), Ontario Secondary School Teachers' Federation.

King, A.J.C., & Peart, M. (1992). *Teachers in Canada: Their work and quality of life.* Kingston, ON: Canadian Teachers' Federation and Queen's University Social Program Evaluation Group.

King, A.J.C., Warren, W., & Peart, M. (1988). *The teaching experience.* Toronto: Ontario Secondary School Teachers' Federation.

King-Sears, M.E. (2008). Facts and fallacies: Differentiation and the general education curriculum for students with special education needs. *Support for Learning, 23*(2), 55–62.

Klassen, R. (2007). Using predictions to learn about the self-efficacy of early adolescents with and without learning disabilities. *Contemporary Educational Psychology, 32*(2), 173–187.

Klassen, R., & Lynch, S. L. (2007). Self-efficacy from the perspective of adolescents with LD and their specialist teachers. *Journal of Learning Disabilities, 40*(6), 494–507.

Kleinert, H. L., Haig, J., Kearns, J. F., & Kennedy, S. (2000). Alternate assessments: Lessons learned and roads to be taken. *Exceptional Children, 67,* 51–66.

Klinger, D. A., DeLuca, C., & Miller, T. (2008). The evolving culture of large-scale assessments in Canadian education. *Canadian Journal of Educational Administration and Policy, 76.* Retrieved on April 12, 2008, from https://www.umanitoba.ca/publications/cjeap/articles/klinger.html.

Klingner, J. K., & Vaughn, S. (1998). Using collaborative strategic reading. *Teaching Exceptional Children, 30,* 32–37.

Kluth, P. (2000). Community-referenced learning and the inclusive classroom. *Remedial and Special Education, 21,* 19–26.

Kluth, P. (2004). Autism, autobiography, and adaptations. *Teaching Exceptional Children, 36*(4), 42–47.

Koellner, K., & Wallace, F. (2007). Alternative uses for junk mail: How environmental print supports mathematics literacy. *Mathematics Teaching in the Middle School, 12,* 326–332.

Kondor, C. A. H. (2007). *One size may not fit all, but the right teaching strategies might: The effects of differentiated instruction on the motivation of talented and gifted students.* (Online submission, Eric Reproduction Service ED497701).

Koscik, R. L., et al. (2004). Cognitive function of children with cystic fibrosis: Deleterious effect of early malnutrition. *Pediatrics, 113,* 1549–1558.

Kosky, C., & Curtis, R. (2008). An action research exploration integrating student choice and arts activities in a sixth grade social studies classroom. *Journal of Social Studies Research, 32*(1), 22–27.

Kouzes, J. M., & Posner, B. Z. (2007). *The leadership challenge* (4th ed.). San Francisco: Jossey-Bass.

Kramer, T. J., Caldarella, P., Christensen, L., & Shatzer, R. H. (2010). Social and emotional learning in the kindergarten classroom: Evaluation of the *Strong Start* curriculum. *Early Childhood Education Journal, 37,* 303–309.

Krogness, M. M. (1995). *Just teach me, Mrs. K.: Talking, reading, and writing with resistant adolescent learners.* Portsmouth, NH: Heinemann.

Kutnick, P., & Kington, A. (2005). Children's friendships and learning in school: Cognitive enhancement through social interaction? *British Journal of Educational Psychology, 75,* 521–538.

Kutnick, P., Ota, C., & Berdondini, L. (2008). Improving the effects of group working in classrooms with young school-aged children: Facilitating attainment, interaction and classroom activity. *Learning and Instruction, 18*, 83–95.

Ladd, H. F., & Zelli, A. (2002). School-based accountability in North Carolina. *Educational Administration Quarterly, 38*(4), 494–529.

Ladd, H. F., & Zelli, A. (2003). School-based accountability in North Carolina: The responses of school principals. *Educational Administration Quarterly, 38*, 494–529.

Lahey, B. B., Pelham, W. E., Loney, J., Lee, S. S., & Willcutt, E. (2005). Instability of the DSM-IV subtypes of ADHD from preschool through elementary school. *Archives of General Psychiatry, 62*(8), 896–902.

Laidlaw Foundation. (2002). *Working paper series on social inclusion.* Toronto, ON. Retrieved from www.laidlawfdn.org/working-paper-series-social-inclusion.

Lambdin, D. V., & Forseth, C. (1996). Seamless assessment/instruction = good teaching. *Teaching Children Mathematics, 2*(1), 294–298.

Langer, E.C. (2007). *Classroom discourse and interpreted education: What is conveyed to deaf elementary school students.* Unpublished doctoral dissertation, University of Colorado at Boulder.

Larivee, B. (2006). *Authentic classroom management: Creating a learning community and building reflective practice* (2nd ed.). Boston: Pearson Allyn & Bacon.

Lawson, J. (2008). Women leaders in high-poverty community schools: Work-related stress and family impact. *Canadian Journal of Education, 31*(1), 55–77.

Learning Disability Association of Canada. (2002). *Official definition of learning disabilities: Adopted by the Learning Disabilities Association of Canada January 30, 2002.* Retrieved from www.ldac-acta.ca/learn-more/ld-defined/official-definition-of-learning-disabilities.

Learning Disabilities Association of Ontario. (n.d.). *The Web Based Teaching Tool (WBTT) Early Screening and Intervention Program.* Retrieved from www.ldaho.ca/WBTT/index.php.

Learning Disability Association of Ontario (2001). *Definitions of LDs.* Retrieved July 20, 2010, from www.ldao.ca/aboutLDs/Definitions_of_LDs.php.

Lee, H-J., & Herner-Patnode, L. M. (2007). Teaching mathematics vocabulary to diverse groups. *Intervention in School & Clinic, 43*(2), 121–126.

Lennon, G. (1995, March/April). Inclusion: Adapting the curriculum. *FWTAO Newsletter,* 22–26.

Lepofsky, M.D. (1997). A report card on the *Charter's* guarantee of equality to persons with disabilities after 10 years-what progress? What prospects? *National Journal of Constitutional Law, 7,* 263–331.

Lesaux, N. K., Pearson, M. R., & Siegel, L. S. (2006). The effects of timed and untimed teting conditions on the reading comprehension performance of adults with reading disabilities. *Reading and Writing, 19*(1), 21–48.

Levac, M. (2004). How exemplary dyads describe their practice of collaborative consultation: An interview study. *Exceptionality Education Canada, 14*(2&3), 115–140.

Lévesque, N. L. (1997). Perceptions of friendships and peer groups: The school experiences of two adolescents with learning disabilities. Unpublished master's thesis, Queen's University, Kingston, ON.

Levin, D. E. (2004). *Teaching young children in violent times: Building a peaceable classroom.* Cambridge, MA: Educators for Social Responsibility.

Levin, B., & Fullan, M. (2008). Learning about system renewal. *Educational Management Administration and Leadership, 36*(2), 289–303.

Levine, T. H., & Marcus, A. S. (2010). How the structure and focus of teachers' collaborative activities facilitate and constrain teacher learning. *Teaching and Teacher Education: An International Journal of Research and Studies, 26*(3), 389–398.

Lewis, B. A., Freebairn, L. A., & Taylor, H. G. (2000). Follow-up of children with early expressive phonology disorders. *Journal of Learning Disabilities, 33,* 433–444.

Lewis, R., & Burman, E. (2006). Providing for student voice in classroom management: Teachers' views. *International Journal of Inclusive Education, 1,* 1–17.

Lim, J., Wood, B. L., & Cheah, P. (2009). Understanding children with asthma: Trouble and triggers. *Childhood Education, 85*(5), 307–312.

Lindberg, J.A., & Swick, A.M. (2006). *Common-sense management for elementary school teachers* (2nd ed.). Thousand Oaks, CA: Corwin Press.

Lipman, E. (2003). Andy versus cystic fibrosis. *Exceptional Parent, 33*(11), 3–31.

Lizzio, A., Wilson, K., & Hadaway, V. (2007). University students' perceptions of a fair learning environment: a social justice perspective. *Assessment & Evaluation in Higher Education, 32* (2), 195–213.

Lloyd, S., Wernham, S., Jolly, C., & Stephen, L. (1998). *Jolly phonics.* Chigwell, UK: Jolly Learning.

Long, L., MacBlain, S., & MacBlain, M. (2008). Supporting students with dyslexia at the secondary level: An emotional model of literacy. *Journal of Adolescent and Adult Literacy, 51*(2), 124–134.

Lord, J., & Hutchison, P. (2007). *Pathways to inclusion: Building a new story with people and communities.* Concord, ON: Captus Press.

Lorence, D., & Chen, Li. (2007). A study of peer-to-peer information in a domain of uncertainty: The case of epilepsy. *Health Informatics Journal, 13,* 303–316.

Lovett, S., & Gilmore, A. (2003). Teachers' learning journeys: The quality learning circle as a model of professional development. *School Effectiveness and School Improvement, 14,* 189–211.

Luciano, S., & Savage, R. S. (2007). Bullying risk in children with learning difficulties in inclusive educational settings. *Canadian Journal of School Psychology, 22,* 14–31.

Lupart, J. L., & Wilgosh, L. (1998). Undoing underachievement and promoting societal advancement for women and girls. *Gifted Education International, 13,* 159–169.

Lutz, S. L., Guthrie, J. T., & Davis, M. H. (2006).Scaffolding for engagement in elementary school reading instruction. *Journal of Educational Research, 100,* 3–20.

MacCuspie, P. A. (1996). *Promoting acceptance of children with disabilities: From tolerance to inclusion.* Halifax: Atlantic Provinces Special Education Authority.

MacKay, W. (2007). *Inclusive education: A review of programming and services in New Brunswick* (Connecting care and challenge: Tapping our human potential). Fredericton, NB: NB Department of Education.

Madden, M., & Sullivan, J. (2008). *Teaching fluency beyond the primary grades: Strategy lessons to meet the specific needs of upper-grade readers.* New York: Scholastic, Inc.

Maker, C. J. & Nielson, A. B. (1996). *Curriculum development and teaching strategies for gifted learners* (2nd ed.) (Report: ED401676). Austin, TX: PRO-ED.

Mandall, S. L., & Gordon, T. A. (2009). Management of Type 1 diabetes in schools: Whose responsibility?. *Journal of School Health 79*(12), 599–601.

Marshall, M. (2005). Discipline without stress, punishments, or rewards. *The Clearing House, 79*(1), 51–54.

Martin, J., Sugarman, J., & McNamara, J. (2001). *Models of classroom management: Principles, applications and critical perspectives* (3rd ed.). Calgary: Detselig Enterprises.

Martini, R., & Shore, B. M. (2008). Pointing to parallels in ability-related differences in the use of metacognition in academic and psychomotor tasks. *Learning and Individual Differences, 18*(2), 237–247.

Mascolo, M. F., Kanner, B. G., & Griffin, S. (1998). Neo-Piagetian systems theory and the education of young children. *Early Child Development and Care, 140,* 31–52.

Masden C. A. (2005). *Social-perspective coordination in gifted early adolescent friendship.* Unpublished doctoral dissertation, McGill University, Quebec, Canada.

Mason, K. L. (2008). Cyberbullying: A preliminary assessment for school personnel. *Psychology in the Schools, 45,* 323–348.

Maté, G. (2000). *Scattered minds: A new look at the origins and healing of attention deficit disorder.* Toronto: Knopf Canada.

Matthews, D. J., & Steinhauer, N. (1998). Giftedness, girls, others, and equity: Theory-based practical strategies for the regular classroom. *Exceptionality Education Canada, 8*(2), 41–56.

Matthews, D. J., Foster, J., Gladstone, D., Schieck, J., & Meiners, J. (2007). Supporting professionalism, diversity, and context within a collaborative approach to gifted education. *Journal of Educational & Psychological Consultation, 17*(4), 315–345.

Mayer, K., & Kelley, M. L. (2007). Improving homework in adolescents with attention-deficit/hyperactivity disorder: Self vs. parent monitoring of homework behavior and study skills. *Child and Family Behavior Therapy, 39*(4), 25–42.

McAllister, R., & Gray, C. (2007). Low vision: Mobility and independence training for the early years child. *Early Child Development and Care 177*(8), 839–852.

McCaleb, S. P. (1995). *Building communities of learners: Collaboration among teachers, students, families, and community.* Mahwah, NJ: Lawrence Erlbaum.

McCord, K., & Fitzgerald, M. (2006). Children with disabilities playing musical instruments: With the right adaptations and help from teachers and parents, students with disabilities can play musical instruments. *Music Educators Journal, 92*(4), 46–52.

McCord, K., & Watts, M. H. (2006). Collaboration and access for our children: Music educators and special educators together: When music educators and special educators work together, all students are likely to benefit. *Music Educators Journal, 92*(4), 26–31.

McCormick Richburg, C., & Goldberg L. R. (2005). Teachers' perceptions about minimal hearing loss: A role for educational audiologist. *Communication Disorders Quarterly, 27*(4), 4–19.

McDougall, J., DeWit, D. J., King, G., Miller, L., & Killip, S. (2004). High school-aged youths' attitudes toward their peers with disabilities: The role of school and student interpersonal factors. *International Journal of Disability, Development and Education, 51,* 287–313.

McEwan, E. K. (2002). *10 traits of highly effective teachers.* Thousand Oaks, CA: Corwin Press.

McGhie,-Richmond, D., Underwood, K., & Jordan, A. (2007). Developing effective instructional strategies for teaching in inclusive classrooms. *Exceptionality Education Canada, 17*(1), 27–52.

McHugh, M. W. (2006). Governor's schools: Fostering the social and emotional well-being of gifted and talented students. *Journal of Secondary Gifted Education, 17*(3), 50–58.

McIntosh, R., & Vaughn, S. (1993). So you want to teach social skills to your students: Some pointers from the research. *Exceptionality Education Canada, 3*(1&2), 39–59.

McIntyre, E., Kyle, D. W., & Moore, G. H. (2006). A primary-grade teacher's guidance toward small group dialogue. *Reading Research Quarterly, 41*(1), 36–66.

McPhail, J. C., & Freeman, J. G. (2005). Beyond prejudice: Thinking toward genuine inclusion. *Learning Disabilities Research and Practice, 20,* 254–267.

McPhail, J. C., Pierson, J. M., Goodman, J., & Noffke, J. B. (2004). Creating partnerships for complex learning: The dynamics of an interest-based apprenticeship in the art of sculpture. *Curriculum Inquiry, 34,* 463–493.

McQueen, T. (1992). *Essentials of classroom management and discipline.* New York: HarperCollins.

Meenakshi, G., Jitendra, A. K., Sood, S., Sacks, G. (2007). Improving comprehension of expository text in students with LD: A research synthesis. *Journal of Learning Disabilities, 40,* 210–225.

Miedijensky, S., & Tal, T. (2009). Embedded assessment in project-based science courses for the gifted: Insights to inform teaching all students. *International Journal of Science Education, 31*(18), 2411–2435.

Miller, C., Leonard, L., & Finneran, D. (2008). Grammaticality judgments in adolescents with and without language impairment. *International Journal of Language and Communication Disorders, 43*(3), 346–360.

Mishna, F, Scarcello, I., Pepler, D., & Wiener, J. (2005). Teachers' understanding of bullying. *Canadian Journal of Education, 28,* 718–738.

Moss, L. J., & Grover, B. W. (2007). Not just for computation: Basic calculators can advance the process standards. *Mathematics Teaching in the Middle School, 12,* 266–271.

Monroe, B. W., & Troia, G. A. (2006). Teaching writing strategies to middle school students with disabilities. *Journal of Educational Research, 100,* 21–33.

Montague, M. (2008). Self-regulation strategies to improve mathematical problem solving for students with learning disabilities. *Learning Disability Quarterly, 31,* 37–44.

Montague, M., & Applegate, B. (2000). Middle school students' perceptions, persistence, and performance in mathematical problem solving. *Learning Disability Quarterly, 23*(3), 215–228.

Montague, M., Warger, C., & Morgan, T. M. (2000). Solve it! Strategy instruction to improve mathematics problem solving. *Learning Disabilities Research & Practice, 15,* 110–116.

Moon, T. R. (2005). The role of assessment in differentiation. *Theory Into Practice, 44,* 226–233.

Moore Johnson, S. M., & Kardos, S. M. (2008). The next generation of teachers: who enters, who stays, and why. In M. Cochran-Smith, S. Feiman-Nemser, & D. J. McIntryre (Eds.), *Handbook of research on teacher education* (3rd ed., pp. 445–467). New York: Routledge.

Moore Johnson, S., and the Project on the Next Generation of Teachers. (2004). *Finders and keepers: Helping new teachers survive and thrive in our schools.* San Francisco: Jossey-Bass.

Morgan, P. L., Farkas, G., Tufis, P. S., & Sperling, R. S. (2008). Are reading and behavioral problems risk factors for each other? *Journal of Learning Disabilities, 41*(5), 417–436.

Moss, L. J., & Grover, B. W. (2007). Not just for computation: Basic calculators can advance the process standards. *Mathematics Teaching in the Middle School, 12,* 266–271.

MTA Cooperative Group. (1999). A 14-month randomized clinical trial of treatment strategies for attention deficit/hyperactivity disorder. *Archives of General Psychiatry, 56,* 1073–1086.

Munk, D.D., & Bursuck, W.D. (2001). Preliminary findings on personalized grading plans for middle school students with learning disabilities. *Exceptional Children, 67,* 211–234.

Munk, D. D., & Bursuck, W. D. (2004). Personalized grading plans: A systematic approach to making the grades of included students more accurate and meaningful. *Focus on Exceptional Children, 36*(9), 1–12.

Muscular Dystrophy Canada. www.muscle.ca.

Myers, P. A. (2006). The princess storyteller, Clara clarifier, Quincey questioner, and the wizard: Reciprocal teaching adapted for kindergarten students. *Reading Teacher, 59*, 314–324.

Nachshen, J.S., Garcin, N., & Minnes, P. (2005). Problem behavior in children with intellectual disabilities: Parenting stress, empowerment and school services. *Mental Health Aspects of Developmental Disabilities, 8*, 105–114.

Nachshen, J. S., & Minnes, P. (2005). Empowerment in parents of school-aged children with and without developmental disabilities. *Journal of Intellectual Disability, 49*, 889–904.

Nagel, L., & Brown, S. (2003). The ABCs of managing teacher stress. *Clearing House, 76*(5), 255–258.

National Center for Education Statistics (NCES). (2007). *Indicators of school crime and safety*. Washington, DC: NCES. Retrieved from http://nces.ed.gov/programs/crimeindicators/crimeindicators2007.

National Reading Panel. (2000). Publications and materials. [www.nationalreadingpanel.org]. (November 15, 2008).

Nesbit, J.C., & Adesope, O.O. (2006). Learning with concept and knowledge maps: A meta-analysis. *Review of Educational Research, 76*(3), 413–448.

Nelson, B. W., Awad, D., Alexander, J., & Clark, N. (2009). The continuing problem of asthma in very young children: A community-based participatory research project. *Journal of School Health, 79*(5), 209–215.

Newfoundland and Labrador Department of Education. (2007). *Focusing on students: The Individual Support Services Plan (ISSP) & Pathways Commission Report*. St. John's: Government of Newfoundland. Retrieved from www.ed.gov.nl.ca/edu/publications/k12/Focusing_on_Students.pdf.

No Child Left Behind Act. (2001). Pub.L. 107–111, 115 Sttat. 1425 enacted January 8, 2002. Retrieved from www2.ed.gov/policy/elsec/leg/esea02/index.html.

Noddings, N. (1996). On community. *Educational Theory, 46*, 245–267.

Northfield. S., & Sherman, A. (2004). Acceptance and community building in schools through increased dialogue and discussion. *Children and Society, 18*, 291–298.

Norwich, B. (2008). Dilemmas of difference, inclusion and disability: International perspectives on placement. *European Journal of Special Needs Education, 23*(4), 387–304.

Nowacek, E.J., & Mamlin, N. (2007). General education teachers and students with ADHD: What modifications are made? *Preventing School Failure, 51*(3), 28–35.

Nyman McMaster, K., & Fuchs, D. (2002). Effects of cooperative learning on the academic achievement of students with learning disabilities: An update on Tateyama-Sniezek's review. *Learning Disabilities Research & Practice, 17*, 107–117.

Obenchain, K. M., & Abernathy, T. V. (2003). 20 ways to build community and empower students. *Intervention in School and Clinic, 39*(1), 55–60.

Olson, C. B., & Land, R. (2007). A cognitive strategies approach to reading and writing instruction for English language learners in secondary school. *Research in the Teaching of English, 41*, 269–303.

Olson, B. F., Teuber, S., & Bruhn, C. M. (2009).Development of an educational packet for persons with life-threatening food allergies. *Journal of Food Science Education, 8*(3), 73–77.

Olson, H. C., Jirikowic, T., Kartin, D., & Astley, S. (2007). Responding to the challenge of early intervention for fetal alcohol spectrum disorders. *Infants and Young Children, 20*, 172–189.

Olweus, D. (2003, March). A profile of bullying. *Educational Leadership*, 2–17.

Ontario Department of Education. (1968). *Living and learning: Report of the provincial committee on aims and objectives of education in the schools of Ontario* (The Hall-Dennis Report). Toronto: Ontario Department of Education.

Ontario Ministry of Community and Social Services. (2005). *Accessibility for Ontarians with Disabilities Act*. Retrieved from www.mcss.gov.on.ca/en/mcss/programs/accessibility/index.aspx.

Ontario Ministry of Education. Ontario Secondary School Literacy Course www.edu.gov.on.ca/extra/eng/ppm/127.html.

Ontario Ministry of Education. (1998). Ontario's Regulation 181/98. Retrieved from www.e-laws.gov.on.ca/html/regs/english/elaws_regs_980181_e.htm#BK9.

Ontario Ministry of Education. (2000a). *Individual education plans: Standards for development, program planning, and implementation*. Toronto: Ontario Ministry of Education. Retrieved from www.edu.gov.on.ca/eng/general/elemsec/speced/iep/iep.html.

Ontario Ministry of Education. (2000b). *Standards for school boards' special education plans*. Toronto: Queen's Printer for Ontario. Retrieved from www.edu.gov.on.ca/eng/general/elemsec/speced/iepstand/iepstand.pdf.

Ontario Ministry of Education. (2001). *Special education: A guide for educators*. Toronto: Ontario Ministry of Education. Retrieved from www.edu.gov.on.ca/eng/general/elemsec/speced/guide/specedhandbooke.pdf.

Ontario Ministry of Education. (2004). *The individual education plan (IEP): A resource guide*. Toronto: Ontario Ministry of Education. Retrieved from www.edu.gov.on.ca/eng/general/elemsec/speced/guide/resource/iepresguid.pdf.

Ontario Ministry of Education. (2004). *Leading math success, mathematical literacy Grades 7-12. (The report of the expert panel on student success in Ontario)*. Toronto: Queen's Printer for Ontario. Retrieved from www.edu.gov.on.ca/eng/document/reports/numeracy/numeracyreport.pdf.

Ontario Ministry of Education. (2005). *Education for All* (The report of the expert panel on literacy and numeracy instruction for students with special education needs, kindergarten to grade 6). Toronto: Queen's Printer for Ontario.

Ontario Ministry of Education. (2007). *First Nations, Métis, and Inuit education policy framework*. Toronto: Ontario Ministry of Education.

Ontario Ministry of Education. (2007). *Shared solutions: A Guide to preventing and resolving conflicts regarding programs and services for students with special education needs*. Toronto: Ontario Ministry of Education. Retrieved at: http://www.edu.gov.on.ca/eng/general/elemsec/speced/shared.html.

Ontario Ministry of Education. 2008. Ontario Provincial Report Card, Retrieved from www.edu.gov.on.ca/eng/document/forms/report/1998/report98.html.

Ontario Ministry of Education. (2008). *Finding common ground: Character development in Ontario schools K-12*. Toronto: Queen's Printer for Ontario. Retrieved from www.edu.gov.on.ca/eng/document/reports/literacy/booklet2008.pdf.

Ontario Ministry of Education. (2008). *Growing success: Assessment, evaluation and reporting in Ontario's schools, first edition covering grades*

*1 to 12*. Toronto: Ontario Ministry of Education. Retrieved at: http://www.edu.gov.on.ca/eng/policyfunding/success.html.

Ontario Ministry of Education. (2008). *Report of the Safe Schools Action Team: Shaping a culture of respect in our schools: Promoting safe and healthy relationships*. Toronto: Queen's Printer for Ontario. Retrieved from www.edu.gov.on.ca/eng/teachers/RespectCulture.pdf.

Ontario Ministry of Education. (2009). *Aboriginal perspectives, a guide to the Teacher's Toolkit: Teaching resources and strategies for elementary and secondary classrooms*. Toronto: Queen's Printer for Ontario. Retrieved from www.edu.gov.on.ca/eng/aboriginal/Guide_ Toolkit2009.pdf.

Ontario Ministry of Education. (2009). *Learning for All K-12* (Draft). Retrieved from www.ontariodirectors.ca/L4All/L4A_en_downloads/LearningforAll%20K-12%20draft%20J.pdf.

Ontario Ministry of Education. (2010). *Keeping our kids safe at school: Reporting and responding to incidents*. Toronto: Queen's Printer for Ontario. Retrieved from www.edu.gov.on.ca/eng/safeschools/KeepKidSafeSchool.pdf.

Ontario Ministry of Education. (2010). *Making Ontario's schools safer: What parents need to know*. Toronto: Queen's Printer for Ontario. Retrieved from www.edu.gov.on.ca/eng/safeschools/pdfs/safer-Schools.pdf.

Ontario Ministry of Education – Provincial Schools Branch: W. Ross Macdonald School. Retrieved August 8, 2010, from www.psbnet.ca/eng/schools/wross/index.html.

Ontario Royal Commission on Education. (1950). *Hope report*. Toronto: Ontario Department of Education.

Ontario Royal Commission on Learning. (1995). *For the love of learning*. Toronto, ON: Government of Ontario.

Ostad, S. A., & Sorensen, P. M. (2007). Private speech and strategy-use patterns: Bidirectional comparisons of children with and without mathematical difficulties in a developmental perspective. *Journal of learning Disabilities, 40*, 2–14.

Overholt, J. L.., Aaberg, N., & Lindsey, J. F. (2008). *Math stories for problem solving success: Ready-to-use activities based on real-life situations, grades 6-12*. San Francisco, CA: Jossey-Bass.

Owen, R. L., & Fuchs, L. S. (2002). Mathematical problem-solving strategy instruction for third-grade students with learning disabilities. *Remedial and Special Education, 23*, 268–278.

Palincsar, A. S., & Brown, A. (1984). Reciprocal teaching of comprehension-fostering and comprehension-monitoring activities. *Cognition and Instruction, 1*, 117–175.

Palincsar, A. S., & Herenkohl, L. R. (2002). Designing collaborative learning contexts. *Theory into Practice, 41*, 26–32.

Palisano, R. J., Shimmell, L. J., Stewart, D., Lawless, J. J., Rosenbaum, P. L., & Russell, D. J. (2009). Mobility experiences of adolescents with Cerebral Palsy. *Physical & Occupational Therapy in Pediatrics, 29*(2), 133–153.

Patterson, D. (1996). Becoming a change agent in your elementary classroom. In J. Andrews (Ed.), *Teaching students with diverse needs: Elementary classrooms* (pp. 14–37). Scarborough: Nelson Canada.

Paterson, D. (2007). Teachers' in-flight thinking in inclusive classrooms. *Journal of Learning Disabilities, 40*(5), 427–435.

Pedersen, K.S., & Kitano, M.K. (2006). Designing a multicultural literature unit for gifted learners. *Gifted Child Today, 29*(2), 38–49.

Pepler, D., Jiang, D., Craig, W., & Connolly, J. (2008). Developmental trajectories of bullying and associated factors. *Child Development, 79*(2), 325–338.

Peterborough Victoria Northumberland and Clarington Catholic District School Board. *Educational assistants resource guide*. Retrieved from www.pvnccdsb.on.ca.

Peterson, L. D., Young, K. R., Salzberg, C. L., West, R. P., & Hill, M. (2006). Using self-management procedures to improve classroom social skills in multiple general education settings. *Education and Treatment of Children, 29*, 1–21.

Pewewardy, C., & Hammer, P. C. (2003). Culturally responsive teaching for American Indian students. *ERIC Digest*. (ERIC Document Reproduction Service No. ED 482325).

Phelps, L. A. C. (2003). High schools and authentic and inclusive learning practices; Selected features and findings. *Research to Practice Brief*. (ERIC Document Reproduction Service No. ED 481547).

Philpott, D.F., & Dibbon, D. (2007). A review of the literature on Newfoundland and Labrador's model of Student Support Services: A global perspective on local practice. (Appendix G, Literature review). In *Focusing on students: A report of the ISSP & Pathways Commission* (pp. 177–219). St. John's: ISSP & Pathways Commission.

Pierangelo, R., & Giuliani, G. A. (2007). *Special education eligibility: A step-by-step guide for educators*. Thousand Oaks, CA: Corwin Press.

Piggott, A. (2002). Putting differentiation into practice in secondary science lessons. *School Science Review, 83* (305), 65–71.

Pilling, N., McGill, P., & Cooper, V. (2007). Characteristics and experiences of children and young people with severe intellectual disabilities and challenging behaviour attending 52-week residential special schools. *Journal of Intellectual Disability Research, 51*(3), 184–196.

Polloway, E. A., Bursuck, W. D., & Epstein, M. H. (2001). Homework for students with learning disabilities: The challenge of home-school communication. *Reading & Writing Quarterly, 17*, 181–187.

Pompeo, M. (2004). *When your "problem" becomes mine: Siblings' perspectives on having a brother or sister with disabilities*. Unpublished master's thesis York University, North York, ON.

Preddy, L. B. (2009).Reaching advanced readers in the middle grades. *School Library Media Activities Monthly, 25*(10), 19–21.

Preiss, R. W., & Gayle. B. M. (2006). A meta-analysis of the educational benefits of employing advanced organizers. In B. M. Gayle, M. Allen, R. W. Preiss, & N. Brunell (Eds.), *Classroom communication and instructional processes: Advances through metanalysis* (pp. 329–344). New York: Erlbaum.

Premji, S., Benzies, K., Serrett, K., & Hayden, K. A. (2006). Research-based interventions for children and youth with fetal alcohol spectrum disorder: Revealing the gap. *Child: Care, Health and Development, 33*, 389–397.

Pressley, M. (2002). *Reading instruction that works: The case for balanced teaching* (2nd ed.). New York: Guilford.

Pressley, M., Roehrig, A., Bogner, K., Raphael, L. M., & Dolezal, S. (2002). Balanced literacy instruction. *Focus on Exceptional Children, 34*, 1–14.

Prevatt, F. F., Heffer, R. W., & Lowe, P. A. (2000). A review of school reintegration programs for children with cancer. *Journal of School Psychology, 38*, 447–467.

Prior, J., & Gerard, M. (2004). *Environmental print in the classroom: Meaningful connections for learning to read*. Newark, DE: International Reading Association.

Pyryt, M. C. (2007). The giftedness/perfectionism connection: Recent research and implications. *Gifted Educational International, 23*(3), 273–279.

Rakow, S. (2007). All means all: Classrooms that work for advanced learners. *Middle Ground, 11*(1), 10–12.

Ramsay, J. (2007). *A case study of an effective working relationship involving an educational assistant and an educator*. Unpublished master's thesis, Queen's University at Kingston, ON.

Randolph, J. J. (2007). Meta-analysis of the research on response cards: Effects on test achievement, quiz achievement, and off-task behavior. *Journal of Positive Behavior Interventions, 9,* 113–128.

Reed, V. (2005). *An introduction to children with language disorders.* Boston: Allyn & Bacon.

Regan, K., & Page, P. (2008). Character building: Using literature to connect with youth. *Reclaiming Children and Youth, 16*(4), 37–43.

Reithaug, D. (1998). *Orchestrating academic success by adapting and modifying programs.* West Vancouver: Stirling Head Enterprises.

Renzulli, J. S. (2005). Applying gifted education pedagogy to total talent development for all students. *Theory Into Practice, 44*(2), 80–89.

Renzulli, J.S. (2008). Teach to the top: How to keep high achievers engaged and motivated. *Instructor, 117*(5), 34–38.

Renzulli, J. S., Gentry, M., & Reis, S. (2003). *Enrichment clusters: A practical plan for real-world, student-driven learning.* Mansfield, CT: Creative Learning Press.

Reschly, A.L., Huebner, E.S., Appleton, J.J., & Antaramian, S. (2008). Engagement as flourishing: The contribution of positive emotions and coping to adolescent' engagement at school and with learning. *Psychology in the Schools, 45*(5), 419–431.

Ridgway, A., Northup, J., Pellegrin, A., LaRue, R., & Hightshoe, A. (2003). Effects of recess on the classroom behavior of children with and without attention-deficit hyperactivity disorder. *School Psychology Quarterly, 18*(3), 253–268.

Riendl, P. A., & Haworth, D. T. (1995). Chemistry and special education. *Journal of Chemical Education, 72,* 983–986.

Rimm-Kaufman, S. E., La Paro, K. M., Downer, J. T., & Pianta, R. C. (2005). The contribution of classroom setting and quality of instruction to children's behavior in kindergarten classrooms. *The Elementary School Journal, 105,* 377–394.

Roach, A. T., Niebling, B.C., & Kurz, A. (2008). Evaluating the alignment among curriculum, instruction, and assessments: Implications and applications for research and practice. *Psychology in the Schools, 45,* 158–176.

Roberts, M., White, R., & McLaughlin, T. F. (1997). Useful classroom accommodations for teaching children with ADD and ADHD. *B.C. Journal of Special Education, 21*(2), 71–90.

Robinson, C. S., Menchetti, B. M., & Torgesen, J. K. (2002). Toward a two-factor theory of one type of mathematics disabilities. *Learning Disabilities Research & Practice, 17,* 81–89.

Robinson, D. H., Funk, D. C., Beth, A., & Bush, A. M. (2005). Changing beliefs about corporal punishment: Increasing knowledge about ineffectiveness to build more consistent moral and informational beliefs. *Journal of Behavioral Education, 14,* 117–139.

Rodabaugh. (1996). Institutional commitment to fairness in college teaching. *New Directions for Teaching and Learning, 66,* 37–45.

Rogers, C. (2007). Experiencing an 'inclusive' education: Parents and their children with special educational needs. *British Journal of Sociology of Education, 28,* 55–68.

Rollins, K., Mursky, C. V., Shah-Coltrane, S., & Johnsen, S. K. (2009). RTI models for gifted children. *Gifted Child Today, 32*(3), 20–30.

Rosenthal-Malek, A., & Greenspan, J. (1999). A student with diabetes is in my class. *Teaching Exceptional Children, 31*(3), 38–43.

Rotter, K.M. (2004). Simple techniques to improve teacher-made instructional materials for use by pupils with disabilities. *Preventing School Failure, 48*(2), 38–43.

Running Wolf, P., & Rickard, J. (2003). Talking circles: A Native American approach to experiential learning. *Journal of Multicultural Counseling and Development, 31,* 39–43.

Rusby, J. C., Forrester, K. K., Biglan, A., & Metzler, C. W. (2005). Relationships between peer harassment and adolescent problem behaviors. *Journal of Early Adolescence, 25,* 453–477.

Rushowy, K. (2009, October 13). Coming soon: Report cards that make sense – province reworking jargon-filled documents. *TorStar News Service.* Retrieved from www.tyndale.ca/libraryblog/2009/10/ministry-demands-for-ontario-reprot-cards-to-be-written-in-plain-english.

Russell, E. (2005). Starting school: The importance of parents' expectations. *Journal of Research in Special Educational Needs, 5,* 118–126.

Rustique-Forrester, E. (2005). Accountability and the pressure to exclude: A cautionary tale from England. *Education Policy Analysis Archives, 13*(26). Retrieved from http://epaa.asu.edu/epaa/v13n26/.

Ryder, J.F., Tunmer, W.E., & Greaney, K.T. (2008). Explicit instruction in phonemic awareness and phonetically based decoding skills as an intervention strategy for struggling readers in whole language classrooms. *Reading and Writing: An Interdisciplinary Journal, 21,* 349–369.

Rynders, J. E., & Horrobin, J. M. (1990). Always trainable? Never educable? Updating educational expectations concerning children with Down syndrome. *American Journal on Mental Retardation, 95,* 77–83.

Sabbatino, E. D., & Macrine, S. L. (2007). Start on success: A model transition program for high school students with disabilities. *Preventing School Failure, 52*(1), 33–39.

Sands, D. I., Guzman, L., Stephens, L., & Boggs, A. (2007). Including student voices in school reform: Students speak. *Journal of Latinos and Education, 6,* 323–345.

Salvia, J. & Ysseldyke, J. (2007). *Assessment in special and inclusive education* (10th ed.). Boston, MA: Houghton Mifflin.

Sarason, S. B. (1993). You are thinking of teaching? Opportunities, problems, realities. San Francisco: Jossey-Bass.

Sarason, S. B. (2002). *Educational reform.* New York: Teachers College Press.

Saskatchewan Learning (2001). *Aboriginal elders and community workers in schools: A guide for school divisions and their partners.* Regina, SK: Saskatchewan Education.

Saskatchewan Learning (2004). *Building communities of hope: Effective practices for meeting the diverse learning needs of children and youth.* Regina: Saskatchewan Learning.

Scorgie, K., Wilgosh, L., & Sobsey, D. (2004). The experience of transformation in parents of children with disabilities: Theoretical considerations. *Developmental Disabilities Bulletin, 32*(1), 84–110.

Schalock, R. L., Luckasson, R. A., & Shogren, K. A. (2007). The renaming of mental retardation to the term intellectual disability. *Intellectual and Developmental Disabilities, 45*(2), 116–124.

Schlachter, S. (2008). Diagnosis, treatment and educational implications for students with attention-deficit/hyperactivity disorder in the United States, Australia, and the United Kingdom. *Peabody Journal of Education, 83,* 154–169.

Segers, M., Gijbels, D., & Thurlings, M. (2008). The relationship between students' perceptions of portfolio assessment practice and their approaches to learning. *Educational Studies, 34*(1), 35–44.

Shankweiler, D., & Fowler, A.E. (2004). Questions people ask about the role of phonological processes in learning to read. *Reading and Writing: An Interdisciplinary Journal, 17*(5), 483–515.

Shaw, S. R., & McCabe, P. C. (2008). Hospital-to-school transition for children with chronic illness: Meeting the new challenges of an evolving health care system. *Psychology in the Schools, 45,* 74–87.

Shaywitz, S. E., Morris, & R. Shaywitz, B. A. (2008). The education of dyslexic children from childhood to young adulthood. *Annual Review of Psychology, 59,* 451–475.

Sheetz, A. H. et al. (2004). Guidelines for managing life-threatening food allergies in Massachusetts schools. *Journal of School Health, 74*(5), 155–160.

Siegel, L. S. (1999). Issues in the definition and diagnosis of learning disabilities. *Journal of Learning Disabilities, 32,* 304–319.

Siegle, D. (2005). Six uses of the internet to develop students' gifts and talents. *Gifted Child Today, 28*(2), 30–36.

Silliman, E. R., & Wilkinson, L. C. (Eds.) (2004). *Language and literacy learning in schools.* New York: Guilford Press.

Silva, M., Munk, D. D., & Bursuck, W. D. (2005). Grading adaptations for students with disabilities. *Intervention in School & Clinic, 41*(2), 87–98.

Simmons, B. (2002). Facilitative conferences: Parents and teachers working together. *Clearing House, 76,* 88–93.

Slater, W. H., & Horstman, F. R. (2002). Teaching reading and writing to struggling middle school and high school students: The case for reciprocal teaching. *Preventing School Failure, 46,* 163–166.

Smith, C.R. (2004). Advocating for our students in the current sociopolitical climate: One perspective on the challenges we face. In L.M. Bullock, R.A. Gable, & K.J. Melloy (Eds.), *Effective Interventions for classrooms, schools, and communities* (pp. 1–9). Tampa, FL: Council for Children with Behavioral Disorders.

Smith, P.K., Smith, C., Osborn, R., & Samara, M. (2008). A content analysis of school anti-bullying policies: Progress and limitations. *Educational Psychology in Practice, 24,* 1–12.

Smith, T. E. C., Polloway, E. A., Patton, J. R., Dowdy, C. A., McIntyre, L. J. & Francis, G. C. (2008). *Teaching students with special needs in inclusive settings (3rd Canadian ed.).* Toronto, ON: Pearson Education Canada.

Stanovich, K. E. (1994). Constructivism in reading education. *Journal of Special Education, 28,* 259–274.

Stanovich, K. E. (2000). *Progress in understanding reading: Scientific foundations and new frontiers.* New York: Guilford Publications.

Stanovich, K.E. (2005). The future of a mistake: Will discrepancy measurement continue to make the learning disabilities field a pseudoscience? *Learning Disability Quarterly, 28*(2), 103–115.

Stanovich, K.E., & Stanovich, P.J. (1995). How research might inform the debate about early reading acquisition. *Journal of Research in Reading, 18,* 87–105.

Stanovich, P. J. (1999). Conversations about inclusion. *Teaching Exceptional Children, 31*(6), 54–58.

Stanovich, P. J., & Jordan, A. (1998). Canadian teachers' and principals' beliefs about inclusive education as predictors of effective teaching in heterogeneous classrooms. *Elementary School Journal, 98,* 221–238.

Stanovich, P., & Jordan, A. (2004). Inclusion as professional development. *Exceptionality Education Canada, 14*(2&3), 169–188.

Steele, M. M. (2008). Helping students with learning disabilities succeed. *Science Teacher, 75*(3), 38–42.

Steiner Bell, K. (1998). *Teaching emotion and belief as adapted curriculum for children with autism: A first step in addressing mind-blindness.* Unpublished master's thesis, Queen's University, Kingston, ON.

Steiner Bell, K. (2005). *Social understanding in the friendships of persons with a developmental syndrome.* Unpublished doctoral dissertation, Queen's University, Kingston, Ontario, Canada.

Stenhoff, D. M., & Lignugaris/Kraft, B. (2007). A review of the effects of peer tutoring on students with mild disabilities in secondary settings. *Exceptional Children, 74,* 8–30.

Stiggins. R. (2006). Assessment for learning: A key to motivation and achievement. *Edge: The Latest Information for the Education Practitioner, 2*(2), 1–19.

Stiggins, R., & Duke, D. (2008). Effective instructional leadership requires assessment leadership. *Phi Delta Kappan, 90,* 285–291.

Stoch, S. A. (2000). *Zak: An adolescent with learning disabilities at home, at camp, and at school.* Unpublished master's thesis, Queen's University, Kingston, ON.

Stojanovik, V., & Riddell, P. (2008). Expressive versus receptive language skills in specific reading disorder. *Clinical Linguistics and Phonetics, 22*(4-5), 305–310.

Stough, L. M., & Palmer, D. J. (2003). Special thinking in special settings: A qualitative study of expert special educators. *The Journal of Special Education, 38,* 174–186.

Strickland, C. A. (2007). *Tools for high quality differentiated instruction.* Alexandria, VA: Association for Supervision and Curriculum Development.

Strike, K. A. (2008). Small schools: Size or community? *American Journal of Education, 114*(3), 169–190.

Sturm, J. M., & Rankin-Erickson, J. L. (2002). Effects of hand-drawn and computer-generated concept mapping on the expository writing of middle school students with learning disabilities. *Learning Disabilities Research and Practice, 17,* 124–139.

Sugai, G., & Horner, R. H. (2008). What we know and need to know about preventing problem behavior in schools. *Exceptionality, 16*(2), 67–77.

Sugai, G., & Horner, R. H. (2009). Responsiveness-to-intervention and school-wide positive behavior supports: Integration of mulit-tiered system approaches. *Exceptionality, 17*(4), 223–237.

Sullivan, N. A. (2004). *Walking with a shadow: Surviving childhood leukemia.* Portsmouth, NH: Praeger Publishers.

Sullivan, N. A., Fulmer, D. L., & Zigmond, N. (2001). School: The normalizing factor for children with childhood leukemia. *Preventing School Failure, 46*(1), 4–13.

Sundmark, J. (2003). *Voices from the field: The practice of educational assistants working with students with severe behaviour disorders.* Unpublished doctoral dissertation, University of Alberta, Edmonton.

Swanson, H. L., & Deshler, D. (2003). Instructing adolescents with learning disabilities: Converting a meta-analysis to practice. *Journal of Learning Disabilities, 36,* 124–135.

Talbot, R. P. (2002). Carpe diem: Andy's story. *Reclaiming Children and Youth, 11*(1), 47–51.

Tannock, R. (1998). Attention deficit hyperactivity disorder: Advances in cognitive, neurobiological, and genetic research. *Journal of Child Psychology and Psychiatry, 39,* 65–99.

Tannock, R. (2007). The educational implications of attention deficit hyperactivity disorder. *What works? Research into practice* (Research Monograph No. 3). Toronto: Literacy and Numeracy Secretariat & the Ontario Association of Deans of Education. Retrieved from www.edu.gov.on.ca/eng/literacynumeracy/inspire/research/whatWorks.html.

Tannock, R., & Martinussen, R. (2001, November). Reconceptualizing ADHD. *Educational Leadership,* 20–25.

Taras, H., & Potts-Datema, W. (2005). Chronic health conditions and student performance at school. *Journal of School Health, 75*(7), 255–266.

Thapar, A., Langley, K., Owen, M. J., & O'Donovan, M. C. (2007). Advances in genetic findings on attention deficit hyperactivity disorder. *Psychological Medicine, 37,* 1681–1692.

Theisen, T. (2002). Differentiated instruction in the foreign language classroom: Meeting the diverse needs of all learners. *Communiqué LOTE CED Issue 6* Retrieved from www.sedl.org/loteced/communique/n06.html.

Thornberg, R. (2006). Hushing as a moral dilemma in the classroom. *Journal of Moral Education, 35*, 89–104.

Tobin, R., & McInnes, A. (2008). Accommodating differences: Variations in differentiated literacy instruction in grade 2/3 classrooms. *Literacy, 42*, 3–9.

Tomlinson, C.A. (1999). *The differentiated classroom: Responding to the needs of all learners.* Alexandria, VA: Association for Supervision and Curriculum Development.

Tomlinson, C. A. (2000). *Leadership for differentiating schools & classrooms.* Alexandria, Va.: Association for Supervision and Curriculum Development.

Tomlinson, C. A. (2003). *Fulfilling the promise of the differentiated classroom: Strategies and tools for responsive teaching.* Alexandria, VA: Association for Supervision and Curriculum Development.

Tomlinson, C. A. (2005). *How to differentiate in mixed-ability classrooms.* (2nd ed.). Columbus, OH: Pearson Merrill Prentice Hall.

Tomlinson, C. A. (2008). Making a difference. *Teacher, 2*(1), 26, 28–31. Retrieved from www.edweek.org/tsb/articles/2008/09/10/01tomlinson.h02.html.

Tomlinson, C. A., Brimijoin, K., & Navarez, L. (2008). *The differentiated school: Making revolutionary changes in teaching and learning.* Alexandria, VA: Association for Supervision and Curriculum Development.

Tomlinson, C. A., & Cunningham Eidson, C. (2003). *Differentiation in practice: A resource guide for differentiating curriculum, grades K-5.* Alexandria, VA: Association for Supervision and Curriculum Development.

Tomlinson, C. A., & McTighe, J. (2006). *Integrating differentiated instruction and understanding by design: Connecting content and kids.* Alexandria, VA: Association for Supervision and Curriculum Development.

Tomlinson, C. A, & Strickland, C. A. (2005). *Differentiation in practice: A resource guide for differentiating curriculum, grades 9-12.* Alexandria, VA: Association for Supervision and Curriculum Development.

Topping, K. J. (2005). Trends in peer learning. *Educational Psychology, 25*, 631–645.

Touchette, N. (2000).Kids and Type 2: Type 2 diabetes, the kind that only adults used to get, is on the rise among America's youth. *Diabetes Forecast, 53*(11), 79.

Trautwein, U. (2007). The homework-achievement relation reconsidered: Differentiating homework time, homework frequency, and homework effort. *Learning and Instruction, 17*, 372–388.

Trent, S. C., Artiles, A. J., & Englert, C. S. (1998). From deficit thinking to social constructivism: A review of theory, research, and practice in special education. *Review of Research in Education, 23*, 277–307.

Tretter, T. R. (2010). Systematic and sustained: Powerful approaches for enhancing deep mathematical thinking. *Gifted Child Today, 33*(1), 16–26.

Triplett, C. F., & Hunter, A. (2005). Talking circle: Creating community in our elementary classrooms. *Social Studies and the Young Learner, 18*(2), 4–8.

Turnbull, A., Zuna, N., Young Hong, J., Hu, X., Kyzar, K., Obremski, S., Summes, J. A., Turnbull, R., & Stowe, M. (2010). Preparing families to be partners in making educational decisions. *Teaching Exceptional Children, 42* (3), 42–53.

Turnbull, R., Turnbull, A., Shank, M., Smith, S., & Leal, D. (2002). *Exceptional lives: Special education in today's schools* (3rd ed.). Columbus, OH: Merrill, Prentice-Hall.

Udvari-Solner, A., & Kluth, P. (2007). *Joyful learning: Active and collaborative learning in inclusive classrooms.* Thousand Oaks, CA: Corwin Press.

Underwood, M., & Buhrmester, D. (2007). Friendship features and social exclusion: An observational study examining gender and social context. *Merrill-Palmer Quarterly, 53*, 412–438.

Urdan, T., & Schoenfelder, E. (2006). Classroom effects on student motivation: Goal structures, social relationships, and competence beliefs. *Journal of School Psychology, 44*, 331–349.

Vacc, N. N. (1995). Gaining number sense through a restructured hundreds chart. *Teaching Exceptional Children, 28*(1), 50–55.

Valeo, A., & Bunch, G. (1998). Teachers, attitudes, inclusion, and the curriculum. *B.C. Journal of Special Education, 21*(3), 6–19.

Valverde, L.A. (Ed.). (2008). *Latino change agents in higher education: Shaping a system that works for all.* San Francisco: Jossey Bass.

Van den Bos, K. P., Nakken, H., Nicolay, P. G., & van Houten, E. J. (2007). Adults with mild intellectual disabilities: Can their reading comprehension ability be improved? *Journal of Intellectual Disability Research, 51*, 835–849.

Van der Molen, M.J., Van Luit, J.E.H., Jongmans, M.J., & Van der Molen, M.W. (2007). Verbal working memory in children with mild intellectual disabilities. *Journal of Intellectual Disability Research, 51*(2), 162–169.

VanDeWeghe, R. (2007). What about vocabulary instruction? *English Journal, 97*(1), 101–104.

Van Garderen, D. (2004). Reciprocal teaching as a comprehension strategy for understanding mathematical word problems. *Reading and Writing Quarterly, 20*, 225–229.

VanWeelden, K. (2001). Choral mainstreaming: Tips for success. *Music Educators Journal, 88*(3), 55–60.

Varga-Toth, J. (2006, February). *Meeting the needs of children and adolescents with special needs in rural and northern Canada: Summary report of a roundtable for Canadian policy-makers* (Research Report F 54). Thunder Bay, ON/Ottawa, ON: Lakehead University/Canadian Policy Research Networks, Inc.

Vass, E. (2002). Friendship and collaborative creative writing in the primary classroom. *Journal of Computer Assisted Learning, 18*, 102–110.

Vaughn, S. (1991). Social skills enhancement in students with learning disabilities. In B. Y. L. Wong (Ed.), *Learning about learning disabilities* (pp. 407–440). San Diego, CA: Academic.

Versnel, J. (2005). *Transition preparation program: Linking motivation and learning strategies for youth facing challenging transitions.* Unpublished Ph.D. dissertation, Faculty of Education, Queen's University.

Vieira, M. C. L. (2010). *Theory of mind in autism spectrum disorders: A case study describing an intervention to teach ToM concepts.* Unpublished master's project, Queen's University, Kingston, Ontario, Canada.

Villa, R.A., Nevin, A., & Thousand, J.S. (2007). *Differentiating instruction: Collaborative planning and teaching for universally designed learning.* Thousand Oaks, CA: Corwin Press.

Villeneuve, M. (2009). A critical examination of school-based occupational therapy of collaborative consultation. *The Canadian Journal of Occupational Therapy, 76*, 206–219.

Villeneuve, M. (2010). *Enabling outcomes for students with developmental disabilities through collaborative consultation.* Unpublished manuscript, Queen's University, Kingston, Ontario, Canada.

Volkmar, F. R. (Ed.). (2007). *Autism and pervasive developmental disorders* (2nd ed.). Cambridge, UK: Cambridge University Press.

Voytsekhovska, S. (2008). *Reading in a grade 9 mathematics classroom: A case study.* Unpublished master's thesis, Queen's University, Kingston, ON, Canada.

Vygotsky, L. (1978). *Mind in society.* Cambridge, MA: Harvard University Press.

Vygotsky, L. S. (1986). *Thought and language.* Cambridge, MA: MIT Press.

Vygotsky, L. S. (1996). *Thought and language* (Revised). Cambridge, MA: MIT Press.

Walczyk, E. B. (1993). Music instruction and the hearing impaired. *Music Educators Journal, 80,* 42–44.

Walker, A., & Nabuzoka, D. (2007). Academic achievement and social functioning of children with and without learning difficulties. *Educational Psychology, 27*(5), 635–654.

Walker, K.T. (2008). *A bittersweet existence: The lived experiences of four young women with diabetes mellitus.* Unpublished master's thesis, Queen's University, Kingston, Ontario.

Walpole, S., & McKenna, M. C. (2007). *Differentiated reading strategies for the primary grades.* New York: Guilford Pub.

Webb, N. M., Nemer, K. M., & Ing, M. (2006). Small group reflections: Parallels between teacher discourse and student behavior in peer-directed groups. *The Journal of the Learning Sciences, 15,* 63–119.

Webster, A. A., & Carter, M. (2007). Social relationships and friendships of children with developmental disabilities: Implications for inclusive settings, a systematic review. *Journal of Intellectual and Developmental Disability, 32,* 200–213.

Weinstein, C. S., Tomlinson-Clarke, S., & Curran, M. (2004). Toward a conception of culturally responsive classroom management. *Journal of Teacher Education, 55,* 25–38.

Weisgerber, R. A. (1993). *Science success for students with disabilities.* New York: Addison-Wesley.

Welch, A. B. (2000). Responding to student concerns about fairness. *Teaching Exceptional Children, 33*(2). 36–40.

Whitley, J., Lupart, J. L., & Beran, T. (2007). The characteristics and experiences of Canadian students receiving special education services for a learning disability. *Exceptionality Education Canada, 17*(3), 85–109.

Wiener, J., & Tardif, C. (2004). Social and emotional functioning of children with learning disabilities: Does special education placement make a difference? *Learning Disabilities Research and Practice, 19,* 20–32.

Wiggins, G.P., & McTighe, J. (2005). *Understanding by design.* Alexandria, VA: Association for Supervision and Curriculum Development.

Wilgosh, L., & Chomicki, S. (1994). Parents' views on inclusive education for young people with disabilities. *Developmental Disabilities Bulletin, 22*(2), 29–35.

Wilgosh, L., & Scorgie, K. (2006a). Fostering teacher understanding of parent issues when a child has a disability: A brief report. *Developmental Disabilities Bulletin, 34,* 127–136.

Wilgosh, L., & Scorgie, K. (2006b). Theoretical model for conceptualizing cross-cultural applications and intervention strategies for parents of children with disabilities. *Journal of Policy and Practice in Intellectual Disabilities, 3,* 211–218.

Wilhelm, J. D. (2006). The age for drama. *Educational Leadership, 63*(7), 74–77.

Willard, N. E. (2007). *Cyberbullying and cyberthreats: Responding to the challenge of online social aggression, threats, and distress.* Champaign, IL: Research Press.

Williams, D., & Happe, F. (2010).Representing intentions in self and other: Studies of Autism and typical development. *Developmental Science 13*(2), 307–319.

Willows, D. (2002). The balanced literacy diet. *School Administrator, 59,* 30–33.

Winebrenner, S. (2007). *Teaching gifted kids in the regular classroom: Strategies and techniques every teacher can use to meet the academic needs of the gifted and the talented* (3rd ed.). Minneapolis: Free Spirit Publishing.

Witzel, B. S., Riccomini, P. J., & Schneider, E. (2008). Implementing CRA with secondary students with learning disabilities in Mathematics. *Intervention in School and Clinic, 43*(5), 270–276.

Wodrich, D.L., & Cunningham, M.M. (2007). School-based tertiary and targeted interventions for students with chronic medical conditions: Examples from Type 1 Diabetes Mellitus and epilepsy. *Psychology in the Schools, 45*(1), 52–62.

Wodrich, D., Kaplan, A. M., & Deering, W. M. (2006). Children with epilepsy in school: Special service usage and assessment practices. *Psychology in the Schools, 43*(2), 169–181.

Wolford, P. L., Heward, W. L., & Alber, S. R. (2001). Teaching middle school students with learning disabilities to recruit peer assistance during cooperative learning group activities. *Learning Disabilities Research and Practice, 16,* 161–173.

Wolraich, M. L. (2006). Attention-Deficit/Hyperactivity Disorder: Can it be recognized and treated in children younger than 5 years? *Infants & Young Children, 19*(2), 86–93.

Wood, T., & McCarthy, C. (2002). *Understanding and preventing teacher burnout. ERIC Digest.* (ERIC Document Reproduction Service No. ED 477726).

Working Forum on Inclusive Schools. (1994). *Creating schools for all our children: What 12 schools have to say.* Reston, VA: Council for Exceptional Children.

Wormeli, R. (2006a). Differentiating for tweens. *Educational Leadership, 63*(7), 14–19.

Wormeli, R. (2006b). *Fair isn't always equal: Assessing and grading in the differentiated classroom.* Portland, ME: Stenhouse Pub.

Wright, P. M., White, K., & Gaebler-Spira, D. (2004). Exploring the relevance of the personal and social responsibility model in adapted physical activity: A collective case study. *Journal of Teaching in Physical Education, 23,* 71–87.

Wysocki, T., & Gavin, L. (2006). Paternal involvement in the management of pediatric chronic diseases: Associations with adherence, quality of life, and health status. *Journal of Pediatric Psychology, 31,* 501–511.

Xin, Y. P., Grasso, E., Dipipi-Hoy, C. M., & Jitendra, A. (2005). The effects of purchasing skill instruction for individuals with developmental disabilities: A meta-analysis. *Exceptional Children, 71,* 379–402.

Xu, Y., Gelfer, J., & Perkins, P. (2005). Using peer tutoring to increase social interactions in early schooling. *TESOL Quarterly, 39*(1), 83–106.

Yamaki, K., & Fuijura, G. T. (2002). Employment and income status of adults with developmental disabilities in the community. *Mental Retardation, 40,* 132–142.

Yssel, N., Prater, M., & Smith, D. (2010). How can such a smart kid not get it? Finding the right fit for twice-exceptional students in our schools. *Gifted Child Today, 33*(1), 54–61.

Zajac, R. J., & Hartup, W. W. (1997). Friends as coworkers: Research review and classroom implications. *Elementary School Journal, 98,* 3–13.

# Name Index

# Subject Index

teaching strategies
  Asperger syndrome (AS), 92
  communication exceptionalities, 69–71
  learning disabilities, 61, 62–63
  teaching around the mismatch, 118
  teaching through the mismatch, 118
*Teens: The Company They Keep,* 75
test administration, 154–155
test construction, 153, 154
testing, 141
test marking, 155
tiering, 119
time out, 66, 176
Tourette syndrome, 100, 101
TTYPA, 198

**U**

UDL. *See* universal design for learning (UDL)
United States
  inclusion, 15
  large-scale assessment, 145–146

*Universal Declaration of Human Rights,* 6
universal design for learning (UDL), 9,
  119, 120
University of Calgary, 204
University of Ottawa, 60
University of Regina, 204
University of Toronto, 19, 35, 64–65, 129,
  142, 150, 204
University of Western Ontario, 46, 62

**V**

verbal reprimand, 66, 176
vision teacher, 95
visual art, 133–134
visual impairment, 95–97
  assessment, 97
  characteristics of students with, 95
  classroom adaptations, 95–97
  learning implications, 95–97
  organization, 96
  presentation of information, 96

resources, 96, 97
  tips for teachers, 96f
vocabulary, 123–124
vocabulary strategies, 126–127
voice synthesizer, 86

**W**

WBTT. *See* web based teaching tool
  (WBTT)
web based teaching tool (WBTT), 31
written expression, 127–128
  DARE strategy, 128
  SEARCH strategy, 128
  story-planning sheet, 127

**Y**

York University, 19

**Z**

zone of proximal development (ZPD),
  122, 189